WITHDRAWN

891.43934 B595RO

BILGRĀMĪ, ʻABDULLĀH ḤUSAIN

THE ROMANCE TRADITION IN URDU

DATE DUE

DEC 22 1994

MAR 24 1995

JUL 09 1998

APR 02 1999

D1596642

Niles Public
Library District

6960 Oakton Street
Niles, Illinois 60648
(708) 967-8554

WITHDRAWN

The Romance Tradition in Urdu

بہ عون صانع مکین و مکان و فضل خلاق زمین و زمان نسخہ
داستان امیر حمزہ
مطبع منشی نولکشور میں بطرز مطبوع مقبول چھپا ہوا

The Romance Tradition in Urdu

Adventures from the Dastan of Amir Hamzah

TRANSLATED, EDITED, AND
WITH AN INTRODUCTION BY

Frances W. Pritchett

COLUMBIA UNIVERSITY PRESS
NEW YORK

Columbia University Press
New York Oxford
Copyright © 1991 Columbia University Press
All rights reserved

Library of Congress Cataloging-in-Publication Data

Bilgrāmī, 'Abdullāh Ḥusain
[Dāstān-e Amīr Ḥamzah. English]
The romance tradition in Urdu : adventures from the Dastan of Amir Hamzah / translated, edited, and with an introduction by Frances W. Pritchett.
p. cm.
Translation of the Bilgrāmī version of Dāstān-e Amīr Ḥamzah, one of several Urdu versions of the Romance of Amīr Ḥamza.
Includes bibliographical references.
ISBN 0-231-07164-7 : $35.00
I. Pritchett, Frances W., 1947– . II. Romance of Amīr Ḥamza. English. III. Title.
PK2199.B495D3713 1991
891'.43934—dc20 90-24247
CIP

Casebound editions of Columbia University Press books are Smyth-sewn and printed on permanent and durable acid-free paper

Printed in the United States of America
c 10 9 8 7 6 5 4 3 2 1

COLUMBIA UNIVERSITY PRESS WISHES TO EXPRESS ITS APPRECIATION OF ASSISTANCE GIVEN BY THE PUSHKIN FUND IN THE PREPARATION OF THIS TRANSLATION.

THE DECORATIVE DEVICES, ILLUSTRATIONS, AND CAPTIONS ARE ALL FROM THE *Dāstān-e amīr Ḥamzah* PUBLISHED BY THE NAVAL KISHOR PRESS, LUCKNOW, IN 1871, AND ATTRIBUTED TO 'ABDULLAH BILGRĀMĪ, REPRINTED WITH THE PERMISSION OF THE BRITISH LIBRARY BOARD.

RULER OF MEN,
BESTOWER OF CROWNS ON KINGS,
STRINGER OF SLAVE-RINGS IN THE EARS
OF THE INTRANSIGENT,
SLAYER OF FIRE-BREATHING SERPENTS,
HUNTER AND TAKER OF BLOODTHIRSTY,
TIGERS,
BREAKER OF TILISMS,
DESTROYER OF THE DEVS OF QAF AND THE
DARK REGIONS,
CHAMPION OF THE WORLD,
SAHIB-QIRAN OF THE AGE,
EARTHQUAKE OF QAF,
YOUNGER SOLOMON,
FATHER OF GREATNESS,
AMIR HAMZAH BIN ABDUL MUTTALIB,
LORD OF ARABIA.

Contents

A Note on Transliteration

The letters of the Urdu alphabet have been transliterated as follows:

alif as: a, i, u, ā
b p t ṭ ṡ
j ch ḥ ḳh
d ḍ ż
r ṛ z zh
s sh
ṣ ẓ
ṭ̤ ẓ̤
ʻ ġh
f q
k g
l m
n
vā'o as: v, ū, o, au
h
ī
baṛī ye as: y, e, ai
nūn-e ġhunnah: ñ
hamzah: '
iẓāfat: -e

For the sake of consistency, Persian words have been transliterated as they are pronounced in Urdu. Indic words have been treated as though they were written phonetically in Urdu script.

Acknowledgments

My dastan work goes back for more than ten years now, and from the start I have had the support of my teacher and friend, C. M. Naim of the University of Chicago. As the work progressed, M. A. R. Barker of the University of Minnesota most generously lent dastan volumes from his own collection for microfilming, as did Ralph Russell, formerly of the School of Oriental and African Studies, London. William L. Hanaway of the University of Pennsylvania, to whose work on Persian dastan I am immensely indebted, has also been a most valuable friend and counselor.

At Columbia, I have been fortunate in my colleagues: for readings, comments, and general encouragement I particularly thank John S. Hawley, Barbara Stoler Miller, Theodore Riccardi, David Rubin, James Russell, and Ehsan Yarshater.

In South Asia too, I have had generous help from friends and colleagues. These have included, in India, Dr. Gopi Chand Narang of Delhi University and Dr. Naiyar Masud of Lucknow University; and in Pakistan, Dr. Farman Fatahpuri of the Urdu Dictionary Board, and Jamiluddin Aali and Dr. Aslam Farrukhi of the Anjuman Taraqqi-e Urdu, in Karachi. Maulvi Niyaz ud-Din of the Kutubkhanah Anjuman Taraqqi-e Urdu, in Urdu Bazaar in Delhi, has long been the best and most consistent supplier of rare books, and my work would have been much the poorer without his help. The India International Centre, New Delhi, provided ideal living and working arrangements during several long visits to Delhi; the Centre's support has contributed a great deal to the successful completion of the project.

Libraries too have been of the greatest help at all stages of the work. Kenneth Jones and Ismat Jahan of the Library of Congress office in New Delhi not only found things for me, but also made it possible to preserve rare dastan texts in microform versions. In London, the India Office Library and Records, the Oriental Reading Room, and other parts of the British Library maintain unparalleled collections, and have an altogether cooperative and helpful group of staff members; I am especially indebted to Qazi Mahmud ul-Haq. Dastan microfilming in the United States was made possible by the good offices of Maureen L. P. Patterson of Regenstein Library at the University of Chicago, and of Henry

Scholberg of the Ames Library at the University of Minnesota. First Cecelia Shores, and then Ray Boylan, arranged for the forty-six-volume microfilm version to find a safe home at the Center for Research Libraries in Chicago. In New York, the Columbia University libraries and the New York Public Library have been most helpful.

I've also had the benefit of several research grants for dastan-related projects: a short-term Senior Research Fellowship from the American Institute of Indian Studies (1984), and two successive summer grants (1985, 1986) from the Council for Research in the Humanities, Columbia University.

Jennifer Crewe, Jonathan Director, Jennifer Dossin, Susan Clark, Teresa Bonner, and Leslie Bialler of Columbia University Press have been extremely helpful, and a pleasure to work with. I've had a truly magical companion as well: my faithful and intelligent computer, equipped with the astonishing brainpower of Nota Bene.

In fact my dastan work all along has had a magical quality, like the Water-flask of Khizr. As the work has progressed, as its demands have become clear, unexpected resources have always appeared, and they have always been just sufficient for the needs of the moment. The dastan world has proved to be the ultimate tilism: its wonders keep changing, but they never diminish.

And first, last, and always, I've had the invaluable help of Shamsur Rahman Faruqi, my best collaborator and friend. This project, like so many others we've worked on during the past twelve years, really belongs to us both.

Frances W. Pritchett
New York, 1990

Introduction

The Medieval Persian Romance Tradition

Dāstān and *qiṣṣah*[1] in Persian both mean "story," and the narrative genre to which they refer goes back to medieval Iran. At least as early as the ninth century, it was a widely popular form of storytelling: dastan narrators practiced their art not merely in coffeehouses, but in royal palaces as well. They told tales of heroic romance and adventure —stories about gallant princes and their encounters with evil kings, enemy champions, demons, magicians, Jinns, divine emissaries, tricky secret agents called *ʿayyārs*, and beautiful princesses who might be human or of the *Parī* ("fairy") race.

Dastans had no official religious or social purpose within their culture, and therefore no externally prescribed form. They existed for the sheer pleasure of the storytelling experience: created by the narrator's artistic authority, they were sustained by the listeners' responsiveness, by the perpetual question, "Then what happened?" Dastan narrators drew on the revered national verse epic *Shāh nāmah (The Book of Kings)* (c. 1010),[2] and incorporated into its framework folk traditions of all kinds, creating narratives that were swept along by the strong currents of the imagination. Their ultimate subject matter was always simple: *"razm o bazm,"* the battlefield and the elegant courtly life, war and love.

A number of such dastans were current in medieval Iran, and their well-known plots offered frameworks upon which each narrator practiced his own kind of embroidery. As a professional, the dastan narrator provided passages of elaborate rhyming prose at high points in the story (especially when describing gardens, nights, women, or battlefields), inserted verses from well-known poets, and in general catered most carefully to the mood and tastes of his listeners.

William L. Hanaway, who has made a close study of Persian dastans, describes them as "popular romances" which were "created, elaborated, and transmitted" by professional storytellers. He mentions five as the principal ones surviving from the pre-Ṣafavid (i.e., fifteenth century and earlier) period: those which grew up around the adventures of the world-conqueror Alexander, the great Persian king Darius, the Prophet's uncle Ḥamzah, the legendary king Fīroz Shāh, and—an interesting counterpoint—a humbly born trickster-hero named Samak the ʻAyyār.[3] Only a few translations of these texts into Western languages have ever been made.[4]

It is hard to be certain about the earliest sources and origins of such romances; inevitably, the surviving manuscripts leave many questions unanswered. Moreover, since the dastans lived at their fullest in performance, the written forms they were given from time to time cannot speak with complete authority about their "real" lives. The romances, even in the written "scripts" we have, are so clearly designed to be narrated orally and *heard* by a listening audience, that our lack of access to the medieval performance tradition must always remain a source of regret. According to one observer, the Ḥamzah story in particular was a staple of Teheran coffeehouse performances as recently as the early 1930s.[5] It is hard to know to what extent we can extrapolate from modern parallels. An excellent study done in 1974–75 found the coffeehouses of Teheran playing host to resident professional narrators who spun out long, complex tales for a relatively stable clientele, filling in the crevices of the *Shāh nāmah* with material from their notebooks, memories, and opinions.[6] Another modern study found the Ḥamzah story occasionally told by Turkish coffeehouse narrators in Azerbaijan.[7]

Of all the early dastans, the Ḥamzah romance is thought to be the oldest;[8] it probably originated in the eleventh century.[9] In Hanaway's view it also shows the "greatest direct influence" of the *Shāh nāmah;* it is "structurally the simplest of all the romances," since Ḥamzah himself "comes on the scene early and dominates it throughout the story." Hanaway finds, however, one "glaring example of padding" in the plot: the "strangely incongruous" episode in which Ḥamzah goes to the land of Qāf and spends eighteen years among the non-human Devs (demons) and Parīs. The incongruity lies in the insertion of such a fantastic episode into "a very earthbound book"—a book which otherwise contains "practically nothing of the marvelous or supernatural." Hanaway concludes that the whole Qāf episode has no apparent "structural function," and could even be "deleted without any serious damage to the story." Apart from the Qāf episode, the Ḥamzah story thus has the virtue of simplicity, though it lacks the "variety and movement" of, for example, the later romance about Samak the ʻAyyār, in which "numerous strands are woven harmoniously together," and even a flashback—Samak's recounting of a childhood experience—appears.[10]

The romance of Ḥamzah goes back—or at least purports to go back—to the life of its hero, Ḥamzah ibn ʻAbd ul-Muṭṭalib, the paternal uncle of the Prophet. According to the earliest biographical source, Ḥamzah was the strongest man of his tribe and "the most unyielding." He was an outdoorsman, "fond of hunting." After he accepted Islam, he was impetuously willing to use force in its defense: even in the early days at Mecca, he once struck a violent blow at someone who had been reviling the Prophet, and cried out, "Will you insult him when I follow his religion, and say what he says? Hit me back if you can!" Ḥamzah followed the Prophet to Medina, became one of the earliest standard-bearers on expeditions, and fought in the battle of Badr. Finally, in the battle of Uḥud (625 C.E.), as he fought "like a great camel, slaying men with his sword, none being able to resist him," he was struck in the groin by a javelin. The javelin thrower was a slave who had been promised his freedom in return for Ḥamzah's death; his act was instigated by a woman named Hind bint ʻUtbah, whose relatives Ḥamzah had killed at Badr. Hind bint ʻUtbah then went to the battlefield and mutilated the dead Ḥamzah's body, cutting off his ears and nose, cutting out his liver and chewing it to fulfill the vow of vengeance she had made. Later, when the Prophet conquered Mecca, Hind bint ʻUtbah "came veiled and disguised" before him, fearful of punishment; she accepted Islam, and was pardoned.[11]

It has been argued that the romance of Ḥamzah may actually have begun with the adventures of a Persian namesake of the original Ḥamzah: Ḥamzah ibn ʻAbdullāh, a member of a radical Islamic sect called the Ḳhārijites, who was the leader of an insurrectionary movement against the caliph Hārūn ur-Rashīd and his successors. This Persian Ḥamzah lived in the early ninth century, and seems to have been a dashing rebel whose colorful exploits gave rise to many stories. As these stories gained circulation they were eventually transferred to the earlier Ḥamzah, who was an orthodox Muslim champion acceptable to all.[12] This conjecture, though attractive, rests on circumstantial evidence alone; it cannot be substantiated, as far as I know, from any evidence within the manuscripts themselves. What the romance claims to be about is the life—and grisly death—of the Arab Ḥamzah, the Prophet's uncle; though this life is seen through very Persian eyes.[13]

In early medieval Iran, the romance about the life of Ḥamzah was only one of a number of similar stories, and did not particularly stand out among its peers; it was, as we have seen, on the brief, simple and straightforward side, while other early romances had been more elaborately developed. Yet the Ḥamzah story was unique in its ability to grow, to ramify, and to travel: it gradually spread over immense areas of the Muslim world. It was soon translated into Arabic; there is a twelfth-century Georgian version, and a fifteenth-century Turkish version twenty-four volumes long.[14] It also exists in sixteenth-century Malay and Javanese versions,[15] and in Balinese and Sudanese ones as well.[16] Moreover, even in Iran the story continued to develop over time: by the mid-nineteenth century the Ḥamzah romance had grown to such an extent that it was printed in a version about twelve hundred very large pages in length.[17] By this time the dastan was often called *Rumūz-e Ḥamzah (The Subtleties of Ḥamzah)*. And by this time, the Ḥamzah romance had made itself conspicuously at home in India as well.

The Persian Ḥamzah Romance Comes to India

Persian-speakers began to establish themselves in Sind from the early eighth century, and in large regions of northwestern South Asia from the early eleventh century onward. They came as military adventurers, and stayed to become founders of dynasties. The cultural prestige of Persian was so commanding at the time that even those rulers whose native language was Turkish tended to use Persian as their court language. But of all the Persian romances, only the story of Ḥamzah took firm root in the new soil. Annemarie Schimmel judges that the Ḥamzah story "must have been popular in the Subcontinent from the days of Mahmud of Ghazna"[1] in the early eleventh century, and it is tempting to suppose so. The earliest solid evidence, however, seems to be a late fifteenth-century set of paintings that illustrate the story; these were crudely executed, possibly in Jaunpur, perhaps for a not-too-affluent patron.[2]

By the beginning of the Mughal period the Ḥamzah story was well established across a wide region. In 1555, Bābur noted with disapproval that the leading literary figure of Khurasan had recently "wasted his time" in composing an imitation of the cycle.[3] The great emperor Akbar (r. 1556–1605), far from sharing his grandfather's attitude, conceived and supervised the immense task of illustrating the whole romance. As Akbar's court chronicler tells us, Ḥamzah's adventures were "represented in twelve volumes, and clever painters made the most astonishing illustrations for no less than one thousand and four hundred passages of the story."[4] The illustrated manuscript thus created became the supreme achievement of Mughal art: "of all the loot carried off from Delhi by Nadir Shah in 1739 (including the Peacock Throne), it was only the *Hamza-nama*, 'painted with images that defy the imagination,' that Emperor Muhammad Shah pleaded to have returned."[5] Akbar was so fond of the Ḥamzah story that he even used to tell it himself, like a qissah-khvan or qissah narrator, in the harem.[6] Akbar's personal qissah-khvan—himself the son of another professional narrator—was so constantly present in court that he is said to have earned the nickname of "Darbār Ḳhān."[7] Akbar's successor Jahāngīr (r. 1605–1627) also retained a Persian qissah-khvan, Mirzā Asad Beg Shīrāzī, whose skill he valued and rewarded.[8]

The Ḥamzah story left traces in the Deccan as well. One Persian romance narrator, Ḥājī Qiṣṣah-ḳhvān Hamadānī, records his arrival in 1612 at Hyderabad, at the court of Sultan ʿAbdullāh Quṭb Shāh (r. 1611–1672) of Golconda. The Ḥājī writes, "I had brought with me a number of manuscripts of the *Rumūz-e Ḥamzah*. When I presented them in the king's service, I was ordered, 'Prepare a summary of them.' In obedience to this order this book *Zubdat ur-rumūz (The Cream of the Rumūz)* has been prepared."[9] The prestige of the written word in this oral performance tradition can be clearly seen: a professional oral narrator, a qissah-khvan, can think of no better way to introduce himself at the court of a potential patron than by presenting written texts. The king graciously responds by ordering the qissah-khvan to make a written digest of these texts—an offer which no doubt included a pension, permission to attend at court, and a chance to practice his oral art as well. At least two other seventeenth-century Indo-Persian Ḥamzah manuscripts survive, dated A.H.1096 (1684–85) and A.H.1099 (1687–88), as well as various undated and later ones.[10]

By the eighteenth century, the Ḥamzah story was so well-known in India that it inspired an indigenous Indo-Persian imitation, the massive *Bostān-e ḳhiyāl (Garden of "Ḳhiyāl")*. The future author of this work, Mīr Muḥammad Taqī, who had chosen as his pen name "Ḳhiyāl" ("dream, vision"), came to Delhi from Ahmedabad, hoping to improve his none-too-promising fortunes.

> Near the house where he was staying was a gathering place where a number of people came every day, and before them a qissah-khvan

> used to narrate the qissah of Amīr Ḥamzah, which is well-known in the whole world. Poor Mīr Taqī too, with a view to lifting his spirits, joined the gathering on one or two occasions, and listened silently to the qissah. The qissah-khvan, seeing this person poorly dressed and looking like a student, one day said tauntingly before the people of the gathering, "A man can, according to his capacity, learn every discipline and science. But the art of qissah narration is so subtle and difficult that it can never be acquired at all—except by someone whose temperament is naturally suited to it."

The young Ḳhiyāl is supposed to have responded to the taunt by vowing to create a "colorful story of such a style that not even the sky itself—much less mere human beings—will ever have heard the like!"[11]

The result of his boast was an original Persian dastan that kept getting longer and longer: over a thirty-year period (1726–1756) Ḳhiyāl composed a dastan long enough to fill fifteen massive manuscript volumes which averaged something like 500 extraordinarily large-sized pages in length; during most of this time he lived on patronage from various local rulers. To speed up the process of composition, one eager patron is said to have bestowed on him "fifteen swift-writing scribes with fine penmanship."[12] Ḳhiyāl's original work was never printed, but it circulated widely in manuscript form, and as a basis for oral narrative it indeed became the only serious rival to the Ḥamzah cycle throughout North India.[13]

The degree to which the Ḥamzah romance had become a part of Indo-Persian language and culture can be seen in some of the most famous Indo-Persian dictionaries: they define a number of characteristic terms from the story as full-fledged words in the Persian language.[14] In the course of countless retellings before faithful audiences, the Indo-Persian Ḥamzah story seems to have grown generally longer and more elaborate throughout the seventeenth and eighteenth centuries. Oral narration in Persian continued well into the nineteenth century. Writing in 1834, James Forbes describes the household of a Persianized navab at Cambay, near Ahmedabad, as containing the usual contingent of professional "kissa kawn, a class of people well known to the admirers of Persian and Arabian tales." Forbes then tells an anecdote about an English friend who was ill with a dangerously high fever: "the nabob sent him two female story-tellers, of respectable Mogul families, but neither young nor handsome. Placing themselves on each side of his pillow, one of them in a monotonous tone commenced a tale, which in due time had a soporiferous effect." Whenever the patient woke, "the story was renewed exactly where it had left off." The women relieved each other day and night by his bedside, until they "wrought a cure."[15]

Even in the second half of the nineteenth century, it appears that written Persian dastans of considerable length were circulating among the educated elite in North India. The great Urdu (and Persian) poet Mirzā Asadullāh Ḳhān Ġhālib (1797–1869), writing around 1861, speaks of his delight at receiving "a book of the dastan of Amīr Ḥamzah about fifty or sixty *juzv*s long, and a volume of the same size of *Bostān-e ḳhiyāl*."[16] The length of a *juzv* in Delhi was usually sixteen pages, which would yield a book 800 to 960 pages long.[17] No Urdu version of such length then existed, so Ġhālib was surely reading a Persian narrative—but was it an indigenous Indo-Persian work, or an import from Iran? Was it some manuscript descendant of the sixteenth-century text which Akbar caused to be illustrated in the *Ḥamzah nāmah?*[18] Was it an offshoot of Ḥājī Qiṣṣah Ḳhvān Hamadānī's massive manuscript *Zubdat ur-rumūz* (c. 1612)? (We do not know the full length of either of these works, since only fragments of the former remain, and our only existing copy of the latter is incomplete.) Or had Ġhālib perhaps received the newly published *Kitāb-e rumūz-e Ḥamzah,* printed in Teheran in 1857–59? The questions are tantalizing, and the answers still all too few. In the case of *Bostān-e ḳhiyāl* as well, Ġhālib almost surely read a Persian (manuscript) text;[19] for a few years later he took elaborate and celebratory notice of two different Urdu translations, as though he had never seen one before.

Near the end of his life Ġhālib paid one last conspicuous tribute to the dastan world. When his patron Navāb Kalb-e ʻAlī Ḳhān of Rampur (r. 1865–1886) expressed interest in the Ḥamzah romance, Ġhālib addressed to him a Persian praise-poem *(qaṣīdah)*[20] in which every verse contained a witty reference to one or more characters in the dastan. Of a total of forty-seven references, eight were to Ḥamzah himself, five to his trickster companion, ʻAmar ʻAyyār, and the rest to about thirty-three other characters; Ġhālib arranged the references so cleverly, and made them so evocative of the various characters' individual roles, that he clearly knew the dastan extensively and well. In an accompanying letter (1865), he gave his own account of the history of the Ḥamzah romance, calling it a "fictional" *(mauẓūʻī)* work "written by talented men of Iran in the days of Shah Abbas II [1642–1666]." In Iran, he said, it was called *Rumūz-e Ḥamzah,* while in India it was known as *Dāstān-e amīr Ḥamzah.* "It was written something over two hundred years ago, but is still famous and always will be."[21]

By the nineteenth century, however, Persian as an Indian language was in a slow decline, for its political and cultural place was being taken by the rapidly developing modern languages. But even into the early twentieth century, there was at least some market in India for short Persian versions of the Ḥamzah romance: one such version was published in Bombay as recently as 1909.[22]

The Ḥamzah romance spread gradually, usually in its briefer and less elaborate forms, into a number of the modern languages of South Asia. Pushtu and Sindhi were particularly hospitable to the Ḥamzah story, and at least in Pushtu it continues to flourish today, with printed pamphlet versions being produced.[23] In Bengali it was popular among Muslims as early as the eighteenth century, in a long verse romance called *Amīrhamjar pūthī* which was described by its authors, Fakīr Garībullāh and Saiyad Hamjā, as a translation from the Persian;[24] this romance was printed repeatedly in pamphlet form in the nineteenth century, and even occasionally in the twentieth. Various Hindi versions were produced, as we will see. But above all, the story of Ḥamzah flourished in Urdu.

The Ḥamzah Romance in Urdu

From the sixteenth to the eighteenth centuries, an important change was gradually taking place, first in the Deccan and then in North India: Urdu was developing as a literary language. It was equipping its Indic grammar with an extensive overlay of sophisticated Persian words, expressions, and idioms. It was also appropriating every Persian genre it could possibly use. Both Urdu poetry and Urdu prose seem to have developed initially in the Deccan, then gradually migrated northwards. The various genres of poetry, led by the ghazal *(ġhazal)*, made the transition quickly and easily.

Prose, however, was another matter. Dakkani ("Deccani") Urdu may have been, as was Persian, a medium for oral dastan narration; there is little evidence either way. But it could certainly boast the qissah-like allegorical prose romance *Sab ras* (1635) and the Ḥamzah-influenced verse narrative *Ḳhāvar nāmah* (1649). The latter in particular was full of battles in which Ḥaẓrat 'Alī, the Prophet's son-in-law, "fought with Devs and Paris, and confronted dragons, tigers, and ghosts"; the action also included "wars with hundreds of kings, and in between, some romantic episodes."[1] The Ḥamzah story itself exists in a late Dakhani prose version called *Qiṣṣah-e jang-e amīr Ḥamzah (Qissah of the War of Amir Ḥamzah)* (1784). This work was probably translated from a Persian text, but we cannot be sure; very little is known about its background. Dakhani Urdu was also the medium of a number of other, generally shorter qissah narratives with the typical themes of magic, romance, and adventure. These qissahs were produced from the seventeenth to the nineteenth centuries; the earlier ones were mostly in verse, the later ones in prose.[2]

Despite this early cultivation in the Deccan, written Urdu prose seems to have been a late migrant to the North: ordinary people were illiterate, and literate people, even if they spoke fluent Urdu, wrote in Persian.[3] "Until the end of the eighteenth century," according to Gyan Chand Jain, "the writing of prose in Urdu was such a unique thing that several authors . . . thought they had invented it."[4] A few manuscript works like Faẓl-e 'Alī Faẓlī's *Karbal kathā (The Story of Karbala)* (1732), a tragic narrative about the battle of Karbala; Mīr Muḥammad Ḥusain 'Aṭā Ḳhān Taḥsīn's *Nau ṭarz-e muraṣṣa' (A New Style of Adornment)* (1780), an elaborately told version of the Persian *Qiṣṣah-e cahār darvesh (Qissah of the Four Dervishes)*; and the Mughal king Shāh 'Ālam's *'Ajā'ib ul-qiṣaṣ (Wonder among Qissahs)* (c. 1790), also a traditional qissah, stand as rare examples—and even they tend to be heavily and somewhat clumsily Persianized in style.[5]

Azīz Aḥmad states flatly that pre-nineteenth-century Urdu prose developed an "intricate and interminable" romance tradition that "lost itself into the fantasies of the dastan, chiefly of the cycle of Amir Hamza,"[6] but there is not yet enough evidence to establish the point. It is easy to show that during the eighteenth century the Islamicized North Indian elite patronized the Ḥamzah romance in Persian; but even when Ḳhiyāl set out to challenge the dominance of the Ḥamzah romance he wrote, as we have seen, not an Urdu dastan, but another Persian one. If the Urdu Ḥamzah romance was cultivated, either in oral narration or in manuscript form, in eighteenth-century North India, no clear proof of its presence has yet been found.

There are a few vague traces, but they are exasperatingly blurred by the constant interpenetration of Persian and Urdu. One such murky trace is a verse by the great early ghazal poet Mīr (c. 1722–1810): "The story-teller's boy—how can I tell you, he's so worth seeing! / My and his qissah is, friends, worth hearing."[7] The verse is in Urdu, but were the stories? In the 1770s the Urdu poet Mīr Ḥasan composed, in Persian, a *tażkirah* or anthology of Urdu poets. In it he said of one contemporary poet, "He earns his living through qissah-khvani; in this art he is the pupil of the late Mīr Aḥmad, who was famous for his qissah-khvani."[8] A casual statement, showing that qissah-khvani was a well-known and long-established profession. But was its medium Urdu or Persian? An even more tantalizing trace appears in Ḳhiyāl's manuscript itself. Ḳhiyāl writes that when he had completed *Bostan-e ḳhiyāl* and was reading it in a coffeehouse, to the listeners' approval, a qissah-khvan made some objections, one of which was: "This man tells this story in Persian, but a sweet story is one which is told in Hindi [=Urdu]."[9] The qissah-khvan's remark itself is recorded in Persian, as is the whole anecdote. Do we here see the only real evidence of a parallel tradition of Urdu dastan narration in the eighteenth century, as Rāz Yazdānī argues? Were qissah-khvans like the one quoted here bilingual in their narrative skills, choosing Persian or Urdu according to the capacities of their listeners? We do not at present have enough evidence to be sure.

Once we move into the nineteenth century, however, we are immediately on firmer ground. In 1800 the famous Fort William College in Calcutta was founded, to teach Indian languages to newly arrived English agents of the East India Company. Fort William commissioned, and printed in various modern Indic languages (and Persian, Arabic, and Sanskrit as well), a number of simple texts that could be used as readers for language training. Most of the works Fort William published were prose fairy tales, romances, and fables, often didactic in intent. In the case of Urdu, the Fort William text *Bāġh o bahār (Garden and Spring)*, also known as *Qiṣṣah-e cahār darvesh (Qissah of the Four Dervishes)* (1801), by Mīr Amman, is recognized as one of the masterpieces of prose narrative in the language. The Fort William versions of well-known traditional North Indian folk narratives like *Sinhāsan battīsī (Thirty-two [Tales] of the Throne)* (1801), *Baitāl paccīsī (Twenty-five [Tales] of the Vampire)* (1802), *Gul-e bakāvalī (The Bakāvalī Flower)* (1803), and *Ārā'ish-e maḥfil (Adornment of the Gathering)*, also known as *Qiṣṣah-e Ḥātim Ṭā'ī* (1803), have enjoyed long and successful careers. All these works, including *Bāġh o bahār*, have been perennial favorites of the popular publishing industry from its very inception, in the 1880s, to the present.[10]

Fort William's Hindustani department included on its staff a "qissukhaun," or qissah-khvan, no doubt to give the students listening practice; we have, alas, no record of his tales.[11] We do know, however, that another member of the Hindustani department, Ḳhalīl ʻAlī Ḳhān Ashk, composed one of the first, and longest, Fort William books to be published: the 500–page *Dastan-e amir Ḥamzah* (1801). Ashk writes in his preface,

> Let it be known to all that this interesting qissah was created in the time of Sulṭān Maḥmūd Bādshāh. And in that era, all the sweet-tongued narrators sat down together to narrate and commemorate plans for battles and fort-seizures and conquests of countries. Especially for the king they wrote down fourteen volumes of the qissah of Amīr Ḥamzah. Every night they used to narrate one dastan in His Majesty's presence, and attain rewards and honor. Now in the era of the noble Shāh ʻĀlam Bādshāh, in the year 1215 Ḥijrī, that is to say, 1801 A.D., Ḳhalīl ʻAlī Ḳhān, who uses the pen-name Ashk, according to the desire of Mister Gilchrist Ṣāḥib of great glory and high praise, for the use of those who have just started to learn the Hindi [=Urdu] language, wrote this qissah in the language of *Urdū-e muʻallā* [i.e., standard Urdu] so that it would be easy for the beginning Ṣāḥibs to read, by His bounty and grace.[12]

In this notable preface to the first known North Indian Urdu dastan, Ashk brings together two classic dastan themes that are worth examining in a bit more detail: the claim of ancient, remote, and prestigious origins; and the claim to tell a story of great length.

Ashk claims that the story he is telling goes back to the time of Maḥmūd of Ghazna, in the early eleventh century; he implies that his present text is a translation, or at least a rendering, of the written, presumably Persian text that the distinguished dastan narrators of Maḥmūd's court first set down. Once again, we can see that Ashk envisions these narrators' oral dastan narration as closely linked to the production of written texts: they composed written dastans which they then narrated to the king. The actual historical claim involved is highly doubtful, for a fourteen-volume dastan would be a major undertaking, and we have no evidence that Maḥmūd of Ghazna ever sponsored the production of such a work. Gyān Chand thinks that Ashk in fact based his version on the Dakhani *Qiṣṣah-e jang-e amīr Ḥamzah* (1784),[13] which was itself probably translated from a Persian source. Certainly there are enough Persianisms of usage and idiom in Ashk's text to make it overwhelmingly likely that he had a Persian source, either directly or indirectly. His plot agrees in many important particulars with the early Persian *Qiṣṣah-e Ḥamzah,* but it disagrees in many others. In our present state of knowledge we cannot say whether he used a Persian text from which he sometimes departed, or used a divergent Indo-Persian text. The point to be noted is his finely cavalier attitude about the whole business: questions of plausibility and textual access and historical possibility simply don't arise. The claim's the thing, and the more sweeping and impressive the better.

In this he is merely continuing a classic dastan tradition. The early Persian Ḥamzah romance has been said to have been commissioned by Ḥamzah the Ḳhārijite;[14] the later Indo-Persian Ḥamzah romance has been said to have been composed by Faiẓī for Akbar.[15] The *Zubdat ur-rumūz* actually gives two conflicting origin stories: first, that after Ḥamzah's death anecdotes in his praise were told by ladies living near the Prophet's house, in order to get the Prophet's attention, and that one Mas'ūd Makkī then produced the first written version of these stories, in order to to divert the Meccans from their hostility to the Prophet; and second, that the romance was devised and recited by wise courtiers to cure the brain fever of one of the 'Abbāsid caliphs.[16] The 1909 Indo-Persian version also gives two conflicting sources: first, that the dastan was invented by 'Abbās, who used to tell it to the Prophet, his nephew, when he was feeling sad, to cheer him up with stories of his other uncle's glory; or, second, that the dastan was invented during the reign of Mu'awiyā (r. 661–679), to keep loyalty to the Prophet's family alive among the people despite official hostility and vilification.[17]

The point seems to be that the story should be ascribed to some irreproachably ancient and picturesque source, which will envelop the dastan in an additional veil of interest by evoking a bygone time and place; and also that the remoteness of the original source from the present audience will make incongruities or inconsistencies in the story seem no more than what one would expect. Dastans never begin with a "Once upon a time" formula, but invoking the mysterious aura of the past serves to create the same effect. The whole pretense of chronicle-writing and consultation of ancient "writers" or "narrators" which most dastans keep up (though only sporadically) is far from being a real historicity; it is in fact anti-historical, and serves to remind the audience that the dastan world is inaccessible, unchallengeable, wrapped in layer after layer of the past.

Ashk also claims that his sources, the narrators of Maḥmūd's court, compiled fourteen volumes of Ḥamzah's adventures. The implication is that the dastan is immensely large in relation to any individual narrator's resources of time and energy. (*Bostān-e ḳhiyāl,* with its fifteen

500–page volumes, had taken even the resolute Ḳhiyāl thirty years to create.) The single 400–page book that Ashk actually composed consists of twenty-two dastans, or chapters, grouped into four "volumes."[18] But apparently Ashk's plan for his work was at some point much more expansive—or at least so he told his patron, John Gilchrist, head of the Hindustani department at Fort William College, for Gilchrist wrote with suitably patronizing approval,

> If, as KHULEEL KHAN, one of the learned natives of the College, and who now considers himself the Hereditary Story Teller of the Emperor, Princes, and Nobles of India, asserts, the Historical Romance of Umeer Humzu itself, which he is now translating, will consist of 15 or 20 large Volumes, the patrons and admirers of the Hindoostanee may, in this branch alone, hail an inexhaustible fund of legendary narrative and diversion. Though oriental knight errantry and Harlequinism can hardly possess many charms for the present age, it may nevertheless exhibit in the wonderful feats and ingenious pranks of Umeer Humzu's squire Omr-yar, and such other heroes of Asia, some instructive lessons, as the first models of several of our most excentric ideal characters, in modern times.[19]

Even if Ashk never actually intended to write so many volumes, the numbers had a fine, grandiloquent effect: they were a rhetorical flourish, sufficiently impressive in their own right, and they served to call attention to the vastness of the Ḥamzah cycle. Moreover, by confirming that the ultimate size of the dastan was far greater than the text he had (so far) written, Ashk left ample scope for future dastan-writers to create "pre-legitimated" expansions and additions. Interestingly, at least one later nineteenth-century dastan-writer took very explicit advantage of this legitimating process: he claimed that of the original fourteen volumes produced at Maḥmūd's court, Ashk had translated only four, then had tacked on Ḥamzah's martyrdom from the fourteenth—and so he himself would now translate volumes five through eight![20]

During the early and middle nineteenth century, we start to have glimpses of Urdu dastan narration in public places. We know that the famous Qiṣṣah-ḳhvānī Bāzār in Peshawar was a celebrated institution, and that dastan narrators figured commonly in fairs and festivals, catering to mixed audiences of Muslims and Hindus.[21] We know from a travel book about Delhi called *A Tour of the Sights* (1820?) that nightly performances took place at the Jāma' Masjid: "On the stairs on the north side in the evening a qissah-khvan comes and does qissah-narration."[22] Writing in 1847, Sir Sayyid Aḥmad Ḳhān amplified this description of the Jāma' Masjid's northern stairs: "In the evening a qissah-khvan arranges a reed stool, sits down, and narrates the dastan of Amīr Ḥamzah. To one side the qissah of Ḥātim Ṭā'ī is being told, and somewhere else the dastan *Bostān-e ḳhiyāl.* Hundreds of men gather to hear the performances."[23] No less a literary figure than Ġhālib, who as we have seen took a strong interest in dastans, wrote in 1864 of arranging private dastan performances at his own house: "Muḥammad Mirzā comes [to my house] on Thursdays and Fridays at the time of dastan [narration]."[24]

Now that dastans were narrated in Urdu, the language of the general population, they could be enjoyed beyond the narrow ranks of the educated and elite; romance narration became much more like the popular, street-corner, coffeehouse tradition it had always been in Iran. From about 1830 on we begin to know the names of individual dastan narrators.[25] At some point during this period, "dastan" came to be used as a special name for the longer, more elaborate romances, like that of Ḥamzah, and "qissah" became a residual category of shorter, simpler stories that were more like traditional fairy tales;[26] but this distinction was never absolute.

While oral dastan narration was well launched in popularity during the first half of the century (if not before), dastan printing necessarily lagged behind. Ashk's text was reprinted several times, and two one-volume Urdu "translations" of *Bostān-e ḳhiyāl*—Calcutta, 1834,[27] and Bhagalpur, 1842[28]—were published. But dastans could not be printed on a large scale until sufficient presses were available. Presses had been in the hands of Englishmen, missionaries, educators, local rulers, newspaper editors, and others with various axes to grind, since at least the beginning of the century. Not until the second half of the century, however, did presses gradually come into the hands of enterprising businessmen with a keen eye for what large numbers of people really wanted. It was the second half of the nineteenth century that saw the Urdu dastan tradition, in both oral and printed forms, at its height.

The Dastan of Amīr Ḥamzah in Oral Narration

During the latter half of the nineteenth century, the Ḥamzah romance in Urdu reached a peak of popularity all over North India, among people at social levels from the highest to the lowest. Oral dastan narration became so widespread, in fact, that local styles are said to have developed in different cities. Suhail Buḳhārī claims to have identified styles associated with Delhi (simple and short), Lucknow (ornate and lengthy), Rampur (influenced by Lucknow style), and Akbarabad (a hybrid of Delhi and Lucknow styles).[1] In my opinion such claims go considerably beyond the evidence; it seems more probable that each city asserted the uniqueness of its local dastan narration on principle, as a form of proper civic pride. Most such claims of local oral styles are ultimately founded on the famous Delhi-Lucknow polarization; this great divide has been shown to be largely an artifact of cultural history in the case of poetry,[2] and I believe it is so in the case of dastan narration as well, though it is often taken for granted by scholars writing in Urdu.

In any case, local styles had to accommodate considerable movement of the most celebrated dastan-gos from one patronage center to another, especially when the rebellion of 1857 and its aftermath caused many narrators to leave Delhi. Lucknow became, and remained, the single most important center of Urdu dastan cultivation. For ordinary people, there were almost daily public performances by dastan-gos in Chauk, starting "when the lamps were lit." And for the elite, there were private sessions—even for ladies. Upper-class women kept their own female dastan-gos and storytellers, who were treated with real respect. Storytelling sessions often went on and on in the early evening "until the dining-cloth was spread."[3]

The Lakhnavī cultural historian "Abdul Ḥalīm Sharar assigns to dastan narration, which he defines as an art of "extemporaneous composition," a preeminent place among the verbal arts of his city. Sharar writes of this period,

> The famous dastan-gos of Delhi began to come to Lucknow. The opium-users valued them so much that they made listening to dastans a major part of their social gatherings. Very soon the practice had become so popular in Lucknow that there wasn't a rich man to be found who didn't have a dastan-go in his entourage. Hundreds of dastan-gos appeared. . . .
>
> The dastan consists of four arts: *razm* (war), *bazm* (elegant gatherings), *ḥusn o 'ishq,* (beauty and love), and *'ayyārī* (trickery). The dastan-gos of Lucknow have shown such expertise in all four arts that without seeing and hearing one cannot imagine it.[4]

This makes the dastan-gos sound like versatile all-rounders. By contrast, Viqār 'Aẓīm maintains that the Lakhnavī dastan-gos "cultivated their own special styles, and each one was known as unique and distinctive in his style." Their styles sound rather narrow: "One was excellent at portraying battle scenes; another was unequalled in describing elegant gatherings; another made the dastan pleasurable by including many verses; another's dastan was so humorous that whoever heard it rolled on the floor with laughter." Yet 'Aẕīm also agrees with Buk̤ẖārī about the presence of a distinctive Lakhnavī style of narration.[5] There are obvious gaps in our knowledge here, and we have no way of filling them.

While the art of dastan narration was cultivated longer and more intensively in Lucknow and Rampur, the dastan-go about whose career we have the most substantial information was a Dihlavī, and remained in Delhi all his life. We know somewhat more about him because his career extended into the twentieth century: born in 1850, he lived until 1928. Mīr Bāqir 'Alī Dihlavī was the last famous dastan-go, and by all accounts a great one; among his admirers was the "Grand Old Man of Urdu," Maulvī 'Abdul Ḥaq himself.[6] Mīr Bāqir 'Alī was born into a family of Persian emigrés, and was trained in dastan narration by his maternal uncle, Mīr Kāẕim 'Alī, also a professional dastan-go.[7] Several anecdotal descriptions of Mir Baqir 'Ali's performances have survived.

> He never *told* dastans—he presented lively, moving pictures; or rather, you could say that he himself became a picture. If he described a battlefield, you felt that you had seen the combat of Rustam and Isfandyār. If he evoked a romantic gathering, an air of intoxication began to pervade the atmosphere.
>
> His memory was so extraordinary that everything was at the tip of his tongue. If food was the topic, he described every sort of delicacy; if the subject of clothing came up, then how could any sort of dress escape mention? He not only knew the name of every kind of jewelry, but was thoroughly acquainted with its form and style. If anyone interrupted to challenge him, then what rivers of knowledge began to flow! His style was so fluent that once he had begun the dastan, he never paused for breath till it was finished.
>
> He was a thin, slightly built man, but while he was reciting the dastan, if a king appeared in the story, the listeners felt themselves standing before an imperious monarch. Sometimes, if he spoke the words of some old woman, he adopted the very style of speech of respectable elderly ladies, and even (despite his teeth) became quite toothless!

> . . . In his old age, he settled in Bhojlā Pahāṛī [in Delhi]. He kept up the tradition of dastan-narration to his last breath. Every Saturday evening, listeners came from miles away, placed two pennies in a niche in the wall, and sat respectfully down in a corner. Till the last watch of the night, held enchanted by his magic of speech, they sat breathless and still as if turned to stone.
>
> . . . Mīr Ṣāḥib was a regular user of opium, and unless he was intoxicated he could never recite a dastan.[8]
>
> He knew thousands of verses by heart. He also had the knack of using them appropriately. He had such a command of language that poets and writers accepted Mīr Ṣāḥib as an authority. . . .
>
> People used to say that some of Mīr Ṣāḥib's dastans went on for ten or twelve years and still weren't finished. From this one can guess what a great master of his art and language he was.[9]
>
> He never told even a small episode of the dastan of Amīr Ḥamzah in less than three hours. . . . If he began to enumerate the names of weapons, then he named thousands . . . the same with ornaments and jewelry, in fact with everything. In short, he was an encyclopedia of knowledge. When he described *'ayyār*s, people would laugh till their sides split. . . . Before beginning the dastan, he would wrap a pellet of opium in cloth, and dissolve it in a silver cup. With great refinement, he would slide into a state of intoxication.[10]

From the above and similar accounts, a few basic devices of oral dastan recitation can be pieced together: mimicry and gestures, to imitate each dastan character; insertion of verses into the narrative; recitation of catalogs, to enumerate and evoke all items of a certain class as exhaustively as possible;[11] maximum prolongation of the dastan as an ideal goal. Moreover, the association of dastan narration with opium is mentioned in so many contemporary accounts that it should not be overlooked. If both dastan-go and audience were slightly under the influence of opium, they might well enjoy the long catalogs and other stylized descriptive devices, which slowed down the narrative so that it could expand into the realms of personal fantasy.

Except for such fragmentary material as the above, however, dastan narration as an oral art is essentially beyond our reach. We are several generations removed from the last expert practitioner, and the secrets of his art died with him. No folklorist ever made a transcript—much less, of course, a tape recording—of an oral dastan performance. Nor would it normally occur to any listener to make such a transcript; and even if it did occur, he would find it almost prohibitively difficult under actual performance conditions.

Therefore we must be cautious about accepting what purport to be tantalizing fragments of just such a transcript. In his memoir *Dillī kī chand 'ajīb hastiyāñ (Some Remarkable People of Delhi),* Ashraf Ṣubūḥī includes long excerpts from what he declares to be one of Mīr Bāqir 'Alī's narrations. The performance probably took place in 1911[12] —but the book was not published until 1943. About his transcript Ṣubūḥī says candidly, "How could I remember the whole dastan—I am not such a memorizer, and it wasn't just yesterday. But some fragments have remained in my memory."[13] Judging from his book, Ṣubūḥī does have a vivid memory for detail, and Gyān Chand accepts the accuracy of his account without hesitation.[14]

The performance takes place in Mīr Bāqir 'Alī's house. Some visiting gentlemen from Lucknow, where dastan narration is still popular, have come to hear "a Delhi-style dastan"; there is an air of patronizing antiquarianism in their interest, since in Delhi dastan narration has fallen on hard times. Mīr Bāqir 'Alī takes a cup of a marijuana preparation and a cup of tea, then sits back on his heels and prepares to recite. After two introductory verses in Persian, he begins:

> The most humble one presents this delightful dastan from the point at which the *daftars Kochak bāḳhtar (The Lesser West)* and *Bālā bāḳhtar (The Upper West)* have ended, and the luckless Laqā, expelled from the court of Zumurrud Shāh of Bāḳhtar, has fled from combat with his Worship the Wealth-winning, World-illuminating Sun, the Planet-brightening Moon of the Sultanate of Bāhirah, the Chastiser of the Arrogant of the World, the Highly-respected Ruler, the Revered and Auspicious Lord of Arabia and Persia [i.e., Amīr Ḥamzah]; and many arrogant ones have already bent their proud heads at his fortunate door.
>
> In this time of joyful outcome, it happens one day that in the midst of the Palace of Solomon, the World-sustaining Court is being held. One or two hundred dancers, producers of pleasure, are in attendance. The *tablah* is being played. The trill of the *sārangī* and the deep tones of the drum reach to the skies. Various kinds of musical instruments—[here twenty-five kinds are named]—are being played. The rosy cup-bearers, bringing wine-flasks and cups, are stealing away men's senses. . . .[15]

At this point occurs the first of a number of breaks in Ṣubūḥī's transcription. Of the whole amount of text which he does provide, almost half consists of elaborate descriptive material like that quoted above. There are catalogs: champions' names; wild animals; boats; wrestling equipment (nineteen kinds named); wrestling holds (forty-three kinds named); 'Amar 'Ayyār's appearance and equipment. There are lengthy, sensuous, set-piece descriptions: a country scene in the monsoon season, a group of lovely Parī maidens, the Parī princess herself. There is ornamental verse, inserted freely and supplemented by many sets of doubled descriptive phrases sharing rhythm and end-rhyme. The effect is rich, ornate, self-consciously poetic.

These more dense and static passages occur like islands within a narrative stream that otherwise tends to be plain, colloquial, direct, and fast-flowing. As a sample of the simple narrative style, here is 'Amar 'Ayyār cleverly winning the confidence of a lovesick young prince, one of Amīr Ḥamzah's sons, who has fallen in love with a Parī princess and has just been reproached by his father for his distracted condition:

> "Son, I'm quitting right now! What reward can you expect from somebody who's so stony-hearted toward his son? He's forgotten his own youth—how he used to wander around babbling with love for Princess Mihr Nigār! He was ready to comb the dust of Mount Qāf itself for Princess Raushan-tan. And even now, if he sees a pretty face—I can't even describe the state he gets in. But not a thought for his son! He tells me to cool the fire of love by reasoning with you. So, my dear boy, understand: throw dust on the flames of love. But I've seen something of life myself. 'There's no more patience in a lover's heart, than water in a sieve.'[16] If your life were a burden to me, *then* I'd talk to you about patience and endurance!" At this he pretended to weep.
>
> The prince, finding 'Amar sympathetic, said, "Uncle, if you care about me, get me the address of that devastating beauty!"

'Amar pretends to demur, but allows himself to be persuaded by a gift of ten thousand rupees; extracting even more money from Ḥamzah himself, he prepares to set out in search of the Parī. And 'Amar setting out in his "real form" is an unforgettable sight: "Head like a coconut, face like a bread-bun, nose like a pine-cone, eyes like cumin seeds, chin like a sponge-cake, with a few hairs on it like a goat's beard only straight, shoulder blades like betel trees, chest like a basket, hands and feet like string, stomach like an earthenware pot, navel like a cup inverted over the pot, and adorned with '*ayyārī*-weapons." The inventory of his '*ayyārī* equipment which follows runs to twenty-three items; at this piquant point, Mīr Bāqir 'Alī's narration ends.[17]

In early Persian dastans Hanaway finds a similarly alternating diction, one which moves back and forth between complexity and simplicity of syntax and rhetoric. He identifies it as a characteristic "romance style," in which "simple narrative passages are combined with elaborate descriptive passages."[18] It seems highly probable that such an alternation of styles was a common feature of dastan recitation, in both Persian and Urdu, with the formal set pieces used to embellish the more colloquial narrative prose. But we cannot quite prove it. Hanaway is working from written texts. And since Ṣubūḥī's transcript was done from memory after a considerable lapse of time, we cannot be quite sure whether the exact choice of words originates in Mīr Bāqir 'Alī's oral narrative, or Ashraf Ṣubūḥī's writing style.

One other conspicuous feature of Ṣubūḥī's transcript is its thorough grounding in a larger narrative framework well known to the audience. Unless Ṣubūḥī has completely falsified the transcript, which seems unlikely, we can reasonably ascribe this major structural pattern to the dastan-go himself. Mīr Bāqir 'Alī names two well-established *daftar*s (large sections) of the dastan, refers casually to the most recent previous events, and takes up the action without further ado. Moreover, the narration itself is by no means a self-contained, complete episode. Rather, it is a bundle of introductory material, the beginnings of several adventures which are unashamedly left dangling at interesting and inconclusive points. The whole dastan itself was the narrative context presupposed by the dastan-go: it was relied upon to integrate and make meaningful the extremely minute, fragmentary threads of narrative which were embroidered into any individual performance. If Mīr Bāqir 'Alī presented such a narration even before a temporary audience of guests from another city, it seems safe to assume that narrations presented to the usual relatively stable audiences were similarly constructed.

Mīr Bāqir 'Alī enjoyed, as we have seen, a reputation as a dastan-go whose stories went on "for ten or twelve years and still weren't finished"; this reputation is adduced as evidence of "what a great master of his art and language he was." The interminable dastan, suggested both by Ashk in his grandiose vision of "15 or 20 large Volumes" and by Ḳhiyāl in his 7,500 pages, is a concept which lies at the very heart of oral dastan narration. The dastan-go could flaunt his power precisely by invoking and controlling this interminability: by a display of prowess called "arresting the dastan" *(dāstān roknā)*. The assertive power of this display was so well understood and admired that it could form the basis for a legendary battle royal of dastan narration.

> Once in Lucknow there was a contest between two master dastan-gos, as to how long each could arrest the dastan. One dastan-go brought his story to a high point: the lover has drawn near to his beloved. Between two frustrated hearts, between the lovers' thirsty eyes, only a curtain intervenes. When the curtain is lifted, the separated ones will meet. At this point, the spellbinding storyteller arrested the dastan. The listeners were eager for the curtain to be lifted, and the meeting to be described. But the dastan-go, through his capability, knowledge, and command of language, kept sagely describing the emotions of both parties, and the hanging curtain. This took some days. Every day the listeners came believing that on that day the curtain would surely be lifted, for there was nothing left to be explained. But they went home at night, and the curtain had still not quite opened. In this way the master kept the dastan arrested for more than a week.[19]

The reason length was so greatly valued in oral dastan-narration is not far to seek: length provided the direct and ultimate measure of a dastan-go's skill. For the prolonging of his narration depended on his audience's active interest and consent. The rapt attention of his listeners was both his supreme achievement, and the medium in which he worked. As Viqār 'Aẕīm puts it, it "follows from a dastan-go's situation that his object and goal is simply to cause the listener to ask in his heart every moment, 'What happened next?' "[20] To command this degree of audience attention grows more difficult over time; thus a longer dastan narration, like a longer tightrope walk, is inherently superior to a shorter one.

This vision of the interminable dastan, so central to the oral narrative tradition, was extended during the latter half of the nineteenth century to printed dastans as well. The combination of a new technology with an old narrative art produced, as we will see, extraordinary results.

The Dastan of Amīr Ḥamzah in Print

As we have seen, a few dastans had begun to appear in print in the first half of the nineteenth century. Only in 1858, however, when Munshī Naval Kishor founded his famous Lucknow press, did the real era of

dastan publishing begin. Naval Kishor, born in 1836 in a village near Mathura, was educated in the Aligarh area, where he studied Persian and Arabic in a traditional school *(maktab)*; the medium of education was undoubtedly Urdu. Though his family were Hindu landed gentry, his classical and Islamicized education was not at all unusual: it was in fact quite the normal thing in his day, for cultural traditions derived from the Mughal period retained much of their prestige, and Hindi had not yet been sharply divided off from an Urdu which belonged to everybody.[1] The young Naval Kishor did so well in school that he was sent to the English-style Agra College to complete his education—also quite a normal thing, for anyone could see that the times were changing and some concessions to the new order were necessary. During the five years that Naval Kishor spent at Agra College, he began to write articles for the local newspaper; these were well received, and he was awarded a government scholarship. His literary interests ranged so widely that by the age of seventeen he had added not only English but also some Sanskrit to his array of languages.

Naval Kishor learned the newspaper and book publishing business while working for a press called Koh-e Nūr, in Lahore. He then decided to settle in Lucknow and establish his own publishing house. In 1858 he obtained a hand press and set himself up in business, with the strong encouragement of Colonel S. A. Abbot, the Commissioner. At first he published short books that were guaranteed a quick sale: basic religious books, grammars for schoolchildren. But Colonel Abbot gave him government printing contracts, and soon he was able to expand his operations, though he still did most of the work himself. He then started the *Avadh Akhbār*,[2] a long-lived and immensely influential newspaper, and began to enlarge his list of books.

One of his early publications in the 1860s was Ashk's *Dāstān-e amīr Ḥamzah* (1801). This Fort William College production, the first printed Urdu dastan, had a head start on its few competitors, and Naval Kishor was not the only one to reprint it. In fact, its very popularity prompted the search for a successor. Naval Kishor eventually replaced Ashk's version, with a revised and improved *Dāstān-e amīr Ḥamzah* (1871), explaining to the public that the Ashk version, although it had been printed "in thousands of copies in Calcutta, Bombay, and Delhi" as well as at his own press, was marred by its "archaic idioms and convoluted style."[3] In 1871, therefore, he published the *Dāstān-e amīr Ḥamzah* in a new version by 'Abdullāh Bilgrāmī. This version proved extraordinarily successful: Naval Kishor and his heirs have kept it in print, with

relatively minor modifications, from 1871 to the present. Although it has always had competitors—and continues to have them today[4]—it has always outsold and outlasted them. The Bilgrāmī version has almost certainly been more often reprinted, and more widely read, than any other in Urdu. Thus it has been selected for translation in the present volume, and will be discussed at length below.

No doubt because of the popularity of the Ashk and Bilgrāmī versions in Urdu, Naval Kishor also brought out in 1879 a counterpart work in Hindi called *Amīr Hamzā kī dāstān,* by Paṇḍits Kālīcharan and Maheshdatt. This work was quite an undertaking in its own right: 520 large pages of typeset Devanāgarī script, in a prose adorned not with elegant Persian expressions but with exactly comparable Sanskritisms, and interspersed not with Persian verse forms but with Indic ones like *kavitt, soraṭhā,* and *chaupā'ī.* The text described itself in its frontispiece as telling of "courage and heroism like that of Ālā [=Ālhā] and Ūdal," the heroes of the widely popular North Indian folk epic *Ālhākhaṇḍ.*[5] In view of the great fame of the Ḥamzah story, the text sought to offer "to the enjoyers of Nāgarī [script] and the cravers for qissahs, knowledge of such an unprecedented dastan and conversance with worldly customs."[6] At the front of the volume Naval Kishor also included a list of his other Devanāgarī script publications: these were without exception Sanskrit or Sanskrit-based works on astrology, traditional medicine *(vaidya),* and religious topics. The addition of the Ḥamzah story to such a list represented a radical departure indeed, and bears witness to the story's widespread appeal among Hindus as well as Muslims; the story must in fact have sold well, for Naval Kishor reprinted it in 1883.[7] The *Amīr Hamzā kī dāstān,* with its assimilation of a highly Islamic content into a self-consciously Sanskritized form, offers a fascinating early glimpse of the the development of Hindi. The heirs of Naval Kishor apparently published a 662–page Hindi version of the dastan as late as 1939, but I have not been able to locate a copy. (Substantial twentieth-century Hindi pamphlet versions, undated, have also been published by presses in Delhi and Mathura.[8])

As if two versions of the Ḥamzah story were not enough, during this same period Naval Kishor added a third. He began to publish a verse rendering of the romance: a new *maṡnavī* by Ṭoṭā Rām Shāyān called *Ṭilism-e shāyān ma'rūf bah dāstān-e amīr Ḥamzah.* This version, which Naval Kishor published (probably for the first time) in 1862, was almost 30,000 lines long—making it the longest Urdu *maṡnavī* ever written in North India, with the exception of versions of the *Arabian*

Nights. Yet Shāyān, the "most prolific" writer in the genre, is said to have composed it in only six months.[9] This version too apparently found a good sale, for by 1893 Naval Kishor was printing it for the sixth time.[10]

All these were one-volume works; but most dastan-gos of the later nineteenth century would have scorned to confine their genius to the narrow space of a single volume. Dastans, now increasingly popular, were growing ever longer and more elaborate; professional rivalry among narrators was surely a contributing factor. Sharar describes the *Dāstān-e amīr Ḥamzah* as the "dastan narrators' real and essential arena,"[11] and most written dastans of the period, like most oral ones, indeed consisted of direct expansions and adaptations of parts of the Ḥamzah cycle.

Two extreme cases give an idea of the amazing written output of the dastan-gos of the period. Mirzā 'Alīm ud-Dīn of Rampur (1854–1927) had to his credit nine dastans. Six of these dastans consisted of five, one, two, eight, four, and five volumes respectively, for a total of twenty-five volumes; the other three consisted of at least one volume each, and probably more, for a lifetime total of at least thirty or so manuscript volumes. He was the most productive dastan writer at Rampur, but even he was outdone by a Lucknow rival, Sayyid Mīran Ābrū Riẓvī Lakhnavī, who produced eight dastans of two, four, four, three, two, two, ten, and four volumes respectively, and three dastans of at least two volumes each, for a total of at least thirty-seven volumes. Both these industrious dastan-gos used as their stock-in-trade plots involving enchanted worlds created by magicians, giving their works titles beginning *Ṭilism-e . . .* (*The Enchantment of . . .*). Sayyid Mīran Ābrū Riẓvī in particular gave to the world *The Ṭilism of the Land of the Jinn* (2 vols.), *The Deadly Ṭilism* (4 vols.), *The Ṭilism of Jamshed's Pleasure-house* (4 vols.), *The Ṭilism of the Underworld* (3 vols.), *Sāmirī's Elegant Ṭilism* (2 vols.), *Jamshed's Splendid Ṭilism* (2 vols.), *The Ṭilism of Nine Kingdoms* (10 vols.), *The Ṭilism of the Valley of Islam* (2 vols.), etc. The crucial concept of the *ṭilism*, or magic world, will be discussed below. Most of these *ṭilism*-filled dastans existed only as bound manuscripts in court libraries, conferring status upon their owners. Sayyid Mīran Ābrū Riẓvī did in fact show his manuscripts to the Naval Kishor Press, but none were ever published.[12]

Munshī Naval Kishor, whose business continued to thrive, steadily enlarged his list of publications. In dealing with dastans, he could afford to pick and choose. When in 1881 he finally began publishing his own elaborate multi-volume Ḥamzah series, he did not accept haphazard manuscripts, but maintained control over every stage of the production process. He hired Muḥammad Ḥusain Jāh, Aḥmad Ḥusain Qamar, and Taṣadduq Ḥusain, who were among the most famous Lucknow dastan narrators; one account has it that they simply "used to come [to the press] every day and recite the stories, and the scribes would write them down."[13] Another account adds that the dastan-gos worked together in relays, each picking up the story in turn as his predecessor tired, so that every volume was a collective effort.[14] Internal evidence suggests, however, that at least part of the time the dastan narrators wrote down their texts themselves. Jāh, for example, says of his own working methods,

> I write on oath that I left the manuscript alone and didn't even make a clean copy. Whatever emerged from the pen the first time, I retained. I made the style of every volume different. Battles, magic, *razm o bazm,* descriptions of beloveds and gardens and deserts, etc. —although they are all the same, this humble one has described them all in different ways. Still it won't be surprising if envious ones say that I have lengthened the story. [Although] everyone knows that even when children tell stories, as far as they are able they say [not merely "a garden" but] things like "a garden of flowers, with lovers' bowers, with nightingales singing, with all kinds of fruit on the trees." Truly, "the only pleasure of a short story is in prolonging it."[15]

By whatever hybrid methods they were produced, the forty-six volumes of this *Dāstān-e amīr Ḥamzah* were an extraordinary achievement: not only the crowning glory of the Urdu dastan tradition, but also surely the longest single romance cycle in world literature, since the forty-six volumes average 900 pages each. Publication of the cycle began with the first four volumes of *Ṭilism-e hoshrubā (The Stunning Tilism)* by Muḥammad Ḥusain Jāh; these volumes were published between 1883 and 1890, after which Jāh had differences with Naval Kishor and left the press. These four volumes by Jāh proved immensely popular, and are still considered the heart of the cycle. After Jāh, the two main architects of the cycle, Aḥmad Ḥusain Qamar (nineteen volumes) and Taṣadduq Husain (nineteen volumes) took over the work from 1892 to its completion around 1905.

The final arrangement of the cycle was into eight *daftars* or sections. The first four *daftars*—the two-volume *Naushervān nāmah (The Book of Naushervan)*; the one-volume *Kochak bāḳhtar (The Lesser West)*;

the one-volume *Bālā bāḳhtar (The Upper West)*; and the two-volume *Īraj nāmah (The Book of Iraj)*—were closer to the Persian romance, and were linked more directly to Ḥamzah's own adventures, especially those of the earlier part of his life. Then came the fifth *daftar*, the *Ṭilism-e hoshrubā* itself, begun by Jāh (four volumes) and completed by Qamar (three volumes). The remaining three *daftars*, though they make up the bulk of the cycle in quantity, emphasize the adventures of Ḥamzah's sons and grandsons, and are generally of less literary excellence. A list of all the forty-six volumes, along with much additional information about them, is provided in Gyān Chand's invaluable study;[16] a revised version of this list, incorporating new research, appears below as Part C of the Bibliography. Though no library in the world has a full set of the forty-six volumes, a microfilm set at the Center for Research Libraries in Chicago is on the verge of completion.

What does this immense cycle claim about its own origins? It sees itself as a translation of a (mythical) Persian original written by Faiẓī, one of the great literary figures of Akbar's court; this claim is made repeatedly on frontispieces, and here and there within the text. Like this purported Persian original, the Urdu version thus contains exactly eight *daftars*—even though as the Urdu cycle grew, the eighth *daftar* had to become longer and longer until it contained twenty-seven volumes. That the dastan claims to have a prestigious Persian source which was merely "translated" into Urdu should come as no surprise; in this case such claims have been decisively disproved.[17] The dastan-gos frequently speak of themselves as translators—but frequently boast of their authorship as well. Once in a while they make distinct claims of original invention, as for example Qamar does for the "*Haft balā*" section in volumes six and seven of *Ṭilism-e hoshrubā*. Occasionally they mention senior and contemporary dastan-gos whose versions are being incorporated or improved upon, or cite classical dastan-gos whose work has served as a model. Occasionally they refer to volumes not yet written at the time—or to volumes that never actually were written at all, but that they plan to write or could write if Naval Kishor should so wish. Occasionally they slip in snide remarks about each other—Qamar boasts of his superiority over Jāh, and Taṣadduq Ḥusain indirectly sneers at Qamar. All of them occasionally refer to "the dastan-go" who will embellish their written descriptions in the telling.[18]

And after all, what is their work like? An evaluation by Shams ur-Raḥmān Fārūqī, who has so far read forty-one of the forty-six volumes, suggests the following conspicuous qualities of this version as against the short one-volume versions: a much larger vocabulary of both Persian and indigenous words, many of them technical; an unimaginably more sumptuous verbal texture, with far more elaborate and prolonged wordplay, and more detailed and colorful descriptions; far more colorful and resonant names; a faster movement of events, and a larger, more complex variety of incidents, outcomes, and whole subplots; a tone much more amoral; a more erotic, less scatological interest in the body; much more humor; frequent use of long letters; a greater development of the concepts of kingship and *ṣāḥib qirānī;* a new notion of rivalry between the "right-handers" and the "left-handers," champions who sit on either side of Ḥamzah's throne. Fārūqī also notices much less reliance on Devs and Parīs, and much more inventiveness in the kinds of characters who appear: for example, human magicians who aspire to replace God, and who have magic artifacts such as submarines, flying spheres, etc.; immensely powerful but almost subhuman creatures called *dīvānah*s, "madmen"; a category of *qazzāq*s, "robbers," who are occasionally led by members of Ḥamzah's own family.[19]

This astonishing treasure house of romance, which at its best contains some of the finest narrative prose ever written in Urdu, was the delight of its age; many of its volumes were reprinted again and again, well into the twentieth century. But by the time of Mīr Bāqir 'Alī's death in 1928, dastan volumes were being rejected by the educated elite in favor of Urdu and Hindi novels—many of which were in fact very dastan-like.[20] In our century, dastans have been much neglected, though popular retellings and even reprints of parts of the cycle have kept appearing. Now there are signs of a welcome change: the whole *Ṭilism-e hoshrubā* in facsimile has just been reprinted in Pakistan, and is currently being reprinted in India.[21] While the forty-six volumes cannot be discussed in more detail in the present limited space, the best of them deserve a kind of serious literary attention which they have not yet been given even in Urdu, much less in English.

But whatever the fate of dastan literature in the twentieth century, toward the end of the nineteenth century dastans reached an extraordinary peak of popularity. Although the *Dāstān-e amīr Ḥamzah* and its extravagant *ṭilism*-filled offshoots dominated the scene, there was ample room left for the cultivation of *Bostān-e ḳhiyāl.* Not merely one, but actually *two* notable Urdu translations of this huge Indo-Persian dastan were prepared and published: one in Delhi, and one in Lucknow. The Delhi version, its first half by Ḳhvājah Amān and its second half (after his death in 1879) by other translators, was published in ten massive volumes (1866–1887) by various firms in Delhi and Meerut; judging by its survival rate in old book stores, it seems to have been the more popular of the two. The situation in Lucknow was more complex, for Naval Kishor and his competitors engaged in intrigues over the publishing rights, but finally a set of nine volumes (1882–1891) emerged, translated by various people and published by different firms. There were still other manuscript translations that were never actually published.[22]

The great poet Ġhālib himself, whose strong interest in dastans we have already noted, wrote a preface for the first volume of Ḳhvājah Amān's translation of *Bostān-e ḳhiyāl;* in it he praised dastans for allowing one to hear "what no one had ever seen or heard." He maintained that even the learned, who make a point of preferring histories, are susceptible to the appealing and charming power of romances—and furthermore, "aren't there impossible events in histories too?"[23] Ġhālib was equally enthusiastic about still another translation, this one by his "nephew" Farzand Aḥmad Ṣafīr Bilgrāmī, whom he congratulated on translating *Bostān-e ḳhiyāl* and getting "two volumes" published in Patna.[24] Ġhālib wrote, "This is a great kindness on your part—in particular, to me, and in general, to all those in India with mature taste *(bāliġh naẓarān).*" Later he helped to publicize the translation among his friends.[25]

To Ġhālib, dastan reading was an exquisite, escapist pleasure. In his old age, he wrote to a friend that he was "in clover": as we have seen, he reported receiving one massive volume of the dastan of Amīr Ḥamzah, and one of *Bostān-e ḳhiyāl.* "And there are seventeen bottles of good wine in the pantry. So I read all day and drink all night. 'The man who wins such bliss can only wonder / What more had Jamshed? What more Alexander?' "[26] The distracting pleasures of the romances were equally evident to the great reformer Ḥālī, who remarked acidly in 1880, "As long as our fellow-countrymen's ears are full of the sounds of the *Dāstān-e amīr Ḥamzah* and *Bostān-e ḳhiyāl,* nobody can possibly hear any unfamiliar voices."[27]

And dastans *were* seductive; everybody knew it. Virtuous women were strictly enjoined not to read them.[28] Dastans were some of the hottest literary properties of their day: combining the extravagant fantasy of Tolkien with the fast action of James Bond, they virtually cornered the market in sophisticated popular literature. They had everything—*razm o bazm,* adventure and romance, trickery and magic, and a lively sense of humor as well.

Dāstān-e amīr Ḥamzah: The Bilgrāmī Text

In the long run, Naval Kishor turned out to be a more important patron of the Urdu dastan than any prince or aristocrat: he was responsible for creating and preserving most of the texts which today provide our only real access to the tradition. As we have seen, Naval Kishor started with the Ashk version of the story. After printing and reprinting it, in 1871 he replaced it with another version which proclaimed itself a great improvement:

> Although [the Ashk version], because of its appeal to great and small, has been printed in thousands of copies in Calcutta, Bombay, and Delhi, and at the *Avadh Akhbār* Press, it has always been disliked by purists for its archaic idioms and convoluted style. With the greatest effort and energy Maulvī Ḥāfiẓ ʻAbdullāh Ṣāḥib, teacher at the Arabic school *(madrasah)* of Kanpur, has made modern additions and alterations and corrections in the language and idioms, at the desire of the Master of the Press. And under the supervision of the employees of the press of Munshī Naval Kishor, situated in Lucknow, in the month of November 1871 A.D., at the special request of Janāb Maulvī ʻAbdul ʻAzīz Ṣāḥib Bookseller of Lucknow, who has generously promised before publication to buy a great number of copies, with the greatest haste it has undergone publication.[1]

This new ʻAbdullāh Bilgrāmī version obviously sold excellently, for it was reprinted in 1874 with a note at the end expressing great satisfaction at its popularity. As the note complacently observed, the Bilgrāmī version had joined a growing tradition of successful Ḥamzah printings all over North India, editions which were selling out seemingly as soon as they were placed on the market:

> Although every dastan has a certain rank, nevertheless that pinnacle of speech the dastan of Amīr Ḥamzah has a rank even higher and more perfect. . . . For everyone seeks it with his whole heart and soul, from east to west it is in great demand. Previously it was printed a number of times in Calcutta and Delhi, and still is printed there. It sold so fast that in the presses not even one copy could be found—not even under dire necessity! . . . [Our new edition has] a thousand

> ornaments and improvements, and has become collyrium to the eyes of those who have been watching for it.[2]

The buyers of this collyrium must indeed have been numerous, for as we have seen, the continuing success of the Bilgrāmī version was followed by the Hindi *Amīr Hamzah kī dāstān*, by Shāyān's verse rendering, and by the immense forty-six-volume version of the cycle, as well as a number of other one-volume versions by other publishers. Throughout this whole period, and indeed up to the present, the Bilgrāmī version seems to have been kept constantly in print. It even inspired an English translation, though the work was never completed.[3]

About the author of the version, 'Abdullāh Bilgrāmī, we know only a little. He is identified by the 1874 edition as the "head teacher of the Arabic school of Kanpur," and described as a "Maulvī," or man of religious learning; as a "Sayyid," or descendant of the Prophet; as a "Ḥāfiẓ," or memorizer the whole of the Qur'ān; and as a "Bilgrāmī," coming from the small but intellectually sophisticated town of Bilgram, northwest of Lucknow. This official Naval Kishor description suggests a pious, learned schoolteacher of simple tastes, sitting blamelessly in Kanpur revising and improving the sometimes defective language of the Ashk version.

The truth, however, is much more complex, dubious, and interesting, for we now know exactly where Bilgrāmī obtained the text from which he worked: he plagiarized it. He did not base his work on the Ashk version at all, but took a version published by one Ġhālib Lakhnavī in Calcutta in 1855, embroidered it in various ways, and passed it off as his own. I know of only two surviving copies of this Ġhālib Lakhnavī text,[4] but they suffice to make the case clear. Ġhālib Lakhnavī[5] describes himself in his introduction as the son-in-law of the oldest son of Ṭīpū Sulṭān (r. 1783–1799), and claims—perhaps even accurately, for all we can presently tell—to be translating from a Persian text into colloquial Urdu, to oblige his friends who thought that the Ḥamzah story should be made more accessible to ordinary people. Of his narrative organization he says, "Since in this dastan there are four things, *razm*, *bazm*, *ṭilism*, and *'ayyārī*, the translator has made the fourteen volumes of the Persian into four."[6] The figure of fourteen volumes does arouse suspicions: could Ġhālib too, like Ashk, be claiming descent from the legendary Maḥmūd of Ghazna version? Ġhālib's version of the story closely resembles Ashk's throughout its first volume—then veers away considerably, with occasional similar episodes embedded among completely different ones.

Bilgrāmī followed Ġhālib not only in his general structure of four sections (he calls them *daftars*) but in an almost literally line-by-line way: though he sometimes added phrases of his own, he usually took Ġhālib's phrases and slightly modified them, most often by adding a rhyming echo-phrase. While Ġhālib's work contains almost no rhyming prose, Bilgrāmī's contains more than any other dastan text I have seen. Ġhālib's very simple, lively, fast-moving narrative is slowed into greater elaborateness by Bilgrāmī's additions—which, since they are being inserted into a pre-existing text, cannot really advance the story and must merely repeat and amplify what has already been said. Here, for example, is a Bilgrāmī passage with his additions to Ġhālib's original text italicized:

> *The arrangers of colorful reports and the news-bearers of variegated effects, the mystery-knowers of the arenas of event-understanding and the subtlety-speakers of the ranks of literary skill gallop the steed of the pen into the field of composition in this way, tell the agreeable story in this way:* When the Khvajah *after traveling a long way and traversing many stages* arrived near Mecca the Great, *from his halting place* he wrote to Khvajah 'Abdul Muttalib, who was chief of the tribe of Bani Hashim, a letter like this: This lowly servant has come to worship at Mecca the Great, and also longs to wait on you. *I hope that you will gladden me with a meeting, and show hospitality to a traveler.* Khvajah 'Abdul Muttalib, having read the letter, was very pleased. Taking all the nobles of Mecca with him, he went to welcome Buzurchmihr; he escorted him with the greatest honor and respect, *and had many fine houses vacated for him to stay in.* First Buzurchmihr made his pious visit to the Kabah with Khvajah 'Abdul Muttalib. Afterwards, he met the nobles of the city with great magnificence. Giving rupees and gold pieces to every one, he said, "The King of Iran says, 'I am most happy with you all, and know you all as my well-wishers, and want you always to pray for me.'"[7]

Bilgrāmī's additions were, as can be seen even in this small sample, much more extensive in the static parts of the story: in particular, he added the highly Persianized introductions considered very elegant at the time. He also inserted fairly long descriptive verse passages at some points in the story—including a conventionalized head-to-foot description *(sarāpā)* of Mihr Nigār, Ḥamzah's beloved, that ran to a hundred and fourteen lines. His additions tended to create the classic two-layered romance style, with its alternating complex and simple passages, that has been described by Hanaway.

The original 1871 edition was reprinted in a second, freshly calligraphed edition in 1874. An edition printed in 1887 describes itself as the fifth, and claims to have been newly revised by Taṣadduq Ḥusain.[8] However, the 1874 and 1887 editions correspond page by page and line by line, so the "revisions" are obviously the publisher's attempt to create new interest in a standard product. As the Bilgrāmī version was reprinted again and again over the years, a trend toward simplification eventually set in. It was a late and slow trend, however; even the self-described seventh edition, in 1927, retained most of Bilgrāmī's elaborate prose and verse interludes. At some point fairly soon thereafter, as well as can be judged from comparing the vague notes at the back of different editions, 'Abdul Bārī Āsī, a well-known scholar who was an employee of the Press, performed a more radical kind of surgery, stripping away almost all the elaborate passages, which were by then going rapidly out of fashion. In the eleventh and most recent edition, printed in 1969, the introductory part of the passage given above has been simplified to read, "The arrangers of colorful reports tell this agreeable story in this way," while the rest of the passage remains unchanged. The lengthy *sarāpā* description of Mihr Nigār has been eliminated, and other deletions of the same sort have been made throughout the work. These changes over time have made the story simpler and more translatable; they have certainly given the dastan the shape that it has today—and will continue to have in the future, for a new twelfth edition, virtually unchanged from the eleventh, is expected to come out soon. (All the modern editions are published by the Tej Kumār Press of Lucknow, owned by one of Naval Kishor's heirs.) It is the eleventh (1969) edition which has been used in making the present translation. All further discussion of the text and narrative will therefore be based on this eleventh edition.

By using the most recent edition of the most popular dastan text, I have adopted a number of editorial choices made over time within the tradition. However, since I have here translated only about one quarter of the 544-page Urdu text, I have had to make many additional choices myself. On the largest structural level, I have ignored the section *(daftar)* divisions entirely, and have taken liberties with the chapter breaks as well. This reshaping has not resulted in too great a loss, for the division of the text into four sections and seventy-nine chapters, called dastans, appears to be quite arbitrary. The breaks between Section One (27 chapters), Section Two (27 chapters), Section Three (8 chapters), and Section Four (17 chapters) sometimes occur in the midst of stories, at seemingly haphazard points. As for the chapters themselves, they range in length from one to twenty-two pages; some begin with elaborate, Persianized introductory phrases, while others begin in the midst of the action. Sometimes quite minor events are accorded chapters of their own, while much more important events are run together in a single long chapter with a title which does not refer to them at all. I have preserved the original chapter titles where possible, and in the remaining cases have provided titles of my own, identified by square brackets; all deletions within chapters are indicated either by ellipses, or by bracketed summaries of intervening events.

In the interests of clarity, the transitional comments between translated passages do not necessarily summarize all the material omitted; they aim only at making the following passages comprehensible. Footnotes too have been kept to a minimum. Diacritics have been omitted from the translation, but all important names and terms are highlighted by an asterisk on their first appearance, and will be found fully transliterated and briefly explained in the Glossary.

Since the Urdu text flows on from beginning to end, interrupted only by chapter divisions and occasional line drawings, I have also had to add punctuation: all the periods, commas, exclamation points, quotation marks, and even paragraph breaks are mine. I have punctuated with as light a hand as possible, aiming for intelligibility but not overdetermination. I have also had to decide about meaningful names: whether Ḥamzah's horse should be called "Siyah Qitas" (Siyāh Qīṭās) or "Black Constellation," whether Naushervan's vazir should be called "Buzurchmihr" or "Great Sun." My decisions about names have been based on considerations of English style and sound, and have not been consistent; all the important characters, however, appear in the Glossary, where their names are given in accurate Urdu transliteration and are (if meaningful) translated.

There remains the larger question of how, and how much, presenting only one-fourth of the original text has reshaped the narrative. Certainly the broad contours of the story have survived intact: Ḥamzah's birth, his early exploits at Naushervān's court and elsewhere, his prolonged stay in Qāf, his most important martial and marital adventures, his children and family affairs, and finally the circumstances surrounding his death, have been carefully preserved, with crucial episodes translated in full. The life and exploits of his closest companion, 'Amar 'Ayyār, have also been well represented. The cuts have been made in peripheral material and in recurrent adventures.

Cutting peripheral material has meant omitting the independent adventures of certain secondary characters: Landhaur, Bahrām Gurd, 'Ādī, and some of Ḥamzah's offspring figure much less prominently in the translation than in the original, while Naushervān's father Qubād and his courtiers, whose adventures occupy the first thirty-four pages of the Urdu text, have been excised entirely. Cutting recurrent adventures has meant that certain standard kinds of episodes have been represented by selected instances only, with many other similar events omitted: Ḥamzah's single combats, his journeys and encounters with strange champions, his killing of monsters and Devs, and his wanderings in the deserts of Qāf; 'Amar's feats of fort-capture, trickery, and *'ayyārī;* the visits of divine emissaries bearing gifts and injunctions—all these events occur far more often in the original than in the translation. Making the best of an inevitably idiosyncratic business, I have been careful to include my own favorite episodes, hoping that the reader will enjoy them with me.

What I have tried hardest to preserve has been the actual verbal texture of the dastan; I have tried to reflect it in English with a minimum of distortion. I have, of course, translated prose as prose and rhymed verse as rhymed verse; most of the verse is of minor literary merit, so not too much has been lost. To retain the rhymed prose was impossible, since Urdu, with its highly regular verbs at the ends of phrases, makes rhyme feel unforced and fluent in a way impossible to capture in English. I have, however, provided a sample of rhymed prose—in Chapter One, when Buzurchmihr predicts the newborn 'Amar's destiny. I have also retained the repeated phrases, even without their rhyme, and have tried to give them a certain texture and interest of their own. And I have been careful to carry over into my translation the strong tendency for sentences to begin with the name of a character, to use common, colloquial, "least marked" verbs and syntax, and to be organized paratactically—simply "one fact laid end to end with the next"—in a straightforward temporal sequence.

In studying and understanding the structure of the text, I have found one work particularly helpful: *Romance and Chronicle,* P. J. C. Field's study of Malory's prose style. Bilgrāmī's text, like Malory's *Morte Darthur,* puts "romance material into chronicle form": among the features common to both works are a simple, self-effacing, "matter-of-fact" narrative line; a heavy reliance on parataxis and temporal sequence to organize the narrative; sentences that begin with "and," "then," etc. rather than making "zero starts"; a sparing use of adjectives and adverbs; much repetition; and a reliance on "the rhetoric of popular speech," including formulas, agglomerative repetitions, heightened and simplified descriptions, etc.[9] Anyone with a literary or linguistic interest in prose romance will find Field's analysis valuable.

Beyond its obvious universe of other Indo-Persian and Urdu dastans, and its historical antecedents in medieval Persian dastan, a text like the present one can be studied from a wide variety of perspectives. Perhaps most immediately obvious is the cross-cultural comparison to be made with medieval European romance.[10] Moreover, since all romances are full of fairy-tale elements, and the line between short simple romances and long complex fairy tales is ultimately impossible to draw,[11] the work of folklorists like Max Lüthi is often extraordinarily suggestive.[12] Since even written dastans are so palpably shaped by the oral storytelling situation, scholars of oral performance too have useful insights to offer.[13] In the realm of formal literary theory, a number of new perspectives on narrative that have been developed in recent years can be tried out on dastans.[14] All these lines of inquiry offer opportunities for interesting future work.

Since the Urdu Ḥamzah cycle has developed entirely in South Asia, one further question suggests itself: what affinities does the cycle have with indigenous Indic story-telling traditions? The most obvious candidate for comparison to Ḥamzah is surely Rāma: he too is a gallant, virtuous hero, a demon-slayer, predestined to Divine favor, who earns his bride through his amazing prowess, lives a wandering life for many years away from his home, endures a forcible separation from his beloved, pines for her in her absence, receives aid from both divine agents and animal allies, and finally returns home in triumph—only to lose his wife again. Within the *Mahābhārata*, the figure of Arjuna suggests itself, while Bhīma might be said to have things in common with 'Amar (and with 'Ādī). In at least two Indo-Persian dictionaries, Landhaur has been explicitly identified—though on rather unpersuasive grounds—with Karna.[15] To the best of my knowledge, such correspondences are after-the-fact—though this by no means diminishes their interest—and do not prove any direct interaction or influence between the traditions.

When Naval Kishor published his Hindi *Amīr Hamzā kī dāstān* in 1879, his frontispiece made what is to me a much more suggestive Indic connection: it advertised the dastan as depicting "courage and heroism like that of Ālhā and Ūdal." The *Ālhākhaṇḍ*, a widely popular North Indian folk epic, indeed has certain resemblances to the Ḥamzah cycle. Ālhā and his brother Ūdal, its heroes, are warriors of lowly birth but amazing prowess, who win wives, conquer disdainful neighboring kings and their fortresses, and constantly achieve fresh feats of arms against incredible odds. In the end everyone dies except Ālhā himself, who has received the boon of immortality from the goddess Shāradā and wanders off into the Kajarī (=Dark) Forest.[16] Most of the cycle's episodes are called "The Battle of . . ." *(. . . kī laṛā'ī)* and/or "The Marriage of . . ." *(. . . kā byāh)*—a pattern reminiscent of the dastan cult of *razm o bazm.*

More to the point, it can be demonstrated that the two traditions have had at least some contact. I own a remarkable Hindi work well over a thousand pages long, called *The True Ālhākhanḍ: Magic Battles.*[17] In format, verse style, etc., it is a genuine *Ālhākhanḍ,* but the normal episodes are interwoven with *ṭilisms* and a variety of other magical adventures, all obviously influenced by dastan tradition. At one point, Ālhā and Ūdal themselves are trapped in a *ṭilism.* In true dastan style, the narrator first describes their misery and despair, then declares, "Leave them here in the *tilasm*—I'll tell more about them later," and turns his attention elsewhere.[18] This work and its "magic battles" would well repay further study. Moreover, while studying oral *Ālhākhanḍ* performers, Dr. Karine Schomer encountered one singer who claimed to narrate the Ḥamzah story as well.[19] This kind of tentative connection obviously needs much more work, but the possibilities are there. Ḥamzah may prove to have more Indic connections than have yet been recognized.

While a translator can never be wholly satisfied, I feel at least a bit content. It is altogether frustrating to try to translate ghazals, but by comparison it *is* possible to bring much of the flavor of Ḥamzah's life and adventures over into English. My work is emphatically not a "transcreation"; far from trying to "improve" the style or structure of the original, I have tried to retain it as faithfully as possible. I have been inspired by the work of translators like R. A. Nicholson and Reuben Levy, who know how to let a text be itself and speak its own kind of language.

Dāstān-e Āmīr Ḥamzah: The Narrative

The real action of the dastan—speaking now of the Bilgrāmī version which has been chosen as our text—begins with Ḥamzah's birth and ends with his death. His birth is the fulfillment of prophecy: although he is born in Mecca, an obscure corner of the Persian empire, he is sought out and honored by the vazir of the mighty emperor Naushervān, for he is destined to rescue Naushervān from his enemies. Along with Ḥamzah his two closest companions, 'Amar 'Ayyār and Muqbil the Faithful, are also born; the wise vazir Buzurchmihr predicts great destinies for them all. All three boys lose their mothers at birth, and grow up together in the house of Ḥamzah's father, 'Abdul Muṭṭalib. As they grow older, their characters develop along very different lines: Ḥamzah appears as the perfect knightly hero, strong, pious, generous and brave, loyal and trusting; 'Amar as the consummate trickster, clever, cruel, greedy, selfish, and unscrupulous, yet finally loyal to Ḥamzah; Muqbil as quiet, disciplined, self-effacing yet proud, a great archer, the one companion whom Ḥamzah will always keep with him when he sends all the rest away. The boys are soon honored by divine favor, in the form of specially efficacious gifts and powers bestowed on them by a series of venerable emissaries. Adventures and challenges begin to come their way.

Ḥamzah's exploits now take him on long journeys, but these always seem to begin and end in Ctesiphon (Madā'in), the imperial city, where the vacillating Naushervān alternately rewards and betrays him. He meets the love of his life, Naushervān's daughter Mihr Nigār, and sets out to win her hand. His battles and conquests, and his chivalrous behavior, steadily enlarge his small band of devoted companions. Despite all vicissitudes, Ḥamzah's life is on a rising curve, and things are going his way: he finally wins Naushervān's grudging consent to his marriage with Mihr Nigār. Just before the wedding, however, he is wounded in a battle, and rescued by the vazir of the Parī king Shahpāl, ruler of the realm of Qāf. In return for this act of kindness, Ḥamzah gallantly agrees to subdue the rebellious Devs who have seized Shahpāl's kingdom. The whole expedition to Qāf is to take eighteen days, and Ḥamzah insists on fulfilling this debt of honor before his wedding. We learn, however, that he is destined to be detained in Qāf not for eighteen days, but for eighteen years. At this point, the shape of the story radically changes: adventures take place simultaneously in Qāf and on earth, and the dastan moves back and forth in reporting them. While Ḥamzah in Qāf is killing Devs, trying to deal with Shahpāl's powerful daughter, Āsmān Parī, whom he has been forced to marry, and looking desperately for ways to get home, 'Amar in the (human) World is holding Ḥamzah's forces together, moving from fort to fort, and trying to defend Mihr Nigār from Naushervān's efforts to recapture her.

After eighteen years, much suffering, and more divine intervention, Ḥamzah does finally escape from Qāf; he makes his way home, and is reunited with his loyal companions. In the longest and most elaborate scene in the dastan, he marries the faithful Mihr Nigār. But by this time, the story is nearing its end. About two-fifths of the text deals with Ḥamzah's early years, about two-fifths with the years in Qāf, and only one-fifth with the time after his return. The remaining years of Ḥamzah's long life are filled with activity; some of it is fruitful, but usually in a kind of equivocal way. Ḥamzah and Mihr Nigār have one son, Qubād, who is killed at an early age; soon afterwards, Mihr Nigār herself is killed. Ḥamzah, distraught, vows to spend the rest of his life tending her tomb. But his enemies pursue him there, kidnap him, and torment him; his old companions rally round to rescue him, and his old life reclaims him. He fights against Naushervān and others, travels, has adventures, marries a series of wives. His sons and grandsons by various wives appear one by one, perform heroic feats, and frequently die young. He and 'Amar have a brief but traumatic quarrel. Toward the very end of his life he must enter the Dark Regions, pursuing a series of frightful cannibal kings; while their incursions are directly incited by Naushervān, 'Amar's own act of vicarious cannibalism (chapter thirty-six) seems somehow implicated as well. Almost all Ḥamzah's army is lost in the Dark Regions, and he returns in a state of grief and desolation. Finally he is summoned by the Prophet, his nephew, back to Mecca to beat off an attack by the massed infidel armies of the world. He succeeds, losing all his companions except 'Amar in the process, but dies at the hands of the woman Hindah, whose son he had killed. She devours his liver, cuts his body into seventy pieces, then hastily accepts Islam to save herself. The Prophet and the angels pray over every piece of the body, and Ḥamzah is rewarded with the high celestial rank of Commander of the Faithful.

It can be seen that there are a few shreds of tenuous historicity in parts of the story. The dastan-Ḥamzah, like the historical one, is born in Mecca, the son of 'Abdul Muṯṯalib; he is thus the Prophet's uncle. He is a strong and gallant defender of the true faith, who serves the cause of the Prophet and of emerging Islam (associated in the dastan with the monotheistic faith of Abraham). The dastan-Ḥamzah dies a somewhat historically realistic death: he is murdered by a vengeful woman who mutilates his corpse and later accepts Islam; his body is prayed over and honored by the Prophet. His geopolitical situation is also somewhat plausible: Mecca was in fact on the far borders of the Persian empire at the time, while Ctesiphon was the imperial city. The dastan-'Amar seems to have borrowed his name from a genuine early Muslim figure.[1] The dastan-Naushervān too has a real source for his identity: there had recently been a Sasanian king called Ḳhusrau Anūshīrvān (r. 531–579) and there was currently one called Ḳhusrau Aparvīz (r. 591–628); it is easy to see how the two might have been conflated.

Apart from these extremely limited correspondences, however, the dastan is clearly not historical. It can best be called Persian-traditional, since its debt to the *Shāh nāmah* is immense and obvious. It is the *Shāh nāmah*, not historical fact, which establishes Kasrā Nūshīrvān as a king famous for justice, and tells numerous anecdotes about his wise and virtuous vazir Buzurgmihr.[2] Above all, a number of Ḥamzah's feats and adventures clearly correspond to those of Rustam, setting up a kind of emulative rivalry which Ḥamzah himself proclaims at the end of chapter five.[3] Apart from many changes and additions of detail in Ḥamzah's specific adventures, the substantive changes from the early Persian *Qiṣṣah-e Ḥamzah* into Ashk's, Ġhālib's, and Bilgrāmī's Urdu versions are largely shifts in emphasis: a decreased respect for Naushervān; an enhanced respect for Ḥamzah and his one Indian companion, Landhaur; a livelier interest in 'Amar and his feats, especially vulgar ones; a much more serious concern with Ḥamzah's visit to Qāf and with other elements of supernatural adventure. It was not for nothing that Ġhālib Lakhnavī added two new elements to the traditional Persian ones: according to him, as we have seen, the dastan is made up of *razm, bazm, ṭilism,* and *'ayyārī*—in effect, war, courtly life and love, magic, and trickery.

All of which does not prevent the Bilgrāmī text from maintaining, however erratically, a pretense of historicity. Two rival schools of historians are quoted near the end of chapter twenty-seven; 'Amar's own testimony is cited by the narrator in chapter fifteen; numerous chapter introductions emphasize the purported derivation from chroniclers' reports. This claim to historicity seems at times to have created awkward consequences within the tradition: one recent Urdu version devotes its last twenty-eight pages to explaining most carefully and emphatically that 'Amar does *not* represent the Caliph 'Umar.[4] Some modern Urdu critics have made a point of ferreting out glimpses of South Asian cultural history from dastans;[5] this is, it seems to me, a doubtful project, of no more than peripheral interest at best.

The narrative itself constantly undercuts the pretense of historicity by playing fast and loose not only with historical accuracy but with consistency as well. A classic religious potpourri occurs in chapter thirteen, for Hell-cave Bāno's funeral procession features Brahmans, conches, bells, invocations of "one hundred seventy-five gods," fireworks, praise for Lāt and Manāt, and a group of fire-worshipers. There are also flagrant, explicit anachronisms: Buzurchmihr gives rupees to the nobles of Ctesiphon (chapter one), ʻAmar recites a verse explicitly attributed to the nineteenth-century Urdu poet Ṣābir Bilgrāmī (chapter eight). The dastan's claims to historicity were not of course taken seriously by the sophisticated; Ġhālib, as we have seen, praised dastans for allowing one to hear "what no one had ever seen or heard." It makes no more sense to expect—or even want—historical accuracy in a dastan, than to read James Bond books as a reliable source of information about the British Secret Service. At the heart of all romance lies the dream-nightmare double vision, the free play of fantasy over time and space.

The story of Ḥamzah should be taken for what it is: a romance which has traveled through long distances in space and time, and has developed a complex history of its own. As Hanaway has noted, the dastan is organized above all by its focus on Ḥamzah's life, from birth to death. Not too surprisingly, therefore, Ḥamzah's relationships with a few crucial characters serve to shape the whole story. Among all such characters, Ḥamzah's foster brother, ʻAmar, holds pride of place. He is in fact almost an alter ego for Ḥamzah: as greedy as Ḥamzah is generous, as unscrupulous as Ḥamzah is honorable, as vulgar as Ḥamzah is refined, as roundabout as Ḥamzah is straightforward.

ʻAmar is an *ʻayyār*—and what is that? Any answer we can give must be based on extrapolation, for nowhere do we have a definitive origin myth or code of rules for *ʻayyārī*.[6] The dastan treats it as a special kind of profession, passed on from master to pupil; there is an *ʻayyārī* dress and an *ʻayyārī* language by which members of the profession can recognize their peers. (Interestingly, Ḥamzah too knows this language, for he and ʻAmar are described as using it for secrecy in times of danger; Baḳhtak also uses it.) *ʻAyyār*s seem to be a normal part of a courtly retinue, and can defect to another king or feudal lord if discontented; kings have whole troops of them, though only a few emerge as individuals. They specialize in reconnaissance, espionage, disguise (impersonating women with implausible ease), commando tactics (scaling walls, tunneling into fortresses, killing sentries, knocking enemies unconscious with drugs), and other forms of guerrilla warfare, thievery, and dirty tricks. *'Ayyārs* are not really part of the courtly elite, and so have less dignity to uphold; they are tremendously given to playing practical jokes, especially vulgar ones, on each other and on their enemies. Bausani refers to them as "trickster figures."[7] The description of 'Amar's *'ayyārī* equipment near the end of chapter four is, in my opinion, one of the high points of the whole text.

'Amar, unlike Ḥamzah, has what can truly be called a wicked sense of humor. At times he laughs at himself, and far more often he manages to laugh at others. Apart from the running joke of 'Ādī's gargantuan appetite, 'Amar is responsible for virtually all of the considerable amount of humor in the dastan. Not only is the content of 'Amar's humor entertaining, but the very fact of its presence is notable as well, for humor has been held to be dangerous to the "high style" of romance. As Field notes, Malory uses a minimum of humor: "The strong and simple emotional responses which romance educes demand that humor be carefully controlled if introduced at all, or it may deflate the reader's whole reaction."[8] But in chapter nine, the sublime heights of Ḥamzah's rapture over Mihr Nigār, and the scatological crudity of Baḳhtak's being forced to foul his clothing and carpet, occur literally in the same room at the same time—yet thanks to the interposed figure of 'Amar, Ḥamzah's dignity is not jeopardized. By the same token, Ḥamzah keeps 'Amar's unbounded, cruel humor within some kind of necessary restraint. It is not surprising that John Gilchrist of Fort William College, the first Westerner to comment on the Urdu Ḥamzah romance, singled out, as we have seen, "the wonderful feats and ingenious pranks of Umeer Humzu's squire Omr-yar" for special praise.

Ḥamzah and 'Amar together are a natural, narratively effective pair. They are two halves of a whole: the adult and the child, the king and the jester, the feudal knight and the wild barbarian, the straightforward soldier and the devious guerrilla, the patron and the manipulator, the man who recognizes certain limits and the man who recognizes none. In classic fairy-tale style, the dastan expresses conflicts not by internalizing them within a single character's mind, but by embodying clashing values in different characters and then examining their interactions. It might even be said that in the course of the story Ḥamzah learns the limits of his power over 'Amar. Compare, for example, his reaction on two occasions, first in chapter thirty-five and then in chapter thirty-six, when 'Amar kills a prisoner without permission: on the first occasion, wrath and retribution; then, after he has seen the results of his behavior, silent resignation when the same thing happens again.

Ḥamzah and 'Amar act together while they can—that is to say, during the first and last parts of the story. During the middle period of their lives, Ḥamzah is trapped in Qāf, so the two do not see each other for eighteen years. They do, however, appear to each other in instructive or cautionary dreams. As the story zigzags unpredictably back and forth between ʿAmar in the World and Ḥamzah in Qāf, its variety, richness, and movement are augmented, while the suspense is very much heightened by narrative delays and postponements. For the most part events in the two realms progress independently. But who could predict that, for example, Ḥamzah's jealous wife Āsmān Parī would send down a hand *(panjah)* out of the sky to try to snatch Mihr Nigār from the roof of the fort, and would only narrowly fail; that ʿAmar in his anxiety and relief would go so far as to strike Mihr Nigār with a whip for going to the roof without permission; and that the sheltered Mihr Nigār would then actually run away from ʿAmar? Who could predict that a mysterious Veiled One Dressed in Orange would come to ʿAmar's rescue again and again in time of peril—and insist on preserving the secret of his identity for Ḥamzah's return? If Ḥamzah and ʿAmar were not so closely bound together, yet so painfully and radically separated, many of the dastan's most effective episodes would be impossible. Hanaway found, as we have seen, the whole Qāf episode to be a "strangely incongruous" case of "padding," and concluded that it could be "deleted without any serious damage to the story." In Urdu—and especially in the Ġhālib/Bilgrāmī text—it is almost the other way around: Ḥamzah's time in Qāf is at the heart of the story.

Qāf is the place of magic, of strange non-human races, of *ṭilisms*. Ġhālib Lakhnavī was right to add *ṭilism* and *ʿayyārī* to the list of basic dastan elements, for in Urdu they are of central importance. While feats of *ʿayyārī* are ubiquitous and easy to relish, the nature of *ṭilisms* is not so transparent. A *ṭilism* is an enchantment created by a magician; it can be as small as a brief magic effect or spell—or as spacious and potent as a whole world. (Enormous *ṭilisms*, though they do not occur in the present text, are everywhere in the forty-six-volume version; one scholar has recently argued that they are allegorical representations of Sufi parables about the deceptive nature of the "real" world.[9]) The essence of a *ṭilism* is illusion: nothing is what it appears to be, so that fantastic and frightful encounters are able to overwhelm the unwary. The victim of a *ṭilism* often thinks he knows what is going on, but he does not. *Ṭilisms* cannot normally be escaped from, only broken; the breaking of a *ṭilism* usually results in the death of the magician who has made it. A *ṭilism* can be broken only by its predestined destroyer, and then only by means of some special knowledge not deducible from anything within the *ṭilism* itself.

Thus when Ḥamzah enters his first *ṭilism* (chapter twenty-one), he is provided with a tablet *(lauḥ)* of detailed instructions—but he often forgets to consult it. The most common source of power within *ṭilisms* is the use of a secret, esoteric Name, which somehow invokes the power of the one named; virtuous characters use one of the known Names of God, or even the legendary unknown Great Name. Only constant aid and prompting from the Unseen enable Ḥamzah to thwart *ṭilisms* while still, as a good Muslim, refusing to dabble in magic himself. For he often finds himself bewildered: Qāf is full of strange species like the frightful demon Devs, but in addition to the "ordinary" Devs of Qāf there are the magic Devs inside *ṭilisms*, who don't respond to any of the usual forms of combat, who come back to life when killed, who often multiply themselves many-fold. Gorgeous Parīs inside *ṭilisms* may be demons in disguise—or authentic Parīs, trapped there. In a way *ṭilisms* show imagination raised to its ultimate power, cut loose and floating free, detached not only from the real world but even from the "real" dastan world. They show how dastans can command the farthest reaches of both dream and nightmare. Ḥamzah's courage, despair, vanity, and simple curiosity all lure him up to the heights, and down to the depths; of course his destiny is involved too, as the dastan frequently asserts (but never explains).

Ḥamzah's destiny is so arranged that the most important people in his life, after 'Amar, are two daughters of kings: Mihr Nigār, daughter of Naushervān the King of Kings (of the Realm of the World), and Āsmān Parī, daughter of Shahpāl the King of Kings of the Realm of Qāf. A few obvious parallels can be noted. Ḥamzah rescues both kings from usurpers and restores their thrones to them; both kings realize that accepting Ḥamzah as a son-in-law, despite his lesser lineage, would be a proper reward for this service. Both princesses see Ḥamzah before he sees them, fall instantly in love with him, and maneuver him into noticing them. Here, however, the similarities are replaced by sharply drawn oppositions. Ḥamzah responds to Mihr Nigār with unbounded ardor, and loves her passionately for the rest of his life; he tries in every way to overcome her father's resistance to their marriage. Ḥamzah responds to Āsmān Parī with no more than a brief (although quite evident) infatuation, refuses point-blank to marry her, and reluctantly consents only when coerced by her determined father.

Mihr Nigār, though a princess, has two brothers, and there is never any question of her inheriting the throne; she lives for the most part an irreproachably secluded life. Āsmān Parī, by contrast, seizes power even during her father's lifetime, takes the throne, and drives *him* into a life of seclusion. Mihr Nigār always does as Ḥamzah wishes; Āsmān Parī does exactly as she herself wishes. Mihr Nigār gives birth to a son, Qubād, who respects his mother and whose name links him with the Persian royal tradition; Āsmān Parī gives birth to a daughter, Quraishah, who frequently abuses her mother and whose name links her with Ḥamzah's own Arab ancestry. The dastan shows us, in short, that Mihr Nigār plays by the rules, while Āsmān Parī breaks them; in a way, Āsmān Parī can almost be seen as Mihr Nigār's alter ego.

Āsmān Parī—"Āsmān" means "Sky," with overtones of fate and destiny—can get away with her behavior because she is a Parī, a creature of fire, not bound by human norms; moreover, she is the queen of the Parīs, and much the most powerful of them all. Significantly, Ḥamzah begets with her a daughter, rather than the sons he has with his other wives. In the course of his marriage, Ḥamzah has nothing but trouble with Āsmān Parī; she is simply too strong for him, and he cannot control her. In marrying the queen of the Parīs, Ḥamzah has overreached himself—yet he never wanted to marry her at all, it was simply something that was part of his destiny. On the narrative surface at least, Ḥamzah is an innocent victim of fate: he is simply destined to have trouble with women, in life as in death, and in some way he understands this—as witness his cryptic remark in chapter thirty-four, when he is kidnapped by one of Naushervān's wives and rescued by 'Amar. Like a good Muslim story hero,[10] Ḥamzah must end his glorious rise to almost superhuman stature with a fall back into common human vulnerability.

When the destined eighteen years in Qāf are over, Ḥamzah is finally freed from Āsmān Parī's grasp; surely not coincidentally, his rescuer is another woman. Bībī Āṣifā Bāṣafā, "Lady Āṣifā the Pure," the mother of the venerable brothers Ḳhiẓr and Elias, commands a divinely-given power: she turns Āsmān Parī's fiery nature into literal flames that all but burn her alive. From that point on, Āsmān Parī is a changed woman: rather disappointingly to the modern reader, she loses all her flamboyant bitchiness. Her few remaining appearances in the story are exemplary, with barely a flash of the old fire. She presides over Ḥamzah's long-delayed wedding to Mihr Nigār, bringing wedding gifts from Qāf which reconcile everybody to everything. After a lavish wedding celebration (during which he divides his nights among his several wives)

Ḥamzah is finally able to live the human life he had wanted all along. Mihr Nigār receives the long-deferred recompense for her years of solitude and suffering, and as far as we can tell she enjoys it fully.

Ḥamzah was gone for eighteen years; he is together with Mihr Nigār for about eighteen more, time enough for them to raise their son Qubād to young manhood. Then suddenly 'Amr, Ḥamzah's oldest son, is killed in his sleep by a jealous woman. Soon afterwards Qubād is also killed in his sleep, through the thoughtless machinations of his grandfather, Naushervān. And before long Mihr Nigār herself is killed, while fighting off a long-time suitor who is making a last desperate attempt to abduct her. The crazed grief Ḥamzah shows at this triple bereavement is unlike any of his other emotions in the dastan. He sends away all his companions except Muqbil the Faithful, and plans to live the rest of his life as a *faqīr,* tending Mihr Nigār's tomb.

He is dragged back into the real world, of course, and obliged to resume the life of conquest and adventure to which he was born. He marries other wives—as he has done throughout the dastan, for even in his youthful days he was persuaded by 'Amar to marry Nāhīd Maryam (chapter fourteen), breaking his promise to Mihr Nigār that he would never look at another woman *until* (his exact choice of words) he married her. Ḥamzah's lesser wives are somewhat casually treated, but the Bilgrāmī text seems to recognize eight of them, of whom the following appear in the present volume: Nāhīd Maryam; Raiḥān Parī; Qamar Chahrah or Saman Sīmā Parī; Nāranj Parī; Gelī Savār the warrior-princess; and perhaps we should include the poor Cowhead princess, Arvānah, whom Ḥamzah so callously and inexcusably murders (chapter thirty). Ḥamzah begets with his minor wives a total of seven sons, but only three of these—'Amr bin Ḥamzah, Rustam, and Badī' uz-Zamāñ—are important in the dastan cycle as a whole. None of the women makes more than one or two brief appearances, generally in connection with courtship and childbirth, in the whole course of the story. Once Ḥamzah has lost his two serious wives—Āsmān Parī paying only rare visits from Qāf, and Mihr Nigār dead—his later, somewhat perfunctory marriages only serve to emphasize the winding down of his life. Ḥamzah has sons and even grandsons, but these gallant and promising young men rarely survive for very long; their untimely deaths foreshadow Ḥamzah's own. And Ḥamzah's death, as we in the audience know very well, will come about at the hands of a woman.

Besides his wives and 'Amar, Ḥamzah has a number of other loyalties—to his father, to his close companions (especially Landhaur), to his steeds (especially Ashqar), to Ḳhiẓr, to the kings Naushervān and Shahpāl—that lend additional kinds of motivation and structure to the story. These loyalties give rise to typical situations in which Ḥamzah repeatedly finds himself: arraying his army and directing its movements; presiding over the single combats of his own champions with enemy champions; personally encountering another champion in single combat; deciding the fate of conquered enemy champions; wandering alone or with companions in a strange country; rescuing people besieged in a fort; being urged to marry a local king's daughter, etc. Each individual strand is temporally linear, and the dastan is woven out of such strands like a tapestry. Thus the term "entrelacement" or "interlacing" used by romance scholars, and the phrase "polyphonic narrative": "In music, polyphony is a form in which the various voices move in apparent independence and freedom though fitting together harmonically. This is an apt metaphor for romance narration. . . . [W]e are presented with a thronging, level world, held at a constant distance from us, colourful, full of detail and particularity, ramifying endlessly outwards."[11] Temporal connections are multiplied, as we shift from one scene to another taking place at the same time, but causal links are almost never supplied.

The result is a story that is full of linear recurrences—but always with variations. Andras Hamori has described the use of rhythmic recurrence as a source of "musical pleasure," a means of holding the audience's attention: "You know something is destined to happen again, but you also know that it will come in by a different door, or even a window."[12] My own experience as a dastan reader bears him out. Not only does the constant rapid movement of the story make for variety, but the patterns of recurrence-with-variation actually enable the reader to enjoy the story with increasing subtlety and sophistication.

As a translator, I wanted to show my own readers how this could be the case. At first I felt handicapped in doing so, for the sheer length of the text compelled me to omit many of the repeated episodes that would illustrate my point. Finally I decided to choose one sort of episode, and include multiple examples of it. If I had chosen on the basis of frequency alone, I would have selected some episode of combat. Because of my own interests, however, and because it was convenient to have slightly fewer episodes to work with, I chose to concentrate on Ḥamzah's crucial relationships with women. In a general way, therefore, I have translated most of the episodes in the text about Ḥamzah and women. And as my central example, I have translated virtually every single word Ḥamzah exchanges with Shahpāl and Āsmān Parī on the subject of his departure from Qāf.

Almost as soon as Ḥamzah arrives in Qāf he begins negotiating for his return to the Realm of the World; since he knows that he cannot return without the Parīs' help, he tries to buy his release by cooperating. As his polite, diplomatic requests are met with evasion and deceit, he becomes more and more distraught; the result is a long, tangled series of struggles, interwoven with many other kinds of events taking place in both Qāf and the world, and displaying a number of recurrences. These recurrences include four major confrontations[13] between Ḥamzah and Āsmān Parī, each followed by a desperate effort on Ḥamzah's part to escape to the World. Since these four episodes have much in common, it might seem that they would grow tedious. But in fact, the converse is true: each one presupposes the previous ones, and screws the tension a notch tighter as Ḥamzah's desperation increases. The reader cannot predict exactly how any one of them will develop; memories of the previous ones permit a satisfying sense of recognition, and make the points of branching off, of differentiation, more piquant. Or at least so I would maintain; while the argument cannot be developed here at length, the textual evidence is fully present, and every reader can explore it.

The paratactic structure of the dastan in fact invites every reader to individual speculation. That endless string of seemingly haphazard, repetitive, randomly ordered adventures—does it not hold within itself subtle progressions, developments, meanings? Does Ḥamzah's character not help to make his fate? Does Ḥamzah's life not have some larger shape? Long interlaced strings of beautifully colored beads are held up before us; by the conventions of the genre, they are shown directly, authoritatively, without interpretive clues, without even a sidelong glance from the narrator. The narrator never moves below the surface of the story; but he may be addressing us in a kind of code. Parataxis involves simply "one fact laid end to end with the next"—but there are always "silent intervals," in Vinaver's words, between the facts.[14] What mysteries, what relationships lie in the "silent intervals" generated by parataxis? It is part of the lasting appeal of dastans that the text itself will never answer such questions; we are left to make our own meanings.

Dastans may be studied from any number of perspectives, but always, from any point of view, they belong most of all to their audience. Dastans are built around a "criterion of immediate rhetorical effect":

they abound in wild dreams and nightmares, dizzy ascents and disastrous falls, marvelous and terrible encounters. As the Bilgrāmī text itself explains at the beginning of chapter sixteen, dastans are not a whit more extraordinary than the realm of the World, in which we humans live. "The fickleness of Fortune is well known, the Conjurer's marvelous tricks are clearer than clear. Sometimes right in the midst of merriment, causes of grief make themselves felt; sometimes in the midst of utter despair, the bright face of hope can be glimpsed. Therefore this dastan follows the same pattern." Like all human art, the dastan both protests against the human condition, and in the end somehow affirms it.

NOTES TO INTRODUCTION

THE MEDIEVAL PERSIAN ROMANCE TRADITION

1. Both "dastan" *(dāstān)* and "qissah" *(qiṣṣah)* were used interchangeably, with the latter term predominating. To these terms could be appended either "-go" *(go)*, "teller," or "-khvan" *(ḳhvān)*, "reciter, reader," to refer to the narrators of the tales.

2. An abridged but useful English version of this important text is Levy's *The Epic of the Kings.*

3. Hanaway, "Formal Elements," pp. 140–43. This latter romance has been studied in Gaillard, *Le livre de Samak-e ʻAyyār.*

4. Two abridged English translations are available: Southgate, *Iskandarnamah;* and Hanaway, *Love and War.* One French translation has been begun, but not completed: Razavi, *Samak-e ʻAyyār,* vol. 1.

5. Lang and Meredith-Owens, "*Amiran-Darejaniani;* see p. 474 for discussion of the Ḥamzah cycle's continuing popularity, including this observation made by E. Bloch in 1934.

6. Page, *Naqqali and Ferdowsi,* includes detailed accounts of their narratives. Nowadays these storytellers are called *naqqāl*—derived from *naql,* "anecdote, story"—and according to Page they do not narrate the old romances as such, though they may freely borrow material from them.

7. Basgöz, in "Turkish *Hikaye*-Telling Tradition in Azerbaijan, Iran," finds that both the *Ḥamzah nāmah* and the *Shāh nāmah* are told during the two holy months of the year, when secular *hikaye* narratives are not acceptable (p. 394).

8. Hanaway, "Formal Elements," p. 152. For a conflicting view, see Alessandro Bausani, "Hikaya—Persian," *Encyclopedia of Islam* (new series) 3:373.

9. Lang and Meredith-Owens, "*Amiran-Darejaniani,*" p. 473.

10. Hanaway, *Persian Popular Romances*, pp. 196, 230, 237–38. The Ḥamzah text on which he bases his discussion is Ja'far Shi'ār, ed., *Qiṣṣah-e Ḥamzah*.

11. A. Guillaume, trans., *The Life of Muhammad; A Translation of Ibn Ishaq's Sirat Rasul Allah* (London: Oxford University Press, 1955), pp. 131–32, 283, 299, 375–76, 385–87, 553.

12. Lang and Meredith-Owens, "*Amiran-Darejaniani*," pp. 475–77.

13. Somewhat confusingly, there also exists a traditional Arabic Ḥamzah romance, the *Sīrat Ḥamzah*, but its hero is "an entirely different person who is, however, some relative of the Prophet." See G. M. Meredith-Owens, "Ḥamza b. 'Abd al-Muṭṭalib," *Encyclopedia of Islam* (new series) 3:153.

14. Lang and Meredith-Owens, "*Amiran-Darejaniani*," pp. 471–74.

15. Van Ronkel, *De Roman van Amir Hamza*.

16. Meredith-Owens, "Ḥamza b. 'Abd al-Muṭṭalib," *Encyclopedia of Islam* (new series) 3:152–54.

17. This printed version, *Kitāb-e rumūz-e Ḥamzah* (Teheran, A.H. 1274–1276 [1857–1859]), is in the British Library.

THE PERSIAN ḤAMZAH ROMANCE COMES TO INDIA

1. Schimmel, *Classical Urdu Literature*, p. 204.

2. Karl Khandalavala and Moti Chandra, *New Documents of Indian Painting—a Reappraisal* (Bombay: Board of Trustees of the Prince of Wales Museum, 1969), pp. 50–55, plates 117–26.

3. Bābur described this imitation as a "far-fetched lie, opposed to sense and nature." Annette S. Beveridge, trans., *The Babur-nāma in English* (London: Luzac and Co., 1969), p. 280.

4. H. Blochmann, trans., *Ain i Akbari*, 2nd ed. (Lahore: Qausain, 1975), p. 115.

5. Stuart Cary Welch, *Imperial Mughal Painting* (New York: George Braziller, 1978), p. 44. Only about 150 of these paintings are known to survive today.

6. Lang and Meredith-Owens, "*Amiran-Darejaniani*," p. 473. For an attempt to outline the story as Akbar knew it, see Glück, *Die Indischen Miniaturen des Haemzae-Romanes*; see also the more scrupulous Faredany-Akhavan, *The Problems of the Mughal Manuscript of the Hamza-Nama*.

7. H. Beveridge, trans., *The Akbar Nama* (Delhi: Ess Ess Publications, 1977), 2:343.

8. Gyān Chand, *Naṡrī dāstāneṅ*, p. 106.

9. Ḥājī Qiṣṣah-ḳhvān Hamadānī, *Zubdat ur-rumūz*, p. 2. The manuscript, which is in the Khudabakhsh Library in Patna, is unfortunately incomplete.

10. Aḥmad Manzavī, comp., *A Comprehensive Catalogue of Persian Manuscripts in Pakistan* (Islamabad: Iran Pakistan Institute of Persian Studies, 1987), 6:933–39.

11. Amān, "Dībāchah-e kitāb natījah-e fikr-e tarjamah nigār," an introduction to *Ḥadā'iq-e anẓār*, p. 3. (This is the first volume of Ḳhvājah Amān's Urdu

translation of *Bostān-e ḳhiyāl.*) In typical dastan style, there is another origin myth as well: that in his youth Ḳhiyāl invented one new qissah every day, at the command of a woman with whom he was in love. See Ibn-e Kanval, *Hindūstānī tahżīb*, pp. 24–25.

12. Ibn-e Kanval, *Hindūstānī tahżīb*, p. 25.

13. Gyān Chand, *Nas̱rī dāstāneñ*, pp. 598–600.

14. These dictionaries include *Burhān-e qāṯi'* (mid-seventeenth century), *Bahār-e 'ajam* (early eighteenth century), *Chirāġh-e hidāyat* (early eighteenth century), and *Shams ul-luġhāt* (printed in the early nineteenth century, but based on much older dictionaries). Examples of such linguistic incorporation are being compiled by S. R. Fārūqī as part of a larger study of the Persian and Urdu Ḥamzah tradition.

15. James Forbes, *Oriental Memoirs; a Narrative of Seventeen Years Residence in India* (London: Richard Bentley, 1834), 2:235–36.

16. Mirzā Asadullāh Ḳhān Ġhālib, *Ḳhuṯūṯ-e Ġhālib*, edited by Ġhulām Rasūl Mihr (Lahore: Panjab University Press, 1969), 1:385.

17. 'Abdul Qādir interprets the length as "960 pages." Sir Abdul Qadir, *Famous Urdu Poets and Writers* (Lahore: New Book Society, 1947), p. 42.

18. Only bits and pieces of this text survive, mostly on the backs of the famous illustrated leaves which are now dispersed in museums around the world. For a thorough and fascinating study of these fragments, see Faridany-Akhavan, *The Problems of the Mughal Manuscript of the Hamza-Nama.*

19. The one existing printed Urdu version (1842) was much shorter. There were, however, some Urdu manuscript volumes done at Rampur, at the Navāb's command, from 1842 onwards; see Ibn-e Kanval, *Hindūstānī tahżīb*, pp. 28–29.

20. Ġhālib, *Kulliyāt-e Ġhālib fārsī* (Lahore: Majlis Taraqqī-e Urdū, 1967), 2:390–95. I am grateful to C. M. Naim for bringing this *qaṣīdah* to my attention.

21. Russell and Islam, trans. and eds., *Ghalib*, p. 321. See also Ġhālib, *Qaṣā'id o mas̱naviyāt-e fārsī*, edited by Ġhulām Rasūl Mihr (Lahore: Panjab University, 1969), pp. 470–75. Apparently Ġhālib knew nothing of Akbar's *Ḥamzah nāmah*, which antedates the reign of Shāh 'Abbās II by more than half a century.

22. Mirzā Muḥammad Ḳhān Malik ul-Kuttāb, *Kitāb-e dāstān-e amīr Ḥamzah ṣāḥib qirān*. This version is in Butler Library, at Columbia University. Two other late printed Indo-Persian versions—Bombay, 1895, and Lucknow, 1906—are in the British Library. Each of the three is about 250 large, closely-printed pages long.

23. For this information I am indebted to Dr. Wilma Heston of the University of Pennsylvania, who has made an extensive study of modern Pushtu folk narrative. One substantial 324–page printed verse version in modern Pushtu, Jān Muḥammad Mullā, *Dāstān amīr Ḥamzah* (Peshawar: Miyān Ḥājī 'Abdul Ḳhāliq, 1949), is documented in Iqbal Ali Jatoi, *Bibliography of Folk Literature* (Islamabad: National Institute of Folk Heritage, 1980), p. 76.

24. Mannan, *Emergence and Development of Dobhasi Literature*, pp. 79–133.

THE ḤAMZAH ROMANCE IN URDU

1. Farmān Fatḥpūrī, *Manẓūm dāstāneñ*, p. 90.

2. Ibid., pp. 118–20; Gyān Chand, *Naṡrī dāstāneñ*, pp. 130–39.

3. The great prestige of Persian, which lasted far into the nineteenth century, was lamented by 'Abdul Ḥalīm Sharar in his famous cultural history of Lucknow: "But as for prose, the whole country was interested only in reading and writing in Persian. . . . The result of which was that however sweet and elegant the Urdu language had becoee for colloquial conversation, when it came to writing, everyone was struck dumb." Sharar, *Guẓashtah Lakhna'ū*, p. 181.

4. Gyān Chand, *Naṡrī dāstāneñ*, p. 143.

5. Ibid., pp. 140–47, 729–51.

6. Aziz Ahmad, *Islamic Culture in the Indian Environment* (London: Oxford University Press, 1964), p. 255.

7. Mīr Ṭaqī Mīr, *Kulliyāt-e Mīr*, edited by Zill-e 'Abbās 'Abbāst (Delhi: 'Ilmī Majlis, 1968), pp. 679–80.

8. Mīr Ḥasan, *Taẓkirah-e shu'arā-e urdū* (Lucknow: Uttar Pradesh Urdu Academy, 1985), p. 28.

9. The manuscript is in the Raza Library, Rampur; the anecdote is quoted and discussed by Rāz Yazdānī in his excellent article, "Urdū meñ dāstān go'ī aur dāstān navīsī," p. 9.

10. The modern genre of printed pamphlet literature, called *qiṣṣah* in Urdu and *kissā* in Hindi, to which all these works came to belong, has been studied in Pritchett, *Marvelous Encounters*; see especially chapter 2.

11. M. Atique Siddiqi, ed., *Origins of Modern Hindustani Literature—Source Material: Gilchrist Letters* (Aligarh: Nayā Kitāb Ghar, 1963), pp. 123, 159–60.

12. Ashk, *Dāstān-e amīr Ḥamzah*, p. 2. The "His" in the last sentence is cleverly ambiguous: it can refer either to God or to Gilchrist. In different editions of the Ashk text there are slight variations in the wording of this introduction, but the main points are always clear. I have not yet seen a first edition.

13. Gyān Chand, *Naṡrī dāstāneñ*, p. 134.

14. See Ja'far Shi'ār, *Qiṣṣah-e Ḥamzah*, introduction to volume 1, p. 3.

15. The claim that the Indo-Persian Ḥamzah romance was written by Faiẓī for Akbar is made most insistently by a later Urdu version of the romance, to be discussed below; the claim has been thoroughly discredited, though it lingers on in many library catalogs. See Gyān Chand, *Naṡrī dāstāneñ*, pp. 476–80, for a convincing refutation.

16. Ḥājī Qiṣṣah-ḳhvān Hamadānī, *Zubdat ur-rumūz*, pp. 2–3.

17. Mirzā Muḥammad Ḳhān, *Kitāb-e dāstān-e amīr Ḥamzah*, pp. 2–3.

18. The word "volume" *(jild)* can be used to refer to units of text ranging in length from fewer than 100 pages to more than 1,000 pages; instances at

both ends of the spectrum are easy to find. My observation is that the sense of "volume" shifts toward the large end of the range when claims or boasts of length are being made; but within a single book or manuscript small clusters of chapters are sometimes grouped together, and each of these clusters may also be called a "volume."

19. John Borthwick Gilchrist, *The Hindee Story Teller, or Entertaining Expositor of the Roman Persian, and Nagree Characters* (Calcutta: Hindoostanee Press, 1802), 2:iii.

20. Niyāz Aḥmad Ḳhān, *Dāstān-e amīr Ḥamzah,* p. 4. However, the author's own zeal seems to have failed him after a time: volume 5 is 132 pages long; volume 6, 83 pages; volume 7, 71 pages; and volume 8, entirely lacking (though the work is complete). This text is in my possession.

21. Narayani Gupta, *Delhi Between Two Empires, 1803–1931* (Delhi: Oxford University Press, 1981), pp. 5, 51.

22. Mirzā Sangīn Beg, *Sair ul-manāzil,* translated and edited by Sharīf Ḥusain Qāsimī (New Delhi: Ghalib Institute, 1982), pp. 18, 161.

23. Sayyid Aḥmad Ḳhān, *Āṡār uṣ-ṣanādīd,* edited by Ḳhālid Naṣīr Hāshimī (Delhi: Central Book Depot, 1965), p. 278.

24. Mirzā Asadullāh Ḳhān Ġhālib, *Ḳhuṭūṭ-e Ġhālib,* edited by Ġhulām Rasūl Mihr (Lahore: Panjab University, 1969), 1:329.

25. Rāz Yazdānī, "Urdū meñ dāstān go'ī," pp. 6–7.

26. This is how Sir Sayyid Aḥmad Ḳhān uses the terms in the passage quoted above.

27. Garçin de Tassy, *Histoire de la littérature Hindouie et Hindoustanie* (Paris: Adolphe Labitte, 1870), 1:186, 236.

28. This version, perhaps in the tradition of *Zubdat ur-rumūz,* was called *Zubdat ul-ḳhiyāl.* Ibn-e Kanval, *Hindūstānī tahżīb,* p. 28.

THE DASTAN OF AMĪR ḤAMZAH IN ORAL NARRATION

1. Suhail Buḳhārī, "Urdū dāstān kā fannī tajziyah," p. 96.

2. Carla R. Petievich, in "The Two-School Theory of Urdu Poetry" (Ph.D. dissertation, University of British Columbia at Vancouver, 1986), makes this case effectively.

3. These female storytellers tended to be among the well-bred but impoverished ladies who acted as companions, tutors, and general factotums in wealthy households. Such a lady was called a "Muġhlānī" or an "Ustānī." Mirzā Ja'far Ḥusain, *Qadīm Lakhna'ū kī āḳhirī bahār* (New Delhi: Taraqqī Urdū Bureau, 1981), pp. 168, 434, 453.

4. Sharar, *Gużashtah Lakhna'ū,* pp. 188–89.

5. Viqār 'Aẓīm, *Hamārī dāstāneñ,* p. 22.

6. Taḥsin Sarvarī, "Mīr Bāqir 'Alī dāstān go," pp. 74, 54.

7. Ashraf Ṣubūḥī says of him, "Mīr Kāẓim 'Alī went beyond qissah-khvani and began dastan-go'i" (*qiṣṣah ḳhvānī se baṛh kar dāstān go'ī shurū' kī*); he thus seems to treat these as two separate narrative arts, of which the latter was superior. Ṣubūḥī, "Mīr Bāqir 'Alī," pp. 43–4.

8. Sayyid Ẕamīr Ḥasan Dihlavī, in his introduction to Mīr Bāqir 'Alī's *Ḳhalīl Ḳhān fāḳhtah* (Delhi: Sang-e Mīl Publications, 1966), pp. 7–10. This work, one of a number of potboilers written in Mīr Bāqir 'Alī's old age, is a broad farce rather than a dastan. On these late works see Yūsuf Buḳhārī Dihlavī, "Mīr Bāqir 'Alī dāstān go," pp. 51–58.

9. Taḥsīn Sarvarī, "Mīr Bāqir 'Alī," p. 74.

10. Gyān Chand, *Nas̱rī dāstāneṅ*, pp. 108–9.

11. The dastan-go thus needed a wide technical knowledge in a number of fields. According to Ḥakīm 'Abdul Ḥamīd of the Hamdard Davakhana, Mir Bāqir 'Alī would often come and consult his (the Ḥakīm's) father, about the names and properties of herbs and medicines. S. R. Fārūqī, personal communication, November 1989.

12. Since Ṣubūḥī refers to the "Delhi Darbar" as a contemporary event, the other possible date would be 1903, the date of an earlier Darbar, or royal visit from England.

13. Ṣubūḥī, "Mīr Bāqir 'Alī," p. 49.

14. Gyān Chand, *Nas̱rī dāstāneṅ*, p. 524.

15. Ṣubūḥī, "Mīr Bāqir 'Alī," pp. 42, 49–50.

16. This Persian saying is from the *Gulistān* of Sa'ādī.

17. Ṣubūḥī, "Mīr Bāqir 'Alī," pp. 60–62.

18. Hanaway, *Love and War*, pp. 4, 18–19.

19. Gyān Chand, *Nas̱rī dāstāneṅ*, pp. 56–57. Another such performance is described in Ibn-e Kanval, *Hindūstānī tahẕīb*, p. 18.

20. Viqār 'Aẓīm, *Hamārī dāstāneṅ*, p. 361.

THE DASTAN OF ĀMĪR ḤAMZAH IN PRINT

1. The process of Hindi-Urdu division, with its related Hindu-Muslim mutual self-consciousness, did not really acquire momentum until the last decade of the nineteenth century. For a close look at this process see Christopher R. King, "The Nagari Pracharini Sabha . . . of Benares 1893–1914: A Study in the Social and Political History of the Hindi Language" (Ph.D. dissertation, University of Wisconsin, 1974).

2. Amīr Ḥasan Nūrānī, *Munshī Naval Kishor: ḥālāt aur ḳhidmāt* (Delhi: Idārah-e Iḳhvān uṣ-Ṣafā, 1982), pp. 23–29.

3. Bilgrāmī, *Dāstān-e amīr Ḥamzah* (1871), p. 752.

4. The most recent that I've seen are: Ḥamīd Buk Ḍipo, *Aṣlī mukammal dāstān-e amīr Ḥamzah urdū bataṣvīr;* Mubīn ur-Raḥmān, *Dāstān-e amīr Ḥamzah;* and Jahāngīr Buk Ḍipo, *Mukammal o bataṣvīr dāstān-e amīr Ḥamzah.* All three are divided into eighty-eight dastans, use modern (though minimal) paragraph breaks, and in plot are fairly close to the Ashk version, though they all differ from each other.

5. On the background of this most important modern North Indian folk epic see William Waterfield, *The Lay of Alha: A Saga of Rajput Chivalry as Sung by Minstrels of Northern India* (London: Oxford University Press, 1923). See also Karine Schomer, "Paradigms for the Kali Yuga: The Heroes of the Ālhā

Epic and their Fate," in Blackburn et al., *Oral Epics in India*, pp. 140–54; and Laxmi G. Tewari, "An Elementary Reading of the Ālhākhaṇḍ," in *South Asia Research* 9,1:3–20, May 1989.

6. Kālīcharan and Maheshdatt, *Amīr Hamzā kī dāstān*. This edition is in the collection of the British Library.

7. This second edition is in the Bodleian Library at Oxford.

8. One example: Munshī Badrīprasād Jain, anuvādak, *Amīr Hamzā chāroñ bhāg* (Mathura: Shyāmkāshī Press, n.d.), 248, 222, 136, 207 p.

9. Gyān Chand, *Urdū maśnavī shumālī Hind meñ* (Aligarh: Anjuman Taraqqī-e Urdū, 1969), p. 653. Gyān Chand says it was composed "after 1862," but the British Library has a copy published in 1862.

10. M. A. R. Barker, *A List of Books on Urdu Literature in the Collection of Dr. M. A. R. Barker* (McGill University, Institute of Islamic Studies, 1964), item no. 664.

11. Sharar, *Guẓashtah Lakhna'ū*, p. 188.

12. Gyān Chand, *Naśrī dāstāneñ*, pp. 505–06, 518–20.

13. Ralph Russell, "The Development of the Modern Novel in Urdu" pp. 102–141. Russell discusses this account on p. 108; its source is a letter from Naval Kishor's heirs quoted in Rāz Yazdānī, "Urdū dāstānoñ par," p. 34.

14. Amīr Ḥasan Nūrānī, *Munshī Naval Kishor: ḥālāt aur ḳhidmāt*, pp. 77–79.

15. Jāh, *Ṭilism-e hoshrubā*, 3:920.

16. Gyān Chand, *Naśrī dāstāneñ*, pp. 470–90.

17. See for example Rāz Yazdānī, "Urdū dāstānoñ par," pp. 32–34. The general question of sources is also discussed, and Persian sources disproved, in Gyān Chand, *Naśrī dāstāneñ*, pp. 476–90.

18. Many of these points were made to me by S. R. Fārūqī, to whom I am indebted for so much of my knowledge about the forty-six-volume version.

19. S. R. Fārūqī, personal communication, August 28, 1986.

20. On early Urdu novels see Russell, "The Development of the Modern Novel in Urdu." On early Hindi novels, which were also heavily indebted to the dastan tradition, see Krishnā Majīṭhiyā, *Hindī ke tilasmī va jāsūsī upanyās* (Jaipur: Panchshīl Prakāshan, 1978), especially pp. 32–75 on the ever-popular Devakīnandan Khatrī, whose *Chandrakāntā* (1888) and its successors were full of *aiyār*s and *tilisms*.

21. The Pakistani edition, seven volumes, is a handsome one by Sang-i Mīl Publications, Lahore; the Indian edition, by the Khudabakhsh Library, Patna, will include the two volumes of the related *Baqiyah-e ṭilism-e hoshrubā* and a volume of critical articles.

22. The whole complex situation is discussed in detail, with lists of volumes, in Gyān Chand, *Naśrī dāstāneñ*, pp. 598–613.

23. Mirzā Ġhālib, "Dībāchah," in Ḳhvājah Amān, *Ḥadā'iq-e anẓār*, p. 2. Ġhālib's examples show that he was treating the *Shāh nāmah* as a history; this naturally made it easy for him to prove his case about impossible *(mumtani' ul-vaqū')* events.

24. These were the first of a total of ten. Ibn-e Kanval, *Hindūstānī tahżīb*, p. 29.

25. Ġhālib, *Ḳhuṯūṯ*, ed. by Ġhulām Rasūl Mihr, 2:795. See also Russell and Islam, *Ghalib*, pp. 314–15, 334–35.

26. Russell and Islam, *Ghalib*, p. 255.

27. Alṯāf Ḥusain Ḥālī, *Kulliyāt-e naśr-e Ḥālī*, edited by Shaiḳh Muḥammad Ismā'īl Pānīpātī (Lahore: Majlis Taraqqī-e Adab, 1968), p. 179.

28. As for example by Ashraf 'Alī Thānavī, who includes the *Dāstān-e amīr Ḥamzah* among "Books which it is Harmful to Look Into," in his famous turn-of-the-century handbook for women, *Bihishtī zevar* (Lahore: Maktabah ul-'Azīziyan, n.d.), p. 819. On this attitude see Barbara D. Metcalf, "Maulānā 'Ashraf 'Alī Thānavī and Urdu Literature," in Christopher Shackle, ed., *Urdu and Muslim South Asia: Studies in Honour of Ralph Russell* (London: School of Oriental and African Studies, 1989), pp. 93–100.

DĀSTĀN-E AMĪR ḤAMZAH: THE BILGRĀMĪ TEXT

1. Bilgrāmī, *Dāstān-e amīr Ḥamzah* (1871), p. 752. This text is in the India Office section of the British Library, and is available on microfilm.

2. Bilgrāmī, *Dāstān-e amīr Ḥamzah* (1874), pp. 559–60. The reduction in length from 750 to 560 pages was due to changes in format, not in content.

3. Husain, *The Amir Hamza, an Oriental Novel.* Only Part 1 exists; apparently no more was ever published. The text is in the British Library.

4. It was my great good fortune to discover one surviving copy, battered but complete, in July 1985, and to be able to buy it. A microfiche of it is now in the collection of the Library of Congress. Another copy is in the Panjab University Library in Lahore; see Suhail Buḳhārī, *Urdū dāstān*, pp. 228–29.

5. Ġhālib Lakhnavī, an obscure figure, is mentioned in one *tażkirah*, *Suḳhan-e shu'arā* by 'Abd ul-Ġhafūr Nassāḳh; he is described as a student of the poet Qaṯīl, and a convert from Hinduism. I am indebted to S. R. Fārūqī for this information.

6. Ġhālib Lakhnavī, *Tarjamah-e dāstān-e ṣāḥib qirān*, pp. 1–2.

7. Ibid., p. 30; Bilgrāmī, *Dāstān-e amīr Ḥamzah* (1871), p. 48.

8. This was not the same Taṣadduq Ḥusain who wrote much of the forty-six-volume version, but a man of learning employed as a *muṣaḥḥiḥ*, or editor, at the Naval Kishor Press.

9. Field, *Romance and Chronicle*, pp. 36–82.

10. Gillian M. Beer's *The Romance* includes an annotated bibliography. Also of interest are R. S. Crane's extensive study, "The Vogue of *Guy of Warwick* from the Close of the Middle Ages to the Romantic Revival" in *P.M.L.A.* 30(2):125–194, 1915, and John J. O'Connor's *Amadis de Gaule and its Influence on Elizabethan Literature* (New Brunswick, N.J.: Rutgers University Press, 1970).

11. This point is argued in Pritchett, *Marvelous Encounters*, pp. 164–69.

12. Perhaps the best introduction to his work is Max Lüthi, *The Fairytale as Art Form and Portrait of Man*, translated by Jon Erickson (Bloomington:

Indiana University Press, 1984). See also the useful volume *Folklore Genres*, edited by Dan Ben-Amos (Austin: University of Texas Press, 1976).

13. For a good overview of this complex question, see Walter J. Ong, *Orality and Literacy; the Technologizing of the Word* (London: Methuen, 1982). Also of interest is Michael D. Cherniss, "Beowulf: Oral Presentation and the Criterion of Immediate Rhetorical Effect," in *Genre* 3:214–228, September 1970.

14. Tzvetan Todorov, *The Fantastic: A Structural Approach to a Liberary Genre*, translated by Richard Howard (Ithaca: Cornell University Press, 1975) is of special relevance. Robert Scholes, *Semiotics and Interpretation* (New Haven: Yale University Press, 1982), provides a select and well-annotated bibliography.

15. See Pritchett, "Emperor of India."

16. See Blackburn et al., *Oral Epics in India*, pp. 201–02.

17. Maṭarūlāl Goyal Meraṭhī, *Aslī Ālhākhanḍ jādū kī laṛā'iyāñ* (Delhi: Dehātī Pustak Bhanḍār, n.d. [mid-1960s]).

18. Maṭarūlāl, *Aslī Alhākhanḍ*, "Bhīmsinh kā byāh, Sohangaṛh kī laṛā'ī," p. 188. The variant spelling *"tilasm"* is common in Hindi.

19. Dr. Karine Schomer, personal communication, April 1984.

DĀSTĀN-E ĀMĪR ḤAMZAH: THE NARRATIVE

1. See Louis Massignon, *The Passion of al-Hallāj: Mystic and Martyr of Islam*, translated by Herbert Mason (Princeton: Princeton University Press, 1982): 'Amr bin Umayya Damrī [sic] was a disciple (1:621) of Salmān Fārisī, "the spiritual adviser of the Family of the Prophet," and as Salmān became an important mystical figure in the theology of certain Shī'ite groups (1:300–1, 3:34–35, etc.), 'Amr Damrī sometimes played an ancillary role (2:93). Sharar maintained that the historical 'Amr bin Umayyah Ẓamirī had been, before his conversion, a terrifying, murderous bandit famous for his great speed; see Suhail Aḥmad Ḳhān, *Dāstānoñ kī 'alāmatī kā'ināt*, p. 109.

2. See Levy, *The Epic of the Kings*, pp. 324–34.

3. In fact, in the early Persian *Qiṣṣah-e Ḥamzah* Buzurgmihr is originally sent by Nūshīrvān not to honor the infant Ḥamzah as a predestined rescuer—but to kill him as a predestined rival. Ja'far Shi'ār, ed., *Qiṣṣah-e Ḥamzah*, 1:24.

4. Ratan ainḍ Kampanī, *Dāstān-e amīr Ḥamzah mukammal chār ḥiṣṣe*, pp. 308–36. 'Amar is a (deliberately mispronounced) variant of 'Amr, the diminutive of 'Umar.

5. See for example Rāhī Ma'sūm Riẓā, *Ṭilism-e hoshrubā*, and Ibn-e Kanval, *Hindūstānī tahżīb*.

6. For a discussion of the subject see Sayyid Aḳhtar Mas'ūd Riẓvī, "Kuchh 'ayyāroñ ke bāre meñ," in his *Fikrī kāvisheñ* (Peshawar: Maktabah-e Shāhīn, n.d.), pp. 5–29.

7. See Bausani, "An Islamic Echo of the 'Trickster'?"

8. Field, *Romance and Chronicle*, p. 109.

9. Suhail Aḥmad Ḳhān, *Dāstānoñ kī ʻalāmatī kā'ināt*, pp. 65–101.

10. J. A. B. van Buitenen outlines a broad contrast between Hindu and Muslim story heroes in "The Indian Hero as Vidyadhara," in *Traditional India: Structure and Change*, edited by Milton Singer (Philadelphia: American Folklore Society, 1959), pp. 99–105.

11. Beer, *The Romance*, pp. 20–21.

12. Andras Hamori, *On the Art of Medieval Arabic Literature* (Princeton: Princeton University Press, 1964), p. 172.

13. These quarrels occur in the beginning of chapters twenty-three, twenty-four, and twenty-six, and at the end of chapter twenty-seven.

14. Eugene Vinaver, *The Rise of Romance* (Oxford: Clarendon Press, 1971), p. 6.

The Dastan of Amir Hamzah: Index of Chapters

1. Khvajah Buzurchmihr goes to Mecca and makes inquiries everywhere about Amir Hamzah's birth.
2. Amir Hamzah's cradle goes to the Realm of Qaf, and takes that sun of perfection to Mount Qaf.
3. The dastan of how the Amir and Muqbil and Amar were given looks of empowerment by the Friends of God.
4. The Amir comes to Mecca the Great, and Naushervan's letter reaches him.
5. [The Amir kills a lion on the way to Ctesiphon, and Amar makes use of its skin.]
6. Gustahm arrives in the city of Ctesiphon, bringing Bahram Gurd, the Emperor of China, with supreme grandeur and glory and splendor.
7. [The Amir goes with Naushervan to the Garden of Justice, where Amar contrives to join them.]
8. [Amar humiliates Bakhtak, and the Amir is stricken with love.]
9. The Amir's first meeting with the foremost among the beautiful ones of the age, that is, with Princess Mihr Nigar.
10. [The Amir sets out for Sarandip to conquer Landhaur bin Sadan, Emperor of Hindustan.]
11. The Amir's ships are again storm-tossed, and those unlucky ones fall into the Whirlpool of Alexander, then emerge from the hurricane and arrive in the land of Sarandip.
12. Landhaur makes war on the Sahib-qiran, and is finally subdued by that lordly World-conqueror.
13. [The Amir and Landhaur return to Naushervan's court, where Landhaur narrowly escapes execution.]
14. The Amir sets out for Greece, and contracts a marriage with Nahid Maryam, a charming beauty.
15. The pigeon's letter arrives in Ctesiphon, and plans are made to kill Muqbil, etc., and Amar suddenly arrives. Amar sets out for Egypt

after the pigeon and kills it by the city gates and frees the Amir from captivity, after grief and despair.

16. Abdur Rahman the Jinn, vazir of the King of Kings of the Realm of Qaf, comes to bear away the Amir.
17. Naushervan discovers that the Amir has gone to Qaf, and sends an army off to Mecca.
18. Directing the reins of the steed of the pen toward writing about the Sahib-qiran, the World-conqueror, Amir Hamzah of great magnificence, the possessor of generosity and kindness.
19. Qarin Elephant-neck sets out to chastise Amar, and dies at the hands of the Veiled One.
20. [Amar pretends that he will give Mihr Nigar to Zhopin in marriage, and thus acquires fresh provisions for the fort.]
21. Ifrit Dev takes refuge in the tilism of the City of Gold, at the advice of his mother, Malunah Jadu.
22. Dastan about the situation of the Sahib-qiran of the Age, the Earthquake of Qaf, the Younger Solomon, Amir Hamzah the glorious.
23. [The Amir tries in vain to return from the Realm of Qaf to the Realm of the World.]
24. [The Amir is persecuted by Asman Pari, and tricked by the White Dev.]
25. The dastan of Khvajah Amar Ayyar's going from his previous fort to the fort of Devdad, with Princess Mihr Nigar and the army of Islam.
26. [The Amir marries Raihan Pari, in an attempt to reach the World.]
27. Asman Pari goes with a powerful army to the fort of Sabz-nigar, lays waste to the city, makes captive Sabz-qaba the Jinn and Raihan Pari, punishes Sabz-qaba the Jinn, and imprisons Raihan Pari in the Dungeon of Solomon.
28. Zuhrah of Egypt disappears from the roof of the fort, and comes before Asman Pari.
29. [The Amir tries again to leave Qaf, and again is unwillingly reunited with Asman Pari.]
30. [The Amir is helped by Asifa Basafa to escape from Asman Pari and leave Qaf.]
31. [The Amir is joyfully reunited with Mihr Nigar and all his old companions.]

1. Khvajah Buzurchmihr goes to Mecca and makes inquiries everywhere about Amir Hamzah's birth.

[The great emperor Qubad Kamran, whose realm extended from his capital city of Ctesiphon throughout Iran and the whole Seven Realms, had only one son, *Naushervan. Before he died, he advised Naushervan never to do anything without consulting the virtuous vazir *Buzurchmihr, and never to heed the words of the unscrupulous courtier *Bakhtak.

Naushervan married the beautiful *Mihr Angez; in time they had two sons, *Hurmuz and *Faramarz, and a lovely daughter, *Mihr Nigar. One night Naushervan had an ominous dream. Buzurchmihr, skilled in divination, was able to interpret it. From the eastern city of Khaibar a prince, Hisham bin Alqamah, would rise against him and steal his throne; but from the western city of Mecca a boy named *Hamzah would come to overpower the usurper and restore the throne. Naushervan at once sent Buzurchmihr off to find this boy, honor his family with gifts, and see to his proper upbringing.]

The arrangers of colorful reports tell this agreeable story in this way: When the *Khvajah, after traveling a long way and traversing many stages, arrived near Mecca the Great, from his halting place he wrote to Khvajah *Abdul Muttalib, who was chief of the tribe of Bani Hashim, a letter like this: "This lowly servant has come to worship at Mecca the Great, and also longs to wait on you. I hope that you will gladden me with a meeting, and show hospitality to a traveler." Khvajah Abdul Muttalib read the letter and was very pleased. Taking all the nobles of Mecca with him, he went to welcome Buzurchmihr; he escorted him with the greatest honor and respect, and had many fine houses vacated for him to stay in.

First Buzurchmihr made his pious visit to the *Kabah with Khvajah Abdul Muttalib. Afterwards, he met the nobles of the city with great magnificence. Giving rupees and *gold pieces to every one, he said, "The King of Iran says, 'I am most happy with you all, and know you all as my well-wishers, and want you always to pray for me.'" With these words, Buzurchmihr sent for the drummer and had the proclamation made: "From today on, all the baby boys who are born will become servants of the King of Iran. At their birth let each guardian come to me, and show the newborn to me, so that I may determine an allowance for his upbringing on behalf of the king, and may give him a name." Since Buzurchmihr was accompanied by a numerous army, a camp was made outside the city; because of their numbers the army stayed outside the city. But Khvajah Buzurchmihr always used to come into the city to visit Khvajah Abdul Muttalib, and sometimes Khvajah Abdul Muttalib too came to visit Khvajah Buzurchmihr.

One day, after fifteen or twenty days, when Khvajah Buzurchmihr came at the appointed time to visit Khvajah Abdul Muttalib, Khvajah Abdul Muttalib, after greeting him, said, "Yesterday a son was born to this servant, the Eternal God bestowed a male child." Buzurchmihr instantly sent for the boy and looked at his face, and threw the *divining-dice and cast his horoscope, and realized, "This is the very boy who will take tribute from the kings of the Seven Realms, and make the whole world obey him! All the high-handed ones in the Realm of the *World and Mount *Qaf will fall beneath his hand, and the great lords on the face of the earth will be brought low when face-to-face with this star of the heights of accomplishment. Unbelief will decline and Islam will grow, justice will increase and tyranny will diminish."

Buzurchmihr kissed the boy on the forehead and named him Hamzah; pleased, he congratulated Khvajah Abdul Muttalib, and they all began to exchange greetings and felicitations with each other. All those who were present turned with Khvajah Buzurchmihr toward the Great Kabah; with hands uplifted, they recited the prayer of thanksgiving, prayed for *Amir Hamzah's safe and long life, and gave thanks to the True Creator. Buzurchmihr gave a number of boxes of gold pieces to Khvajah Abdul Muttalib for the upbringing of Amir Hamzah, and presented him with many valuable jewels and silken shawls and items of clothing.

Khvajah Abdul Muttalib prepared *sherbet, according to Arab custom, and wanted to serve it to those present, and to send it to neighbors and relatives. Buzurchmihr said, "Please be patient for a little while, and let two more people come, for their sons will become your noble son's companions and well-wishers, quick to support him, loyal, and ready to lay down their lives." Even as Buzurchmihr was saying this, a slave of Khvajah Abdul Muttalib's named Bashir brought his son and said, "In this slave's home too a servant has been born." Buzurchmihr named that boy *Muqbil the Faithful, and gave Bashir a bag of gold pieces for his upbringing, and said, "This boy will be clever in the art of archery, skilled in marksmanship and arrow-shooting."

When Bashir took his leave and went toward his home, on the way he chanced to meet a camel-driver named Umayyah Zamiri. Umayyah asked Bashir, "Where are you coming from, and how does it happen that you are bringing this bag of gold pieces along with you?" Bashir told him the whole story. Umayyah Zamiri very joyously went home and told the whole story, and went in and said to his wife, "You constantly say, 'I'm pregnant'! Have a boy quick, so we can get money and gold pieces, and live happily in luxury and enjoyment." She said, "You know better, show a tiny trace of sense! It's the start of my seventh month, God forbid that I should give birth now! Let my enemies have labor pains so prematurely!"

Umayyah said, "You just start groaning and forcing yourself—a boy will surely come! If a son is born now, that's exactly what's wanted, but if it comes two months from now, then what will I get out of it?" In irritation she said, "The wretched man has lost his mind, the bully is trying to make me give birth without labor! It's not force or tyranny, just lack of sense, the way he glares at me!" Umayyah grew annoyed. He struck such a blow to her stomach that the poor woman fell to the floor writhing in pain; the child burst out of her stomach and she breathed her last.

Umayyah instantly wrapped the boy up in the sleeve of his cloak, and bringing him before Buzurchmihr, said, "Excellency, this eater of your salt too has had a son, my good fortune has begun; I've brought him here so you can have a look, I've come to have his name recorded in the royal book." Khvajah Buzurchmihr laughed at the sight of him, and said to Khvajah Abdul Muttalib, "This boy will be king of the *ayyars of the age, sharp and fleet, and full of deceit. Many grand and glorious kings and mighty champions, the envy of *Rustam and *Nariman, will tremble when they hear his name: when it's mentioned in their ear they will wet their pants in fear. He'll seize hundreds—no, thousands of forts all alone, and defeat mighty armies on his own. He'll be very greedy and treacherous, full of conniving art; he'll be cruel, bloodthirsty, without fear of God, without a heart. But he'll be Amir Hamzah's companion and friend, he'll be true to his salt and keep faith till the end."

When Buzurchmihr, after saying this, took the baby in his lap, it began to scream and cry. Khvajah Buzurchmihr put his finger in its mouth. The baby slipped the ring off Buzurchmihr's finger with its mouth, then grew quiet and didn't shed a tear. When the Khvajah didn't see the ring on his finger, he looked for it in the pockets of his robe; when he didn't find it, he deliberately kept silent. When everyone drank sherbet, the Khvajah put a drop of sherbet in the baby's mouth too, and when its mouth opened, the ring fell out of its mouth. Buzurchmihr picked the ring up, laughing, and said to Khvajah Abdul Muttalib, "This is his first theft—he has inaugurated his career on me!"

After saying this, he said, "I name him *Amar."[1] Giving two boxes of gold pieces to Umayyah, he said, "Raise him with great care, do not spare any pains; devote yourself fully to bringing him up." Umayyah took the boxes of gold pieces, but said, "His mother died as soon as he was born! How can I raise him?" Buzurchmihr said to Khvajah Abdul Muttalib, "Hamzah's mother has died, and these two boys' mothers have also died, so it's proper for you to keep these two boys in your house as well. *Adiyah Bano, *Adi Madikarab's mother, to whom *Hazrat *Abraham has come in a dream, and whom he has ennobled by conversion to Islam, and whom he has commanded to be Hamzah's wet-nurse, is just arriving. Please welcome her and escort her in, and have her give the milk of her right breast to Hamzah and the milk of her left breast to Muqbil the Faithful and Amar Ayyar." Khvajah Abdul Muttalib, following Khvajah Buzurchmihr's order, welcomed Adiyah Bano and escorted her in and showed her due hospitality. He gave her sherbet to drink and had her hands and feet washed, and put all three boys in her lap, and gave them into her charge for breastfeeding.

When six days had passed after the Amir's birth, and the sixth-day ceremony had taken place, Buzurchmihr said to Khvajah Abdul Muttalib, "In the morning, please have the Amir's cradle put on the upper story. If the cradle should disappear, then don't be disturbed, for the Creator of the World has made the most extraordinary kinds of creatures with His supreme power, and has ordained for every kind its own separate place of residence and means of earning a livelihood. Thus the inhabited quarter of the world is surrounded by a great and glorious river. In it are very spacious and populous islands and harbors. Among these one is the dwelling-place of various creatures and the sons of the *Jinns, and they call it Mount Qaf; around it are many cities in which Jinns, *Paris, *Devs, Ghouls, Camel-feet, Cow-feet and Cow-heads, Elephant-ears, Half-bodies, Leather-strap-legs, Horse-faces, etc., live. And the king of that place is *Shahpal bin Shahrukh, very stately and comely and beautiful, like the sun. *Abdur Rahman is his vazir, who in the present age has no peer or equal: he is wise, resourceful, and ingenious; night and day he remains absorbed in the worship of God. He will order Hamzah's cradle brought before his king, and after seven days will send it back again to you. That visit will bring numerous benefits; various kinds of advantages and objects will be achieved in that realm." Having said this, he took leave of Khvajah Abdul Muttalib and went to his own camp. Khvajah Abdul Muttalib waited for that time, he constantly waited for that appointed moment.

2. Amir Hamzah's cradle goes to the Realm of Qaf, and takes that sun of perfection to Mount Qaf.

Now the narrator of sweet speech tells to the lovers of old stories and fables, a few words of the dastan of Qaf. One day Shahpal son of Shahrukh, ruler of Mount Qaf, was seated on the Throne of *Solomon in royal state and infinite grandeur. From all parts of the Realm of Qaf eighteen kings who rendered service to him, and paid the tribute due him, were in attendance at court, and also countless nobles and dignitaries, who stood respectfully with hands folded, waiting upon the king.

The chamberlain presented himself, made obeisance to the king, and gave the good news that a star of the sign of auspiciousness and chastity, a Venus of the heaven of rectitude and purity—that is, a princess with the qualities of Jupiter and the beauty of the sun, had adorned the cradle, and increased the radiance of the brilliant family. The king spoke to Khvajah Abdur Rahman, who was his vazir, and was the companion and disciple of Hazrat Solomon, and was eminently learned in all the arts, and commanded, "Give this girl a name, and look at her fate; tell me how it will be, and what her star of fortune foretells."

Khvajah Abdur Rahman, according to the king's command, named the princess *Asman Pari. Throwing the divining-dice and casting her horoscope, he put the patterns together, and most joyously told the king the good news: "Let Your Majesty be congratulated. This girl will reign over all eighteen realms of Qaf, and will rule and govern these kingdoms in grandeur and glory. But in the eighteenth year from now, those high-handed Devs, who at present are under your hand, will grow thoroughly arrogant; rebelling utterly, they will step outside the path of obedience and behave insolently. Except for *Garden of Iram, all the cities—Gold, Silver, Ermine, etc.—will slip from Your Majesty's control. But at that time a son of *Adam, coming from the inhabited region of the world, will destroy and break those rebels with his might, retake the land, and give it back into Your Majesty's hand."

The king, hearing this, was extremely happy, almost beside himself with delight, and commanded, "See if that boy has been born or not—has he filled his mother's lap with radiance, or not? In what land does he dwell? Of what happy constellation is he the shining star?" Khvajah Abdur Rahman threw the divining-dice and said, "In the land of Arabia is a city, Mecca; he is the son of the chief of that place, and today is the sixth day since his birth. He has been named Hamzah, and today his father has put his cradle on the upper story." The king ordered, "Let four *Parizads go and bring his cradle here before me, let this light of the eye of magnificence and grandeur appear before me."

The king was still celebrating when the Parizads brought Hamzah's cradle and set it down before the throne, and for this good service the

Amir Hamzah is put to sleep on the roof, and the Jinns carry him off, with his cradle, to the land of the Paris.

Jinns began demanding a reward. All the onlookers stood transfixed like painted images, wonderstruck at his beauty; the Parizads almost fainted, thunderstruck by his form and graces. The king, lifting the Amir from the cradle into his lap, kissed him, and sending for the *Kohl of Solomon, put it in his eyes, and ordered that the ayahs and nannies and wet-nurses should attend him. As commanded, they all immediately came, and for seven days fed him the milk of Devs, Paris, Jinns, Ghouls, tigers, and leopards. Khvajah Abdur Rahman said, "According to *geomancy, it seems that Princess Asman Pari will marry this very boy, and sons of Adam and sons of the Jinns will know kinship and joy."

The king happily ordered from his palace a cradle with rods and feet of emerald, and sides of ruby, inlaid with many precious jewels. In it he laid the Amir and most carefully put him to sleep. Causing many night-glowing rubies to be strung on red silken thread, he put them in the cradle, and had many other valuable stones put in the cradle. And the king commanded the Parizads who had brought him, "Take him back most carefully to the place where you found him; then come tell me all about the trip, and about the boy and the land where he lives." As soon as they were given the order the Parizads returned the Amir's cradle to the same upper story from which they had taken it, and after a little while they happily described the whole trip to the king in detail.

3. The dastan of how the Amir and Muqbil and Amar were given looks of empowerment by the *Friends of God.

[Amar, Hamzah, and Muqbil were raised together. In their infancy, the greedy Amar even stole extra milk from the nurse's breast. He grew into a surpassingly dextrous and mischievous thief. When the boys were sent to school, Amar played ruthlessly humiliating tricks on their pious old schoolmaster. Sometimes Amar ran off, or was sent away; then Hamzah wept bitterly and refused to eat until he was found and brought back.]

The noble riders upon the fingers of previous scribes urge the steeds of their well-paced pens into the field of narration in this way: One day the Amir, with Muqbil and Amar, was seated on the verandah of his mansion, he was sitting there with friends and companions, when he saw a large number of people going past him in one direction. Seeing this, he told Amar, "Go and inquire where these people are going, find out quickly and inform me." Amar came back and told him, "Some merchants have come with horses, a number of caravans have arrived from abroad. People are going to see the horses, they'll look to their heart's content and then return. If Your Excellency should wish, you can make an excursion, have a look, and come back." The moment he heard the word "horse," the Amir set out in that direction. He was so eager that he went on foot, taking with him his friends and companions.

[When they reached the place, Amar wagered with one of the merchants that the Amir could ride a wild, unmanageable horse; the Amir eagerly mounted the animal.] When the Amir pressed with his thighs, the horse began running like the wind. His mouth was so hard that although the Amir sawed on the reins, the horse wouldn't stop. He ran all-out for a hundred miles. Finally the Amir, using his full strength, broke the horse's back; he showed him the fruits of his mischief and bad behavior. The horse died.

The Amir, on foot, turned back toward his home. He was not in the habit of walking, he never went around on foot. His feet grew blistered; it was impossible for him to reach his home. When he tried to take a step, his feet wouldn't move. Tired out, he sat down under a tree. In a little while, what did he see but a veiled horseman coming, leading a riderless horse, a piebald equipped with an elegantly decorated saddle. When the veiled elder came near, he greeted the Amir with "Peace be upon you," and said, "Oh Hamzah, this horse has been the mount of the *Prophet Isaac, peace be upon him. The horse's name is *Black Constellation, and he runs as swiftly and lightly as the spring breeze. At the Lord's command, I've brought him for you to ride, and as the Lord has ordered I've come to give you a look of empowerment.[2] No champion will overcome you; if God wills, your ascendant fortune, in the competition among fortunes, will never be brought low. Everyone will be under your hand, and all will obey you. Remove this heap of stone before you, and dig in the earth beneath it. There you will find a chest of the Prophets' armor, and every kind of weapon, of the very best quality, beyond measure and beyond limit. Arm yourself with them, and test their mettle when the time comes."

The Amir at once removed the stone, and found so much strength in his arms and legs that it couldn't be conceived; he had never imagined having even a fourth part of this strength. He tested this immense strength while digging in the earth. In the chest he found the cloak of

Hazrat Ishmael, the helmet of Hazrat *Hud, the chain-mail of Hazrat *David, the gauntlets of Hazrat Joseph, the anklets of Hazrat *Salih, the belt and dagger of Rustam, the swords *Samsam and Qamqam which had belonged to *Asif Barkhiya, the shield of *Gurshasp, the mace of *Sam bin Nariman, the dagger of *Suhrab, and the spear of Hazrat Noah the Prophet, peace be upon him. Taking them out, he examined them, and adorned his body with those weapons and garments. Saying "In the name of God," he mounted Black Constellation, and the veiled elder disappeared from view. They write that the veiled elder was Hazrat *Gabriel, peace be upon him, that it was he himself who at that time aided and assisted the Amir. "And God knows the truth best."[3] The Amir set out toward Mecca, he headed for his home.

Now please hear about Amar, who for twenty miles had followed the Amir, halting and stumbling. He didn't give up his loyalty, he never stopped pursuing the Amir. When the soles of his feet had been pierced so full of acacia thorns that they looked like wasps' nests, he could go no further. He lost consciousness, and fell beneath a tree. Through the Lord's power Hazrat *Khizr, peace be upon him, drew near where Amar lay, and began to comfort and reassure him. He lifted Amar up from the ground, gave him a look of empowerment, and commanded, "Amar, rise. At the Lord's command I have given you a look of empowerment. No one will be able to overtake you." With these words, he disappeared from view, the Lord knows where he went! Amar got up and made a bound, by way of experiment; he tested what the Hazrat had told him. He realized, "In truth I can run faster than the wind—even the steed of Thought could never manage to overtake me!" Prostrating himself in gratitude, he set off in search of the Amir, he went on in the direction in which the Amir had gone.

He had hardly taken more than a few steps when the Amir came into view before him. Both of them expressed their pleasure and relief, and described the difficulties they had encountered on the road. Amar, seeing the armor and horse, was astonished, and said to the Amir, "Oh Arab, what have you done to the merchant's horse? And tell me the truth: who did you kill to seize this horse and equipment?" The Amir replied, "Killing other people is *your* style! What foolish things are you saying? At the Lord's command, I've been given a look of empowerment by Hazrat Gabriel, I've been entrusted with the armor of the Prophets, peace be upon them! This horse, named Black Constellation, has been the mount of Hazrat Isaac, and the Generous Provider has bestowed the rest of the Prophets' armor on me."

Amar replied, "I'll only believe you, and only know that you're telling the truth, when your horse outruns me, and I end up even a small bit behind in the race." The Amir said to himself, "What is he babbling about, this jester has gone mad! Can a man ever run as fast as such a horse, how can a man possibly have the strength to outrun him?" The Amir then said aloud, "All right, come on, show your paces against my horse." Amar said, "First please agree to a couple of wagers, and make me feel reassured." The Amir said, "Whatever you wish, I will agree to wager." Amar said, "If I outrun this horse, I will take ten camels from you; and if this horse outruns me, then my father will graze your father's camels for one year, with no wages or reward."

The Amir agreed, and took up his horse's reins. Amar too positioned himself alongside. They went for twenty miles. Amar and the horse ran neck-in-neck, they were shoulder to shoulder. They both amazed the spring breeze with their swiftness. The Amir, when he saw Amar's speed, was astonished, he was stupefied by Amar's cleverness. Amar said, "Oh Amir, I too have been given a look of empowerment by Hazrat Khizr, peace be upon him, I've been favored by a great Prophet."

. . . It's proper to hear about Muqbil the Faithful, we ought to observe the faithfulness of that loyal well-wisher. When he learned that the Amir and Amar had been given looks of empowerment by Gabriel and Khizr, peace be upon them, that through the grace of the Lord both had been chosen for such an honor, he said to himself, "How can I live with them, since they've been singled out for such an honor? Both of them have high resolve and high courage—how can I get along with them? It's better for me to go and enter Naushervan's service, and live for a while at his court. If the Lord wills, I might be chosen for some post of honor there, and my prospects might improve, my sleeping fortune might awaken. There everyone is treated with the same respect, in the royal service all are equal." With this kind of stew boiling in his mind, he left the city, and set out toward Ctesiphon.

He had gone about eight or ten miles, when he felt tired and sat down under a tree. He said to himself, "A life like this is worse than death, it's better to die than to be shamed like this! I have no provisions for the road, and no horse—how difficult and humiliating it all is!" With this thought he climbed the tree, tied one end of his cummerbund-sash to a branch, made a noose with the other end and placed it around his neck, leaped, and dangled there, thrashing his arms and legs. The bird of his soul was about to take flight from the cage of his body, in another breath or two he would have passed beyond this transitory world, when the Lion of God, the One Addressed by God, the King who destroyed Khaibar, the Second of the Five Pure Ones,[4] arrived and gave a call. Muqbil fell to the ground.

The Hazrat lifted him up, bestowed on him five arrows and a bow, and said, "I have bestowed on you the art of archery, I have made you peerless and unequaled in this art. The greatest masters in the world will be proud to be your pupils, in this art the most dextrous archers of the age will not be able to compare with you." Muqbil asked, "If anyone should ask me who has given me a look of empowerment, what should I tell him, what answer should I give to everyone?" The Hazrat replied, "Say you are under the protection of the Lion of God, the Victorious, you are in the service of that very family."

Muqbil, taking the five arrows and the bow, joyously set out toward Mecca. For their part, the Amir and Amar, not seeing Muqbil, had grown anxious, and Amar had set out in search of Muqbil. He had scarcely set foot outside the city, when he saw Muqbil coming toward him. Most happily he ran and embraced Muqbil, and took him to the Amir. Muqbil presented himself in the Amir's service, showed his arrows and bow, and told all about how he had been given a look of empowerment. The Amir was very happy, and they all lived contentedly together.

4. The Amir comes to Mecca the Great, and Naushervan's letter reaches him.

[In the course of various adventures, Hamzah acquired the first members of his group of loyal companions. Hisham bin Alqamah of Khaibar had indeed attacked and looted Ctesiphon, as Buzurchmihr had predicted, and had carried off the royal crown and throne. Hisham then moved toward Mecca, but Hamzah intercepted him, fought and killed him, freed all his prisoners, and recovered the crown and throne. Hamzah sent Muqbil to Naushervan with this reassuring news, and then returned to Mecca.]

The sweet-tongued narrators relate that when the Amir arrived in Mecca, first he paid his holy visit to the Kabah and gave thanks for his victory. He made Adi repent of highway robbery, and made him swear to live righteously and observe the

THE AMIR AND HISHAM ARRAY THEIR RANKS FOR BATTLE, AND HISHAM IS KILLED, WITH HIS MOUNT, BY A SINGLE BLOW FROM THE AMIR'S HAND.

rituals of Islam. Afterwards he arranged to visit his father, he went to kiss the feet of his venerable father. When Khvajah Abdul Muttalib heard the news of Hamzah's arrival, the inhabitants of Mecca congratulated him on the Amir's return. Taking the nobles of the city with him, Khvajah Abdul Muttalib set out to welcome the Amir; along with all his relatives, the Khvajah went out to meet him.

On the road, father and son met. The Amir kissed his father's feet. The Khvajah lifted the Amir's head and pressed it to his breast, and scattered gold and silver for the beggars to pick up. The beggars and poor began to gather up the alms, and the nobles of the city began to bless the Amir: "May the Ultimate Victor make you always victorious, and always over vile foes triumphant and glorious!" When the Khvajah took the Amir into the house and seated himself in the audience hall, the nobles of the city came as well. The Amir presented *Manzar Shah of Yemen, Numan bin Manzar Shah, Suhail of Yemen, *Sultan Bakht of Maghrib, and *Tauq bin Haran to the Khvajah; he introduced and praised each one of them. The Khvajah was very happy. He showed kindness to every one of them, and treated each one with honor and respect according to his rank.

One day the Amir heard it mentioned that Adi was the son of Adiyah Bano. The Amir was very happy: "He is my brother, by the mother's milk we have shared!" That very day the Amir made Adi general of his armies, herald of his troops, and superintendent of his audience hall, his storehouse, and his drum-storehouse; he gave Adi a title and a robe of honor consisting of eighteen items. Amar, at the Amir's command, requested Adi, "Whatever provisions you need for your meals, just give the order, so the chief of the kitchen can bring them from our store every day, or cook and send the dishes to your door every day." Adi said, "This is my own house, after all—I'll only ask for enough to keep body and soul together! All I want is to do my duty as a servant at the Amir's door." Amar said, "Please tell me the name and quantity of everything, so the chief of the kitchen can send it to you every day. Why speak in a roundabout way? Showing diffidence and hesitation before your gracious master is far from respectful!"

Adi said, "All right, brother, tell the chief of the kitchen that in the morning, I eat twenty-one camels for breakfast. At midday, I eat kabobs made from twenty-one deer and twenty-one fat-tailed sheep, washed down with twenty-one bottles of wine. In the evening, the curried meat of twenty-one camels and a like number of deer and fat-tailed sheep and buffalo is served to me—and with both meals, twenty-one *maunds of flour made into bread. Although this doesn't really fill me up as it should, at least it quiets the pangs of hunger." When the Amir heard this, he ordered: "Every morning let the chief of the kitchen send twice this amount of food to Adi's kitchen, and never hesitate or fall short in this." Accordingly, the rations were arranged, and the food went every single day.

After some days, the Amir heard that Naushervan's emissaries had come, bearing a robe of honor and a letter. Khvajah Abdul Muttalib and Amir Hamzah, with the chief men of the city, went out to welcome the emissaries. . . . The next day when Nature, the chiefest of cooks, took the freshly baked hot cake of the sun out of the oven of the sky, and spread the glowing tablecloth of the sun's reflected light on the carpet of the earth, Khvajah Abdul Muttalib gave a feast for Naushervan's emissaries, and had all the nobles and dignitaries of the city come to the feast as well. After the eating and drinking were over, the emissaries gave the Khvajah the letter addressed to him. When the Amir read it, he regretted his own self-sacrificing devotion and loyalty to Naushervan. [He sent back the robe, and with it a reproachful letter.]

The king, having looked at the contents of the Amir's petition, and the style of his own letter, and that unworthy robe which the king would not have given even to his own latrine-sweeper, began to rage at Bakhtak: "Oh you petty creature, what wickedness you've done, what baseness and mischief you've perpetrated!" Instantly he fined him a thousand *tumans of bright gold, and banished him from the court for a number of days. And he wrote a letter of apology to the Amir with his own hand. . . . Giving the letter and a royal robe of honor even more valuable than the former one to Khvajah Buzurchmihr, he commanded, "Send this by the hand of *Buzurg Ummid to Amir Hamzah. And look, take care: let there be no negligence, and no meddling by anyone else!"

Khvajah Buzurchmihr went home and, at an auspicious hour, made a magic banner in the shape of a serpent, such that when the wind blew through its mouth into its stomach, the cry "Ya *Sahib-qiran!" came from its stomach three times without a break, and reached the ear of every friend and foe; and all the soldiers' noses were overpowered by its perfume, musk and ambergris were put to shame by its perfume; and when it came before the eyes of the enemy, fear of the Amir's army stole over them. Together with this banner he also sent the pavilion of Hazrat Daniel for Hamzah's use. Having added four hundred forty-four pieces of weaponry in the art of *ayyari for Amar, he confided them all to Buzurg Ummid's care and commanded, "Take these to Amar from me." Teaching Buzurg Ummid the way to put on the garments, he said, "Put them on Amar with your own hands in just the same way." After explaining this, he sent Buzurg Ummid off with a brigade of soldiers, having instructed him all about the ups and downs of the road, the stages and stopping-places.

When Khvajah Buzurg Ummid was eight miles from Mecca, he halted. As fate would have it, that day Amar passed that way on a tour of inspection. Buzurg Ummid recognized him by his appearance: "Undoubtedly this is Amar!" Calling him over, he embraced him and said, "You and I are brothers, we are seekers of each other's love. In the name of God, get down here and stay a while! My revered father has bestowed some gifts. For you he has sent an ayyari outfit; take off your Arab dress, so that I can put it on you and tell you its method." Amar took off his clothing. Buzurg Ummid gave the clothing into his men's custody, kept Amar naked for a whole hour, and said, "Never again become naked out of foolish covetousness! Now you must continue to wear this dress of nakedness—accept the will of God, and stay naked like a child!"

Then Amar became distraught: he began to weep and plead violently, "Give my clothes back to me, don't keep me naked among so many men! I'll be grateful and bless you forever. I renounce your robe and gifts—I'll set out for home!" Buzurg Ummid laughed and said, "Oh *Father of the Runners of the World, you'll make many people naked and anxious, and take off the clothes of many! Therefore I've made *you* naked, so you'll remember this time in the future." Amar said, "I am Your Excellency's pupil."

Buzurg Ummid sent for the gifts from the storeroom. First he put on Amar a pair of drawers without a codpiece; the moment he pulled them up, Amar's private parts were exposed. Amar said, "My dear father, you are marvelously generous—you haven't even provided a hand's breadth of codpiece in the drawers!" Buzurg Ummid pulled out an *afat-band;* Amar saw that there was a small velvet bag also: roses and sprigs had been embroidered on it with seven colors of silk, and a ruby button had been fixed on its cord, so that it was most expensive and priceless. Buzurg Ummid, having put Amar's private parts in this and wrapped it up like a loincloth, said, "This is called an *afat-band,*[5] have even your elders seen or heard of such garments?" And he told its benefits: "First, while running and leaping around no injury will be done to the testicles, and second, when swimming in water there will be no need to loosen the drawstring of the drawers." Amar said, "May God bless your worthy father, for if he has sent a robe for me, he has also robed my private parts!"

Buzurg Ummid put two robes on Amar, one of silk and one of fine light linen, and told him their benefits, and said, "The soft one is for bodily comfort, and the other is for moderation of the wind." He put on him a green vest embroidered in gold; and a gold-embroidered turban, on which was a parrot made of emerald with its stomach full of musk and ambergris for the delight of the nose; and a gold turban-ornament with a plume, and a jewelled aigrette. He put over his forehead an umbrella made of the skin of a Chinese deer, to keep out the heat of the sun. He attached to Amar's waist a sling wrapped with seven colors of silk and worked with various kinds of gold embroidery; and nooses and snares for trickery, in every loop of which were clusters of emeralds and rubies, which outshone the full light of the sun with their brilliance; and five daggers with jewel-studded hand-grips, and forty-four small cymbals.

He taught him twelve musical tones, twenty-eight ways to improvise, six high-pitched notes, twenty-four melodies, and six ways of wearing a false beard and of putting on socks to hide footprints. He placed at his waist a glass flask full of naphtha and tied it very tightly; and a bit of prepared medicinal silk-cotton that had been soaked in wine and then dried, so that if it was soaked in water, the water would become wine, would give the effect of rose-red wine. He gave him a small box of wax-and-oil for disguises; a perfume-vessel, extremely elaborately worked and full of the essence of mischief; a little box full of a sovereign antidote; a wonderfully attractive fly-whisk made from a peacock's tail-feathers; a water-skin full of water; a finely tempered sword that flashed lightning all around it; a round shield equal to the disk of the sun; a quiver; a curved bow which put the rainbow to shame; Khurasani and Isfahani hunting knives, incomparable, unrivaled, peerless.

He gave him an ayyari-cloak, long and wide, reticulated like a fishnet from head to foot, so that no one wrapped in it would be suffocated, or anxious, or in danger of death; a pair of slippers for the feet, softer, lighter, and more delicate than cotton, fitted with double broadcloth tassels; two shells plaited in silk to be tied to the shoes, such that even after running thousands of miles, the feet would not grow tired or refuse to move. In this way Amar was fitted out from head to foot with four hundred forty-four novel weapons of ayyari designed by Buzurchmihr, and his body was adorned and equipped with every sort of the most choice, sophisticated, valuable, and jewel-adorned weapons.

Amar took leave of Buzurg Ummid, and in this dress went and waited upon the Amir. He told his whole story in detail, and said, "Naushervan has sent, in answer to your letter, by the hand of Khvajah Buzurchmihr's son—whose name is Khvajah Buzurg Ummid and who is camped four miles outside the city—a letter of apology and a resplendent robe of honor. Khvajah Buzurchmihr has also sent a banner in the shape of a serpent, and the pavilion of Daniel, as a gift for you. And he has bestowed on me a set of clothing, together with four hundred forty-four pieces of ayyari weaponry that I am wearing and have on my body right now, and his noble son put all the items on me and told me the properties of each item!"

When the Amir heard this good news he was very happy; with his companions and soldiers and all his horsemen, most ceremoniously, he rode outside the city to welcome Khvajah Buzurg Ummid. Buzurg Ummid treated the Amir with respectful honor, caused him to read Naushervan's letter of apology, and presented the robe of honor which Naushervan had sent him. When the Amir read the royal letter, he was joyful, and at that very moment put on some of the garments of the robe of honor. After this Buzurg Ummid presented to the Amir the banner in the shape of a serpent, and the pavilion of Daniel, and said most respectfully, "My father has sent you his blessing, and has sent you this gift; and in truth this gift, a wonder of the age and a marvel of the world, is suitable only for you." The Amir was thoroughly delighted and grateful to the Khvajah for this, and entrusted the banner to Tauq bin Haran and the pavilion to Adi. Buzurg Ummid with his victorious-appearing army went toward the city. When they arrived there, the Amir introduced him to Khvajah Abdul Muttalib and the nobles of the city, and for many days arranged festive gatherings for Buzurg Ummid.

5. [The Amir kills a lion on the way to Ctesiphon, and Amar makes use of its skin.]

One day Buzurg Ummid said to the Amir, "The king must be waiting for you, he must mention you again and again in court. It's best that you now set out for Ctesiphon, and gladden the people there too with your beauty and radiance." At once the Amir, having visited the Kabah and taken leave of Khvajah Abdul Muttalib, set out for Ctesiphon together with Manzar Shah of Yemen and Numan bin Manzar Shah and Suhail of Yemen and Sultan Bakht of Maghrib and Adi Madikarab and Tauq bin Haran and a detachment of thirty thousand bloodthirsty, enemy-killing horsemen. Stage after stage and day after day, crossing land and sea on the way, he and his companions and servants pressed on without delay, until a crossroads appeared.

The Amir asked Khvajah Buzurg Ummid, "Since you came this way, you must know where these roads go, and which lands' borders they lead to." Buzurg Ummid said, "Both roads go to Ctesiphon. One road is free from fear or danger, but the travel time is longer: it takes six months on that road. The other road gets to Ctesiphon very quickly, but it has been closed for five years because it goes through the Beneficent Forest. In this forest is a lion: whenever any poor traveler comes along it smells him, and leaps out from a reed-thicket and kills him. No matter how strong and powerful the man may be, he dies after a single blow. So no one goes by this road, everyone saves his life." The Amir said, "That harmful beast causes vexation to God's creatures; it is necessary for me to kill it." With these words, he went along with the dagger-wielding runner, that is, Khvajah Amar Ayyar, on this dangerous road toward Ctesiphon. His soldiers and companions went with Khvajah Buzurg Ummid on the road that was free from fear or danger, and the Amir ordered them to proceed at double-quick time. Although Manzar Shah, etc., begged to ride by his side, the Amir did not agree.

The next day in the late afternoon, the Amir and Amar arrived at a reed-thicket in the Beneficent Forest. Finding the breeze refreshing, they dismounted and saw a spring, rivaling the stream of the *Water of Life, with pure, clear, extremely sweet water, and wonderfully attractive foliage on its bank. Here and there stood shade trees with beautiful, colorful, melodious birds singing in them. The Amir and Amar spread out their saddle-blankets on the bank and sat down, and Amar began grazing his horse and enjoying the forest breeze—when suddenly within the reed-thicket a rustling occurred, the sound of an animal's coming was heard, and a lion emerged from it.

Amar had never seen so much as a clay lion in his whole life; the moment he saw the lion he let go of his horse in fear, and climbed a splendid big tree, and began calling to the Amir: "Hamzah, a huge tall lion has come out of the reed-thicket and is heading in your direction! For the Lord's sake escape from the spring and come over here with me, or climb a tree at once!" When the Amir heard these words of Amar's he laughed very much and said, "Oh you cowardly creature, why are you so petrified? You must be half out of your mind! I came along this road in order to kill the lion, I've come all this way just for that purpose, and have left my army behind—and you want to frighten me and make me run away from the lion, you want to turn me into a eunuch here in the forest!"

With these words, he turned his attention to the lion, and saw that in truth it was a very big one, extremely terrifying, over forty-five feet long to its tail, and taller than a cow. The Amir challenged the lion,

"Come here, jackal, where are you running off to? I, your challenger, have arrived!" Hearing the voice, the lion at once leaped at the Amir. The Amir slid to one side and avoided its charge, then raised the battle-cry *"God is great!" so loudly that the whole reed-thicket echoed. Seizing the lion's hind legs, he gave such a jerk that its spinal column broke, and after six hours the lion died, screaming. Amar kissed the Amir's hands.

THE AMIR LIFTS UP THE LION AND HURLS IT TO THE GROUND, AND THE LION DIES, AND AMAR COMES DOWN FROM THE TREE.

In the morning Amar removed the lion's skin and cleaned it, and scrubbed it very well inside, and stuffed it with straw, and brought wood from the forest. He had a new trick in mind to try out: making a cart, he seated the lion on it in such a way that any beholder would take it for a living lion; and catching hold of a porter, he put it on his head and went along with the Amir. The Amir knew that the army would arrive in Ctesiphon only after many days. Wherever he and Amar found plenty of birds and a pleasant breezy place, they camped and hunted. Thus the Amir and Khvajah Buzurg Ummid arrived in Ctesiphon at the same time. The Amir went to his army's encampment, and Amar seated that straw-stuffed lion atop a hillock under the wall of the fort, in such a way that it exactly resembled a living lion.

Thus the next day when the city gate was opened, and the grass-cutters passed by that hillock on their way to cut grass, the eye of one of them happened to fall on the lion. He let out a shriek and fainted, his throat choked with fear. His companions began to look around: "What did he see so terrifying that he screamed and fainted, that he passed out and fell to the ground?" As they were looking, their eyes met those of the lion. They all screamed, "A lion, a lion!" and ran toward the city, no one kept hold of himself.

When the grass-cutters spread this news, a tumult broke out in the city: "A lion has come, a huge big one, it's sitting on the hillock, any moment it's likely to come after us! One of our men fainted and fell unconscious there—just wait and see if he ever comes home, or if he'll be a tidbit for the lion!" Everything was topsy-turvy for a while, everyone was stunned and anxious: some began shutting up their doors, others strapped on their muskets and went to sit upstairs, no one went out or sat outside. All the outpost guards were ordered to be careful and keep close watch. In the city the word was, "Wait and see—if, God forbid, the lion heads this way, it'll murder thousands!" When the king heard this news, he went out onto the viewing balcony of the fort, and the great nobles of the court and the soldiers and champions distinguished for courage went with him. They saw that indeed a lion was sitting on the hillock; and whoever saw it trembled.

It happened that Muqbil came out of his tent, which had been pitched outside the city, and went to meet the king; when he passed by the hillock, the lion could be seen. He pulled an arrow out of his quiver, strung it on his bow, and approached the lion. When he came closer and looked attentively, he found no sign of life in the lion; it appeared to be a fake. He thought, "Such a trick could hardly occur to anyone except Amar, this is just in character for that refined gentleman! For the Amir, hearing of the lion's attacks, came by way of the Beneficent Forest, and must have freed the forest of that harmful and bloodthirsty lion, and killed it. Amar has stuffed its skin with straw and set it up on this hillock to frighten people, he has fixed up a trick." He told his idea to the king. The king was persuaded of it too. Pleased, the Refuge of the World bestowed on Muqbil boxes of gold pieces, and granted him a robe of honor and valuable jewels, and said, "Look, where is the Amir staying, in which quarter of the city has he alighted? Go yourself quickly, and send runners, and find out and tell me at once."

Muqbil took leave of the king and left the fort, and went toward the Beneficent Forest. By chance Amar, having escorted the Amir to the army camp, was coming toward the city, on his way to tell the king about the Amir's arrival. From afar he saw that a party had emerged from the fort and set out toward the Beneficent Forest. Amar followed them; as he drew quite near, he saw, "It's Muqbil the Faithful, my old friend." Muqbil, seeing Amar, began asking, "Where is the Amir, where has his tent been pitched?" This displeased Amar: "He neither greeted me, nor asked how I was, nor alighted from his horse and embraced me—in fact, he didn't even shake hands!"

Addressing Muqbil he said, "Listen, oh you wretch, did the Amir send you to remain in attendance upon the king, or to stroll around at your pleasure?" Muqbil said, "I've heard that the Amir has arrived, that he has just entered this region; I am going to wait upon him, not strolling around. I'm going in the king's service." Amar said, "It was very wrong of you to go to meet him." Muqbil said, "Amar, have you gone mad, that you set yourself up as an equal to me?" Amar was just looking for an excuse, he grew angry and said, "Oh son of a slave, do *you* have the nerve to speak to me like that? Naushervan gave you a mere three boxes of gold pieces, and you lose your senses and imagine yourself a Khvajah!" With these words, he at once pulled out his sling from his turban, and removed from his ayyari-pouch a stone chiselled and chased, seasoned in sunlight and moonlight, nourished in a riverbed, and put it in the sling. He whirled it, aimed it, and flung it at the target. It struck Muqbil's forehead; a fountain of blood began to gush out.

In this state Muqbil went before the Amir, and began to weep and moan. The Amir, who at first thought the people of Ctesiphon had bathed him in blood, that some ill-bred villain had given him a severe blow, was quite annoyed; but Muqbil complained against Amar. The Amir called Amar and said, "What is all this, why do you have such enmity between you?" Amar petitioned, "This is like the proverb, 'Go alone before the judge, come back satisfied.' Please listen to my side too, then assign the blame." The Amir replied, "What do you have to say? I'll listen; what's your answer?"

Amar said, "Oh Dispenser of Bounty, a man hopes for help even from strangers, and when abroad even a casual acquaintance is so heartening: at least he is a companion! Muqbil and I met after quite a while; he neither greeted me, which is a mark of Islam and humanity, nor dismounted and embraced me, which is a sign of affection. And it's clear that he and I are juggling-balls from the same bag, let me have justice! We two are equal before you, neither is superior to the other, both are equal! I was standing there to meet him, and he with total arrogance reined in his horse and began asking me about you. When I said in a friendly way, 'Oh you wretch, did the Amir send you to remain in attendance upon the king, or to stroll around at your pleasure? You are acting very badly in strolling and wandering around,' then in answer to this what does he say to me—'Do you set yourself up as equal to me'! Your Excellency, judge us, let me have justice: except for the fact that through Your Excellency's grace the Lord has permitted him to wear a decorated robe given by Naushervan, and he has gotten three boxes of gold pieces, in what other way is he superior? But what can I do, he only cares about his own elevation and haughtiness! It has been truly said, 'May the Lord not give power to the petty-minded, or fingernails to the bald, and may He not bestow high position on the low-minded.' "

The Amir, having heard this speech of Amar's, said to Muqbil, "It's true that in this case the fault is yours for having treated Amar disdainfully. Arrogance and pride are out of place between you two. Go on, be reconciled with each other." Muqbil approached to be reconciled, but Amar refused and said, "He is a gentleman of family and position, a gentleman of glory and splendor! I am a wretched commonplace ayyar, what do he and I have in common, what position do I have compared to him?" Muqbil, when Amar would not be reconciled, gave him a box of gold pieces and said, "Take it, brother; now forgive my offense, clear your heart of anger against me." Amar was the greedy sort, after all: he took the gold pieces and was reconciled with Muqbil.

The next day Khvajah Buzurg Ummid attended upon the king, and told him the whole story of his journey and the Amir's return. The king was delighted and, as advised by Buzurchmihr, decided to go the next day with the nobles of the court to welcome the Amir. . . . The king mounted a throne borne by four elephants, and with pomp and ceremony, and a retinue of all the nobles, went to receive Hamzah; the nobles of the court and the great lords rode with him. When they had gone about four miles, a cloud of dust appeared before them. When the shears of the wind-gusts had cut open the collar of the dust, and the effect of the breeze had cleaned the dust from the face of the field, thirty banners of thirty thousand horsemen became visible; the flags on the standards, lifted on the shoulder of the breeze, raised their heads high. In the circle of horsemen the Amir, under the shadow of the serpent-shaped banner, mounted on Black Constellation, came into view.

At his right hand famous kings, at his left hand dignified champions could be seen. And in front of the Amir the Father of the Runners of the World, the Chief of the Generals of the Age, the King of the Dagger-Wielding Ayyars, Khvajah Amar Ayyar, with his gold-embroidered turban on his head; his vest embroidered in gold; his broadcloth socks; his ayyari-sling adorned with trickeries; his sword, bright from being dipped in the brilliance of lightning, in its scabbard; his jewelled dagger in his belt; his arrow-quiver slung on his shoulder; his nooses and snares for trickery, the worry of foolish enemies, in his hands; and shaping with his mouth six high notes, twelve tones, twenty-four melodies, and twenty-eight improvisations, he advanced, surrounded by his pupils. On both sides troops were arrayed: the right flank and the left flank, vanguard and rearguard, foot-soldiers and horsemen, experienced in war, sated with the wine of courage, resembling the radiant appearance of God's power.

The king saw the Amir, who was fifteen or sixteen years of age, with the down just appearing on his face, before whose beauty the sun in the sky was a worthless particle of dust. With valor and generosity and bravery and benevolence and splendor he sat, mounted on Black Constellation, such that the eye of the heavens would never have seen another hero of his elegance on the face of the earth. Hardly anyone in the world would ever have heard of such a summation of perfections both bodily and mental, a hero so forbearing, peaceful, dignified, and noble. Naushervan's eyes were fastened on the Amir's figure from head to foot as though he was turned to stone, and the gaze of all the mighty champions with powerful bodies and strong arms who were with the king became fixed on this sun of glory and splendor. Each one knew his own pretensions to be false, each one's ambitions were brought low.

The Amir, the moment he saw the king's throne, leaped down from his horse and came forward for the honor of attendance, and kissed the foot of the throne; and placed the Throne of King Cyrus, which Hisham (who was now in Hell) had taken, on his own head, and offered it, together with the crown and royal regalia, to the king. The reason the Amir lifted the throne on his head was that when King Cyrus, having subdued Turan, had taken Iran, Rustam bin Zal had lifted the throne

THE AMIR, WITH DIGNITY AND GRANDEUR, PLACES THE THRONE ON HIS HEAD AND GOES TO KISS THE KING'S FEET, AND THE KING EMBRACES THE AMIR.

onto his head and gone thirty steps for the honor of the king; therefore the Amir also did the same for the grandeur of Naushervan. He lifted the throne onto his head and went forty steps. Lifting this weighty throne like a flower, he considered it a mere turban-ornament: "I am ten times stronger than Rustam, I am chief of the champions of the world and of the mighty ones of the age!"

Naushervan was extremely happy at this deed of the Amir's, and gestured to his servants and retainers: "Take the throne down quickly from the Amir's head, and place it on your own heads as is proper." And he himself, descending from his throne, approached the Amir and began to regard him with the greatest affection and joy. The Amir too advanced with extreme humility and eagerness; he came forward very, very quickly, and with the utmost submissiveness kissed the king's feet. Naushervan seized both the Amir's arms and embraced him like a loved one, and at once told Hurmuz and Faramarz, his two sons, to embrace the Amir. He introduced him to all the chiefs, and informed him of the name and rank and position, in order of importance, of every single one.

6. Gustahm arrives in the city of Ctesiphon, bringing Bahram Gurd the Emperor of China, with supreme grandeur and glory and splendor.

After ten or twelve days, the king was informed that Gustahm was bringing *Bahram Gurd the Emperor of *China and four thousand Uzbek champions whom he had captured. . . . Then the king sent to tell the Amir, "We are going to welcome Gustahm; you come too, and bring your army and companions."

The king had gone about two miles out of the city when he saw Gustahm bin Ashk, wearing golden slippers and a coat of chain mail with shoulder-guards, riding on a rhinoceros, twirling his mustaches, coming along under the shade of his wolf-shaped banner; and he looked as though now that he had captured and brought Emperor Gurd of China, he didn't consider anybody else's courage and bravery and prowess except his own worth anything at all. Seeing him, the *Sasanians were delighted: "Now he has come, he will subdue the Amir! Our heart's desire has been obtained." Gustahm, dismounting from his horse, kissed the foot of the king's throne, and told the whole story of his bravery, and of the capture of Bahram, the Emperor of China, and of the battle, with the most perfect eloquence. The king prostrated himself in gratitude before his one hundred seventy-five gods, and turned back toward the fort. At a sign from Bakhtak, Gustahm remained behind, and did not go with the king. On their way back, the king's party met the Amir on the road. The king said to the Amir, "Come and meet Gustahm, listen to his conversation and be entertained for a little while." The Amir said, "Very good, what cause could I have to hesitate? To obey you is my honor and good fortune."

Now please hear about Bakhtak. Complaining to Gustahm about the Amir, he said, ". . . Thank heavens you've arrived! Come quickly, and when you embrace him, squeeze him so tightly that you soften up his bones! That way he'll be warned, and in the future such deeds of vanity and arrogance will not occur in your presence." Gustahm said, "It will be just as you say."

In the meantime the Amir and his retinue arrived and entered Gustahm's pavilion. When Gustahm saw the Amir, he dismounted and came forward to welcome him. The Amir too got down from his horse; both drew near to embrace each other. When they embraced, first Gustahm squeezed the Amir with his whole strength, and uttered words of warmth and enthusiasm. Then the Amir too expressed his enthusiasm, and then squeezed him so hard that several times wind came out of Gustahm's asshole. Embarrassed, he said in the Amir's ear, "Oh Amir, you are chivalrous. Don't tell anybody about this, don't make me ashamed and embarrassed; let it remain a secret just between us." The Amir said, "It will be just as you say." Gustahm set out toward the fort, and his army went with him.

The Amir began to stroll in the meadow, and his companions, following him, were exchanging anecdotes and pleasantries, when they chanced to notice a coffin tightly bound in chains, and four thousand fierce horsemen following behind it. The Amir asked the guards, "What is in this coffin?" They said, "Bahram Gurd the Emperor of China is shut up in it, he whose chivalry and courage are of high renown in the world." The Amir said, "Does anyone shut up champions and kings and transport them like this? Does anyone capture chivalrous warriors and torment them like this?" He had the box put down on the ground, and at once caused his servants to open it. In it he saw a handsome young man, in iron fetters, lying unconscious.

The Amir, removing him from the box, released him from captivity, and sprinkled rose-water and restoratives on his face, and gently dropped apple and pomegranate sherbets (which the Amir's porters had been carrying with them) into his mouth. . . . The Amir took Bahram to his own camp, and treated him with favor and generosity: he set aside a kitchen and a stable for him, and forty of his own special horses with gold and silver saddles, and seven rows of humped camels loaded with equipment, and forty donkey-loads of gold and silver coins, and a quarter of the annual tribute of the lands of Yemen, and the entire booty seized from Hisham. And he wrote everything that had happened so far in a letter, and sent it through Amar to Khvajah Abdul Muttalib.

. . . The custom was that the king held court for a week, then spent a week in retreat with his moon-faced ladies, enjoying himself. At this time the king was absorbed in festivities within the harem, devoting himself to music and melody. Gustahm said to the Amir, "This week we are at leisure; if you will visit this worthless one's garden, and spend the week in enjoyment and pleasure, then it will be the highest graciousness on your part, and a source of honor and pride for me."

The Amir, taking Bahram Gurd, the Emperor of China, and Muqbil and some other companions with him, set out with great pomp and ceremony for Gustahm's garden, and joyously brought his radiant presence to enhance the gaiety of the garden. Gustahm had carpeted the ground from the gate to the pavilion in velvet and brocade and satin, and had spread a regal carpet in the pavilion. Seeing his enthusiasm, the Amir was delighted, and praised Gustahm's good taste to his companions. Gustahm offered them fresh and dried fruits and presents from Ctesiphon, and summoned silver-bodied cupbearers; wine-cups began to circulate. And Gustahm himself, with his robe tied up like a servant's, on the pretext of serving the guests, began biding his time. He began to look over each friend and loyal companion, seeing who among them was weak and who cowardly.

Before the Amir's arrival Gustahm had secretly hidden four hundred trusted champions in a corner of the garden, and had said to them, "When I give three knocks to summon you, come at once and slash the Amir and his well-wishers and companions to death with your harsh swords. And above all do not be the least bit afraid, not even for a moment, of punishment by the king and Buzurchmihr." In short, when Gustahm saw that the night was half over, and the Amir and his companions were so drunk that they couldn't tell black from white, he went from the pavilion into the servants' passage and knocked three times in sequence. Very forcefully he clapped his hands three times; his people emerged from their ambush and, together with Gustahm, confronted the Amir and his companions.

Looking the Amir in the eye, Gustahm said, "Oh Arab, you held your head very high, you thought the nobles of the kingdom low and insignificant. Now look: your time has come, Death is standing beside you!" With these words he aimed for the Amir's head, and struck a blow at him with his sword. Bahram, although he was thoroughly drunk, threw himself down on top of the Amir and made himself a shield. That sword-blow of Gustahm's did not reach the Amir, it fell on Bahram's side and laid it open from here to there; the blow disemboweled him from one side to the other, and all the intestines came out of his stomach.

Muqbil had cleverly been alert, for he had drunk very little wine; he had been drinking only a little and had been noticing how the party was going. Instantly seizing his bow, he began to shoot arrow after arrow, so that he stretched more than a hundred warriors out on the ground, the bodies lay piled in heaps in the garden. Gustahm believed he had killed the Amir; he thought, "I've already finished Hamzah off. Now if I stay here any longer I'll needlessly become a target for Muqbil, I'll lose my life for nothing." Together with those of his companions who had escaped from Muqbil's hands, he fled for his life and ran off somewhere or other.

When the Amir recovered from his intoxication, he said to himself, "Oh, wonderful! The gathering has a strange air, this is a peculiar kind of party! The whole pavilion and the paths before it are so bloody they're like a rose garden—a new kind of spring has come to the garden. Bahram, lying with his stomach torn open, is groaning and gasping for breath, and more than a hundred warriors are lying dead, struck by arrows." He asked Muqbil what had happened. Muqbil replied, "Gustahm did it. That eunuch, with a pretense of friendship, tried to kill you."

. . . In the meantime, the Father of all Runners, the Chief of the Tricksters of the World, the Shaver of Infidels' Beards, the Ayyar of the Age—that is, Khvajah Amar bin Umayyah Zamiri, arrived, and happily told the Amir of the health and well-being of Khvajah Abdul Muttalib. But seeing Bahram's condition, he burst into tears, and began saying to the Amir, "What, oh Sahib-qiran! Do people treat their companions this way? Do noble ones show this kind of consideration to their supporters? Do they torment and destroy those whom they favor?" The Amir said, "Oh Amar, this is not the time for exhortation, this is not the place for veiled taunts and jeers! We must think of a way to cure Bahram, we must take the best care of this unfortunate one."

Amar said to Khvajah Buzurchmihr, "You, by the grace of God Almighty, are the physician of all physicians; what treatment do you propose? I am thinking about it myself, I'm putting my mind to it." The Khvajah said, "It's a deep slash, which is considered to be the worst of all types of wound. Unless the intestines go back into the stomach, and take their proper place, we cannot put stitches in it; and it's impossible for the intestines to go back into the stomach. The intestines are completely dry and tangled into a knot; the moment we touch the artery of the heart, he will die, and then nothing can be done. And it's impossible to carry out any scheme for sewing up the wound without touching the artery of the heart." Amar said, "Khvajah, really you are an infallible physician, and my own true teacher, but the fact is that medicine is a difficult art—who in our day truly understands it?"

With these words, he pulled a razor out of his pocket. Holding Bahram down between his two legs, he advanced his hand toward Bahram's stomach. Khvajah Buzurchmihr asked Amar, "What is your intention, what has your mind hit upon?" Amar said, "Those intestines which have come out of the stomach I will cut off, through my dexterity of touch, so that the wound can be sewn up and I can apply salve and cure him." The Khvajah was dumbfounded: "What is he saying? Is he determined to take this poor man's life?" Bahram, when he heard these words of Amar's, was stunned; despairing of his life, he was thoroughly terrified. As he gave a deep gasp of sadness, all his intestines went back into his stomach, and settled themselves in their own proper places.

Amar said to the Khvajah, "There you are, now your object has been attained! Just look, was there any problem? Please put in the stitches and sew up the wound." Buzurchmihr praised Amar's wisdom and said, "Well done!" All those present laughed uncontrollably, and in chorus began lauding and praising Amar's cleverness. . . . Since the Amir held Bahram in great affection, he decided to stay right there with his friends, and gave his companions the order to remain.

7. [The Amir goes with Naushervan to the Garden of Justice, where Amar contrives to join them.]

The next day the king went to the Garden of Justice, and sent for the Amir, and arranged a seat for him near his own couch. The Sahib-qiran took Adi and Muqbil with him, and presented himself before the king. He saw the garden: it was twelve miles in length and width, and delightfully overflowing with the ebullient atmosphere of spring. The description of this garden I will leave, to save time, in the hands of the qissah-khvan,[6] for I have already praised the Garden of Justice before. The Amir sat down at the king's right hand, beside Crown Prince Hurmuz; Muqbil the Faithful and Buzurchmihr and the Amir's other officers remained at the king's left hand. Musicians who soothed the heart, singers with lovely voices, and dancing girls able to enhance pleasure, presented themselves. A luxurious and joyous party began, and wine-drinking started. On the first day the king held the festivities in one of the pavilions.

. . . Now please listen to a few words about that disturber of the alert-minded ones of the age, Khvajah Amar Ayyar, and a few delightful sentences about the trickery and shrewdness of that prankster of the age. When he had not seen the Amir for a night and a day, Amar grew anxious and left his house; searching and inquiring, he arrived at the gate of the garden. There he saw that Adi was seated in an elegant chair, drinking wine, and people were placing all kinds of snacks before him. Adi was eating with relish, and things were so arranged that not even a bird could fly over the top of the gatehouse into the garden, not even the bird of Thought could come anywhere near the garden. Amar began asking everyone, "What is all this? The Amir is in the garden; why is Adi sitting outside?" Someone blurted out, "The king has ordered that Amar and Bakhtak should not be allowed into the garden, so the Amir has stationed Adi at the door, to keep Bakhtak and Amar from getting in."

Amar, greeting Adi, sat down in a chair. Adi asked, "Khvajah, what are you doing here, and what's on your mind?" Amar said, "I hadn't seen you for two days—the world was growing dark before my eyes, so I came halting and stumbling along to see you! Good fortune brought me here without much trouble. Although you've been ignoring me, I haven't forgotten the esteem that I feel for you." Adi invited Amar to have wine and kabobs, and placed snacks before him as well. Amar drank a cup, and said to Adi, "Today I bought a ruby, and I think it was a bargain. Just take a look, and make sure I wasn't cheated." Adi was inwardly delighted: "Amar thinks me a connoisseur of jewels, that's why he's come to have me judge the ruby, he's brought such a jewel to show me!" Adi said, "Khvajah, who else is such a jewel-expert as you? Who could cheat you—who would have the nerve? But anyway I'll look, I'll do as you wish."

Amar, putting his hand in his pocket, pulled out a fistful of sand and dashed it into Adi's eyes. Adi, rubbing his eyes, said, "Curses on you, Amar, you've blinded me!" And everyone anxiously rushed to look after Adi, and began to brush away the dust from his face and clothing.

Amar, with one bound, entered the garden and reached the lawn. Adi, when he had washed and wiped his eyes, and cleaned off the dust and dirt, and when the throbbing in his eyes had lessened, grew suspicious. He asked everyone, "Where did Amar go?" But no one could tell him which way Amar had gone, in which direction he had vanished. Adi concluded, "He's fled because he fears me."

Amar, seeing the blossoming garden, felt his heart open out and bloom, for never in his life had he seen or heard of such a garden. Strolling among the flowerbeds, he headed for the palace where the king and the Amir were adorning a gathering, and the whole company were enjoying themselves. Close to that palace, at the edge of a water-channel, was a chinar tree; Amar sat down beneath it and, strumming a two-stringed lute, began to sing. Amar's singing could revive the dead, and recall the sleepers in graves to consciousness.

When the Amir heard the sound, he said to Muqbil the Faithful, "I hear a voice like Amar's, and a faint sound like that of his lute. I told Adi not to let Amar into the garden, not to let him even set foot near it, so how did he come here? Go and bring Adi here." The king, seeing Hamzah angry, said, "There's no need to call Adi, I forgive Amar his fault."

. . . The king, holding the Amir's hand, came out of the palace; strolling through the gardens, he made for the place where Amar had seated himself and was singing. Amar saw that the king and the Amir, with their party, were coming, they were heading toward him. With one bound, he fell at the king's feet and kissed them, and blessed the king, and said, "I never thought that Your Majesty would consider me a disturber of the company, and would not command my presence in this joyous and festive gathering. And as for Hamzah, he's a great one for kindheartedness and loyalty to his friends: he goes off alone to enjoy himself, and takes the first occasion to forget his old tried-and-true comrades!" The king laughed; seizing Amar's hand, he betook himself to the Turquoise Palace.

When the king had settled himself on the throne, he ordered Amar to pour out the wine. Amar began to fill and refill the cups, and to show off his clever tricks. He served as cupbearer all night, and when the pale light of dawn began to appear, Amar put together his seven-part flute and played, and sang as sweetly as David, so that the king and the Amir and their companions wept copiously, and began to drench handkerchief after handkerchief. The king filled Amar's pockets and lap with pearls, and bestowed many gifts and robes of honor on him. Leaving the

Turquoise Palace, the king went with the Amir and brightened with his appearance the Golden Palace, which had walls made of golden bricks and lattices hung with vines inlaid with precious stones.

Now I will say a few words about Bakhtak's doings and amuse my listeners. When he heard the news of Amar's entry into the Garden of Justice, he was agitated, and went around obsessed by the thought, "What a calamity, that Amar is in the Garden of Justice and I can't get in there, I can't join that heavenly gathering! Now that Amar has a clear field, God knows what thorns he'll strew in my path, what seeds of mischief he'll sow in that garden!" [Bakhtak tried to bribe Adi, but in vain; so he was forced to think of another scheme.] When night came, he covered himself with a felt rug, and with his clothes in a bag under his arm, sneaking along furtively like a thief, keeping out of sight of the guards, he arrived beneath the wall of the Garden of Justice, and threw his bundle into the garden, and himself slid in through a drainage gutter.

Please hear about Khvajah Amar: in the Golden Palace he was acting as cupbearer to the king, he was filling crystal goblets with rose-red wine, when his ribs twitched, and the fire of mischief flared up in his heart—that is, he reflected, "In just this way Gustahm too feasted the Amir, and seemingly showed complete hospitality and affection for him. May this not be the same situation, and the same kind of feast! I must just discreetly take a turn around, and have a look at things here and there." With the excuse of a call of nature, he left the Golden Palace. Wandering along the paths, strolling in the gardens, looking around right and left, he arrived near the gate.

Adi was just then saying to someone, "Today Bakhtak came and tried to bribe me; he took me for a traitor like his father, who could be bribed to let him into the garden!" When these words reached Amar's ears, he realized with a start, "Since Bakhtak came here with that intention, he'll certainly enter the garden somehow or other!" He began to examine everything, shrub by shrub, flower-bed by flower-bed, plant by plant, and to search through everything, path by path, trail by trail, garden by garden. Suddenly his eye fell on a bag; he discerned its possibilities. From a distance he could see that the bag was lying under the wall of the garden, tied tight and very full of clothing, etc. Opening it, he discovered Bakhtak's clothing.

Amar had obtained the wish of his heart, he was in ecstasy, he could hardly contain himself. He hid the bag in a corner under some leaves, and began searching: "Now, how could a thief find entry into this garden? People are so well protected here that a thief would be killed at once." When his eye fell on the gutter, he looked carefully, and saw somebody stick his head out and look all around, then pull his head back again. He decided, "It's definitely Bakhtak, that ingrate!"

Going to Khvajah Alfalfa-robe, who was chief of the gardeners, he said, "You are negligently having a cozy sleep, while a thief is trying to slip into the garden through the gutter! I heard a footfall and came to tell you. Knowing you as a prudent man, I came to warn you secretly out of affection. Now it's up to you: you know your job, you know the king's arrangements. If anything untoward happens, then in the morning—there's you, and there's a prison cell, and you'll see what garden you'll be tending!"

8. [Amar humiliates Bakhtak, and the Amir is stricken with love.]

Frightened, Khvajah Alfalfa-robe got up. Taking some gardeners with spades, he went and stood against the garden wall by the gutter. The moment Bakhtak emerged from the gutter, the gardeners fell on him and seized him. However much he said, "I'm Bakhtak!" no one believed him. Tying him up to the branch of a tree, they all began to thrash him: they were most attentive and took care of him really thoroughly. When Bakhtak's bones had been well tenderized, and his ribs and back were swollen, Amar called out to Khvajah Alfalfa-robe and asked, "Khvajah Alfalfa-robe, what is it, is everything all right? Why are you making all this noise and commotion?" Khvajah Alfalfa said, "Everything's fine. We've captured a thief and tied him to a tree."

When Bakhtak heard Amar's voice, when the sound of it fell on his ear, he called out to Amar and said in ayyari-language, "Khvajah Amar, rescue me from the hands of these brutes, release me from the clutches of these gardeners! I'll be grateful to you all my life, I'll never disobey you in anything!" Amar went up to Khvajah Alfalfa-robe and vouched for Bakhtak, saying, "In truth, this is Bakhtak, the king's vazir. What a disaster the Lord has ensnared him in! Release him right now, let him go at once!"

All the gardeners began bursting open like buds, they began clamoring, "Khvajah Sahib, what are you saying, this is an extraordinary thing you're saying! How could Bakhtak be so ill-fortuned as to come here crawling naked through the gutter? He's one of those close to the king—how could he turn himself into a thief? This is definitely some thieving ruffian, this bastard who has been rash enough to venture in here! He must be punished for his rashness, he must taste the fruit of his entry into the garden!" [Amar thus left Bakhtak in the gardeners' custody.]

Amar presented himself before the king, and all night long he kept pouring the wine. When full dawn came, Amar recited to the king a verse by Sabir Bilgrami:[7]

> "The garden is fragrant, now that it's spring,
> How the flowers have bloomed! How the nightingales sing!

The breeze is cool and crisp, the dawn breeze is gusty, the dawn has broken; it's time for a stroll. Sweet-voiced birds are twittering, the roses are smiling, the buds are bursting, the dust has been settled by a fall of dew, the earth is wet with dewdrops." The king too felt the mood, he seized the Amir's hand and went out with all the company toward the gardens to refresh himself. Amar, beguiling the king, led him toward the spot where Bakhtak, completely naked, was tied to a tree.

Bakhtak, seeing the king, began to clamor, "Oh my Lord and Guide, look what the gardeners have done to me!" And from the other side Khvajah Alfalfa-robe presented himself and said, "During the night a thief entered the garden through the gutter, so this slave tied him to a tree. When he was thoroughly beaten, then he said, 'I'm Bakhtak, the king's vazir; chance and foolishness have led me into this trap!' " When the king and the Amir looked carefully, they saw that it was indeed Bakhtak, tied to a tree.

Amar came forward and said, "Well here's a rose of a different color! Bakhtak is very intelligent and alert, a gentlemen of courage and dignity; what kind of ill fortune could have caused him to come here and ensnare himself in such a disaster? Perhaps some *ghost has come in the guise of Bakhtak, and is staging this trick for Your Majesty's entertainment! Probably after a while he'll vanish into thin air, and nobody here will see him any more." While Amar was saying this, and the king was approaching, Hamzah realized, "Beyond a doubt, Amar is mixed up in this, that refined gentleman has certainly had a hand in this!" [The king was angry at Bakhtak, but the Amir placated the king and treated Bakhtak kindly. The royal party passed the day in elegant amusements.]

When the peacock of the sun went to nest in the western mountains, and the red crane of the moon began to strut and preen itself on the bank of the green river of the heavens, the lamplighters lit camphor-white candles in the chandelier, the dancing girls presented themselves, and the joyous and elegant party began afresh. All night Amar was pouring out pure wine for the company, and entertaining them with jests.

When morning came, the king brightened the Palace of Forty Pillars with his appearance; the Amir, seeing the masterful craftsmanship of that palace, was enraptured. In short, every day the king took the Amir to a new palace, and decreed joyful and luxurious gatherings, and delighted the Amir in all kinds of ways.

Since for five days and nights the king had had not a wink of sleep, finally he dozed off. The Amir too left the Palace of Forty Pillars in order to change his dress, and his companions and friends went with him. As they were strolling along, they entered one corner of the garden and saw a water-channel so delicate that the mirror of the moon would look dingy beside it; its water ran through lattices into the palace. The Amir said to Muqbil, "I will bathe and change my dress." Muqbil helped the Amir remove his clothes, and at once sent for new clothing for him to change into. The Amir began to bathe and enjoy his bath.

It happened that Princess Mihr Nigar, daughter of Naushervan the Most Just, was sitting in a screened balcony in the upper story of the palace, enjoying the gardens. She was looking this way and that, when her glance fell on the Amir; the arrow of love for him passed straight through her heart, and she fainted. Pierced by the arrow of love, she said to herself, "The arched bow of his eyebrow has wounded me; just casually sitting there, he has dealt me the wound of love and the scar of passion. It's not right that he should escape unscathed; it does not suit me for him to get clean away!" Taking off her necklace, she flung it at the Amir. It fell on the Amir's shoulder.

When the Amir looked that way, the glory of the creative power of the Absolute Creator appeared before him. He could not restrain himself:

"I saw an idol—uniquely elegant, with a rare style and a fairy face,
Only ten years old, but a fierce disaster sent by God to the human race!"[8]

The Amir collapsed and fell flat in the water. Muqbil jumped in and supported him, and took him in his lap and lifted him out of the water-channel. The Amir heaved such a burning sigh that the golden harvest of pleasure caught fire and burned up, the flame of love began to blaze in his heart, tears of sadness began to fall from his eyes. Muqbil exhorted him, "This is not the occasion for self-abandonment! Please change into your new clothes and join the party." At length the Amir heeded Muqbil's advice: he changed his dress and betook himself to the Palace of Forty Pillars. But his mind was elsewhere, he was quite distracted.

And on her part Princess Mihr Nigar was in a miserable state. Her nurse and her ladies surrounded her. One gave her water to drink from a consecrated bowl,[9] another recited the *Verse of the Throne and blew it over her, another recited a praise of Ali and blew on her. She could not eat or drink or sleep. Someone massaged her hands and feet. When the princess recovered somewhat, she said to herself, "The secret must not be revealed, Love must not sow thorns in my garden." She said to her ladies, "There's no cause for alarm, I just somehow felt dizzy. But now I'm fine, I'm perfectly all right; don't make such a fuss, don't be anxious."

Now please hear how it was on the other side: the Amir kept waiting, moment by moment, hour by hour, for the day to be over, so that he could find some cure for his heart's restlessness; and for the evening to come, so that his heart could be calmed. Finally somehow or other he got through the day, and sat keeping hold of himself until the first watch of the night. At length his agitation guided him, he couldn't endure it any longer. He petitioned the king, "Tonight is the sixth night, your humble servant has not even closed his eyes. If the command is given I will rest a bit, I will go into some corner of the garden and sleep." The king said, "Go in the name of God, I confide you to the Lord's care."

The Amir, with Muqbil the Faithful, at last came away from the gathering, and then made his way to a spot beneath the screened balcony, but didn't find any means of climbing up. But then he saw a splendid big tree right by the wall of the palace; its branches spread out over the roof and touched the parapets. Stationing Muqbil under this tree, he himself climbed the tree and reached the roof of the palace.

9. The Amir's first meeting with the foremost among the beautiful ones of the age, that is, with Princess Mihr Nigar.

The heart-torn pen of the pulse-readers of true lovers, the pen of the knowers of those who are ill with separation—that is, the pen which has a tumult in its head—brings themes of passion and desire to its tongue, and tells the dastan of separation and union. The Amir saw, from the roof of the palace, that Princess Mihr Nigar was seated amidst a group of Pari-like ladies with faces bright as the moon; and a flask filled with rose-colored wine was before her. A crystalline cup in her hand was brimming, purple wine was glistening in the cup. But a string of tear-pearls ran continuously from the tips of her eyelashes down to her mouth, the fire of love blazed in the furnace of her breast. Deep sighs were on her lips, and she gave herself over to laments.

. . . Eventually, through everyone's persuasions, the princess's tears ceased. And *Fitnah Bano, who was the daughter of the princess's nurse, put a cup of wine into her hand and said, "Drink it up." The princess said, "I will drink after everyone else, I'll have a cup in a little while. First all of you drink to your own pursuers, let me have a bit of respite." First of all Fitnah Bano filled her cup to the rim, and coquettishly drank it in the name of Amar Ayyar. When the Amir heard this, he was perturbed: "How did Amar get in here?" He was still brooding over this when the second beauty drank a cup of rose-red wine to Muqbil the Faithful. And in this way all those present in the gathering drank cups of tulip-colored wine. The Amir reflected, "Well, well! I had no idea of all these secret affairs!"

The princess put the cup of scarlet wine to her lips with these words: "I drink in tribute to the slayer of Hisham bin Alqamah of Khaibar, to the one who released you all from captivity." When the Amir heard this he was overjoyed, and he learned a great deal from their confidential and affectionate talk. For fully three hours the lively wine-drinking party went on; the princess drank every cup in the name of the Sahibqiran. When more than two watches of the night had passed, the party broke up. The princess went and lay down in a curtained bed. She tossed and turned, but the thought of the Sahib-qiran kept sleep away; she went on weeping profusely. Finally she wore herself out with tears. The Sahib-qiran saw that the princess had gone to sleep, and every other woman had gone to her own quarters and was asleep as well. He came down the stairs from the roof, and went on tiptoe to the princess's bed.

. . . For a long time he gazed at her dazzling face. He told himself, "You've taken a lot of trouble to come here, you've gone through so much to get this close to her! So indulge your heart's desire." Somehow or other the Sahib-qiran rested his hands on the small cushions behind her head and wanted to kiss her sweet lips and place a kiss on her radiant cheek as well. The Amir's hands slipped from the small pillows and touched the princess's breasts. She awoke with a start. Not imagining that it could be the Amir, she screamed, and began to cry out "Thief, thief!" Her ladies awoke and came running from every direction.

The Amir said, "My dearest, I am the slayer of Hisham bin Alqamah of Khaibar, and I've been slain by the charm and coquetry of Mihr Nigar the Pari!" The princess recognized the Amir, felt very ashamed of having made such a commotion, and began to apologize; she instantly hid the Sahib-qiran under her bed. She put off her ladies with this excuse: "I had a nightmare, and it made me scream. It's all right, you all go back to sleep, return to your own quarters." They were all groggy with drowsiness anyway, they returned to their own quarters and went back to sleep.

The moment they left, the Sahib-qiran emerged from underneath the bed, he came up and sat next to Princess Mihr Nigar. The princess had only seen him from afar; now that she saw him close at hand she fell into an even deeper faint, she lost consciousness completely. When the Sahib-qiran put his mouth against hers and made her breathe his sweet breath, after a little while she was restored to her senses. In the meantime the white light of dawn appeared; the Sahib-qiran's narcissus eyes filled with tears of longing like dewdrops, and he said, "Oh dearest, may the Lord protect you! Now the slayer of Hisham bin Alqamah of Khaibar can stay no longer, for there's a risk of our secret becoming known. I came away by giving the king the excuse that I wanted to go to sleep. If I live that long, I will come to you again by night, and may I take all your misfortunes upon myself! But don't forget this one who has been wounded by the dagger of your charm, don't let this victim of separation slip out of your heart."

The Amir and Mihr Nigar sit close together in the pavilion, on a jewel-adorned couch.

The princess gave a deep sigh and said, with tears in her eyes, "But I don't know how I'll get through such a long day, how my restless heart will be soothed! All right, I entrust you to the Lord's keeping, I confide you to God's care.

All right, you can go now, I agree
As for me, whatever will be will be.
For a little while I must endure the pain
Slowly, slowly my heart will find peace again."[10]

After this the Amir took his leave, and climbed back down from the roof. Taking Muqbil the Faithful with him, he went to join the gathering.

. . . The Amir was as restless as heated quicksilver: he couldn't manage to control his heart at all. Every second moment he rose, left the gathering, gazed toward Princess Mihr Nigar's palace, and returned. Buzurchmihr, seeing the Amir's restlessness, guessed: "Beyond a doubt, the Amir has given his heart to someone." He made a sign to Amar. Amar said, "I realized it before you did, I have guessed it already: His Honor has fallen in love with someone, the restlessness of his heart shows it." Bakhtak too, seeing the Amir's agitation, concluded, "The Amir is mad about someone! This restlessness is not without meaning, this much agitation shows that his heart is drawn toward someone."

Bakhtak petitioned the king, "Some people are constantly getting up and going out, and the pleasure of the party is spoiled; they are breaking the mood of the gathering. Please command that anyone who leaves the gathering unnecessarily will have to pay a fine of a hundred tumans." The king, liking the idea, said to the Amir, "Anyone who goes out from now on will pay a fine of one hundred tumans." The Amir said, "That's quite proper." Despite his agreement, the Amir twice grew restless, left the gathering, and paid two hundred tumans by way of a fine. Buzurchmihr said to Amar, "We must devise some scheme at once so that Bakhtak will leave the gathering and make himself scarce; he must not be allowed to stay here any longer." Amar said, "Why that's a trifling matter, he'll be gone like the wind; a word or two from me, and he'll take to his heels."

With these words, Amar promptly obtained the royal ear, and petitioned the king, "How wonderful the mood is right now! If Your Majesty is pleased to give the command, this slave will serve Your Majesty a few cups of wine with his own hands." The king said, "What could be better? I like the idea very much." Amar took the cup and flask in his hand, revolved them, and began to warm the party up. When he had served three or four cups in a row to the king, he served one to Crown Prince Hurmuz, then one to the Amir, then afterwards one to Khvajah Buzurchmihr. Moving around in this way, he placed a cup to the lips of Khvajah Wild Pig of the Faith,[11] that is, Bakhtak.

Bakhtak felt a bell ring in his brain: "Now there's something fishy about this, something's definitely up! Amar's request to play cupbearer is not without purpose, he's surely up to some mischief." He said to Amar, "As of yesterday I swore off wine; I won't have any." Amar called out to them all, "Here's a remarkable thing! All the members of the gathering, even up to the Refuge of the World, have allowed me to be cupbearer. But Bakhtak has not, he has turned up his nose. He doesn't realize that if Satan himself had drunk a cup from my hand, he would have prostrated himself thousands of times before Hazrat Adam, he would never have lifted his swollen head from the ground!"[12] The king and all the members of the gathering laughed at this jest of Amar's, and said to Bakhtak, "In point of fact, Amar's performance as cupbearer is not without sophistication! It's astonishing that you refuse!" Having no choice, Bakhtak took the cup from Amar and swallowed the wine like poison.

Since Amar had mixed a raw laxative herb extract into the wine, it was not long before a painful rumbling and a wrenching gurgle began in Bakhtak's stomach. He rose, asking leave of the king: "This hereditary slave is going to answer of call of nature and will be back in a moment." When he had relieved himself and returned, not even a moment passed before a painful pressure again began in his stomach. He was obliged to rise and go out. Amar said, "Now where are you going? You've just come back from outside!" He said, "To the privy." Amar said, "Are you all right? You've just come from there, and you want to go again?"

Bakhtak, paying the fine of one hundred tumans, answered the call of nature. He had not been back in his seat for even a moment when again he felt a twinge, but for fear of the fine he controlled himself and remained seated. When the need grew very strong, he could not restrain himself: his bowels opened and excrement flowed down the legs of his pyjamas.

Amar was just waiting for this to happen. Putting down the winecup, he petitioned the king, "Your Majesty's senses have been heightened by wine. If you are pleased to stroll among the flower-beds, you will be doubly diverted, you will enjoy it very much; and through Your Majesty's grace others also will amuse themselves, and will be able to fill the skirt of longing with pleasure." The king said, "Amar, I was just now thinking the same thing."

The king, seizing the Amir's hand, prepared to set out toward the gardens; all those present rose as well. Among the king's retinue, Bakhtak too was obliged to be one of the first to rise. Everyone saw that Bakhtak's couch was full of filth, and filth was flowing down his pyjama-legs also. The Kirmani carpet which had been spread out to sit on had also been soiled. Amar informed the king, and told him of this situation. The king was already disgusted at Bakhtak's previous behavior, and when he heard about this state of affairs he grew extremely furious. He sent for Adi and commanded him, "This defecating boor is not fit for our company. Put him out of the garden, remove him from our presence!" Adi was already poisonously angry at Bakhtak; the moment the order was given he seized Bakhtak by the beard and dragged him away.

Khvajah Buzurchmihr said to himself, "Although our shrewd move has removed Bakhtak from the royal gathering, the Amir's agitation keeps growing moment by moment. God knows what's causing it! The king must not draw unfavorable conclusions and grow suspicious of him; that would alter everything." With hands respectfully folded he petitioned the king, "Hamzah is very grateful for the esteem shown by Your Majesty. He will be indebted and obliged his whole life long; as long as he lives he will praise the esteem shown by the Sultan of the World. Now let the Center of the World go and make the royal throne radiant with his presence, for God's creatures are waiting for the king's judgment, the king's subjects are hoping for a sight of him." These words of Buzurchmihr's pleased the king very much. Giving the Amir a royal robe of honor, he permitted him to depart. And he himself went into the audience hall, and busied himself with giving decisions and rendering justice.

10. [The Amir sets out for Sarandip to conquer Landhaur bin Sadan, Emperor of Hindustan.]

[Overcoming all difficulties, Hamzah and Mihr Nigar took great risks in order to see each other. She managed to find her way into his camp at night, and he into her palace. They talked, drank wine together, pledged their love, and vowed to keep faith forever. She accepted Islam. One night Hamzah was almost caught in her apartments, and had to fight his way out with much bloodshed; he was wounded, and was in despair at the fearful consequences of being recognized as the night intruder. But he prayed for God's help—pointing out that he had been engaged in converting an infidel!—and Hazrat Abraham appeared to cure his wound.

In the meantime, Naushervan received a letter complaining about the ominously great strength and arrogant behavior of *Landhaur bin Sadan, Emperor of Hindustan. The letter was from Landhaur's uncle, who wished to steal his throne. In the course of the letter Landhaur was revealed as a descendant of the Prophet Seth, a gallant champion, and the rightful Emperor by direct inheritance from his father. Naushervan promised Hamzah that if he would conquer and kill Landhaur, he could have Mihr Nigar's hand in marriage. Hamzah eagerly agreed, and a formal ceremony of betrothal was arranged in the palace.]

When the Amir had seated himself on a couch, and according to the royal custom had been formally given wedding-sherbet to drink, congratulations and good wishes filled the air. Merriment and joking began among Princess Mihr Nigar's confidantes and girlfriends. By the queen's order, the dancing girls, etc., were given rewards suited to their stations and talents. Queen Mihr Angez said, "Sahib-qiran, Mihr Nigar is a trust I give to you, she is part of your own honor and pride. When you return victorious and triumphant from Hindustan, I will marry her to you: I will fill the skirt of your longing with the flower of your desire."

Amar, looking toward Buzurchmihr, said, "Oh, wonderful, sir! What fairness and compassion, what tender concern! We are off by the king's command to risk our necks in Hindustan, and you don't give us even a glimpse of Mihr Nigar! If the Lord brings us back alive, and with our mission achieved, we won't know whom you are marrying to Hamzah, whom you are tying around his neck! How do we know whether the king's daughter is fair or dark, thin or fat? Let's have a look now, so there won't be any mischief later. We swear by our loyalty to the king, until we see Mihr Nigar we absolutely refuse to take a step outside this house!"

Queen Mihr Angez, laughing at this speech of Amar's, said, "It's not at all customary for the men to have a look! When the women come for the engagement ceremonies, then they see the bride." Amar said, "Your Majesty speaks rightly, but in our camp what aunts and great-aunts do we have, who could enter the ladies' apartments and see the princess? We have only you to care for us and show compassion to us! We know you will look after our interests as is proper, and will grant our petition."

The queen said, "Oh well, she has already become part of your own honor and pride, look at her whenever you want." She said to Buzurchmihr, "All right, Khvajah, bring the Amir behind the curtain, let him have a look at Mihr Nigar, and take him back." Buzurchmihr brought the Amir behind the curtain. When the Amir saw Queen Mihr Angez, he paid his respects to her and presented a formal offering. The queen gave him her blessing. Mihr Nigar, seated with lowered head by her mother's side, with complete shyness and modesty, would not raise her head at all. The Amir, seeing her, was enraptured; he could hardly contain his joy.

When Queen Mihr Angez saw the Amir at close hand, she was boundlessly happy and accepted him with her whole heart and soul as her future son-in-law. Buzurchmihr said to Princess Mihr Nigar, "The Amir faces a long and difficult journey. Please give him some token of yours, so that he can always keep it with him and can constantly think of you." Mihr Nigar removed an emerald ring from her finger and gave it to the Amir. The Amir put that ring on his finger and, giving Mihr Nigar a ring from his own hand, said, "Please keep this token of mine also, so that you won't forget me, so that you'll think of me sometimes."

Amar, with his hands folded, petitioned Queen Mihr Angez, "If you will pardon the liberty, I too will make a submission, I will convey my longing to your auspicious ear." She said, "What do you ask for, what is your desire?" He said, "Since the Amir will, God willing, marry Princess Mihr Nigar, let this slave also without fail marry the daughter of the princess's nurse. So let me also be given a token, and let the lady nurse give me the wedding-sherbet to drink."

Queen Mihr Angez said, "Oh, wonderful! Nurse, do you hear what Amar is saying? That's quite a proposal of his!" The nurse submitted, "May God grant the princess prosperity! It is thanks to her grace that I have heard this proposal. How could my daughter possibly leave the princess? Whatever the princess may please to command, my daughter will do." Mihr Nigar made a sign to the nurse, and the nurse accepted the proposal.

Queen Mihr Angez said to Fitnah Bano, "You too must give a token of yours to Amar." She gave him a perfume-box worth some hundreds of tumans. Queen Mihr Angez said, "Fitnah Bano, you must take something from Amar as well." Amar said, "I have something right here." With these words, he pulled from his pocket one date and two walnuts, and put them in Fitnah Bano's hand, and said, "Take the very best care of these, and keep them with you." All those present went into fits of laughter at this trick of Amar's. Finally the Amir took his leave. . . .

The Amir arrived in his camp, and in lordly style mounted and set out toward the river. Many officers and noble courtiers who were favorably inclined toward the Amir accompanied him, in order according to their rank. Escorting him to the city walls, they asked leave to depart. The Amir confided them all to the Lord's protection, and set out from there at once. After some days he arrived with his army like a wave of victory at *Basra. Reaching the shore, he saw that thirty ships were standing ready, as the king had ordered, waiting for the Amir's arrival. The Amir, with his thirty thousand soldiers, boarded those ships, and prepared to set sail on his expedition to Hindustan.

Amar, getting off the ship, said, "This slave is afraid of Jinns and magic and water, and cannot possibly set out for Hindustan! He will go to Mecca and will beg the True Victor for your victory, he will pray to the Answerer of Prayers." The Amir realized, "He absolutely won't go with me, he will use any kind of ruse to avoid it." He said, "All right, Amar, I am not the one to make you miserable either. But just wait a little, while I write a letter to my father." Amar believed it: "In fact he really will write a letter, he will send me off from right here."

Boarding a small boat, Amar went to the Amir. The Amir, having written a letter, confided it to Amar's care, and said, "Come, brother, let us embrace. God knows when we'll meet again, when we'll find relief from the pain of separation!" Tears gathered in Amar's eyes, and some of them fell. The Amir, embracing Amar, said, "My friend, even in the worst dangers you never left me—at a time like this, how can my heart consent to be separated from you? 'Whatever will be will be, we have set sail out to sea.' " He ordered the captain, "All right, weigh anchor!" It was no sooner said than done: the anchor was hoisted that very moment. When they had gone far from shore, the Amir released Amar.

Amar began feverishly running back and forth on the ship and muttering, "I fulfilled all the duties of friendship toward this Arab, and then he became my mortal enemy!" After they had gone a little further, an island about thirty yards wide came into view. Amar, seeing this island, said to himself, "I'll jump onto it and go home." But what Amar had taken for an island was a fish which had swum to the surface of the water to bask in the sun. When Amar jumped onto it, the impact of his feet caused the fish to dive. Amar began to drown; he was stupefied with shock.

Seeing this state of affairs, the Sahib-qiran enjoined the sailors, "Look out, don't let Amar drown! Look out, don't let him go down a second time! Whoever pulls him out will get a reward." The sailors, throwing chains and ropes, hauled Amar into the ship, brought him into the Amir's presence, and sat him down. It is truly said, "Only he who has been caught in a calamity values security." When Amar was pulled out of the sea, he sat silently, like a wet chicken, in one corner of the ship.

. . . After some days, a small wisp of cloud appeared in the heavens. Within minutes it spread over the whole sky. The wind began to blow strongly, and assumed the form of a hurricane. The light of day grew darker than the longest night of the year; you couldn't see your hand in front of your face. The strong wind grew fiercer, the water in the ocean rose up to the great ocean of the sky, every wave was higher than Noah's flood. Seeing how the slaps of the waves struck the ships' faces, the passengers grew downhearted; despairing of this life as frail as a bubble, they began to weep tears of sorrow. The shore they sought had not come within their grasp: their voyage had brought them within the grasp of death. The Amir said, "Don't be so agitated and buffeted about! Look to the mercy of the True Protector:

> Behind all weeping laughter finds rebirth
> The one who takes a long view is fortunate on earth."[13]

Amar was as though drowned in the ocean of obliteration. Weeping, he began to say, "Oh Captain of the Ship of Oneness, this fleet of Muslims is in Your hands: if You bring it to the shore, then it will reach the shore." Sometimes he said, "Oh Hazrat *Elias, if you will bring this vessel which is caught in the whirlpool to shore, and rescue us from this calamity, then although I'm a useless drop of water with no strength, in your name I will throw a fivepenny packet of sugar into the river! You will have a good deed to your credit,[14] and in addition your brother Hazrat Khizr will be pleased with you—for he has taken me under his protection, yet I'm trapped in this whirlpool of disaster!"

And sometimes he said to the Amir, "Hamzah, this is all your doing and your mischief! If we die here, we will come to a bad end: not a grave, not a shroud, not a funeral procession, not a coffin—and all this is your doing! For this very reason I never set foot in the water, and I was never willing to enjoy the fruits of this disaster. Although the knowledge was rippling on the waters of your heart, and sparkled clearly in your heart, that I, like a flood, run miles away from a river, and that I, like a shore, always stay off to one side! In my whole life I never even dipped my foot into a pool, and when bathing I never poured water over my head! You forcibly brought the vessel of my heart out to sea, and sank it: in the midst of the ocean you've caused me to lose both worlds!" The hearers, who had been distraught, sunk in the ocean-depths of sorrow, opened like flowers at the breath of Amar's speech and burst out laughing.

Finally, after many trials and tribulations, three days later, like tears in the sad eyes of those drowning in the ocean of love, the hurricane blew itself out. The darkness put on a robe of light, the brightness of the heavens displayed itself. The buffeting of the waves ceased, the high billows of the ocean were brought low, the rippling of the ocean-waves became like the phantom waves in a mirage: not the least bit of noise or frenzy remained in the sea. They all rejoiced and began saying to each other, "We had washed our hands of life, we were all but dead, we were done for; but the Creator restored us to life afresh." Someone said, "We had virtually drowned, but the True Captain brought our vessel to shore."

Amar said, "My friend, it was *my* prayer that lifted you drowning ones up, and pulled you out of that whirlpool of disaster! What vows did I not offer, what pious promises did I not make in my heart! Indeed, all of you give me something, so I can make offerings, and can have prayers said over them in the name of venerable elders." Everyone gave Amar some *dinars, and some people promised to contribute later. Amar said, "Uncle Elias, when I reach Sarandip, then I'll buy sugar and offer you your packet! In this salty ocean where can I get sugar to offer you?" Everyone laughed at his pleasantry, and enjoyed it very much.

11. The Amir's ships are again storm-tossed, and those unlucky ones fall into the Whirlpool of Alexander, then emerge from the hurricane and arrive in the land of Sarandip.

The divers in the ocean of historiography, and those who have plunged into the sea of stories of the past, obtain the pearls of narrative in this manner: After the hurricane was over, for some days a favorable wind continually blew. The passengers on the ships were free from all care. The sailors kept trimming the sails, and steadily sailed the ships onward.

One day the ships' lookouts began clamoring and shouting, "Friends, there's an immense hurricane coming! That other hurricane was like a drop of water compared to this one! Let's see which of us God saves. A further problem is that the Whirlpool of *Alexander is very close by. If, God forbid, the ships are sucked in, they'll circle round and round until they sink—we'll all be dragged right down into the depths of the ocean!"

. . . Even as they were speaking, the hurricane enveloped them, and the sea was engulfed in turbulence, and in the wink of an eye the ships were sucked into the Whirlpool of Alexander; revolving, they began to circle around and around. Then all the travelers' minds grew dizzy, and they were very much afraid.

When the Amir looked closely into the hurricane, in the midst of that whirlpool he saw a stone pillar standing, and its length and width were immeasurable. At its summit a tablet made of something like white stone had been fixed, and on it letters had been carved in relief. The inscription was in Arabic. Reading the inscription, he saw that these words were written on it: "At some time the Sahib-qiran's ships will come this way, and they will be caught in this whirlpool. It is necessary for the Sahib-qiran himself to climb this pillar and beat the Drum of Alexander which hangs atop it. Or he may have his deputy climb the pillar, so that the task can be accomplished at his hands. Surely the ships will escape from the whirlpool, and be saved from this disaster."

The Amir said to Amar, "Well, brother, I'll climb this pillar, and say 'In the name of God,' and beat the drum. If through my one life being lost, thousands of lives are saved, then why should I mind? I intend to save the lives of God's servants, under any circumstances." Amar said, "It's also written about your deputy, he too has been given permission to beat the drum! Since I'm your deputy, I will climb the pillar and beat the Drum of Alexander." And inwardly he told himself, "Climb that pillar, and just sit there peacefully! At least you'll be safe from the ocean's turmoil. When some ship passes by, get on it and be on your way somewhere or other. You have no wife or children; as a bachelor, on your own, you'll always manage to survive somehow."

Then, looking toward all the officers, Amar said, "Friends, I am your sacrificial goat,[15] so now open your purse-strings! If perhaps I survive, then I should be rewarded for my labor!" They all wrote out promissory notes. Those who would have given one dinar in cash promised hundreds, and those who would have given hundreds promised hundreds of thousands, and they handed the notes over to Amar. Amar took the notes, reciting this verse:

> "In this bottomless ocean, in this booming storm
> I have thrown my heart, God will bring it safely home."[16]

And, holding his breath, he leaped.

But as he neared the top of the pillar, and had to let out his breath, he fell with a loud noise, and went down. When he looked down, he

The ships come near the Wall of Alexander and enter a whirlpool, and Amar beats the drum atop the tower.

saw a crocodile positioned with its mouth open, waiting for dinner. Amar almost fainted: "Where did this monster come from? Have I escaped the other disaster, only to lose my life here?" When, pulling himself together, he poised his feet on the crocodile's teeth and made a leap, he landed atop the pillar, he reached the summit of the pillar—he crowned all his previous deeds with this one. Everyone praised Amar's agility, and admired his courage and quickness.

Amar saw that in fact there was a drum, and on its drumhead the name of Alexander the Two-horned was written. Amar said "In the name of God" and struck it with the drumstick. A very frightening sound came forth! The sound threw the ocean into turmoil for one hundred twenty-eight miles around. An extraordinary commotion ensued: all the sea creatures swam to the surface, and all the birds that lived on that pillar took fright and flew away. And with the wind created by their wings, the ships escaped from the whirlpool. But Amar remained atop the pillar. Although at first he had longed in his heart for this, the loneliness dismayed him.

After some days, the ships' anchors were lowered at the island of *Sarandip, and the Sahib-qiran, with his army, disembarked on dry land.

For his part, Amar, distressed by the solitude and the sun, was breaking down, and offering prayers to the True Lord, and weeping—when suddenly he heard a voice say, "Peace be upon you." Growing even more fearful, Amar looked all around, and was dumbfounded, and said in amazement, "Besides myself, there's no one else here to greet me and care about me! The *Angel of Death must be arriving to seize my soul, he must have come to take my life. Alas, a thousand times alas! What a bad place death has found me in! I'm not destined to have proper funeral rites, or a shroud wrapped around me; I won't even be buried in the earth!"

In the meantime Hazrat Khizr made himself visible. Amar saw that a radiant form, robed in green, was standing there, with a veil that concealed his noble countenance. Saluting him most respectfully, Amar asked, "What is Hazrat's auspicious name, and how does it happen that he has betaken himself to this place?" Hazrat Khizr said, "I am Khizr, and I have come to deliver you; if God Most High so wills, I will most quickly free you." Amar kissed his feet, and prostrated himself in gratitude to God.

But the ayyar was a slave to his stomach, he didn't stand on ceremony. He said, "Oh Hazrat, I'm powerfully hungry, I hope for your beneficence!" Hazrat Khizr bestowed a *bread-bun on him and said, "Eat this; I'll give you water to drink as well, and I'll release you from this prison of calamity and grief." When Amar saw that bread-bun, he was disgusted and dismayed: "How can this bread-bun satisfy me?" Gripped by the pangs of hunger, he began muttering, "Oh Hazrat, although you are a Prophet of God, and I cannot be of your rank, nevertheless I too am a friend of God's![17] You are joking with me at such a bad time, when I despair of my life! When a man is full of food, that's when he thinks of joking—otherwise he doesn't even like to talk."

Hazrat Khizr said, "Where's the joke? You complained of hunger, I gave you a bread-bun, and I promised to give you water to drink as well." Amar said, "Hazrat, this is a case of 'What good is a cumin seed in a camel's mouth.' What use is this bread-bun to me, it won't fill up even one of my intestines! You've graciously presented me with a little holy crumb!" Hazrat Khizr said, "My good man, first have a bit of faith and eat it, see if you can even finish it! Or do you intend to go babbling on uselessly?" When Amar ate from that bread-bun, even after he was full the bread-bun remained whole, just as it had been.

Khvajah Khizr pulled out a *water-flask two and a half hand-breadths long, and gave him water from it to drink, and said, "You were so impatient before, and now why is the bread-bun still there?" Amar saw that although he had drunk his fill, the water-flask was still full to the lip. Expressing his gratitude, he said slily, "Hazrat, hunger and thirst are constant companions. You'll go away, and what reason would you have to come again? If I'm hungry and thirsty then, whom can I appeal to? If this bread-bun and water-flask were bestowed on me, I'd never worry about food as long as I lived; I'd be most extremely grateful."

Hazrat Khizr accepted Amar's plea, and gave Amar the water-flask and bread-bun. And he said, "Oh Amar, this bread-bun and water-flask will ease your path through the most grievous troubles, and serve your turn in many places. And you must give the Drum of Alexander, with its accessories, to Hamzah—and be warned, don't take anything from among them!" Amar said, "Hazrat, how will I carry this burden, and how will I lift its weight?" Hazrat Khizr, giving him a shawl, said, "Wrap them in this, you won't feel any burden at all." Amar said to himself, "This shawl too is quite a good thing: it will come in handy sometime, and will be comfortable in the cold weather."

Wrapping all the accessories, and the Drum of Alexander, in the shawl, he put the bundle on his head. Placing his feet on the feet of

KHIZR ARRIVES AT THE WALL OF ALEXANDER, AND ACCORDING TO HIS INSTRUCTIONS AMAR, WITH THE BUNDLE, STANDS ON KHIZR'S FEET.

Hazrat Khizr, and closing his eyes, he began reciting the secret Great *Name which Hazrat Khizr had taught him. In the twinkling of an eye he traveled from one place to another. Hazrat Khizr said, "Amar, just open your eyes, and behold the power of God: think where you were before, and where, in the space of a breath, you have arrived; think what difficulties you were trapped in before, and where you are standing now." Amar opened his eyes and found himself standing on dry land; he prostrated himself in gratitude before the True Lord. He set out toward the mountains, in search of the Amir. [During his wanderings he encountered Hazrat Elias, who gave him a blanket that could make him invisible, and a net that could be wrapped around any burden and make it light.]

After some days, Amar arrived near the Sahib-qiran's camp. At first he felt glad at heart: "Praise be to God, I've found the army!" Then he saw that everyone was dressed in black, and looked distraught with grief. Amar said to himself, "May the Lord send me news of Hamzah's well-being, and show him to me safe and sound." Pretending to be a stranger, he asked someone, "Whose army is this, and why is the whole army in mourning?"

The man said, "This is the Sahib-qiran's army, and it's been camped here lately. Amar Ayyar was a brother of the Amir's, and the Amir loved him dearly. But he climbed onto a pillar in the salty sea and died. In mourning for him the Sahib-qiran wears black, because of him the whole army wears black; and the Sahib-qiran has abandoned himself to passionate grief. Today is the fortieth-day ceremony: the prayer for the dead has been recited, and food is being distributed among the mendicants and the poor." Amar said to himself, "Well, the Amir's affection for me has stood the test."

He spent the day among the mendicants who were being fed as part of Amar's funeral ceremonies. At night, wrapping himself in the blanket, he barged into Adi's tent. He saw that Adi was sleeping soundly. He climbed onto Adi's chest and sat there. Adi awoke and began asking, "Who are you, and where have you come from, and what do you have against me?" Amar said, "I am the Angel of Death. Today they were sending Amar's soul to Heaven. He refused to go. He said to the warden of Heaven, 'Adi is my great friend. I won't go to Heaven without him, I won't take one step on the road to Paradise without his company.' They explained to him, 'It will be a long time before he comes, he is not due for quite a while yet.' But when he still refused to consent, I was ordered, 'Go, seize Adi's soul too and bring it.' Therefore I've come to seize your soul, I will take your life."

Adi said, "I'm absolutely not his friend, I'm no comrade or intimate of his! On the contrary: I was always his mortal enemy, and always prayed for his death! In fact I never could stand him, and we never got along at all." Amar said, "If you give me something, I'll let you go, and I'll present what you've said before the High God." Adi said, "Right there is a box of gold pieces—please take the box, and let go of my life!" Amar, taking the box, went and barged into Sultan Bakht's tent, and presented the same speech to him as well. Sultan Bakht too gave a box of gold pieces—he believed that he was saving his life, and freeing himself from the grasp of the Angel of Death.

In short, that night Amar extracted gold pieces from all the officers in the same way, and collected the coins in his net. After Amar's visits they all were feverish and trembling with fright: fear destroyed their peace of mind for the whole night. When morning came, first Adi told the Amir about the night's events. The Amir believed that he had had a nightmare, and laughed very much on hearing his story, and enjoyed it extremely. Sultan Bakht arrived and told his own tale. And all the nobles presented themselves and told the Amir something very similar, they all described the events of the night. The Amir commanded, "Take the tents down at once, have the army move on away from here. It's apparent that Satan has been causing disturbances here! Otherwise, how could everyone have the same dream? What if everyone should go mad, and the camp be possessed by devils?"

The next day Amar played this same trick on the Amir too, he tried the same sort of craftiness even on him. The Amir said, "It's an extraordinary thing—the voice can be heard, but the owner of the voice can't be seen; what wickedness is this?" When the Amir groped about with his hand, he seemed to touch a body. Thinking it to be a Jinn, the Amir seized it with one hand, and with the other hand prepared to strike a blow and pulverize it. Amar said, "Beware, oh Arab, don't strike a blow! You'll injure me, your blow will cause me pain!" And quickly he threw aside the blanket from over his head.

The Amir recognized his voice, and embraced him, and with the greatest happiness pressed him to his breast. Amar recounted all that had happened, and told his whole story. He gave the Amir the Drum of Alexander, with all its accessories, etc. And showing the Amir the bread-bun, the water-flask, the blanket, and the net, he kept them in his own possession and said, "Hazrats Khizr and Elias gave these to me. Nobody else has a share in them, they're mine!"

12. Landhaur makes war on the Sahib-qiran, and is finally subdued by that lordly World-conqueror.

[First Amar, then later Hamzah, climbed a mountain in the wilderness and reached Hazrat Adam's tomb; Hazrat Adam ap-

AMAR MAKES A PIOUS VISIT TO THE GRAVE OF ADAM, AND RECEIVES BLESSINGS FROM ADAM, DAVID, ETC.

peared to each of them and gave him gifts. To Amar, he gave the magic bag *Zanbil which could contain everything and also conferred shape-shifting powers; to Hamzah, he gave an armband which would make it impossible for any foe to overcome him, and would cause his sword-blows to reach the head of any foe—even one a thousand yards tall. Adam also instructed Hamzah in the rules of chivalrous warfare: he must never attack anyone until he himself had been attacked three times, and must never use his battle-cry unnecessarily, since it was so powerful. Adam then gave Hamzah his blessing.

After a time, Amar went in disguise to Landhaur's court, used drugged wine to render everyone unconscious, and stole many jewels and other valuables by emptying them into Zanbil. When Hamzah realized Amar's trick, he sent back the valuables to Landhaur with a graceful message of apology. Landhaur replied that he forgave Amar the trick, and did not want the valuables back, but would like to see Amar in his true form. Amar went to his court again, but tricked him still more cleverly, stealing even his royal robes. Landhaur, however, admired Amar's skill, and was too generous to bear a grudge. Finally Landhaur visited Hamzah's camp. Amar was on his good behavior, and entertained the company with music.]

The Sahib-qiran and Landhaur talked in confidence, they had an affectionate and sincere conversation. When the King of the East entered his tent in the West, the King of Hindustan, while taking leave of the Sahib-qiran, said, "Has my petition been granted, or not? Has my prayer found acceptance, or not?" Hamzah said, "You fulfill all the obligations of friendship, and by your fine courtesy place me in your debt. And yet the King of Kings of the Seven Realms has sent me to fight you—it's a strange kind of duress!"

Landhaur said, "Please abandon this intention—is not peace more gratifying than war? Forget about all this! In real fact Naushervan has sent you not to fight me, but to risk your life in a contrived battle. It's apparent that he is your enemy. When he couldn't subjugate you, he devised this scheme and did this to you. I beg that you take me back with you, and give up this intention. I'll kill him and establish you on the throne. You will rule in comfort, and night and day, with your beloved in your arms, you'll do full justice to the claims of enjoyment with her." The Amir said, "I have taken up the challenge, and sworn to kill you. How can I break my faith with the king, how can this be?"

Landhaur drew his sword, and placed it before the Amir; bowing his head, he said, "If such is your pleasure, then please do so: please cut off this hapless one's head. Take it without pain or hardship, and place it before Naushervan." The Sahib-qiran pressed Landhaur's head to his bosom, and praised his chivalry and courage, and thus made him very happy. But the Amir said, "That would be a task for executioners or cowards. Have the war-drum sounded, and betake yourself in the morning to the battlefield. On the battlefield, whatever will be, will be, and then we'll see."

Landhaur said, "Well then, farewell. If such is your pleasure, please have the war-drum sounded today, and alert your army." The Amir said, "Please first order the war-drum to be sounded in your own camp. You yourself please take the first step; then I will also give the order, and will prepare for battle." The king, under duress, went back to his own army and had the war-drum sounded. The Sahib-qiran too, hearing the sound of his war-drum, ordered the Drum of Alexander to be beaten. The drumstick fell on the drum; the earth of the battlefield trembled.

. . . Now comes the dastan of the battle of Hindustan, the description of the attacks of two lions of the forest of courage and bravery. When King Day, overthrowing his enemy Night, forced him to flee from the field of visibility, and raised the banner of light in the land of the sky, the Sahib-qiran himself donned his helmet, coat of mail, shoulder-guards, padded silken shirt, steel corselet, foot-guards, thigh-guards, and *takori*.[18] He placed his keenly honed sword in his sword-belt, slung his light-flashing dagger at his waist, and mounted Black Constellation. The heralds and mace-bearers, saying "In the name of God," began to pray for victory and success. The Amir, putting his quiver in a weapons-belt on one shoulder, placed his heavy mace on the other; in him the glory of the Provider's power became visible. He took in hand a spear which called to mind the length of lovers' sighs and beloveds' tresses. Tauq bin Haran raised the serpent-shaped standard high over his head.

On one side was Muqbil the Faithful, on the other side Sultan Bakht the brave. In the vanguard the famous runner, the dagger-wielder, the beheader of magicians, the shaver of infidels' beards, Khvajah Amar Ayyar in a circle of twelve hundred ayyars, wearing his gold-embroidered vest, with his broadcloth socks on his feet; with his ayyari-sling, his bundles of nooses in loop after loop, his snare which entangles enemies' lives; wearing falconer's greased gloves on his hands; with his malicious tricks, his scimitar that flashed like lightning, his slashing dagger in his belt; shaping with his mouth six high notes, twelve tones, twenty-four melodies, twenty-eight improvisations, went leaping and bounding along. Thirty thousand armored horsemen, like a river of steel, formed into rank on rank, rode along with the renowned Amir.

From the other direction the King of Hindustan, Landhaur bin Sadan, clad in chain mail, mounted his elephant *Maimunah and hastily took in his train seven hundred thousand bloodthirsty horsemen: Khamachi, Sindhi, Bengali, Karnataki, Maratha, Dakhani, Gujarati, Rangar, Bhil, Siyar, Aghori, Kain, Bhojpuri, Bundela, Rajput, Madrasi, Assamese, Bunaki, Bhutanese covered with steel armor, Bais from Baiswara, Chhatri from the land of Avadh, Thakur, Dichhit, Panwar, Brahman, Shukla, Tiwari, Pande, Dube, Chaube, Bhusre; rustics.[19] They carried weapons, knives, daggers, scimitars, swords, cudgels, broadswords, handguns, carbines, pistols, lances, javelins.

When both armies assembled in the battlefield, wave after wave, troop after troop, squad after squad, group after group, body after body, band by band, rank by rank, and aligned themselves and stood in rows, the Angel of Death pitched his tent between the two armies, and the planet Mars appeared in radiance on every hero's forehead.

The Sahib-qiran grasped his horse's reins, spurred him sharply, and like a roaring lion dashed up to confront Landhaur, and brought this speech to his grace-conveying tongue: "Oh King Landhaur, I have business with you, and you with me. What's the point of spilling the blood of others of the Lord's creatures? This is a point to consider. Use whatever weapon you are expert in, and attack me; satisfy your heart's desire."

Landhaur said, "Oh Sahib-qiran, if I make the first attack, your own heart's desire will remain unexpressed, your own object will not be fulfilled. You make the first attack, and show your mettle." The Sahib-qiran said, "My teacher did not teach me such behavior. Until you attack me three times, I will not attack; I will not raise a hand against you."

Since Landhaur was devoted to the Sahib-qiran, he did not touch his mace: he thrust with his spear at the Sahib-qiran. The Sahib-qiran blocked the spearhead with his own spearhead, and they began a spear fight with each other. When they had each dealt a hundred spear thrusts, and neither had been wounded, and their horses too were drenched in sweat, the Sahib-qiran, blocking Landhaur's spear, gave it such a twist that it was knocked from his hand and fell far away; it flashed and flew like fireworks in the air.

Shame blanched Landhaur's face to whiteness, as though the spear point had passed through his breast. But he pulled himself together and, feeling obliged to acknowledge such merit, said, "Oh Sahib-qiran, the Tailor of Destiny has designed the robe of spear fighting to fit properly and trimly on your body alone; the Almighty Lord has bestowed perfection in this art only on you. As I am a warrior of the battlefield of courage, from now on I will never again take a spear in my hand."

With these words, he lifted up his mace and said, "Oh Sahib-qiran, open the door of reconciliation even now! Realize that peace is better than war. All my life my heart will be scarred with vain regret—don't make me grieve for you!" The Amir said, "This is the time for fighting and dying, not for advice and counsel and exhortation. I've already said that I'm bound by my word. Now I am fulfilling Naushervan's command. Come on, let's see how powerful your mace is! We are still in the early rounds of our combat."

Landhaur, under duress, knelt down, hefted his mace, and struck two blows on the Sahib-qiran's head. The Sahib-qiran, remembering the True Protector, blocked the blows with the shield of Gurshasp, which was not at all affected. Although the Amir sweated from every pore of his body, through the grace of the protective armband given by Hazrat Adam the Amir's arm could not be bent. Landhaur said to himself, "Everyone who has been struck by this mace has had his bones ground to powder, every part of his body has been shattered to pieces. But the Sahib-qiran hasn't reacted at all—his brow hasn't even been clouded!"

A second time, with his whole strength, he again wielded the mace. Although the Sahib-qiran withstood that mace-blow too as steadily as the *Wall of Alexander, inwardly he felt as weak as a child. Landhaur, growing irritated, struck a third blow with his mace on the Sahib-qiran's head, such that if it had fallen on the *Pillarless Mountain, water would have burst out. The Amir withstood that blow too, but all four feet of his horse Black Constellation sank into the ground up to the shanks. The Amir was obscured by whirling clouds of dust, he was covered with dust raised from the ground by the shock of that blow.

Landhaur's face lost its color, and involuntarily the words left his lips, "I've killed him, I've brought him down—my hands have brought low the high-handed one! But alas for the Sahib-qiran's youth! Because of it I kept trying to dissuade him, but his vow would not let him relent." With these words, he got down from his elephant and approached the Amir. Chafing the Amir's arms and legs, he said, "Oh most valued lord! If you are alive, call out, and restore me to life! If you are dead, you and I will not meet till Doomsday; your death has been a devastating shock."

The Sahib-qiran came to his senses, and waved the Whip of David above Black Constellation. His horse extricated all four hooves, and moved to a different spot, and emerged cleanly. The Amir said, "Oh King of Hindustan, whom have you killed, whom have you brought down, what high-handed one have your hands brought low? I'm still here! Strike one more blow, satisfy your heart's desire. The battle has only just begun! If the Lord guards a man's honor, why should he be so agitated? It seems that you haven't encountered a true warrior before, you haven't experienced a tough battle!"

Landhaur was astonished. Getting down from his elephant, he mounted a horse, and drew from his belt a Burdwani sword, steel-blue, like quicksilver, enemy-slaying, reckless, like the counter of a perfumer's shop;[20] with it he launched a blow at the Amir's head. The Amir raised his ornamented shield, adorned with bosses wound with seven-colored silk, and blocked the calamitous blow with it, and said, "Oh Prince Landhaur, I've withstood five of your attacks, and what attacks they were to withstand! Now it's my turn, it's time for my attack, so be warned! Don't say that you were caught off guard, or that I didn't alert you properly!"

With these words, he spurred his horse to the side of Landhaur's horse, seized his sword Samsam, and with complete deftness and cleverness and perfect alertness, launched a blow at the king's head. The king, blocking the blow with his shield, sought to turn it aside and stay the Amir's hand. But the sword, cutting through his shield as though it were soggy cheese, landed on his horse's neck, and felled the horse. The king of Hind freed himself from the saddle, and grew furiously irritated and outraged; drawing his sword, he rushed at the Amir. The Amir said to himself, "Black Constellation must not be wounded and killed at his hands! Half my strength would be gone, and when would I get my hands on such a horse again?" With perfect dexterity he got down from his horse, and with a skillful hand-grip pulled the sword from Landhaur's hand. He grabbed it away to one side, and flung it over toward his own army.

Landhaur closed his hands around the Amir's neck, and the Amir seized him around the waist; both began to exert their full strength. The beholders' knees turned to water. When the Wrestler of the Day set out for his resting-place in the west, and the Master of the Night began to enhance the skills of his students the stars, torches were lit on both sides and burned continually all night long. For three days and nights the Amir and Landhaur wrestled with each other, hand to hand, chest to chest, cheek to cheek, but neither could budge the other.

On the fourth day the Amir gave the cry, "God is great!" and jerked Landhaur up and lifted him up to his chest—but could not raise him as high as his head. He stood there holding that wrestler, who was very heavy. Releasing him, he prepared to stab him with a dagger in his proud ribs, and trample his precious life into the dust of oblivion. Landhaur seized the Amir's hand. Then with folded hands he said, "Oh Sahib-qiran, who besides you has ever been given the strength to dislodge my wrestling-stance from the ground, and to lift me up even a little way? With my whole heart and soul I agree to serve you. From now on I ally myself with you."

The Amir clasped Landhaur to his breast, and at once prostrated himself before God in gratitude, and said, "Oh King, you are like my right arm! I will treat you as a brother and hold you dearer than life. But I have this entreaty: that you go with me to Naushervan, and make me true to my word pledged to him." Landhaur said, "I obey your orders; wherever you command I will go. In the name of God, let's depart, I am at your service. Please order the vanguard to proceed. I've already pledged my word: I have nothing to say even about this matter."

Landhaur at once summoned the officers of his army, and presented them to the Amir, and described the station and rank, etc., of every single one. And he himself joined the Amir, and entered the Amir's tent. The Sahib-qiran gave a great quantity of gold and jewels in charity for Landhaur's sake. Arranging for a celebration, the Amir filled the cup of his eyes to the brim with tears of blood at the thought of Mihr Nigar. Landhaur, seeing this, realized that the Amir was thinking of Mihr Nigar. Wiping the blood-red tears with his handkerchief, Landhaur said, "Why all this tearfulness? Now the time of separation is ending, and the time of union is near."

The Sahib-qiran, gaining control over himself, asked Amar to sing. Amar, settling himself respectfully on his knees, fitted the tip of the plectrum over the end of his finger and began to pluck the strings. Playing the two-stringed lute, first he showed his skill by performing a raga. Afterwards, when he began to sing as sweetly as David, he entranced the Amir, Landhaur, and all those present, whether they were love-torn or not. The Amir's and Landhaur's hearts were enraptured by Amar's singing. Both of them loaded him with gold and jewels in reward.

Afterwards Landhaur placed the keys of his treasury before the Amir, presenting him with rare and valuable gifts from the whole of

King Landhaur sits in glory on the Peacock Throne, and Amar plays the lute and sings.

Hind. Landhaur was ennobled by embracing Islam, and with a sincere heart renounced idol worship. Sending for the major-domo, the cooks, and the carpet-spreaders, and causing scented leather dining cloths to be spread out in one room, the Amir provided a banquet of various kinds of food. The Amir, taking Landhaur with him, ate dinner. Landhaur, after dinner, petitioned, "I am a suppliant for a great honor. I have been hoping for a long time that you with your Paradise-rivaling feet would make my humble home the envy of Heaven, and would be pleased, by taking bread and salt, to let the palate of my soul relish the taste of your kindness." The Amir said, "I accept with my whole heart, I must certainly taste the food of Hindustan."

After this, Landhaur asked leave to depart, and the Amir garbed Landhaur in a royal robe of honor. Landhaur took his leave and went to his own palace. Arranging royal festivities, he brought into his court the Sahib-qiran, along with the famous nobles and dignified champions. A joyous gathering began; slaps fell on the tabla, and it began to resound.

13. [The Amir and Landhaur return to Naushervan's court, where Landhaur narrowly escapes execution.]

[The journey back to Ctesiphon was long and dangerous. Gustahm had Hamzah poisoned with drugged wine purporting to come from Mihr Nigar, and Amar was hard put to cure him. Believing that Hamzah was dead, Naushervan and Bakhtak gleefully arranged for Mihr Nigar to marry another suitor. But Amar in the guise of an astrologer managed to reach Mihr Nigar and reassure her of Hamzah's safety; he found that she had planned to kill herself rather than accept the proposed marriage. When Naushervan heard the unexpected news of Hamzah's survival and return to Ctesiphon, he was very much at a loss, and adopted a scheme of Bakhtak's.]

In the morning, when the Amir came to the court, before anyone else had spoken Bakhtak said to the Amir in a loud voice, "His Majesty says, 'Did I ask you to bring Landhaur's head, or to bring him down on my head, and to introduce a disaster into my city?' "

The Amir disliked this speech of Bakhtak's; he replied, "Was the idea to subjugate him, or to cut off his head to no purpose? He has presented himself here, with his army, in submission. He is not rebellious in any way; with his army he places himself at the king's service." Bakhtak said, "We don't need his submission! He is up to no good. Today he puts his head on the king's feet, and tomorrow he gets high-headed again, and then what will happen?"

The Amir said, "While I am alive, how could he presume to defy the king, or show any kind of rebellion or disobedience? But if this is the king's wish, his head is as good as cut off; my desire is to please His Majesty." Bakhtak said, "The king will be satisfied only with his head! When did the king ever even wish to look at his face? And how can I believe that Landhaur will give up his head on your say-so, and will never be high-handed or high-headed?" The Amir said, "Why this is a trifle! If I give the order, Landhaur will at once bow his head beneath the harsh sword—or rather, he will cut off his head with his own hands." Bakhtak said, "Then why the delay, what are we waiting for? Please send for Landhaur, and tell him what you have just said."

The Sahib-qiran directed Amar, "Bring Landhaur here." Amar came to Landhaur and said, "Come along, the king has ordered your death. The Amir has sent for you in order to cut your head off as the king has commanded." Landhaur rose promptly and said,

> "I'm drunk with the wine of love, to my own self I am dead
> Following love's path, I don't care at all about my head.[21]

My object is to please the Sahib-qiran. Here, tie my hands with a kerchief, and take me before the king."

Amar, hearing Landhaur's words, threw his arms around his neck, and gallantly said, "Oh King Landhaur, who would dare even to give you an evil glance, or to look askance at you? Come with me. Along with your head, first of all there's Hamzah's head. And after that, there are the heads of all the champions, and my head. Gird on your weapons confidently, mount your elephant Maimunah, and come with me." Landhaur, girding on his weapons and carrying his mace on his shoulder, mounted his elephant Maimunah and went to the front courtyard of the palace and dismounted there.

Amar, entering the court pavilion, informed the Amir, "Landhaur, whose head is to be cut off, has presented himself. He seeks the Amir's pleasure, no matter what it may involve." Outside, Landhaur began throwing his mace up into the air and catching it in his hand. All around a tumult arose: "If the mace should slip from his hand, ten or twenty innocent people will die, hundreds will have the bones of their hands and feet broken and be crippled!" The king, hearing the tumult, said, "Is everything all right? What's all that noise? What kind of fuss is going on?" People told him the state of affairs. The king fell silent.

The Amir said, "Bring Landhaur in." Amar went and brought him. Landhaur, with folded hands, asked the Amir, "What is your command? Why did Your Excellency call me to mind?" The Amir said, "The king wants your head; he has misgivings about you." Landhaur said, "I am your servant, I am ready to do whatever you wish. I hold myself in submission to you." The Amir commanded, "All right, take leave of His Majesty, and go and sit in the front courtyard with your head bowed. Whoever receives the royal command will come and cut off your head." Landhaur, after paying his respects, went into the front courtyard and sat down, using his mace as a backrest.

The Amir ordered Adi, "Cut off Landhaur's head and bring it here." Adi told Landhaur the order. Landhaur bowed his head and said, "Thanks be to the Lord, that my head is being cut off at the Amir's order, and I have not fallen short in any way, by even a hair's breadth, in my submission to him." Adi was overcome by Landhaur's submission, and went and sat beside him, saying, "They'll have to cut my head off first, before they can so much as give Landhaur an evil look!"

The Amir, hearing how matters stood, ordered Bahram, "Go and cut off Landhaur's head with your own hands and bring it here." Bahram too was deeply affected by Landhaur's words, and went and sat at Landhaur's other side: "My head also is with Landhaur's head. If the Amir cuts off our heads with his own hand—well, the necks are ours and the hand is his!" The Amir, when he heard what Bahram had said, sent Sultan Bakht of Maghrib. He too came and sat down by Landhaur, and said, "This is a fine kind of bloodshed that the Amir has undertaken! If this is really what he wants, then my head too is with all theirs."

All these people's words came to the ear of the king, and the news-bearers reported directly to him, in detail, everything that had been said. Bakhtak said, "Why shouldn't the royal executioner be ordered to cut off and bring the heads of whichever ones the king should please, and finish off the whole business in a moment?" The Amir said, "You have the authority—send whomever you want." Bakhtak instantly made a sign to an executioner.

The executioner went and stood by Landhaur's head and called out,

"Whose life-star is growing dim, whose life-sun is setting?" Amar saw that the executioner, wearing a tiger-skin vest, with a bloody towel thrust into his belt, and clutching a Burdwani sword, was advancing on Landhaur. Amar had just hastily slipped behind the executioner's back—when the sound of an elaborate royal retinue, the calls of outriders, the cries of heralds, respectful and clear, were heard, and gradually reached the palace gate. When they looked, Queen Mihr Angez and Princess Mihr Nigar were arriving in a palanquin from somewhere or other, and going toward their own palace.

Mihr Angez, looking out through the lattice, asked Mihr Nigar, "What's this? Some kind of turmoil and confusion is going on." Mihr Nigar said, "Why, it's Landhaur." The queen ordered the eunuchs, "Just go and ask what all this confusion is, and why there is such a crowd at the palace gate." The palanquin moved onward very slowly. The eunuchs inquired, and reported the whole situation. The queen said, "It's apparent that the king is bent on bloodshed—he's set out to murder innocent people for nothing! Go, bring Landhaur to my palace."

The eunuchs went to bring Landhaur. The executioner opposed them. The queen, hearing of this, said, "Cut off this executioner's nose and ears, and remove him from the courtyard, and disembowel him and throw his body outside the city walls." When the executioner heard this order he lost his nerve, and stayed silent. Landhaur was freed from this mortal peril and taken to the queen's palace. The queen, giving Landhaur a robe of honor, permitted him to depart. Landhaur, with Bahram and Adi and Sultan Bakht, set out with the greatest joy for *Tal Shad Kam.

. . . The fickleness of Fortune is well known, the Conjurer's marvelous tricks are clearer than clear. Sometimes right in the midst of merriment, causes of grief make themselves felt; sometimes in the midst of utter despair, the bright face of hope can be glimpsed. Therefore this dastan follows the same pattern. The researchers of tales say this: When the king entered the bedchamber of the harem, he asked Queen Mihr Angez, "What was your intention in pardoning Landhaur and rescuing him from execution?"

The queen said, "First, Landhaur is innocent; despite his strength and power, he never grew intransigent. He is constrained by his love for the Amir. Second, Landhaur too is king of a country; kings do not kill kings in this fashion, they don't permit each other to be humiliated in this way. Third, word would spread from country to country, and your reputation would be destroyed: people everywhere would blame you, no one would trust your words or deeds. Fourth, if Landhaur were killed in this way, Hamzah would put out the lights of the whole land to avenge him. Don't you see that Landhaur was ready to give his head only at Hamzah's command? Otherwise, who among all your royal champions could have cut off Landhaur's head? For these reasons I gave Landhaur a robe of honor and permitted him to depart."

The king praised and admired the queen's wisdom, and was very pleased. But then, growing downcast, he said, "It's a pity that no plan has been hit upon for getting rid of Hamzah." *Hell-cave Bano, Bakhtak's mother, was in attendance at the time. With folded hands she said, "If I am ordered, then by means of an elegant scheme I will kill Hamzah, I'll get rid of this pest at once." Naushervan said, "How?" She said, "Tomorrow, before the whole court, let Your Majesty say to Hamzah, 'A week from now your marriage with Mihr Nigar will be celebrated; prepare for the wedding. We will order the royal servants to help as well.' And this handmaiden will take Mihr Nigar to the underground apartments on the pretext of preparing her for the marriage, and will keep her hidden there. Two days later you may falsely announce Mihr Nigar's illness, and on the fourth day after that, the bad news of her death. When Hamzah hears this news, he'll put an end to himself."

[The king acted accordingly. But Amar made a reconnaissance, discovered the scheme, and strangled Hell-cave Bano. Her coffin was then passed off as that of the "dead" Mihr Nigar.]

Hundreds of thousands of torches were lighted, and thousands of men accompanied the bier. Amar saw that the Brahmans were going along sounding conches and bells, and embracing their co-religionists, and reciting the praises of their one hundred seventy-five gods, and setting off fireworks at every step. Amar too, disguising himself, took a bell in his hand, praised *Lat and Manat, and began embracing every single fire-worshipper.

Gradually, he made his way over to Bakhtak. Lighting a "muskrat" firecracker, he put it down Bakhtak's collar, and squeezed him in a very tight embrace. Who besides Amar would do such a thing to Bakhtak? Involuntarily Bakhtak cried out, "Ah! I'm burning! Ah! I'm burning!" and begged, "Amar, let me go, for Hamzah's sake! My whole chest and stomach are burning, my whole body is turning into a blister!" . . . Bakhtak, seeing a pit full of water by the side of the road, threw himself into it; he completely lost control. All those in the funeral procession, who had been weeping, now burst out laughing, and some Brahmans put out the flames on Bakhtak's body. But Bakhtak couldn't bear the pain. He confided his dead mother to the Brahmans' care, and he himself returned, weeping and beating his breast, to his home.

When they had lowered Bakhtak's mother into the grave and returned, all the courtiers saw the king seated in the audience hall grief-stricken and weeping, and began to weep and wail. When Amar looked carefully, he saw that there was an onion in the king's handkerchief: when the king applied it to his eyes, its sharpness made the tears flow. Going very close to him, Amar said softly, "A king as hypocritical as you has never been seen or heard of! Has anybody ever gone back on his pledged word, or deceived nobles and faithful servants, so basely?" The king laughed and said, "The one who was guilty of treachery and deceit has been suitably punished." Although the king said this, he was inwardly very much ashamed, and broke out in a sweat of embarrassment.

. . . Naushervan apologized profusely to the Amir and said, "I was absolutely unaware of this deceit; please don't have such suspicions about me! The one whose trick this was has received her punishment." The Amir said, "In any case, I am at your command, I obey you, heart and soul. Please tell me, now when will the marriage be, when will my house be brightened?" The king said, "After forty days the marriage will be celebrated; your wish will be fulfilled." The Amir, taking his leave, went to Tal Shad Kam.

14. The Amir sets out for Greece, and contracts a marriage with Nahid Maryam, a charming beauty.

The next day when the king, seated on his throne, brightened the court with his radiant presence, and wise men learned in the faith of *Nimrod, and champions of powerful aspect, presented themselves, and the Amir too came and sat in the Seat of Rustam, someone swung the *Chain of Justice. When the sound of the chain came to Naushervan's ears, he sent for the petitioners, and summoned the suppliants into his presence. He saw that some people with their ears and noses lopped off were seeking justice: they were distressed and distraught and in a wretched condition. All those present in court began to regard them, wondering, "Who has done this to them, and slashed off their ears and noses at the root?" The petitioners said, in a very effective way, all the things that Bakhtak had told them to say. [They claimed that the tributary kings of the Seven Lands, all fire-worshipers, were so outraged by Mihr Nigar's impending marriage to a Muslim that they had rebelled.]

Every hair on the Amir's body stood on end with fury, his *Hashimite vein pulsed with rage. Irrepressibly he spoke up, "By the Lord of the Kabah, until I extract tribute from those rebels I will absolutely, absolutely not marry!" He ordered Adi, "Have the vanguard start out this very day for the Seven Lands, and have the army take no more food or drink in this city." Naushervan said, "Oh *Father of Greatness, if this is your wish, then first get this marriage out of the way, and afterwards go and box their ears." The Amir said, "Your humble servant has sworn an oath: until I extract tribute from the rebels in that land, I won't even think of marrying! Let Your Majesty not insist on this, but cheerfully and gladly permit me to depart."

. . . The king gave the Amir a robe of honor, and writing seven letters addressed to the kings of the Seven Lands, he gave them to the Amir and permitted him to depart: "Please send these to all the kings, and insofar as possible, conciliate them." And he sent Qarin the Dev-taker and twelve thousand Sasanians along with the Amir, with orders to do whatever the Amir commanded, and never to fail in obedience to the Amir in any way.

. . . The Amir took his leave and returned to Tal Shad Kam. The king wrote seven letters addressed to the seven kings, and confided them to Qarin. The contents of those letters was this: "We have sent Hamzah this way for good cause. Not to speak of tribute, don't let him even enter your presence. Cut off his head and send it to us." And giving seven drams of deadly poison to Qarin, the king commanded, "When you get the chance, feed this to Hamzah." Honoring him with a robe of honor, he permitted him to depart. Qarin presented himself at the Amir's camp.

The Amir had the departure-drum sounded, and set out with his victorious-appearing army for his intended destination. Amar said to the Amir, "You're in love with the battle-lines—your love for Mihr Nigar is only lip service! However, it's your privilege: go wherever you want, spend your life conquering countries, travel on through new lands and cities, fight on battlefields, organize combats, make your troops and champions fight so you can enjoy the show! This humble servant has wandered with you for a long time, and what disasters has he not narrowly escaped! Now he goes to Mecca; there he will pray for you. If you want to give me any letter for your revered father, please give it, and I will present it in his service."

[Finally, however, Amar did go along. During the journey Qarin tried repeatedly to poison and betray them; he was finally imprisoned, and Amar later killed him. Without Qarin to incite them, most of the kings didn't give the Amir much trouble.]

The adorners of composition clothe the brides of Meaning in jewels of language, and decorate the beauty of expression in various new ways: When the beloved one Victory showed her radiant glory in the mirror of the Amir's heart, the Amir entered the fort of *Aleppo and ordered a week of celebration. Writing all about the tribute and submission of the five lands, and the story of Qarin, and other happenings, he sent a letter with Muqbil to be presented to Naushervan, and he himself set out for Greece. After some days, he crossed the border into Greece and encamped there.

King Faredun, the king of Greece, already knew about the Amir's doings from the reports of his news-writers. As soon as he heard of the Amir's coming, he set out from Greece with substantial offerings, taking his brothers along. On the road he met the Amir, presented his offerings, and with a sincere heart paid reverence to him. With pure intentions he recited the profession of faith and, along with his brothers, was ennobled by Islam.

[The king begged the Amir to marry his daughter; the Amir refused on the grounds of a promise to Mihr Nigar. The king then tried new tactics.] King Faredun, sending for Amar, seated him near the throne with great honor and respect, and presented him with five thousand gold pieces, and said, "Khvajah, my honor is in your hands! For the Lord's sake, somehow or other get my daughter married to the Sahibqiran, and solve this difficulty. After the marriage I will make you an offering of ten thousand more gold pieces. Otherwise, I won't be able to show my face among my peers—I'll have no choice but to take poison or stab myself!"

Amar, giving him many reassurances, said, "Why, this is a small matter! The wedding ceremony will be held this very day. I take full responsibility, don't you be anxious. Please quietly prepare for the wedding." With these words, he took the gold pieces and went to his own quarters.

In private, he praised *Nahid Maryam's beauty and loveliness to the Amir, and thus made him desirous. The Amir said, "Khvajah, I would marry the daughter of King Faredun right now, but what excuse could I give to the princess? For I have sworn to her, 'Until I marry you, even if I'm face-to-face with a Pari I'll consider her a *witch!' "

Amar said, "Oh Sahib-qiran, are you in your right mind? Are men ever truthful in such matters? They make even stronger vows to women, and then always break their word! And then, someone who is a Sahib-qiran, a master of crown and throne, a taker of tribute—he can't keep his trousers fastened merely for Mihr Nigar's sake! You go ahead and marry Nahid Maryam with a good will, and enjoy yourself properly. As for Princess Mihr Nigar, that's her business and mine. If she should say anything to you, just mention my name—I'll quiet her down. I take full responsibility for it."

At length, due to Amar's persuasion, the Amir agreed to the marriage, on this condition: "I will marry her, but I won't share a bed with her until after my marriage to Mihr Nigar." King Faredun willingly and happily accepted this condition, and was most grateful to Amar. In short, that very day Nahid Maryam was rubbed with oil, and preparations were made for the marriage. King Faredun gave Amar, in addition to the ten thousand gold pieces, a valuable robe of honor with costly jewels on it, and said, "Khvajah, I'm at your service; I'll always keep giving you gifts of one sort or another."

Amar was a greedy fellow, after all; he gave King Faredun a great deal of encouragement! Afterwards he praised Nahid Maryam's beauty so lavishly that the Amir grew impassioned. The next night was the night to put on the henna; after performing the henna ceremony the Amir married Nahid Maryam, and for two weeks remained absorbed in enjoyment and pleasure with her.

15. The pigeon's letter arrives in Ctesiphon, and plans are made to kill Muqbil, etc., and Amar suddenly arrives. Amar sets out for Egypt after the pigeon and kills it by the city gates and frees the Amir from captivity, after grief and despair.

[When Hamzah and his party reached Egypt, the *King of Egypt showed them lavish hospitality—but put knockout drugs in their wine. When they awoke, they found themselves in a dungeon, loaded with chains and under constant guard. The King of Egypt sent a letter to Naushervan through a carrier pigeon, asking if he should kill the prisoners.]

When Bakhtak opened the letter and read it, his morose face became all smiles, and his heart expanded in ecstasy. That very instant he presented himself before the king and happily congratulated him, and gave him the letter. Naushervan too, when he read the letter, almost burst the buttons of his robe with happiness.

Bakhtak petitioned, "Now Your Majesty should most quickly write, in answer to this, a warrant authorizing the killing of Hamzah, and Your Majesty should bestow it on me, and should not consult with anybody else about the matter. For this servant has an Egyptian pigeon: if the letter is tied to its neck and it's released in the morning, by evening it will have carried the letter to the addressee." Naushervan said, "In such a difficult matter it is most necessary to have Buzurchmihr's advice, for I wish to act on my father's injunction in all circumstances."

That gallows-bait replied, "As you command. But Buzurchmihr is a Muslim—he will always take the Muslims' side. Mighty ones like Hamzah will hardly fall into your clutches repeatedly; you will not have a chance like this again." The king said, "This consultation will test Buzurchmihr's faith also: his religion will become apparent." With these words, he summoned Buzurchmihr, and gave him the letter to read.

When Buzurchmihr read the letter, he felt that the bird of his senses was about to take wing: what a dreadful disaster! At length, pulling himself together, he said, "May the Lord make this auspicious for you—that you have no part in all this, and yet a great trouble has been removed! But just now it's not proper for you to write ordering that Hamzah be killed. I say this because if the news quickly reaches Landhaur and Bahram and Muqbil, then before the pigeon arrives, there won't be even a bird or beast—not to speak of a human being—left alive in Ctesiphon. And afterwards, God knows what will become of Egypt! First please allow for these people in your plans, then afterwards order that Hamzah be killed."

Bakhtak replied, "That's no great matter—it doesn't need a miracle of intelligence to deal with *those* people! Tomorrow when they present themselves in court, let Your Majesty arrange a feast of meat and wine and, by putting a knockout drug in the wine, make those three pass out on the floor. Afterwards, you should write the letter commanding the King of Egypt to kill Hamzah, then tie it around the pigeon's neck and send it off. You should use the pigeon which is in your humble servant's possession. When Hamzah's head arrives, then you can confidently kill Landhaur, etc., and wipe out a daily threat of mischief and disruption in your country."

Naushervan was very pleased by this idea, and expressed the greatest admiration for Bakhtak's wisdom. Since Bakhtak knew that Buzurchmihr worshiped the Lord, he neither went himself to his house that night nor, with the king's permission, allowed Buzurchmihr to go to his own house.

When morning came, the time for court arrived. Landhaur and Bahram and Muqbil presented themselves at court as usual, and sat in their various places according to their respective ranks. The king behaved very graciously toward them and, as had been decided the night before, arranged a joyous gathering. Wine mixed with knockout drugs began to circulate, Portuguese and French wines began to be poured. Although Buzurchmihr, behind the others' backs, winked at Bahram and Muqbil and Landhaur, none of them understood, none of them paid attention to his signal.

Muqbil, having drunk two cups, realized something of the truth and, on the pretext of a headache, rose and left the gathering, and went straight along by the shortest route to Buzurchmihr's house; arriving there, he lost consciousness and collapsed on the floor. Landhaur and Bahram, having drunk four or five cups, lost consciousness and fell from their chairs and couches. The king had leg-irons put on their feet, iron collars on their necks, chains around their waists, and spiked balls under their arms to torture them; he had them both sent to a dungeon.

Then the king wrote in answer to the King of Egypt, "In truth you have done us a great service by imprisoning Hamzah. It is necessary that the moment you receive this letter, you cut off his head and send it to us, and finish off this affair as soon as possible." Having written the letter, he gave it to Bakhtak: "Put our seal at the top of it, tie it around the pigeon's neck, and tomorrow morning send it off. And be warned—let no one learn of this secret!" Having given this order, the king dismissed the court, and entered the bedchamber of the harem. Buzurchmihr, taking his leave, went to his own house.

Arriving there, he saw that Muqbil was lying unconscious and unmoving, like a dead man. Giving him an antidote to the knockout drug, he brought him to his senses, recounted the whole story, and told him of the entire affair. Muqbil began rending his clothes and wailing, and was ready to give up the ghost. Buzurchmihr said, "This is not the time for wailing and breast-beating, this is the time for strategy! At such a time, to let strategy slip from your hands is highly improper. I have a female camel who can cover two hundred forty miles without stopping. Mount her and rush off: on the road, catch the pigeon wherever you can and kill it, for only if it's killed will things be all right. This is the soundest and most prudent strategy." Muqbil instantly mounted the camel and went off.

[Word came that Amar had arrived.] Buzurchmihr, hearing this, ran barefoot and brought Amar into the house. Telling him the whole story, he began to weep and said, "Khvajah Amar, if you kill this pigeon on its way, then things will be all right, and everything will end well. Otherwise, our goose is cooked!"

Amar too began to weep, and said, "Khvajah, how can I run three thousand miles in one day? I don't have wings and feathers like a pigeon, to fly along through the air!" Buzurchmihr said, "Oh Amar, I have seen in your fortune that three times in your life you'll run as no one ever has run or will run. The first time, you'll cover three thousand miles in one day along with this pigeon. The second time, when enemies tie the Amir between the torture-stakes, you will run thirty-three thousand miles in twelve days to rally the champions of Islam.[22] The third time, in the Wilderness of Alexander you will cover twenty-one thousand miles in seven days for the sake of Hamzah's son,[23] and will never tire at all."

Amar said, "Khvajah, you've told me very dismal news, and have read me a really fine fortune! It appears that my whole life will be spent running—my time will pass in racing around and bearing messages!" The Khvajah said, "Be happy. As wages for it you will receive unimaginable treasures, such as no one has ever even dreamed of—indeed, such as not even the greatest kings have ever heard of. So get ready to leave at once!"

. . . Please hear about the Father of the Runners of the World: calling on the Eternal Creator, he flew along without pausing, in the wing-shadow of the pigeon flying overhead. Wherever a river, a mound, an embankment blocked his way, he crossed it with a bound, and disregarded every obstacle. And with every step he kept his eyes fixed on the pigeon, as if he were a hawk pursuing it.

Now I will tell a little about Muqbil the Faithful, and explain to the eager listeners. When Muqbil mounted the female camel and set out, for one hundred forty miles he went at full gallop. Then, seeing a canal with clear water more sparkling than a pearl, he got down from the camel, took out the food that had been tied up at his waist, and began to eat breakfast. He released the camel to graze in the forest, and he himself at once lay down for a rest. It happened that a good deal of poison grass grew in the forest. When the camel ate the poison grass, she instantly died. Muqbil, distraught, arose and set out on foot. After he had gone a number of miles, his feet grew swollen, and he began to stagger and stumble. Having no choice, he sat down under a tree, and wept and wept until he fainted.

Amar, following the pigeon, went along, and on the way he saw the camel lying dead. He realized, "This is the very camel which Muqbil was riding." Going on a little further, he saw Muqbil lying unconscious under a tree, with his feet swollen and his strength exhausted. Amar at once dripped water into his mouth. Muqbil opened his eyes and began to weep. Amar said, "This is not the time for weeping! Climb on my back quickly, and somehow shoot down that pigeon!" Muqbil, placing the notch of an arrow on his bowstring, prepared himself, and climbed onto Amar's back.

Amar raced on from there with fiery speed, like a blazing meteor. Amar's own words are, "Sometimes I was a bow-shot ahead of the pigeon, and sometimes the pigeon drew near me." The Bird which points toward Mecca had not yet settled in its western nest, and the pigeon was just on the verge of reaching the fortress gates of Egypt and flying over the battlements, when Muqbil released the hawk of his arrow from the nest of his bow. Instantly the pigeon was seized by the talons of the hawk of Death. Even when it writhed itself free, wheeling in circles like a falcon, it fell wounded into the moat before it.

Amar, picking the pigeon up, opened and read the letter; in order to show the letter to the Amir, he placed it carefully in Zanbil. Slaughtering the pigeon, he prepared kabobs and gave them to Muqbil to eat. And with Muqbil he entered the Muslim camp on the bank of the river Nile. Sultan Bakht of Maghrib, seeing Amar, began to weep and wail. Amar, wiping his tears with the handkerchief of consolation, said, "It's hardly the time for anxiety and doubt, for grief and sorrow! If God wills, I'll soon free the Amir and bring him here. If God Most High wills, I'll rescue you all from this disaster, and then just you watch how I straighten out that hypocritical king!"

[Amar found Hamzah and his companions imprisoned in a well called the Pit of Joseph. He lowered himself down to them with a rope.] The Amir embraced Amar, and removed the bonds of all his companions; with the help of the rope he climbed out of the well, and pulled all his companions out also. Amar told the Amir all the events that had occurred from the beginning until that moment, and duly prostrated himself in gratitude to the True God. When he looked toward the sky, he saw that the morning star was shining like the fortune of the Amir, and the whiteness of dawn was about to appear. The Amir, without waiting a moment, turned his attention to the King of Egypt's house, and all his friends went with him. Word spread that the King of Egypt had gone into hiding; however much they searched, they could find no trace of him.

The Amir's companions, entering the royal garden, began to pick guavas, apricots, and mulberries from the trees and eat them. Adi, who was as voracious as a bull, ate God knows how many bushels of fruit. After a little while, Adi feared that his bowels might open; going into the royal privy, he began to obey the call of nature. For some reason the unfortunate King of Egypt had hidden himself there. He was drenched in filth from head to foot, and thought, "Even here I can't escape their attention!" Grabbing Adi's balls, he hung on to them.

When Adi felt the pain in his balls, without cleaning himself he leaped up and fled from there. The King of Egypt, hanging from him, was dragged along too. Adi, weeping and wailing, said, "This city is an extraordinary place—its climate makes men shit men!" Manzar Shah of Yemen, etc., came running, and saw that the King of Egypt had grabbed Adi's balls and was hanging from them. They laughed and laughed until they rolled on the ground.

They seized the King of Egypt and had him bathed, and took him before the Amir in a worn-out condition. The Amir said, "Oh King, what you did has been done to you! Now, are you willing to recognize the One God who has no partners? Why should you delay in reciting the confession of faith in the One God? I have no interest in your country—let your country be yours and welcome! But you must become a Muslim, otherwise it will not be well, you will come to a bad end."

The king, who in reality was a second *Yazid, began to mouthe foolish words. Agha Bulbul,[24] who was standing beside him, at once struck such a blow with his sword that the king's head fell a number of paces away from his body, and his body began to writhe like a slaughtered bird.

The Amir seated *Zuhrah of Egypt on the throne; he made Sarhang the Egyptian steward of all the departments, and bestowed on him a resplendent robe of honor. The Amir advised Muqbil, "Marry Zuhrah of Egypt, release her from the pain of waiting." Muqbil, with his hands folded, said, "Until Your Excellency marries Mihr Nigar, this slave will not marry either."

16. Abdur Rahman the Jinn, vazir of the King of Kings of the Realm of Qaf, comes to bear away the Amir.

[Hamzah returned to Ctesiphon—and found that Naushervan had prudently gone on a hunting trip. He conquered the city, and rescued Mihr Nigar from the underground chamber in which her parents had hidden her. But *Zhopin, trying to retake the city, slipped up behind Hamzah and gave him a deep head wound. Hamzah fainted, and his horse carried him away from the battlefield.]

The narrators of news, and the clerks of archives, recount: Since the vile Devs had rebelled against Shahpal son of Shahrukh, *King of Kings of the Realm of Qaf, and had snatched from him the Silver City, the City of Gold, the Pine City, the Sable City, the Crystal Palace, the Azure Wilderness, the White-Decorated Palace, the Pearl Palace, the Emerald Palace, the Ruby Palace, the Forty Pillars, the Garden of Perpetual Spring, the Garden of Joyful Effects, the Garden of Eight Heavens, the Azure Palace, the Garden of Paradise, the *tilisms made by Hazrat Solomon, and the lands of the Camel-heads, Cow-heads, Cow-feet, Carpet-ears, Half-bodies, etc., only the Garden of Iram remained, so that the King of Kings, with his family, was confined to it.

One day the King of Kings remembered something. He sent for his vazir, Abdur Rahman the Jinn, and said, "Where is that boy Hamzah, that son of Adam whose cradle you caused to be picked up from the land of the Arabs, in the World, and brought here? You used to say, 'One day it will happen that all the Devs of Mount Qaf, rebelling, will snatch away all your lands, and you will be confined to the Garden of Iram. That boy will come and kill them all; freeing the country from their hands, he will give it back to you as before.' Inquire where he is these days, and in what land he makes his home and dwells."

Abdur Rahman, throwing the divining-dice, said, "He has just been involved in a big battle, and during this fight has been wounded in the head with a poisoned sword. If you wish, he can come here right now." The King of Kings said, "What could be better?" At once sending for the Ointment of Solomon, he gave it to Abdur Rahman, and sent with him a great many of the various kinds of fruits of the Realm of Qaf, and ordered, "Now go quickly and apply this ointment to his head, so the wound will be healed. Feed him fruit so that he'll grow strong, and after his recovery, bring him back with you."

Abdur Rahman, mounting a *throne, took some hundreds of Jinns with him and set out from the Realm of Qaf. In a moment he disappeared. When he reached the glade below Mount Abul Qais, he began to look carefully around in every direction. He saw that Hamzah had a deep head-wound, and from the effects of the wound was lying unconscious on the grass. Then, lifting Hamzah onto the throne, he took him away to a cave on Mount Abul Qais. There he most gently and tenderly washed the wound, and anointed it with the Ointment of Solomon, and bandaged it. He spread baskets of fruit from Qaf around Hamzah, so that his brain would be strengthened by their scent, and his spirit would be fortified.

He had changed the bandage for the third time when the Amir opened his eyes and recovered from his faint. Abdur Rahman greeted him with, "Peace be upon you." The Amir returned the greeting and asked, "Who are you, and where are you from, and what is your name and rank? Was it you who brought me here on this throne?" Abdur Rahman said, "I am the vazir of Shahpal son of Shahrukh, King of Kings of the Realm of Qaf. My name is Abdur Rahman."

. . . The Amir asked, "How did you recognize me—what token did you see in me?" Abdur Rahman said, "By signs discerned through wisdom, and your dark mole, and the *lock of hair of Abraham." The Amir was very pleased at Abdur Rahman's good qualities, and began to praise him in a suitable manner. Abdur Rahman presented to the Amir the many hundreds of Jinns who had come with him, and said to the Amir, "I have one plea to make on my own account; I trust to your manly courage. If God Most High wills, you will regain your full strength. Then I will make my petition, and will beg only for your attention." The Amir said, "Before you have even stated your plea, I accept it heart and soul; nothing more need be said about it."

Please hear about Amar. When he went out in search of the Amir, he combed the whole Emerald Border and Mount Abul Qais, but couldn't find a trace of the Amir. [At length, wandering at hazard, he happened upon the cave where Hamzah had taken shelter.] The Amir, introducing Amar to Abdur Rahman, said, "All right, now go. Take the news of my health and well-being to Mecca, but don't tell anyone that I'm staying here." Amar set off toward Mecca.

The Sahib-qiran said to Abdur Rahman, "Now please declare your purpose, tell me what your benevolent master has said." [Abdur Rahman did so.] The Amir said, "Abdur Rahman, if I can kill that Dev, and by the might of my arm liberate the King of Kings' land and return it to him, then I'm ready to set out, I'm thoroughly delighted."

Please hear about Amar. When he left the Amir, he brought word of the Amir's safety and well-being to Khvajah Abdul Muttalib, the nobles of Mecca, the officers of the army, and Mihr Nigar, and said, "If you will not reward me to my heart's content for bringing such good news, then which day will you reward me, when will you fill the skirt of my robe with the hoped-for pearls?" Each one gave Amar as much as he could, and each one in his own way prepared to celebrate.

The next morning Amar again went to the Amir, and brought the story of his arrival and of the celebrations to the Amir's auspicious ear. The Amir said to Amar, "Brother Amar, another journey of some days lies before me yet; let us see what God has in store." Amar said, "Why is this?" The Amir repeated to Amar all that he had heard from Abdur Rahman.

Amar replied, "Oh Hamzah, are you in your senses? To travel for nothing, and to bring Mihr Nigar back with so much labor and exertion, only to leave her sitting alone in a corner! To forego a life of ease and enjoyment—what kind of notion is this? In the light of sound reason, this is a very poor deed." The Amir said, "I am now in Abdur Rahman's debt, for he came and cured my head-wound, he took great pains over my medicines, he constantly had my comfort at heart. As for the rest, you know I'm not afraid even of the fathers of Devs, Jinns, Ghouls, or magicians! The True Protector is my guardian. When have I ever given a thought to such things?"

At this point Abdur Rahman said, "Oh Sahib-qiran, it will take three days to go, and three days to come back, and one day to stay there beforehand, and one day to kill *Ifrit, and one day to celebrate the victory. Altogether, this coming and going will require the space of nine days." The Amir said, "I agree, and even if the time is doubled, and it takes eighteen days, there's no harm done. At such a time as this, to avert your eyes and refuse is to deny the claims of compassion and courage."

Amar said, "Very good, just as you wish! I'll protect Mihr Nigar for eighteen days more. On the nineteenth day, I wash my hands of it—it will be your business to deal with as you choose, and I'll go my own way." The Amir said, "I agree. Go, bring my pen-case, and let me write a letter of counsel to Mihr Nigar and the officers of the army, so that they'll all obey you until I come, and will stay happy and contented. But for the Lord's sake, please don't be too high-spirited, or lord it over the officers too much!" Amar, weeping, emerged from the cave, and set out toward Mecca.

When Amar arrived in Mecca, and Khvajah Abdul Muttalib heard that the Amir would go to the Realm of Qaf, he grew extremely agitated and said to Amar, "The Amir must somehow be persuaded to give up this intention; he must be brought here somehow!" Amar said, "My persuasion had no effect, but let Your Excellency write a letter; if your words can make an impression, perhaps he might be persuaded." Khvajah Abdul Muttalib sent for the Amir's pen-case, and wrote him a letter of counsel, and confided it to Amar. Amar went from there to the camp, and informed the officers of the army about the Amir's trip. They also began weeping and beating their breasts; a Doomsday-like tumult broke out.

When Amar told Mihr Nigar about the Amir's resolve, Mihr Nigar sank to the ground and began to weep and wail aloud; writhing on the ground, she began to bathe her face in tears. Amar said, "Princess, there's nothing to be gained by this weeping and breast-beating! Control yourself, come to your senses. Just as Khvajah Abdul Muttalib has written the Amir a letter of counsel, you write some such letter on your part too, and let's see what response it gets; his real intentions will be disclosed."

Mihr Nigar wrote the Amir a letter of lover's longing, full of counsel. And at the bottom she wrote this too: "If you will not give up the idea, then take me with you when you go! If you go off and leave me, remember that you won't find me alive—I'll spill my own blood, I'll sacrifice myself!" Amar took this letter with him also, along with Khvajah Abdul Muttalib's; quietly slipping the Amir's pen-case under his arm, he went to the Amir.

Placing the pen-case before the Amir, he brought out the letters of Khvajah Abdul Muttalib and Mihr Nigar, and told him something of the situation orally as well. First the Amir wrote a petition in his father's service. After that, he wrote a note to the officers of the army: "An absolutely necessary journey of some days lies before me. At such a time, to avert one's eyes and feign ignorance is utterly unbecoming. Whoever among you want to be my servants and companions should consider Khvajah Amar to be in my place until I return, and should in no way oppose Amar's authority."

And in answer to Mihr Nigar's letter he wrote, "I am going for eighteen days. If God Most High wills, I won't delay beyond that time, I'll come at once. The King of Kings of Qaf sent his vazir to treat my wound, and he came and restored my health. Thus it would be contrary to morality and compassion and chivalry, if I didn't help him in his difficulties, and just turned my face aside from him at such a bad time. If you want to please me, then accept another eighteen days of separation from me. Praise and trust the Lord. It's not as though men take women with them on hard expeditions, that I should take you along, and keep your tent with me during every battle and adventure! If I were going on some pleasure trip or hunt, for amusement, there would be no harm, I'd take you along with me. Until I come, do what Amar says. Consider him your well-wisher, faithful to the death. He will never be unfaithful; never think that in matters affecting your interest he could be at all tricky or treacherous."

He gave the letters to Amar: "Deliver them later to the addressees, and bring me my arms and armor; but don't let anyone know until I'm gone, don't let any mention of my going slip out." Amar left the Amir and went to the city. But he didn't give any of the letters to anyone. Taking the arms and armor, he left and went back to the Amir. The Sahib-qiran was extremely pleased with Amar. Donning his arms and armor, he began planning his departure.

17. Naushervan discovers that the Amir has gone to Qaf, and sends an army off to Mecca.

Naushervan, hearing about this situation, was thoroughly delighted: "In eighteen years, let's see who lives and who dies! Hamzah will surely perish at the hands of some Dev or other—how could he escape from the hands of such a gang? Now is the time to give the Muslims an untimely death, and take vengeance on them for all this."

With this thought he gave to Velam and Qelam—among the Sasanians there was no one mightier than they—thirty thousand horsemen, and sent them off toward Mecca, and said, "Now Hamzah has gone to Qaf. The coast is clear, you have a free hand in every way. Go and devastate Mecca, and bring back Princess Mihr Nigar; let me give my eager eyes a sight of her." The two took their leave of the king, and set out for Mecca.

Now please hear about the King of the Ayyars, Amar Ayyar, the Infidel-Slayer of the Age. When after eighteen days some more days had passed, and the Amir did not come, Amar began to weep uncontrollably and wail aloud. Then he went to Mihr Nigar; he found her distraught as well. . . . Having consoled Mihr Nigar, he went to Muqbil, and said to him, "I am going to Ctesiphon to find out about the Amir from Buzurchmihr, and I'll tell you the plan: you and your forty thousand sharp-shooting archers stay on the alert to protect Mihr Nigar, and station powerful champions at various places on the walls of the fort." Amar himself, donning his ayyari equipment, set out for Ctesiphon by way of the Benevolent Forest.

Some days later, having arrived at his destination, he disguised himself as a grain merchant, and went and stood at Buzurchmihr's door. It happened that Buzurchmihr was just returning from the court. Seeing Amar, he asked, "Who are you?" Amar said, "I am a peasant from your estate. People have very much mistreated me, and have thoroughly cheated me. So I've come as a plaintiff: if you won't give me justice, I'll go and swing the Chain of Justice and tell my wrongs to the king." When Khvajah Buzurchmihr sent for his petition through a servant and read it, he realized that this was Amar. Calling him into a private room, he embraced him, and asked about his welfare and well-being.

Amar said, "How can I tell you what kind of difficulty I'm caught in, and how distressed and anxious I am! When Hamzah left he promised to return in eighteen days, but even beyond that as many days again have passed. There's no telling what disaster may have overtaken him, and what may have befallen him! Mihr Nigar is determined to take poison."

The Khvajah said, "It's true that Hamzah, when he left, promised to return in eighteen days. But he will come and meet you at the fort of the Western Dominion in eighteen years. He will kill all the rebellious

Devs, and no sort of harm will come to him. During this time you will have to confront many challenges: kings and champions of the age will attack you from every direction, and devote themselves to causing you harm. But don't you be alarmed—no one will prevail over you, you alone will be victorious over them all. And now go in haste to Mecca, and look well to your fort, and don't fear anyone. Naushervan has sent Velam and Qelam with thirty thousand horsemen to fight you, and to bring back Mihr Nigar."

Amar said, "Well, even if I die for my friendship and loyalty to Hamzah, I will not hesitate, I am very sure of that. Whatever efforts I can make, I will make, to the point of dying in his service. As for the rest, Velam and Qelam are nothing! If even *Jamshed and King Cyrus should rise up from the grave and come and mention Mihr Nigar's name, they'd be sent right back to the grave, and wouldn't get hold of her! But for your part please write a letter of counsel to Mihr Nigar, so that she'll be comforted and will obey my instructions."

Buzurchmihr, sending for his pen-case, wrote Mihr Nigar a letter full of counsel, and told her how long it would be till the Amir came, and added many comforting reflections, and gave it to Amar Ayyar. Amar, taking this letter, set out toward Mecca by way of the Beneficent Forest; this time he traveled night and day, stage after stage, until he entered the fort and gave Buzurchmihr's letter to Mihr Nigar. She, when she read it, began to weep and sob, and said, "Alas for my destiny, since I am forced to burn in the fire of separation for eighteen more years!" Amar consoled Mihr Nigar: "Oh Queen of the Universe, you will live a long time yet, if God Most High wills. Eighteen years will pass like eighteen days, and he'll be back safe and sound."

After consoling Mihr Nigar, Amar went to the army, and drawing them up in formation, said to everyone, "I have heard from Buzurchmihr's lips that Hamzah will remain in Qaf for eighteen years. Therefore, friends, whoever wishes to leave, let him set out for his home at once, and whoever wishes to stay, let him live here in brotherly unity. When Hamzah returns safely, he will definitely be pleased with each loyal comrade and will accord him great honor and dignity." All the troops present—not to speak of the chiefs and Hamzah's close companions—said with one voice, "Oh Khvajah, we have entered Hamzah's service with our whole heart and soul! We won't abandon our loyal comradeship with him. As long as life is in our bodies, and you are in Hamzah's place, how could we leave you, how could we step outside the bounds of your authority?"

Amar, delighted, embraced them one by one and said, "You're all as dear to me as my own life! I'm your obedient servant, you are my brothers." Those who had to be stationed on the ramparts of the fort, he stationed there, and gave orders for the fullest alertness. And he himself, putting on regal robes, had an ornate carpet spread beneath a gold-embroidered canopy, and displayed his radiant presence on a jewel-encrusted chair. Positioning Muqbil the Faithful with his sharp-shooting archers, he began to wait for Velam and Qelam.

Not even two hours had passed, when before the fort a dark and gloomy cloud of dust appeared, the extent of which caused all the land to be covered with dust. When that dust-cloud came near, the wind blew the dust away, and arms and armor became visible, thirty standards came into view; and leading the vanguard, two mighty champions completely enveloped in steel armor could be seen. Amar knew that these were Velam and Qelam.

These fools, the moment they arrived, said to the army, "Come on, let's surround the fort, kill the Muslims, and bring out Mihr Nigar, so that in recompense for it we can obtain robes of honor and rewards, and fill the skirt of desire with the sought-for pearls. We will quickly return to Ctesiphon, and go and receive exalted rank from the king." At their order, the horsemen spurred their horses into a gallop, and reached the vicinity of the fort. When they came within range of the fort, Amar rained down such a shower of fire-missiles on them that those in front were burned by the fire, and those behind were unable, out of fear, to take a step forward.

. . . Velam and Qelam, holding their shields over their heads and guiding their horses with their knees, managed to reach the moat. When the army saw that their chiefs were standing on the earthworks, shame took hold of them. They all, calling out "Come what may!" urged their horses forward and came up to join their chiefs. Amar thought to himself, "It's a bad thing that the enemy have reached the moat!" At once he took out from Zanbil a fire-box full of naphtha oil, and lit it. Fitting it into his sling, he whirled it two or three times, and slung it at Velam's breast.

As the fire-box struck his breast it burst, and the naphtha-oil spread over his whole body and began burning like a raging fire. Velam tried to extinguish it with his hands, and his fingers started to burn like wicks. And when drops of oil fell on his beard, it burned like cotton-fluff. When he ran his hand over his face, his eyebrows and mustaches sizzled and burned. Qelam saw that Velam was burning and could do nothing to save himself; he was very distressed to see his condition, and went to him. When he began trying to put out the flames, his condition became the same as Velam's. . . . Throwing dust and dirt on them, with the greatest difficulty the army finally extinguished the flames. Then those two found relief. They ran off toward their encampment, and occupied themselves in treating their burns. All military activities were suspended. Amar, now free of care, sat down again comfortably under the canopy in the jewel-encrusted chair.

18. Directing the reins of the steed of the pen toward writing about the Sahib-qiran, the World-conqueror, Amir Hamzah of great magnificence, the possessor of generosity and kindness.

The narrators who cherish speech say that when the Parizads presented white wine, Shahpal with his own hands served a cup of white wine to the Sahib-qiran, and refreshed the bud of the Sahib-qiran's nature with this heart-pleasing spring breeze of delightful wine. The Sahib-qiran, having drunk that cup, kissed Shahpal's throne, and expressed much gratitude for his benevolence and affection. From the hands of the moon-faced cupbearers he drank a good deal of white wine, and his heart attained a certain state of elevation. Rose-colored lines flashed within his eyes, he felt joyful—he was perfectly intoxicated.

When he raised his eyes and looked here and there, all around in that court pavilion he saw multicolored canopies of velvet and satin which would completely daze and dazzle the beholder; they had been made with such artifice that when one beheld them the mind was stupefied. On one canopy, which was hung in the center, pictures of Hazrat Solomon and of the nobles of his court had been painted, all encrusted with jewels; whoever saw them believed with full conviction that Hazrat Solomon was seated in open court. Four thousand four hundred forty-four couches and seats of gold, silver, ivory, ebony, and sandalwood, and high steel chairs plated with gold and drowned in jewels, were arranged in that court pavilion for the champions of Qaf to sit on. And in the center of them all, a throne, extremely large and elegant—Hazrat Solomon used to sit on it, and now Shahpal sat on it—was arranged. The Sahib-qiran, seeing the atmosphere of the palace, was beside himself with delight, and felt the greatest enjoyment.

Let it be noted that Shahpal had a daughter named Asman Pari; in beauty and splendor she was most truly a Pari. She was seated on her own throne, behind Shahpal's throne. Although a jeweled screen stood before her throne and made a curtain between them, when she peeked out from behind the screen at the Sahib-qiran, and saw such a peerless young man, she was ravished with love, she adored him with her whole heart and soul, she began to feel more restless and anxious with every hour that passed.

In short, when a night and a day had passed in this gathering, Abdur Rahman said to Shahpal, "The Sahib-qiran is very much pressed for time. I've brought him with this promise: 'Three days to come and three days to go, one day to be feasted, one day to kill Ifrit, and one day for a farewell feast—altogether you'll need to spend nine days, and all these tasks will be satisfactorily concluded. If beyond this a tenth day should be needed, then I'm in the wrong, and I deserve to be punished by your anger.' "

Shahpal, addressing the Sahib-qiran, said, "Oh Sahib-qiran, what can I say! I've been harassed at the hands of these Devs, and have suffered from their evil conduct. If you will be so kind as to finish them off, I'll be indebted to you as long as I live, I'll remain your obedient servant." The Sahib-qiran said, "This is nothing! God's help is with me. God willing, if I don't cut off the head of every single high-headed one, and return your land to your control as before, then my name isn't Hamzah, and there's no point in expecting anything at all from me. Please have the war-drum sounded, and behold the wonders of God."

. . . This news reached Ifrit as well: "Shahpal has summoned a son of Adam from the Realm of the World to help him; that man has come with great pomp and grandeur and pretensions. Relying on him, Shahpal has taken his army and come out of his city to fight you, and has drawn up his battle-array in the field." Ifrit burst into roars of laughter: "How can a man challenge a Dev? All right, it's for the best: it has brought King Shahpal out of the city." With these words, he ordered the war-drum sounded, and prepared the whole army for war and combat. King Shahpal too had the war-drum sounded in his army, and thus made his martial boasts and challenges before the enemy. Twelve hundred pairs of gold and silver kettledrums began to be beaten incessantly, as though the clouds were thundering. In Ifrit's camp, instead of drums the Devs slapped their own rumps, and clashed huge stones together. In short, throughout the night tumult and commotion reigned in both camps.

When morning came, Ifrit, bringing many hundreds of thousands of Devs, came into the field. Some Devs wore tiger-skins around their bodies, others serpent-skins, others elephant-skins, and they had put iron covers over the horns on their heads. Chains and strips of steel were wound around their throats, arms, waists, and thighs, and they wore garlands of skulls around their necks. Bearing spears, maces, shields of flint, millstones, cypress-tree staves, and crocodile-back saws in their hands, they prepared for battle.

. . . When the Devs saw the Sahib-qiran, they began to behave in strange and bizarre ways. Some of them, coming into the center of the battlefield, danced around, beating their buttocks. Others, giggling and squealing, jumped up and down. Others, clutching their beards, did gymnastic exercises. Others bounded upward toward the sky, and flung themselves into the air, and came somersaulting down to earth. Others, baring their teeth, tried to frighten the Sahib-qiran. Others, taking their tails in their hands, spun round and round. Others, mounting on each other, rode around in circles. The Amir, seeing these antics of theirs, could not help laughing, and their clownish brazenness convinced him of their worthlessness and pettiness.

First of all *Ahriman, the father of Ifrit, whose height was five hundred yards, took his cypress-tree spear in hand, emerged from the ranks, and came forward in challenge. With great power and force he called out, "Where is that *Earthquake of Qaf, that *Younger Solomon, who prides himself on his bravery and courage? Let him come and encounter me, so I can make him taste the flavor of death, and give him his just deserts for his rashness in coming to Qaf and fighting with the Devs!"

The Amir, obtaining Shahpal's permission, came into the field, and did not permit any hesitation or doubt to enter his heart; he gave the battle-cry "God is great!" so forcefully that the whole field trembled. Ahriman said, "Oh Earthquake of Qaf, with such a tiny stature, do you try to frighten us with such a voice? Come on, show me the force of your blow!" The Sahib-qiran said, "It's not my custom to take precedence, or to transgress the bounds of my family tradition. First you make an attack, then I'll make an attack and show you my prowess."

Ahriman said, "If I make the first attack on a tiny weakling like you, what will the Devs say about me? They'll all be astonished, and they'll consider me contemptible! How could you possibly survive my attack, so that you could make an attack on me?" The Sahib-qiran said, "When height and stature were apportioned, you were there; when strength and power were allotted, I was there. Furthermore, you don't know that I'm the Angel of Death! I've come from the Realm of the World to seize your soul; I have brought you the cup of death."

Ahriman attacked the Sahib-qiran with his cypress-tree staff. The Sahib-qiran evaded the blow; and drawing the *Scorpion of Solomon from its scabbard, he said, "Oh you unclean one, don't say that I struck you unawares! Be warned—I'm about to attack, and I'll bathe my glistening sword in your impure blood!" Even as he finished this sentence, he struck such a blow on Ahriman's head that the corpse-eater was split in two and fell to the ground, half on this side, half on that. Shahpal gave thanks, and ordered the Parizads to sound the drum of celebration.

Ifrit groaned and said, "Oh son of Adam, you've done a terrible deed in killing a champion like my father, and separating his head from his body! But you won't manage to escape alive either—just wait and see what blows I inflict on you!" With these words, he sent a Dev who was even more powerful than Ahriman to encounter the Sahib-qiran. The Sahib-qiran dispatched him too to Hell, and sent him to join the dead.

In short, in a brief interval the Sahib-qiran laid lifeless nine powerful Devs who were renowned among Ifrit's army, as he had done to Ahriman. He made Ifrit feel stupefied and distraught. Then Ifrit, trembling, groaning, ordered the retiring drum sounded, and had his father's body lifted up. With weeping and wailing, with utter despair and terror, he set out for his own encampment.

19. Qarin Elephant-neck sets out to chastise Amar, and dies at the hands of the Veiled One.

[Naushervan sent out a huge fresh army under Qarin Elephant-neck, to augment Hurmuz's forces.]

The narrator writes that when Qarin Elephant-neck entered Hurmuz's camp, after completing the stages of the journey, he was delighted to see Hurmuz. That night all the officers of the army, from the greatest to the least, gathered to welcome him, and the wine-flask began to make the rounds, and cups were poured out for everyone. In this state of elevation, Qarin said to Hurmuz, "You've been sitting here for so many days with your army, you've planted yourself on the ground like a mountain! You haven't been able to kill one contemptible worthless little ayyar, or even to capture him—you haven't gotten at him at all, he hasn't fallen for any of your tricks! When people hear this, what will they say? When they hear about it, they'll be astonished!"

Hurmuz said, "Now you've come with a body of a hundred thousand horsemen and foot-soldiers—you've brought great warriors with you, and your own prowess too is clearer than the radiant sun itself. Who is your equal in courage? When you kill him, or capture him, then will be the time to talk like this, and pride yourself on your prowess! As yet you've just arrived. Rest for a few days, see how things are around here, then you and I will both see what happens. When you kill Amar, or capture him, then I'll commend you!"

. . . When morning came, Hurmuz, Faramarz and Zhopin, who had already tasted the experience of battle with Amar, went and arrayed their ranks well out of range of the fort, so that no disaster would befall them and their army, and Qarin would taste the fruit of his rashness. But Qarin, dividing his army into four parts, had his horsemen lead their mounts to all four sides of the fort; with great pomp and grandeur he led his army up to the fort, and brought all four gates of the fort within his reach.

Amar saw that a countless army was approaching the fort on all four sides, and was showing extreme pomp and martial spirit. He told the officers of his army, "Today the fort is under attack; the hostile army is creating a great commotion. It's a test of your dexterity and cleverness. The man who stands firm today is a real hero. Anyone who sets foot within our range must not be allowed to escape alive—he must die where he stands!"

The moment the order was given, from one side Muqbil the Faithful and his twelve thousand archers, fitting their bowstrings into the notches of their arrows, making the arch of their bows bend to their ear-lobes, released the birds of their arrows. Every arrowhead pierced the breasts of four or five infidels. In one attack some thousands of men began writhing like slaughtered birds: the birds of their spirits, slaughtered, began convulsively fluttering. Those cowards whose breasts had not been the nest of any bird screamed and turned backwards like defective bows, and shunned the very thought of battle.

And from the second side, when the stone-slingers, placing carved and chased elephant-killing stones in the pockets of their slings, whirled them three times and hurled them at the infidels' foreheads, they sent rank upon rank of the infidels forcibly to Hell. Some thousands of fire-worshipers bowed their heads as if in prostration, outcasts from both true religion and the world. The rest turned tail and fled, heedless of everything; they fell to the ground in panic.

From the third side the musketeers kept up such a fire that in one round the lightning of death fell on eighty thousand men, the knife of death was passed over all their necks. The survivors, roaring like thunder, fled back the way they had come.

From the fourth side, when a fire-fight started with its fire-bottles and naphtha-vessels, then such a rain of fire poured down that along with each fire-devoured victim, three or four rescuers and helpers too became morsels for the mouth of Hell-fire, and in one moment set out for the realm of Eternity. As they ran hot-footed away, at a blistering pace, their hearts were seared by the loss of their comrades.

Although Qarin's army was in such a state, and his whole army was laid waste like this, Qarin Elephant-neck, protecting his face with his shield, advanced like a maddened elephant to the gate of the fort, and in his passion and fury never thought of the risk to his life. He prepared to break down the gate with his mace. When Amar saw this situation, he grew very anxious and extremely fearful.

. . . The army of Islam had lifted their hands in prayer, when before them a dark black cloud of dust appeared, the extent of which covered the whole earth with dust. The shears of the wind had not yet torn open the collar of the dust when Amar joyously said to the Muslims, "Congratulations, friends! The Granter of Prayers has heard you, your prayer has had effect. Look, help from the Unseen has come! Now you're all saved from the hands of this infidel." Leaning down, he said to Qarin Elephant-neck, "Oh you dead-drunk one, take heed—prepare to die! Someone has come with an elephant-goad to send you to Hell!" When Qarin turned to look, in truth he saw forty banners emerging from the curtain of dust, and this astonishing sight almost stupefied him.

And a *Veiled One Dressed in Orange, spurring his horse, flashed ahead like lightning until he reached the ditch, so that his awesomeness spread fear in every heart. . . . Qarin struck at him with his heavy mace. The Veiled One evaded the blow, and pulling his lightning-forged sword from his belt, he struck with it at Qarin's head, so that darkness spread over Qarin's eyes. Although Qarin protected his head with his steel shield, that sword, traveling like lightning, didn't let him take a breath. Cutting through his steel shield as though it were a ball of soft cheese, cutting through his helmet and head, descending with marvelous sharpness through the vessel of his neck, the sword did not pause even at his breast, but, slicing through his backbone, came down through his horse's back and out beneath the saddle-girth. Cutting every part of him into two halves, it emerged with remarkable grace and force, like lightning. Qarin, with his horse, fell lifeless in four fragments to the ground; in one moment he was obliterated.

The army, seeing what had happened to their general, fell on the Veiled One from all four sides. The Veiled One's army too grasped their swords, they drew their tempered swords from their scabbards. Amar saw that the Veiled One's army was very small, forty thousand horsemen in all. Although every one was brave, the difference between the lesser and the greater was incalculable—that is, on the other side were one hundred seventy-five thousand horsemen and foot-soldiers, the other army was that much bigger. Instantly emerging from the fort with his army, Amar joined forces with the Veiled One for the battle, and prepared to slay Qarin's army. That day such a battle took place that seventy thousand horsemen of Qarin's army were finished off, and on this side no one was even lightly wounded. The infidel army fled at full speed; there was turmoil in their whole army.

Amar said to the Veiled One, "Please tell me your name and rank, and inform me all about yourself, so that when Hamzah comes back from Qaf, he can be told of your generosity and chivalry. In truth, it would have been no time at all until the fort was looted and we were killed! But you graciously arrived and saved our lives, as though you had given us life afresh." The Veiled One replied, "When the Sahibqiran comes, then he will himself become aware of my name and rank. There's no need for me to tell it now; I don't wish to show myself off. Attend to your fort in peace, don't let any anxiety trouble your heart. When it is necessary, if God Most High wills, I'll arrive at once and help you again."

With these words, the Veiled One returned in the direction from which he had come. Amar, taking with him all the tents, pavilions, cash, and property of the defeated army, entered the fort. Through God's blessing, he became entirely tranquil and carefree.

20. [Amar pretends that he will give Mihr Nigar to Zhopin in marriage, and thus acquires from him fresh provisions for the fort.]

The whole army together went with Adi to Amar, and informed him that the food was finished, and told him that the inhabitants of the fort were worried. . . . Amar dived into the ocean of thought. After a moment such a satisfactory piece of ayyari occurred to him that he happily lifted his head; the scheme that had entered his heart caused him to rejoice greatly. So, putting his troops on the alert, he left the fort and went into a mountain valley. Placing his hand on Zanbil, he requested a miracle. From it he received this strange phenomenon: he immediately became forty yards in stature, and a lustrous white beard a foot long appeared around his face—this kind of extraordinary appearance became manifest. Walking along on high wooden sandals, with a tiger-skin sack tucked under his arm, he began looking around like a stranger at Hurmuz's camp and fort, and mumbling extraordinary things.

By chance, Katarah of Kabul the ayyar, who was Zhopin's nephew, came by that way. Seeing Amar's appearance and stature, he was petrified with astonishment—he turned pale with extreme fear and awe, for he had never seen a man of such an appearance. . . . Amar said, "Sad of the *Dark Regions is my name, and I have an important task to perform. I'm the younger brother of Alexander of the Dark Regions, King of the Dark Regions. A man named Hamzah had gone to the aid of Shahpal, King of Kings of the Realm of Qaf. This man showed great hardihood, but when he confronted a Dev named Ifrit—well, one was a Dev and the other a son of Adam! With just one blow his bones were shattered. Shahpal, putting his bones in a leather bag, sent them to my brother, saying 'Your border is nearer the border of the sons of Adam—you can easily accomplish this task. Send this bag through somebody to Naushervan, so he can have these bones buried in a cemetery of the sons of Adam.' "

[Katarah brought the visitor to Zhopin.] Zhopin, showing him great hospitality, said, "Where is that bag? Please give it to me, and accept a receipt for it from me. I'll send the bag very securely to the king, and write all the circumstances in detail and submit them in the king's service." Amar took a serpent-skin bag from his sack, confided it to Zhopin, and thus passed on the burden of his trust to him. Amar said, "You've taken a great load off my mind! I'm very grateful, and I've been extremely pleased to meet you. Well, may the Lord protect you; now I'll take my leave."

. . . Please hear about Zhopin. Taking that bag, he showed it to Hurmuz and Faramarz, told them all about Sad of Zulmat's visit and his strange aspect, and informed them of his appearance and the whole situation. Hurmuz and Faramarz, hearing of Hamzah's fate, were so overjoyed that they could hardly contain themselves. But *Bakhtyarak laughed and replied, "I see Amar's ayyari in this; this trickery strikes me as just in his style!. . . . Whatever kind of appearance he wants, he can assume."

Zhopin said, "On this bag are the seals of four hundred kings of Qaf—why should we consider them unreliable, and accept your foolish opinion without proof?" Bakhtyarak answered, "It's up to you, but I don't believe that his information is accurate or his words trustworthy." Zhopin said, "In any case we should keep silent, and say nothing about this matter. I'll send for news of the fort, and verify how things are there."

. . . Please hear about Amar. From that same day he had stopped the sounding of the drum, and had maintained a kind of silence in the fort. Zhopin's ayyars prowled around the fort for three days, and found absolutely none of the former hustle and bustle, they didn't see the people of the fort showing good cheer. On the fourth day . . . at midnight he told his whole army, "All of you call out the Amir's name, weep and lament loudly, express grief." Cries of "Alas, Sahib-qiran!" and "Oh woe, Sahib-qiran!" were raised. Hurmuz and Faramarz and Zhopin and Bakhtyarak had their ears open. When they heard this they all were filled with joy. When they heard the fort-dwellers' wailing and lamentation, they were so happy they couldn't contain themselves. They had the drum of celebration sounded, and from the least to the greatest, all were convinced of the Amir's death.

The next day Amar tore open his collar, rubbed dust on his face, and came barefooted and bareheaded, beating his breast and head, out of the fort. Going in that condition to Zhopin's tent, he . . . said, with a hundred sobs and laments, "What can I say—I've lost my master, the source of all joy and pleasure is gone! . . . After returning Mihr Nigar to Your Excellency, I'll go to the mountains and bash my head against the rocks and die, and free myself from this distasteful life. Where could I find another judge of my merits like Hamzah, whom I could serve, and to whom I could feel heartfelt gratitude night and day for his understanding of my worth?"

Zhopin pressed Amar's head to his breast, and said with the greatest affection, "Oh Amar, where is your good sense, and why are you so grieved? I'll cherish you as the amulet around my neck—I'll never neglect to show esteem for you!" Amar replied, "I expected no less from you, for you're of the royal family, and you're the most peerless scion of the noble families on the face of the earth. But I'm afraid of the maliciousness of Bakhtak and Bakhtyarak; I'm fearful of their interference. I'm worried that they might misguide you, and make you angry at me—they might turn you toward hostility, and engage in their tricks."

Zhopin replied, "Who are they to dare to look askance at you, or inflict any sort of humiliation on you, or come between you and me, or show enmity toward you? If by chance they ever speak harshly to you, I'll cut them down to size that very moment, I'll crush them and their helpers underfoot! You go and bring Mihr Nigar." Amar said, "I'd bring Mihr Nigar at once, but I'm worried, for how will the officers of the army allow me to? They will say, 'At your instigation, we've committed much rudeness against the princes, and given them much trouble. You'll give Mihr Nigar back and be fine—we'll be condemned, and everyone will call us fools!' "

Zhopin said, "I will maintain them all with more respect and honor than Hamzah did, and give each one a rank according to his worth. You go and persuade them and bring them to me, explain all this and reassure them." [After Amar left, Bakhtyarak expressed grave misgivings.] Zhopin, with a mighty frown, replied, "Oh Bakhtyarak, don't meddle in this business, it's between me and Amar. Why should anyone believe a dolt like you? Amar said beforehand, 'Bakhtyarak will poison the trust between you and me, and move in to ruin this business.' " Bakhtyarak replied, "Why wouldn't he say that? He and I are the same at heart! Well, that's fine, I won't say a word. From now on I absolutely won't open my mouth about this matter, it's between you and Amar. What can anyone say to someone who won't listen? When I see something suspicious, I'll just go on my way!"

[Zhopin prepared a feast for Amar and his officers.] The moment the order was given, the tray-bearer spread the dining cloth, and placed delicate and elegant dishes before them, and the server began to bear the dishes around and serve them. Adi said to the server, with each dish, "Set it here!" . . . Zhopin ordered another round of dishes, and had them all set before Adi. Adi consumed them all too, and didn't even drink any water. Zhopin then asked, "Are you satisfied, or should something more be brought, so you can eat your fill and not leave my house hungry?" Adi said, "If some bread and curried meat appeared, I wouldn't mind. Please order some, and feed them to your servant." Immediately Zhopin ordered bread made from many maunds of flour, and curry. Adi graciously dined on that also.

Zhopin wanted to order even more, and let everyone enjoy the spectacle of Adi's eating. But Bakhtyarak said to him, "Oh Zhopin, do you think you can ever fill up this champion's stomach? You'll never be able to satisfy him! Amar devised this scheme just so that you'd feed him the food of the whole camp, and you wouldn't even be left with enough for one meal. When they don't get fed, the soldiers will be oppressed by hunger, and will go their own ways."

Hurmuz gave him a meaningful look, and said to Adi, "Oh champion, the pots full of food are on the fire, every chef is cooking. While that food is being prepared, whatever food you wish will be brought from the bazaar, so you won't suffer from hunger." Adi replied, "Your Excellency, I'm not such a glutton that I'd give you the trouble of ordering food from the bazaar." With these words he washed his hands, went to his bed and fell comfortably asleep.

Then, having the dining cloth spread a second time, Zhopin had dinner served to all the officers, and ordered more food for them all. When they had all finished eating, cups of rose-red wine began to circulate. The party changed its nature: singers and dancers presented themselves, musicians tuned their instruments for melodies, cries of "Drink up!" and "Cheers!" were raised by the guests. All those present were in a joyous mood—they began talking together with warm friendship, glasses of wine began washing away the malice from their hearts.

In the midst of this Zhopin said to Amar, "Why do you hesitate to bring Mihr Nigar? Your delay in this matter is now improper." Amar replied, "The officers of Islam say, 'It doesn't look nice to hand the princess over like this, it does you no kind of credit.' Please make preparations in your camp for your wedding to her, and set the marriage ceremonies going; invite the army as well to a feast in the fort. Let the marriage be celebrated fittingly, so that everyone can enjoy the merry-making." Zhopin said, "What could be better? This idea of yours is quite suitable." Amar said, "Then some money must be spent on this.

In such a festival money has a part—how could things ever come to fruition without money?'' Zhopin replied, ''That's no problem. Whatever you need is available and at your service; please arrange this function as suits you best.''

. . . Zhopin had his body rubbed with cosmetic paste for seven days, and ate refined foods to improve the condition and coloring of his body. He was absorbed in dance and celebration, and had the whole army as his guests, and delighted himself with the hope of union with Mihr Nigar. When seven days passed, and Amar didn't come even once to see him, Zhopin grew anxious and fearful.

Bakhtyarak asked Zhopin, ''Please tell me, a week has already passed, when will you set out with the marriage procession, and when will you enjoy the nuptial pleasures?'' Zhopin, ashamed and angry, insulted Bakhtyarak freely, and gave him many curses. And he sent ayyars to Amar to say, ''Seven days have already passed, now why do you delay the marriage? Here every kind of preparation has been made, and luxurious adornments of all kinds have been collected.'' The ayyars went, and saw that the fort was four times as well-prepared as before, and every officer was alert at his proper post.

Amar, as usual, seated in a jewel-adorned chair under a pavilion outside the main gate of the fort, was discharging his functions, and delegating tasks to his subordinates. The ayyars, saluting Amar respectfully from afar, gave him Zhopin's message. Whatever words Zhopin had charged them to say, they said them all. Amar sent this message: ''Now for some months I make light of you and Hurmuz and Faramarz, and I don't feel threatened by your army and troops!'' . . . The bird of Zhopin's senses flew away, his complexion paled; learning of this state of affairs made him very distraught. He began biting his lips and feeling agitated: ''This ayyar has outwitted me badly, he has deceived me badly. He has disgraced me from here to Ctesiphon!'' But what else could he do except keep quiet? For to requite the wrong, and to punish him, was most difficult.

21. Ifrit Dev takes refuge in the tilism of the City of Gold, at the advice of his mother, Malunah Jadu.

Now before I return to that dastan, I will tell a bit more of the dastan of the Earthquake of Qaf, the Younger Solomon, the Sahib-qiran, the *World-conqueror, the Father of Greatness, Amir Hamzah. It has already been mentioned that when Ifrit's father, Ahriman, had been killed by the Sahib-qiran, and had died most contemptibly, Ifrit sat mourning for him, absorbed in weeping and lamentation, with a river of tears constantly flowing from his eyes. Shahpal arranged a week of celebrations in the Amir's honor, and adorned the festival hall so lavishly that whoever saw it was enraptured and utterly carried away.

[Hamzah urged the king to renew the battle.] On the eighth day Shahpal ordered the war-drums to be sounded, and made all the preparations for war. The moment the order was given, the drum-beaters took out twelve hundred pairs of gold drums, and twelve hundred pairs of silver drums. The bass drums were warmed, and the trebles were moistened. The drum-beaters began to wield the drumsticks, they began to make the mountains and the earth tremble with the sound of their drums. Since this was the Drum-set of Solomon, its sound could be heard for three days' journey, and no other instrument could possibly equal its sound.

Ifrit was in fact very near. When he heard the sound of the war-drums, and heard such a tumultuous clamor, he pricked up his ears, and grew quite upset. His companions too were terrified. He said to those around him, "I haven't yet finished mourning for my father, my heart hasn't yet found comfort or respite from this heavy grief—and he's had the war-drum sounded and taken the field! This human is surely destined to kill me; undoubtedly I will come to grief through him." After saying this, he wept a great deal, till his face was bathed in tears.

He sent a swift-flying Dev to call his mother. That cursed one, whose name was *Malunah Jadu, was an incomparable magician; to her the spells of *Samiri were child's play. The moment she heard, she came like a whirlwind, as though some disaster had been sent down from the sky. Ifrit threw himself on her neck and began to weep with great sobs;

his teardrops fell one after the other like pearls on a necklace. He told her all about the Sahib-qiran, and revealed the whole secret.

She said, "In truth this human who has come to Shahpal's aid is your mortal enemy, and the enemy of the whole family of high-headed Devs. The best thing will be for you to go and stay in the City of Gold, a tilism I have made. When this human has gone back to the Realm of the World, then we'll have it out with Shahpal, and punish him for his intransigence." Ifrit was very pleased with his mother's advice, and took it to heart. Instantly he set out with Malunah for the tilism of the City of Gold, and told no one about his plan. His whole army was destroyed; Ifrit's pomp and splendor were ruined.

[Hearing this good news, the king ordered another celebration.] After the celebration was over, the Amir said to King Shahpal, "Now please allow me to depart, in your graciousness please permit me to go! My affairs are suffering a great deal—I'm very anxious at being unable to find out how my companions are." King Shahpal said, "Oh Sahib-qiran, it was agreed between us that you would kill Ifrit and then go, and would complete this task before you were given leave to go. But Ifrit has not yet been killed. If you go without having killed Ifrit, and don't send him to Hell with your sword of Islam, after you go he'll lift his head high again, and I'll be compelled to impose on you again, and to call you back from there. It's better for you to first kill Ifrit, then go to the Realm of the World, so that we'll all be comforted by the sight of his corpse; afterwards I'll send you back very quickly, and gladly give you permission to go." The Amir lowered his head, and after a time gave Shahpal this answer: "No matter—I agree to your request."

. . . The king, seating the Amir on a throne, said to four swift-flying Parizads, "Take the Sahib-qiran to the City of Gold, convey him there in great comfort." The Parizads at once took up the throne and flew off. After three days and nights, they descended on a mountain which was green in color and was called the Poison-stone Mountain; strange kinds of people lived there. . . . The Sahib-qiran camped on that mountain, and rested there all night. In the morning, after offering his prayers, he beseeched God to send him victory. . . . He tightened his coat of mail, took the Scorpion of Solomon in his hand, rolled up his sleeves, and went down from the mountain. It was so dark that he couldn't take a step forward, he couldn't even advance one foot in that direction. Again he climbed the mountain. When he looked from there he saw plenty of light. He thought, "Why is this? When I go down, the light disappears!" Again he went down, and found the same darkness; he couldn't even see his own hand. The Amir was astonished. He again climbed the mountain and looked.

Five or six times he climbed up and went down the mountain, trying to unravel this knotty problem. The Parizads thought that the Sahib-qiran was exercising. They asked the Amir, "Oh Sahib-qiran, surely people in the Realm of the World don't exercise like this?" The Amir said, "I'm not exercising! When I go down the mountain, I find such darkness that the longest night of winter would be bright daylight by comparison! There's no way I can find words to describe it. And when I climb the mountain, again the light can be seen. I'm very much astonished and bewildered. What's happening here? What a strange work of the Lord this is!"

The Parizads told him, "Malunah Jadu, Ifrit's mother, who has spread a tilism from here to her fortress, is behind this wonder which has astonished you." The Amir, hearing this, said, "Well, in any case, come what may, now I'll go into that darkness, and go forward trusting in God." With these words, he went down the mountain.

The Amir had only advanced a little way when a voice came from the sky, "Oh Sahib-qiran, don't go any further, don't by any means take even a step—wait until I come, have this much patience!" The Amir stopped, and saw that it was the virtuous *Salasil Parizad. Salasil Parizad saluted the Amir, gave him an emerald tablet with the Names of God written on it, and said, "Abdur Rahman sends you this tablet and says, 'Do nothing without looking at this tablet. Otherwise you'll come to great harm and endure much hardship.' " Salasil Parizad, having given him the tablet, took his leave, and went back to where he had came from.

When the Amir looked at the tablet, after "In the name of God" he found this written: "Oh breaker of the tilism, God the Most Honorable and Glorious showed you much grace when this tablet came into your hands: you won the key to triumph and victory. Read the Name written on its margin, then blow toward the sky, and this darkness will be removed; all the blackness will be hidden, and the road will be full of light." The Sahib-qiran read that Name and blew toward the sky; the darkness completely disappeared. The Amir humbly thanked God and, taking the tablet with him, set out ahead.

When he reached the vicinity of the fort, he saw that a serpent was sitting with its lower jaw on the earth and its upper jaw on the door-lintel, as though it had swallowed the gate of the fort. The Amir, astonished, was regarding it, when suddenly the serpent called out, "Oh breaker of the tilism, enter my mouth, don't feel the least fear or doubt!" The Sahib-qiran looked at the tablet. On it was written, "Breathe this Name over yourself without fear, and leap into its mouth. Do not be at all afraid of this serpent—it is only a trick to frighten you, it is not a real serpent or a malevolent power." The Sahib-qiran had no sooner leaped into its mouth than a loud clamor was heard; utter turmoil and confusion broke out, as if Doomsday had come.

After a time, the Amir opened his eyes. Neither serpent nor fort was to be seen, but a garden in full bloom, the envy of the gardens of Paradise. In it the flowers of all the seasons bloomed at once, the flowering trees were ranged around with perfect elegance and grace; out-of-season fruit hung from the trees, every tree was loaded with fruit. Birds made of jewels sat singing on the trees, creating a marvelous air with their sweet voices. The Amir sat down beside a water-channel and began to look around.

Suddenly from the garden's pavilion a sad voice made itself heard, though there was no face to be seen: "Alas, there's no servant of the Lord here who will free me from the bonds of misery, and find his fair reward before the Lord's throne!" The Amir, hearing this voice, entered the pavilion, and saw a charming girl, very young and most beautiful, sitting bound to a couch. On her wrists and ankles were iron chains instead of jewelry, and in this harsh bondage she was utterly sad and downcast.

The Amir took pity on her condition; seeing her sweet face, he felt very sorry. With the greatest compassion he asked her, "Oh fair one, who are you, and who has imprisoned you here?" She replied, "First please inform me of your name and origin, and tell me about yourself —who you are and where you come from and how you have entered this tilism." The Amir said, "I am the Earthquake of Qaf, the Younger Solomon, the World-conqueror, the Sahib-qiran, the destroyer of the treacherous Ifrit; a servant of God, a member of the community of the chosen Prophet, a worshiper of truth, a follower of the right path." She said, "I am Sosan Pari, daughter of Salim Kohi; how can I tell you of my wretched condition? Ifrit fell in love with me, and asked my father for me in marriage. When he refused, Ifrit brought his army and attacked. . . ."

The Sahib-qiran granted her release from captivity; it was as though he had bestowed on her a new life. She took the Sahib-qiran with her into another garden, and showed him Ifrit's house, and told him all about where he was to be found. The Sahib-qiran saw that there were twelve hundred Devs with weapons at the ready, alert to protect him. Suddenly Sosan Pari threw herself to the ground before the Amir, recited a Name, and rose up into the sky. She ignored such great kindness on the Amir's part, and showed herself unfaithful. When she had flown very high, she called out loudly to those Devs, "Oh Devs, don't just sit there! The destroyer of Ifrit and the ruiner of tilisms stands before you—kill him however you can!"

The Sahib-qiran very much regretted having released her, he was anxious and stupefied at her faithlessness. The Devs surrounded the Amir from all sides and prepared to attack, they drew their weapons to kill him. The Amir, drawing the Scorpion of Solomon from its scabbard, cut every Dev who attacked in two, and sent him to Hell. But all the drops of blood that fell from their bodies turned into Devs! The Amir's arm and hand grew weak from striking and striking; from dealing so many blows his strength was completely exhausted.

Then he remembered the tablet, and fixed his eyes on its words. When he looked, he saw written, "Oh breaker of the tilism, do not release Sosan the Magician from captivity, do not fall into her trap! She is a great deceiver, she will trick and betray you. And if it happens that you make a mistake and she escapes, then when she flies up as high as the stars, and the Devs begin to attack you, breathe this Name over the tip of an arrow and shoot it at her, so that she will disappear and be seen no more." The Amir acted on the tablet's order. Instantly a tumult and confusion broke out: "Beware, let him not escape! The destroyer of Ifrit has entered the tilism, let him be struck down quickly!" After this tumult and confusion, when the Amir looked around, there was no Sosan Pari and no Devs, no noise and no turmoil.

. . . He saw a grand mansion, most elegantly adorned. Its courtyard seemed to be full of water; this surprised the Amir. Then he saw that an opened chest sat in the midst of the courtyard. The Amir extended a foot, to see how deep the water was. That step showed him that it was not water, but a floor of amazingly pure crystal clearer and brighter than water. The Amir said to himself, "I ought to look at this box and see what's in it; it must surely contain some marvels of magic and tilism!" The moment he bent down to look at the box, a Dev who had been lying on his back inside it wrapped both arms around the Amir's neck and clung to him; he clasped him with great force.

The Amir grasped the edge of the chest with one hand and, collecting his strength, used the other hand to bring the tablet before his eyes. He saw written on it, "Traveler in the tilism, beware, beware—do not go near that box, save yourself from such a calamity! If you do go near it, you will never escape from this tilism as long as you live, you will die and stay inside it! On that Dev's breast is a single hair like a stinking piece of rope. It is not a rope, but a snare. A tablet is tied to it. Pull out the tablet and the hair together from his breast, to save yourself from that Dev's attack and to achieve your purpose. Then breathe the Great Name of God over the first tablet and hit him on the head with it. You will see the wonderful power of the Lord, and by the Lord's grace and favor will be freed of all disasters."

The Amir pulled the tablet, together with the hair, out of the Dev's breast, and gave thanks to the Lord when the hair broke. Then he read the Great Name of God over the first tablet, and hit the Dev over the head with it. At once the Dev went off to Hell. At the touch of the tablet a whirling flame came out of his head; the chest began to burn fiercely, a blazing fire arose from it. Voices called out, "Seize him, kill him!" with a tumult and commotion that rose to the skies and reached as far as the mountains: "Be careful, don't let the destroyer of Zarraq the Magician escape! Let him be killed quickly in any way possible!"

When the tumult and commotion ceased, the Amir saw neither crystal floor nor Dev nor palace—only a desolate plain. In the plain was a pool brimful of blood, and in the middle of the pool stood a wheel. The blood flowed through the wheel and into a well. But he could not get a clear impression of what kind of marvel it was, or what sort of magic. The Amir, seeing it, was astonished, and went on.

. . . He saw that there were poppies blossoming for miles around; wherever he looked were fields of roses and sweet basil in full flower. And marigolds were blooming, in large beds so elegantly designed and beautifully decorated as to be beyond description; the tongue is incapable of sufficiently praising them. In the gardens some Parizads with well-tuned instruments were singing and playing, enjoying each other's company in thousands of ways.

When the Amir approached the garden-house and the Parizads saw him, one Parizad girl came running with a cup of wine: "Oh Sahib-qiran, you are thoroughly tired out. Here, drink this, it will take away your weariness and enliven your spirits. Then sit and listen for a few hours to our singing and playing—it will comfort your heart, and remove all the fatigue of the journey, and put you entirely at your ease."

The Amir, having looked at the tablet, took the cup of wine from her hand, recited the Great Name over it, and poured it over her head. He did exactly what the tablet said to do. At once a tongue of flame emerged from her body, and in barely an instant she burned to death; her whole body and all her bones melted in a moment like wax. A tumult and confusion arose: "The breaker of the tilism has killed Asrar the Magician too, and scattered all her companions!"

22. Dastan about the situation of the Sahib-qiran of the Age, the Earthquake of Qaf, the Younger Solomon, Amir Hamzah the glorious.

After a time when the Amir looked around, at the edge of a river he saw a mountain of unimaginable height—the Pillarless Mountain would be a small hillock beside it. From a cave in the mountain came the sound of a drum. The Amir entered the cave. He saw that Ifrit lay in deep sleep, and his snoring resounded far and wide like the sound of a drum, frightening everyone nearby into a state of panic. The Sahib-qiran said to himself, "It's quite unmanly to kill a sleeping foe, it's very heartless."

Drawing the dagger of Rustam from his belt, he thrust it so forcefully into Ifrit's foot that it penetrated to the hilt. Ifrit shook his foot and said, "The mosquitoes are pestering me—where can such an army of mosquitoes have come from? They don't let me sleep in peace, they won't stop biting for a moment!" The Sahib-qiran said to himself, "My God! If this wretch takes a blow like that for a mosquito, then what effect can further blows have on him? How can the miserable creature be affected by them?"

The Amir seized both Ifrit's arms, pressed them hard, and gave the cry "God is great!" so forcefully that it caused the whole mountain and desert to quake. Ifrit woke up, startled. Reeling from the grandeur of that cry, in the daze of sleep he thought that the earth had burst apart, or that the sky had fallen to the ground. When he rubbed his eyes and looked, he saw the face of the Earthquake of Qaf.

Then panic overcame him. Trembling like a willow, he said, "Oh son of Adam, I know and realize very clearly that you are my Angel of Death, you will take away my life. I came and hid here so that perhaps concealed in this corner I could escape from you and live in peace. But you've come even to this place, and you have me in your power. Now come what may, I may live or die, but I won't leave you alive, I won't turn aside from confronting you!"

With these words he struck at the Amir with a cypress-tree staff in which several millstones were embedded; he showed the Amir his demonic strength. The Amir blocked the blow with the Scorpion of Solomon and cut the staff in two. Then the Amir didn't even stop to breathe, but struck a blow at Ifrit's waist and brought him down. Ifrit had been cut in half, but one sinew still held, so that his life was still trapped in his body. Ifrit said, "Now, son of Adam, you've killed me. Strike one more blow, sever the remaining sinew—release my spirit from the pain and torment it feels in this body!"

IFRIT, KING OF THE DEVS, IS KILLED BY THE HAND OF THE SAHIB-QIRAN, AND WHEN THE LAST SINEW IS SEVERED, HUNDREDS OF IFRITS APPEAR AND ATTACK THE SAHIB-QIRAN.

The Sahib-qiran struck one more blow and did as he had asked. Even as the sinew was cut, both halves of the body flew up into the sky, turned into two Ifrits, and swooped down to confront the Sahib-qiran. In short, in the course of the afternoon thousands of Ifrits were born, all kinds of Devs as large as mountains appeared. The Sahib-qiran was very much worried, he was stunned by all this: "Oh God, every one that I kill turns into two and confronts me, and shows his power and strength!"

As he was thinking this, from the right a voice said, "Peace be upon you"; the Amir had received help from God. When the Sahib-qiran turned and looked, he discovered that it was Hazrat Khizr, peace be upon him, it was that Prophet of fortunate destiny. The Sahib-qiran, returning the greeting, laid his complaint before Khizr. Falling at his feet, he said, "Oh Hazrat, both my arms are weak from striking and striking, but it's a strange thing, I'm at a loss and very much worried—every one that I kill becomes two and returns to confront me, not even one of them dies of his wounds and goes to Hell!"

Hazrat Khizr said, "Oh Sahib-qiran, you have brought this grievous task on yourself, and have done everything most carelessly. Otherwise this would not have happened, you would not have wasted your time for nothing! You know that this is a tilism. But you don't look at the tablet, you just do whatever you feel like doing! You don't worry at all about magic devices and tilisms! Now do one thing: take this Name which I will tell you, and the use of which I will teach you, breathe it over the tip of an arrow, and shoot the arrow at that one among the Devs who has a single cornelian gleaming on his forehead, and whose face glows like a ruby. Then this calamity will be warded off, your life will be saved from the magic wiles of these Devs."

The Sahib-qiran acted as Hazrat Khizr advised: he used that auspicious Name and an arrow. When he looked, there were no Devs at all, only Ifrit lying cut in two. The whole field was empty, neither Dev nor monster was to be seen. But Ifrit's head was not on his body. When the Sahib-qiran saw only the body, and no sign of the head, Hazrat Khizr said, "Oh Sahib-qiran, do you understand how all those Devs were created, or not?" The Sahib-qiran said, "God knows, or you! You're the Prophet, you're the one who guides all wanderers who have lost their way."

Hazrat Khizr said, "Ifrit's mother, bearing Ifrit's head, is sitting in this very cave. That treacherous woman worked magic: soaking a leaf of coriander in his blood, she breathed a spell over it and threw it into the sky. In this way one Ifrit turned into two, and came to confront you, and showed you this trick through the power of her magic. Now enter the cave and kill her, slash off her impure head from her body and conquer the tilism." The Sahib-qiran, with Hazrat Khizr, entered the cave; both of them went into it together.

When Malunah Jadu saw Hazrat Khizr with the Sahib-qiran she grew furious; she opened her mouth and spoke: "Oh old man, I know that all this is your mischief, you're seeking to ruin and destroy us! It was you alone who had my son killed at the hands of this son of Adam; you satisfied your malice. Come what may, I won't leave you alive either, I won't forget to take my revenge!" With these words, she began to work magic. Hazrat Khizr recited the Great Name and blew it

KHVAJAH KHIZR, PEACE BE UPON HIM, COMES TO THE SAHIB-QIRAN, AND THROUGH HIS COUNSEL THE TILISM IS BROKEN, AND THE MOTHER OF IFRIT, KING OF THE DEVS, IS KILLED THROUGH HIS INVOCATIONS.

at that cursed one's head. In an instant she reached Hell and joined the other dead. The effects of the tilism were removed.

. . . The Amir said, "Hazrat, I am hungry; please feed me something and show your miraculous power." Hazrat Khizr bestowed on the Amir a bread-bun, he pulled it out of his leather bag and gave it to him. The Amir ate from that bread-bun until his stomach was full, he found peace from the pangs of hunger. But the bread-bun remained just as it was—it didn't diminish even a little bit. Hazrat Khizr also bestowed on him a water-flask full of water; to satisfy his needs he gave him this also.

And he said, "Keep both these things with you, so that as long as you are on Qaf you will not suffer from hunger or thirst, you will not be dependent on anyone for food and drink. And when this bread-bun and water-flask disappear from your possession, and you no longer see them with you, then know that you will soon depart for the Realm of the World, after a long time your own house will be brightened by your footsteps." With these words, Hazrat Khizr took his leave. The Amir, who had eaten his fill from the bread-bun for the first time in some days, felt lethargic. The moment he lay down on that mountain-face—the same one where Ifrit used to sleep—he went to sleep, he lost himself in restful dreams.

. . . When Asman Pari heard the good news of victory, she couldn't control herself, but flew off most rapidly on the wings of her longing to see the Sahib-qiran. She flew off in that direction like a swift wind, and arrived there before all the rest; she found the exact place where the Amir was. She saw that the Sahib-qiran lay asleep by a cave, and the sun was falling on his head—the heat of the sun had darkened the color of his face. Asman Pari shaded the Amir's face with one wing, she sheltered him from the heat and discomfort of the sun, and with her other wing she began to fan him, and adoringly made the *gesture of warding off evil from him onto herself. The Amir felt the comfort; he opened his eyes and looked at her. He saw that Asman Pari was shading him with one wing, and fanning him with her other wing.

He rose and embraced her and showed her much affection, and kissed her cheek which was as radiant as the moon. Seeing her tenderness and love, he felt very much moved; her love and sincerity made him wholeheartedly enamored, and he said, "Oh dearest in the world, oh heart and soul of the Sahib-qiran, why have you come here at such a time? It's quite remarkable that you've come!" Asman Pari replied, "I came when I heard the news of your victory, and I've also brought you a piece of good news: the king too is coming, he is so delighted at your victory and the death of his enemies that he can hardly contain himself.''

The Amir was very happy, and made that charming woman sit down beside him, and treated her most affectionately; he had begun to embrace and caress her, and to declare his passion for her—when King Shahpal's party arrived like a spring breeze. The Amir, seeing his throne, stood up. The king came down from the throne and kissed the Amir's arm and hand. The king embraced him with extreme enthusiasm and, seating the Amir beside him on the throne, took him to Garden of Iram. It was as if every wish of his heart had been granted.

The king arranged a royal assembly, and rejoiced beyond all measure. . . . Abdur Rahman rose and threw a *perfume-orange against the Amir's breast and congratulated him, and delighted his heart. The Sahib-qiran asked, ''Why have you thrown this perfume-orange, and why have you congratulated me?'' Then Abdur Rahman said, ''The king has accepted you as his son-in-law, he has preferred you over all the Parizads.''

The Amir said, ''I do not at all consent! It is not my custom to undertake such things when I'm in the position of a traveler. For if I married Asman Pari, I would have to postpone going to the Realm of the World—I would then stay here with her, absorbed in luxury and enjoyment. And the second problem is that I promised Mihr Nigar, the daughter of Naushervan the King of Kings of the Seven Realms, 'Until I marry you, I won't even steal a glance at anyone else.' Thus I cannot break my vow, and I cannot turn aside from my oath and promise. To break a vow is very improper; it is incumbent upon every person to uphold his vows.''

Abdur Rahman replied, ''Oh Sahib-qiran, you made that promise in the Realm of the World, and this is the Realm of Qaf! It's not at all contrary to that oath and pledge! It's my responsibility to send you to the World; that is a small part of discharging my own pledge to you.'' The Amir said, ''When will you send me to the Realm of the World, and let me take leave of this place?'' Abdur Rahman replied, ''Oh Sahib-qiran, this is a pledge of Qaf—please don't argue about it! Please accept what we tell you, and don't by any means insist. But after one year I'll send you back to the World, I'll see that you reach your native land safe and well.''

The Amir saw no other recourse but to agree, for without their consent he couldn't manage to leave that place. King Shahpal became absorbed in preparing for the wedding: he wrote letters to summon all the kings and chiefs of Qaf, and ordered every kind of decoration. Accordingly the kings of the realms of Emerald, Ruby, Yellow Basin, Yellow Wilderness, Topaz, Darkness, the Dark Regions, etc., came to Garden of Iram, bearing gifts from their various lands, and joined the marriage celebrations with great pomp and grandeur. . . . Then, having put a royal robe of honor on the Sahib-qiran, they mounted him on a horse and escorted him from the Pavilion of Solomon to the royal ladies' apartments; the bridegroom arrived at the bride's house. Look at the marvelous power of the Lord, that a human arrived in the land of the Paris in such style!

When one watch of the night remained, Abdur Rahman joined the Amir with Asman Pari in marriage. Both bride and groom gave their formal consent, both achieved their heart's desire. How many lands of Qaf the king gave to Asman Pari in dowry! Over and above this, he showered many favors on the Amir. Then the Sahib-qiran entered the palace. Through the Lord's marvelous power, on that very night an embryo found lodging in Asman Pari's womb. Through the Lord's marvelous power, a son of Adam made of dust, and a Pari made of fire —both their natures came to be in harmony.

In the morning the Amir bathed, dressed, and entered the court. A joyous and festive gathering began. Through this close kinship, all distance vanished from between them. To make a long story short, every sort of luxury was provided for the Amir night and day, all his desires were at once fulfilled. But night and day, the Amir kept counting the days: "When will the year be over, so I can go to the Realm of the World and have the joy of seeing my near and dear ones, and tell them about this realm, and show them the strange and remarkable gifts I've obtained in the land of the Paris!"

. . . The dastan reciters of ancient stories weigh their words in the following way: When the year came to a close, and the term of pregnancy had achieved its end, a girl bright as the sun was born from Asman Pari's womb; everyone was charmed by her beauty and radiance. The king was very happy. But the Sahib-qiran was thoroughly unhappy at the birth of a girl, and very disturbed in his heart.

The king learned that the Sahib-qiran was unhappy at the birth of a daughter, that he was feeling quite sorrowful. Giving him the Robe of Honor of Solomon, the king said, "Oh Amir, this is the decree of God, and nobody's at fault in it! It's not an occasion for you to be grieved; this is not how the wise behave." Abdur Rahman said, "Oh Sahib-qiran, this girl will be so powerful and favored by fortune that she will subjugate all the high-headed Devs of Qaf, and she'll be called the Sahib-qiran of Qaf! She'll achieve great rank in the whole land of the Paris." The Amir's grief vanished when he heard this, his heart became full of joy. The king celebrated the baby's birth for some months; he gave large amounts of gold, money, and goods of every kind to the needy and faqirs and poor.

When the girl was six months old, the Sahib-qiran said to the king one day, "I have carried out all that you have commanded. Now please send me to the Realm of the World; fulfill your promise." The king said, "Oh Sahib-qiran, in truth I am very grateful, and am very happy with your qualities and behavior. Now I have no objection to permitting you to go, and in every way your happiness is close to my heart. But the Silver Fort, which is to the north of Qaf, is in a bad condition. Two Devs named Kharchal and Kharpal have established themselves there with an army of ten thousand Devs. They are both very high-headed and mischievous. That fort is mine by hereditary right. If you think it proper and if you'll heed my plea, then kill them and clean out the fort before you go—please take that much more trouble! And if not, then as you wish; your happiness is my object, for I am much indebted to you."

[The Amir consented, and easily reconquered the fort.] The king pressed the Sahib-qiran to his breast, and showed him the greatest affection, and said, "After six months I will send you to the Realm of the World, no matter what; I will give you a fine send-off!" The Amir entered his palace, and began to count the days. On the strength of the king's promise, he trusted his soul to patience.

23. [The Amir tries in vain to return from the Realm of Qaf to the Realm of the World.]

Earlier it has already been narrated that the Amir, after killing Kharpal and Kharchal, stayed six more months at the king's request; he was forced to remain there for some time longer. One night the Amir, with Asman Pari, was asleep in the Pavilion of Solomon, on a jewel-adorned bedstead. Suddenly in his dreams the Amir saw Mihr Nigar: she had languished and grown thin as a twig, in the grief of separation her body had wasted away and become thin and bent like the new moon. All her beauty and radiance had gone; she looked like an old woman. And she spoke, weeping, to the Amir, with rivers of tears flowing from her wet eyes: "What is it, oh Father of Greatness? What sin have I committed, how have I displeased you, that you burn me in the fire of separation, while you enjoy yourself with Paris in the Realm of Qaf! Alas, a thousand times alas! The earth is hard, the sky far away, and man is oppressed in every way. If I had the power I'd sink into the earth, or fly up to the sky, and free myself from this devouring grief."

The Amir cried out and suddenly awoke. He saw that he was hopelessly removed from Mihr Nigar and the Realm of the World. Helplessly he began to weep, loudly and uncontrollably, and to drown himself in tears and sobs of sorrow. Hearing the Amir's weeping, Asman Pari awoke with a start, and asked the Amir, "Are you all right? What grief has come over you, that you're sobbing and distressing yourself so much?" The Amir said, "How can I tell you of the wretchedness I feel? I'm so sick of life, I feel like destroying my life with my own hands!" Then she replied, "Please at least say something! Tell me about your grief."

The Amir said, "Asman Pari, for the Lord's sake please send me at once to the Realm of the World—however it can be done, please have me taken there! Just now in my dream I saw Mihr Nigar in the most terrible state, I saw her utterly distraught with grief at being parted from me." Asman Pari asked, "Oh Father of Greatness, who is Mihr Nigar? Do tell me about her, and explain all this fully to me." The Amir said, "She is the daughter of Naushervan, King of the Seven Realms, and she's my beloved. In beauty and radiance she is peerless, and she's my own true love to whom I've lost my heart."

Asman Pari, hearing this, replied, "So now I know! You have an attachment in another place, and you love some daughter of Adam too! So why should you not clamor to go there, why should you not eat your heart out in her absence? Listen, Amir, tell the truth: is Mihr Nigar even more beautiful than I, is she so peerless in loveliness, charm, airs, and graces that even when I'm with you, you pine to see her, and love her with a thousand loves?" From the Amir's mouth there burst out uncontrollably, "Even Mihr Nigar's serving maids are thousands of times more beautiful and charming than you!"

Asman Pari, hearing this, grew enraged and said, "Oh Hamzah, you think me even lower than Mihr Nigar's serving maids, you're so outrageous that you think her handmaidens better than I! Well, we'll see whether you ever get to the World while I'm alive, and whether you ever escape from my clutches!" The Sahib-qiran was incensed, after all —he replied, "If you stand in my way, then I'll kill you and pass on; come what may, I'll get myself there!" Asman Pari answered him, "Don't go boasting that you're the Sahib-qiran, and descended from Hazrat Abraham the Prophet, and superior to me in birth and station! If you're the Sahib-qiran and of noble descent, I too am descended from Hazrat Solomon, I'm the descendant of a most powerful and glorious Prophet. I'm of high birth, I'm not in any way lower than you! When you seek to kill me, I'll kill you instead!"

This speech infuriated the Amir; he was very much enraged by her insolent reply. Drawing his sword, he rushed at Asman Pari. She too, drawing a dagger, flung herself at the Amir, and raised her weapon to kill him. The Parizad ladies, running up, came between them, pulled them both back, and separated them. Someone went to tell the king about this, they informed him of the whole situation. The king was very distressed when he heard this, and came running. He spoke angrily to his daughter: "Oh you shameless one, do you set yourself up against your husband? Have you no fear of God and the Prophet? Aren't you afraid even of me, or of your own ill repute? Go, get out of my sight!"

Having scolded his daughter, he took the Amir into his pavilion, and said, "Let morning come—please be patient for one more night. Then I'll send you off, and give you leave to go." In short, when morning came, the king seated the Amir on a throne, and equipped him with the necessary provisions. And he commanded four swift-flying Devs, "Take the Amir quickly to the Realm of the World; escort him there."

News reached Asman Pari that the king had sent the Amir off, and had permitted him to go to the World. At once she took *Quraishah, the Amir's daughter, in her arms, and went to him, so that when he saw the little girl he would feel love for her. She saw that the Amir had already mounted the throne. Weeping profusely, she began to say, "Oh Sahib-qiran, if you don't love me then you don't, so be it. But don't you have any pity for this little girl either, isn't there any love in your heart for this child? For the Lord's sake, pardon my sin; from now on I'll never talk back to you or show such disrespect!"

The Amir said, "I'm not angry at you, and I do love the little girl. But it's very necessary for me to go there; for the time being I *will* go to the Realm of the World! I'll tell you the truth about my going:

having promised to return in eighteen days, I left my army there, and didn't bring anyone with me. Now so many years have passed, and they must be very troubled: 'What has happened to the Amir, is he alive or dead?' Besides, whenever you call me, I'll come, and convey myself here without hesitation. And where's the necessity for you to call me? You yourself, whenever you feel like it, can come to me, and convey yourself to the World in the space of a breath. Bring Quraishah with you too when you come." With these words, he said, "All right, farewell!" and had the Devs lift up the throne, and set out; he left on the road toward home.

Asman Pari, going to her house, worked herself into a bad state, and felt very sorrowful at the separation. It happened that Salasil Parizad came by to see Asman Pari, and found her in an utterly distraught condition. When he saw this he was grieved and asked, "Why are you distraught, and why have you worked yourself into such a bad state?" Asman Pari, weeping profusely, said, "Today the king has sent Hamzah to the Realm of the World, and has seen him off quite freely. If you'll be so kind as to go and threaten the Devs, and tell them to abandon Hamzah in the Wilderness of Amazement, and not to take him to the Realm of the World, then I'll be extremely happy. If you won't do what I say, then I won't eat or drink! If Hamzah asks why you've come, tell him you've come to say goodbye, that your affectionate feelings have brought you."

Salasil obeyed Asman Pari's order; he instructed the Devs in just that way. The Devs consulted together: "If we disregard Asman Pari's order, and step outside the bounds of obedience to her, it will be impossible for us to stay in Qaf, and through this disobedience our whole clan will be dishonored and brought low. The best thing is for us to abandon the Sahib-qiran in the Wilderness of Amazement, and not act against Asman Pari's order." Having agreed on this policy, in the evening they put the throne down near the Wilderness of Amazement, and paused for a rest. The Amir said, "Why have you stopped here?" They replied, "We're starving! We'll go hunting a bit, to find relief from the pangs of hunger. When our stomachs are filled, then lifting the throne again will not seem a heavy task." The Amir said, "That's fine. You eat and drink something; I too will offer my prayers, and fulfill my duty toward God."

The Amir performed his ablutions in a stream, and offered his prayers atop a hill. When he finished he sat down on the throne and began waiting for the Devs to come and take up the throne. He couldn't see any sign of a Dev; looking out for them, he didn't close his eyes all night. When morning came, he offered his prayer, and again began watching out for the Devs. In this way hours passed. Then the Amir realized, "Beyond any doubt the Devs have abandoned me here out of fear of Asman Pari, and gone on their way; they've gone off most treacherously. However, I should resign myself to my fate: I ought to proceed on foot, and finally somehow or other get through this journey. It's a famous saying, 'Whatever happens to the sons of Adam is sooner or later over.' " With these words, he stood up and went onward; placing his entire trust in God, he set out to leave that fearful wilderness.

At midday he arrived in the desert, where there wasn't the least trace of a tree—to the point that not even grass grew, and water was completely unavailable. No living creature could be seen; not to speak of men, it would have turned even a Dev's blood to water. Wherever one looked, sand dunes glistened like mercury. The intense heat of the sun caused flames to leap up from the sand. The desert wind blew so fiercely that if I were to describe it, the nib of my pen would be blistered and the pages of the book would be scorched. The sun's heat made the desert almost equal to the sphere of fire. The very wilderness itself called out "Help! I surrender!"

Every piece of equipment on the Amir's body grew so hot that merely touching it blistered his hand, merely saying its name raised boils on his tongue. The Amir threw away his weapons on the plain, he took the load off his shoulders. Thirst tormented him so terribly that life almost left him—the bird of his soul was about to take wing from its physical cage, fly to the land of Nothingness, and nest in the branches of the Tree of Paradise. In desperation, he dug a little into one of the sand dunes. When he reached moist and cool earth, he lay down with his chest pressed into it; so through his chest he felt a bit of coolness, and his heart was comforted.

When this sand too grew hot, he scratched his way deeper in, and lay still. The sand dune, which now had no support from underneath, slid down and collapsed from the force of the wind. The Amir was trapped under the sand, so that he couldn't escape from the dune; every limb of his body became useless.

It happened that one day the king asked Abdur Rahman, "Tell me, how far has Hamzah traveled? He must have reached the Realm of the World; he must have known the joy of seeing his near and dear ones." Abdur Rahman, placing the board before him, threw the divining-dice.

He looked up the question in the appropriate table, multiplied the figures together, put their product in the sixteen geomancy boxes, and drew the divining diagram. He found Hamzah trapped under the sand; discovering this situation caused him much sorrow. With an uncontrollable sigh he said, "Alas! Hamzah's young life has been cut off for nothing!"

Then he said to the king, "Now no one will trust you. When things are like this, who will choose to obey you? A man like Hamzah, who killed your enemies and in fact made you King of Kings anew, and saved you from such bloodthirsty foes! You've done an evil deed in sending him off for no reason to such an end!" The king summoned the Devs whom he had sent to carry Hamzah on the throne, and angrily asked them, "Where did you take Hamzah?" They replied, "At Asman Pari's order, we abandoned him in the Wilderness of Amazement. If we had taken him to the World, by the princess' order we would have been killed, or banished from the land."

The king turned red with rage; he was extremely angry, and was very much grieved at hearing this news. Looking toward Asman Pari, he said, "What is this mischief?" She replied, "I don't consent to have Hamzah sent to the World; I can't be happy for a moment in his absence. As for the rest, I'll go myself to search for Hamzah and bring him back—look, I'll mount and be ready to set out!" The king said, "Oh, no doubt, no doubt! How do you expect to find him now? You'll only take pains for nothing, with no benefit!" With these words, the king himself mounted and prepared to leave. He took Devs with him, and set out at once.

Entering the Wilderness of Amazement, he ordered the Devs and Jinns and Paris, "You must search for Hamzah in this desert, you must free him from wherever he is trapped. Whoever finds him and brings him to me will receive jeweled wings, and will be given a high place in my esteem." As they searched, they found Hamzah's weapons lying here and there; they took these weapons and showed them to the king. When the king saw the weapons, he was very much grieved, and felt most sorrowful. Again he urged his people on in the search for Hamzah, and commanded them to look most carefully. [At last they found him under the dune.]

Shahpal instantly ran, barefoot, to that hill. Removing the Amir from the hill, he carried him in his arms and laid him down on his own throne. He placed perfumes near his nose, and caused him to inhale various kinds of sweet scents. Two hours later, when the Amir recovered consciousness, he found himself in a strange situation: he was lying on a throne, and the king was seated beside him, sitting there very sad and melancholy. Gathering his strength, the Amir rose and said to King Shahpal, "What harm did I ever do you, to cause you to punish me like this?" King Shahpal said, "Oh Sahib-qiran, I swear by Hazrat Solomon, and by your life, that I hadn't the slightest hand in this, I never at all wanted you to be tormented. You've done me many great kindnesses, all of us are your servants—as if I would have even the smallest hand in this! Whatever was done, Asman Pari did it; it was *that* fool who dealt you such a blow."

In the midst of this, Asman Pari ran and fell at the Amir's feet, and repeatedly made the gesture of taking his misfortunes onto herself. She said, "Oh Sahib-qiran, truly I'm a sinner, I'm entirely guilty. This once, pardon my sin, and soften your heart toward me! Come for a few days to the City of Gold to take your ease, and give yourself some rest. For you have suffered a great blow, you've endured too much pain. After six months I will definitely send you to the World; I will certainly be faithful to this promise."

The Amir said, "No one can have the slightest confidence in your words and deeds." Asman Pari swore an oath, and invoked the name of Hazrat Solomon. She took the Amir to the City of Gold. For six months Shahpal's army stayed there also, until the Amir could regain his strength and return to full health.

24. [The Amir is persecuted by Asman Pari, and tricked by the White Dev.]

When the period of six months passed, and the Amir didn't get permission to depart, one night he saw Mihr Nigar in a dream. He saw her in the same grief and agitation; weeping profusely, she said, ". . . For the Lord's sake, please come quickly, don't delay any longer! Otherwise you won't find me alive—believe me, you'll be very sorry!" When the Sahib-qiran awoke with a start from his dream and looked around, there was no Mihr Nigar or her house, no slightest trace of anything in his dream. He was there in the Realm of Qaf as usual, sitting there powerless and oppressed. He began to groan and lament and sigh deeply.

When Asman Pari's eyes opened, she saw that the Amir was weeping and could not restrain himself; he was sobbing uncontrollably. Getting up, she wiped the Amir's tears with a handkerchief and asked, "Are you all right? Why are you so distraught, why are you in this dreadful state and suffering so much grief and distress?"

The Amir said, "It's nothing, I'm fine. Weeping is a human trait." Although Asman Pari again and again asked the Amir the cause of his tears and distress, and asked why he was in such a sad and troubled condition, the Amir gave no answer; he kept absolutely quiet. Till morning he sat, soaking handkerchief after handkerchief, weeping continually.

When the king emerged from his bedroom, the Amir went and made obeisance to him, he offered him the customary respectful greeting, and said, "The time of even this last promise is over. Now please send your servant off, give him leave to go!" The king at once seated the Amir on a throne and said to four Devs, "Take the Amir to the Realm of the World, and bring back a receipt with the Amir's signature and seal on it. Convey him carefully there." They lifted the throne to their shoulders and took to the air.

Asman Pari worked herself into a bad state just as she had the first time, she again suffered as before and worked herself into the same distraught condition. And she said to Salasil Parizad, "Somehow or other go and influence the throne-bearing Devs, and give them my order that it will be well for them if they abandon the Amir in the Island of Confusion and return. Let them carry out my order, so that he'll be confused for two or three days and will be lost and bewildered in that forest. Otherwise I'll have their wives and children crushed to death in a wine-press, I'll have each one of them killed most humiliatingly!"

Salasil, flying swiftly, caught up with the Amir and greeted him; outwardly he treated him with great affection and respect. The Sahib-qiran commanded, "Salasil Parizad, your arrival bodes no good! Don't come near me, don't show your face to me!" He replied, "This slave has come to take leave of you; God knows when I'll kiss your feet again. If the stars favor me, I'll someday again have the honor of attending upon you." The Amir said, "Well, you've seen me, and so goodbye. Now please have the goodness to depart, and don't take any further trouble!"

Salasil, as he was leaving, told those Devs the princess' order, and persuaded them to abandon the Sahib-qiran. For a whole day the Devs flew on. When evening came, they descended, and carried out the princess' order. The Amir said, "Why have you set the throne down here? This is a desert; its fearfulness depresses my spirits." They replied, "It's night. It's not good to travel by night; we don't like to fly in the dark. Furthermore, we have to eat something, and we have to rest a bit too. Now we'll eat and drink and rest; in the morning we'll go on."

The Sahib-qiran commanded, "Don't play the same tricks as the former Devs, don't get up to the same mischief as they did!" They replied, "How could we be capable of doing that? Breaking faith is against our principles!" The Amir fell silent. The Devs put the Amir's throne down right there, and themselves, with the excuse of going hunting, set out for Garden of Iram.

The Amir, as he had done before, sat all night on the throne, and stayed awake. When morning came, and the Devs didn't come, he realized that they had deceived him in the same way, and had set out for their own country. He said to himself, "Oh Hamzah, the King of Qaf will not let you go to the Realm of the World, he will always play you false. So set out by yourself—if God should in His graciousness lead you there, and let you see your home again, it wouldn't be surprising."

With this thought, he set out from there. When he grew tired, he sat down under a tree and rested for an hour or two. Afterwards he again stood up and went on, lamenting the King of Qaf's treachery and his own sufferings. In short, he walked the whole day. As evening approached, he saw the same river, the same field, the same wilderness and desert where the Devs had abandoned him and broken faith with him. The Amir was very much surprised: "I toiled and traveled the whole day—and then in the evening I arrive exactly where I set out from in the morning! It's an extraordinary happening, a display of the power of God!" Having no choice, he spent the night in that place.

In the morning he again rose and set out. Although he went off in a different direction, in the evening he again arrived at that same place where the Devs had abandoned him. In short, for three days the same thing happened. On the fourth day he set out in the fourth direction, and traveled till midday; he endured the fatigue of walking and wandering onwards. When the area began to grow hot, the fierceness of the sun made him feel faint; his suffering made him very low in spirits.

In one direction he saw some leafy trees. He went that way, thinking to sit down in their shade and rest a little while. When he looked, he saw an eight-sided marble platform. The air felt cool, and pausing there for even a moment gave a great sense of comfort. The Amir went and sat on the platform. . . . Sitting down with complete tranquility on the platform, he lost himself in enjoyment of the river and the wilderness, he forgot all the troubles of his heart. Suddenly the cool air lulled the Amir to sleep where he sat, its comforting touch banished all his grief and sorrow. The Amir saw Mihr Nigar in a dream: she was standing there weeping, half dead with the grief of separation. The Amir, in the depths of sleep, gave a long helpless groan and abruptly awoke. When he looked around, there was that same limitless wilderness, and the river full of high waves as though in a storm. He said to himself, "I wonder if God will ever bring me to the World, and if I'll ever manage to see Mihr Nigar."

Eventually, it occurred to him that he ought to place his whole trust in God and go down the river, for after all he must find some means for getting out of the wilderness. With this thought, he tore some branches off the trees and made a raft, climbed onto it, and sat down. When he reached the middle of the river, a great storm came and drove the raft back to the bank. The narrator says that the Amir again launched the raft into the river; again a storm came and drove the raft back to the bank. The narrator says that the Amir launched the raft seventy-two times, but whenever it reached the middle of the river, either a tumult arose or a storm came, and the raft was driven back to the bank. For a week the Amir labored hard, but the raft always ended up lodged on the bank; it would never under any circumstances float in the river. [Then the Prophet Noah appeared to Hamzah in a dream and told him how to quiet the river. Hamzah floated down the river, then continued his travels on foot.] On the thirteenth day, blisters appeared on the Amir's feet. Having no choice, he sat down helplessly where he was; the swelling and blisters on his feet prevented him from going on. He thought, "Well, 'Delhi is still far off,'[25] and I'm tired, and my feet are blistered. I wonder if God will bring me to the Realm of the World, and will show me my own country."

Hardly any time at all had passed, when a cloud of dust appeared in the distance. When the dust settled to the ground, he saw a musk-black horse, equipped with saddle and bridle, approaching; it moved so elegantly that watching its gait was a real pleasure. Coming near the Amir, the horse paused. The Amir said to himself, "God has sent this mount to me from the Unseen, He has taken pity on my wretched condition." He rose and mounted, and gave thanks to the Great Lord with his whole heart and soul. No sooner had he climbed on its back, than the horse leaped into the air like *Buraq, it took to the air like a Pari. Although the Amir tried to restrain it, it wouldn't stop. For three days and nights it went on; it never paused for breath or halted even for a moment.

[The Amir continued his travels.] For seventeen days he traveled. On the eighteenth day he arrived at the foot of a mountain; on its peak a very lofty crystal dome could be seen. . . . And when he looked carefully at the pinnacle of the dome, he discovered that a Night-glowing Pearl had been placed atop it, a priceless jewel was mounted there. The Amir reached out by means of the miraculous power bestowed by Hazrat Adam: he stretched out his hand and pulled down the Night-glowing Pearl from the pinnacle. When he placed it next to the Night-glowing Pearl in his own coronet, he couldn't find the smallest difference. The Amir was delighted: "This too is a special gift from Qaf —in the World, how can any king, or king of kings, ever have even seen such a thing!"

. . . Not even an hour had passed when a strong wind came from the forest, so that even the splendid big trees were on the verge of falling; they were almost flattened to the earth by the force of the wind. After this, a Dev, white in color, five hundred yards tall in stature, entered the garden, yelling. His roaring and tumult seemed to tower to the sky: "Who is the thief who has taken out the Night-glowing Pearl, Hazrat Solomon's sacred relic, from the pinnacle of the dome, and deprived the Dome of Solomon of its glory?" The Amir, approaching him, gave his battle-cry, and challenged him with a shout of "God is great": "You big, tall, ugly ball of fat, whom are you looking for? Do you even know me, or not? Do you recognize the destroyer of Devs, the breaker of tilisms, or not? If you recognize me, then take a good look—come before me, and know who I am! I am the Earthquake of Qaf, the Younger Solomon, the slayer of Ifrit and the killer of Ahriman!"

. . . He struck a blow at the Amir's head, using his whole strength, with a cypress-tree staff in which several millstones were embedded. The Amir used the Scorpion of Solomon to cut the staff in two. Then, grabbing the Dev's belt, he lifted him up by main force and hurled him to the ground. Mounting his breast, he placed the dagger of Rustam against his throat. Then the Dev's eyes filled with tears and he said, "Oh Earthquake of Qaf, don't kill me—I'll be very useful to you! Any order that you give, I'll obey with my whole heart and soul." The Amir replied, "If you become a Muslim, then why not? Otherwise, I'll kill you right now with this dagger."

The Dev replied, "Under this mountain are some enemies of mine. If you kill them, then I'll become a Muslim, I'll be your true-hearted

THE WHITE DEV ATTACKS, AND THE SAHIB-QIRAN THROWS HIM DOWN AND CLIMBS ON HIS CHEST, AND HE SAVES HIS LIFE THROUGH TRICKERY AND THEN OPPOSES THE SAHIB-QIRAN.

and faithful servant." . . . The Amir said, "Take me there." The Dev took the Amir beneath the mountain, and showed him their dwelling. The Amir saw a saffron field that extended for many miles, and in its midst was a river which was two hundred yards wide and immeasurably long. Its water was clear and pleasant, and in the midst of this river was a platform of crystal, fifty yards square and fifty yards high. Topaz railings surrounded it; even in the railings, jewels had been inlaid with great craftsmanship. And in the center of the platform was a throne decorated with diamonds; it too was of peerless sophistication. The reflection of the Saffron-field Mountain shimmered on the platform, as though grass were waving in the wind.

The Amir, with a bound, leaped to the platform, stood there, and looked all around. He asked the *White Dev, "Where are those enemies of yours?" The Dev said, "They're in this very saffron field. Please call out and say, 'Oh Seven Monstrous Apes, what do you eat?' They'll answer you, and will appear before you; they'll never delay in coming." The Amir called out and said, "Oh monstrous apes, what do you eat, and where are you? I am eager to meet you! Come out and meet me, show me your faces." A voice came, "We eat saffron. Please wait a minute, we're coming."

Finally the seven monstrous apes came before the Amir, and stood before him in a line. The Amir saw that they were of strange form: their bodies were like men's, and their front teeth were like spears—so sharp that if even a fly should light on one of them, he'd be pierced through! The Amir, drawing the Scorpion of Solomon, leaped among them, and slaughtered all seven with his well-tempered sword. Then he said to the White Dev, "Now your enemies have been killed. All your grief and sorrow has been removed; your heart's desire has been achieved."

The White Dev was delighted; putting one hand on his head and the other on his buttocks, he began to dance. And he replied, "Oh son of Adam, you've killed my enemies, but I, your enemy, am still here! It's the custom of our race to return evil for good; we aren't worried about the consequences." With these words, he lifted up a heavy slab of stone and flung it at the Amir. The Amir warded it off and, drawing his sword, flung himself at the Dev. The Dev ran desperately away, he didn't stop for even a moment. Although the Amir called to him, he wouldn't come close. He said, "I'm not such a fool as to deliberately come near you and lose my life, and purposely get myself slaughtered! When sometime I find you with your guard down, *then* I'll give you a taste of what you deserve!" With these words, he flew away.

The Sahib-qiran said to himself, "It's not good to stay here any longer; it's proper to get away from this place. The White Dev has become my enemy—God knows when he'll see his chance and harm me, and take his revenge on me." He set out at that very moment. The narrator writes that the Amir went on for seven days and nights together through fear of the White Dev, in order to escape from his clutches, and not suffer harm at the hands of that vile creature; he didn't pause to rest for even a moment.

. . . Sitting down on a boulder, he began to weep bitterly at being separated from Mihr Nigar and enduring the absence of his friends. Remembering them all, he grew distraught with grief. As he wept, his eyes gradually closed, and he entered the oblivion of sleep; after many days of fatigue, he was dead to the world. The White Dev was on the alert: seeing the Amir unconscious, he picked him up together with the boulder, and took to the air. He had gone about four miles high, when the strong wind caused the Amir's eyes to open. He saw that the White Dev was flying away with him, carrying him like a bundle on his back. The Amir said, "Oh White Dev, I did good to you, and you're doing evil to me—evil in return for good! Don't you have any fear of God?" The Dev replied, "I've already told you that we return evil for good, that's our habit. Now tell me this: shall I throw you down on a mountain, or in the river?"

The Amir reflected, "Devs have perverse natures. Whatever I say, he'll do the opposite." The Amir said, "Throw me down on a mountain; if you are taking revenge on me, take it like that." The White Dev replied, "Oh son of Adam, I'll throw you into the river, so you'll drown, and you'll never oppress or tyrannize us again!" With these words, the Dev threw him, together with the boulder, into the river, and flew off; he immediately did the opposite of what the Amir had said.

Hazrats Khizr and Elias, by the order of God Most High, took the Amir in their arms and put him down, standing, on the riverbank. The Amir saluted both Prophets, and said, with a thousand tears and lamentations, "Oh Hazrats, Asman Pari has tormented me cruelly, and has caused me the greatest grief! She doesn't allow me to go to the World; she gives me no peace from my sufferings." Hazrat Khizr said, "Oh Amir, there's no cause for anxiety. You are fated to eat the food and drink the water of Qaf for a little longer. When that time is over, you'll leave this place, and return to your homeland, and be at peace. A few more hard days remain; they too, if the Lord wills, will pass. Trust in God and show fortitude; your good days are at hand."

25. The dastan of Khvajah Amar Ayyar's going from his previous fort to the fort of Devdad, with Princess Mihr Nigar and the army of Islam.

The sweetly-speaking narrators write that after a year, the officers said to Khvajah Amar Ayyar, "The provisions in the fort are exhausted. All the people are oppressed by hunger, they're distraught and confused." The Khvajah asked Sayad, "In this area is there any other fort where we could go and stay for a while, and be free of the worry of want?'' Sayad said, ''Two stages' journey from here is a fort named Devdad; it was built by Jamshed and equipped very elegantly with all the comforts. In strength, no fort can equal it—even Mount *Alburz can't compare with it for height and firmness.'' . . . Amar, hearing about the fort, was delighted; sending for the officers, he instructed them, ''Keep very close watch over this fort. I am going to see about another fort, I'm going to carry out a scheme for your comfort.'' With these words, he took off his royal attire, put on ayyari costume, left the fort, and traveled with huge bounds to the fort of Devdad. He circled around the fort, looking for a point of entry, but found none; he couldn't see any way to get in.

Seating himself on a hillock, he looked at the interior part of the fort and marveled at it, for such a fort had never been seen or heard of before. Seeking a means of entry into the fort, he dived repeatedly into the ocean of thought and began to devise plans; various kinds of ideas began to pass through his mind. And what did he see then but an iron balcony with a window. At the window a water-carrier was standing, drawing up water from below, hauling up water as was his appointed duty. Amar reflected that he would never find a better stairway than this for entering the fort, no other stratagem would be available. Keeping out of the water-carrier's sight, he leaped into the water and seated himself in the leather bucket.

When the water-carrier found the bucket heavy, he was astonished. Peering down, he saw that a man of peculiar appearance was sitting in the bucket. In his stupidity he thought, ''My fortune is made—a *merman has come into my bucket! My ascendant star has brought me an infinite treasury!'' He began to draw up the bucket slowly and gently, for fear the merman would fall out and the matchless prize would be lost. When the bucket had risen up to the pulley, he stretched out his hand to seize the merman, and planned to pull him out of the bucket. Amar sprang out to where the water-carrier was, grabbed him by the neck, and threw him down into the water—he played this trick on him. The water in the moat was deep, the water-carrier's cup of life had already been filled to the brim. Rising and sinking a few times, he drowned in the sea of death.

Amar, taking on his appearance, began drawing up the water; he took over the water-carrier's job. When the water-skin had been filled, he reflected, ''I don't know where he normally took his water, or what it was meant to be used for.'' Prudently he lay down. The other water-carriers, who had come to draw water, and had brought their water-skins to that place, waved their hands and asked, "Friend Fattu, are you all right? Why are you lying down like this?" Amar replied, "Oh brothers, I'm feeling feverish right now, the heat has spread into my heart. If you would kindly send word to my home, it would be extremely gracious of you."

A water-carrier informed Fattu's children, "Fattu is lying on the wall of the fort, trembling with fever; he is panting with the heat and his fever." The wife and children went running there as soon as they heard the news, picked him up, and brought him home; seeing his condition, everyone was very grieved. Amar stayed peacefully asleep, and allowed himself a good rest. When about half the night was over . . . suddenly from outside someone called, and yelled out, "Friend Fattu, are you awake or asleep? Just come outside a moment, I have something to say to you. . . . I am the chief of the king's ayyars. . . ." When Amar heard the word "ayyar," he was inwardly uncertain and doubtful, and his heart was overcome by foreboding. He asked the woman, "Has this man come before?" She said, "No, not at all." He felt even more fearful: "Right at the first I've encountered an ayyar—this is a very bad thing! May God protect me!" Helplessly, moaning and groaning, he went out: "Oh God, save me from disaster!"

The chief, when he saw him, said, "Oh *Ayyar and King of Ayyars, peace be upon you!" Amar replied, "Sir, this is the house of Fattu the water-carrier; the house of the King of Ayyars must be down the street!" Ham of Devdad replied, "Oh Khvajah, why hide from me? I too am a Muslim, and I've been longing with my whole heart and soul to meet you. I've been waiting for you for two months, and thinking of you every moment most lovingly!" With these words, he fell at Amar's feet. Amar pressed Ham's head to his breast, and began to say affectionate words. Ham of Devdad said, "Let's go—you can seize the king, you can carry out the task for which you've come. Then after that we'll see what happens, we'll take heed of whatever comes to pass. This servant will share in your fortunes, however dark the night may be."

These two, keeping out of sight of the guards, used their nooses and arrived in the sleeping quarters of Antar of Devdad; through their ingenuity they reached the inner part of the fort. Amar saw that the king, covered by a double-sided embroidered shawl, was sleeping on a bed under a satin canopy made in China. He was all alone, without any servant near him; all the servants were heedless, and he too was deep in the sleep of ignorance. Amar pulled the end of the shawl away from the king's face, and was on the verge of blowing knockout powder into his nose, when the king seized his hand. Amar jerked his hand away, he gave his hand a forceful wrench. Amar's ring stayed in the king's hand. Amar started to leave fast, to be on his way quickly.

The king called out to him, "Oh Khvajah, don't run away from me! Listen to me a moment, and do what I say. Just now Hazrat Abraham appeared to me in a dream, made me a Muslim, told me of your coming, and instructed me to support you. Otherwise, I don't have any mystical knowledge through which to recognize you, or to know your situation without your telling me!" Amar, hearing this speech, stood still. The king rose and embraced Amar, and commanded with the greatest affection and sincerity, "In the morning go and bring all your people, bring them here without any hesitation. This fort is yours. Hurmuz and Faramarz are of no account—if even Jamshed or *Jam came, he couldn't take this fort, or give you any kind of trouble!"

Amar at once took leave of the king, and went to his previous fort. Telling the officers that the fort of Devdad had been taken, he rested during the day. When two watches of the night had passed, he had Mihr Nigar enter a gold-adorned palanquin, and sent her, along with the army, to the fort of Devdad. He himself, having set up paper figures here and there in the old fort, started out last of all. In two days he entered the fort of Devdad, and found every sort of comfort there.

[However, Antar's son, Khvajah Arbab, slipped out to meet with Hurmuz and betray the fort.] Khvajah Arbab said, "Inside your tent will be one end of the tunnel; please have it dug out. The other end will be in my mansion; I will go and have it dug. During the rest of the night, and all of tomorrow, the heat will go out of it, and the breeze will blow through it. Please come early tomorrow evening through the tunnel to my humble home, and honor it with your presence; by means of your inherently auspicious footsteps, please provide me with a resplendent and impressive robe of honor. Be pleased to eat dinner, and enjoy the sights of the place. And when two watches of the night have passed, kill the Muslims and seize Amar as well; when you have him in your power, then do as you wish with him. Please take away Mihr Nigar also, and enjoy the pleasure of her company. But choose many great champions to bring with you, and please enjoin them to show courage and bravery." Hurmuz and Faramarz, giving Khvajah Arbab a robe of honor, allowed him to depart, and ordered their people to perform those tasks.

Khvajah Arbab went back into the fort the same way he had come out of it, and at once brought the diggers to his house and had them start digging the end of the tunnel. Thus as morning dawned, the tunnel was opened up, and Khvajah Arbab made preparations for the princes' dinner; he ordered the requisites for the feast to be collected. It chanced that his daughter, named Dilavez, asked him, "What's all this hustle and bustle today? Please tell me what kind of preparations are going on." Khvajah Arbab, trusting his daughter, told her in detail about his plans for the night; since he had confidence in her, he revealed his deep secret to her.

Dilavez was inwardly very downcast: "That wretch with his futile greed is going to take the blood of so many Muslims onto his head!" Immediately she wrote an account of the whole thing, and sent it by the hand of her old nurse to Amar. She enjoined the nurse, "Go quickly and put this letter into Amar's hands, and return. He'll give you a great reward; he'll make you very happy with cash and valuables." The nurse at once went and gave the letter into Amar's hands, and told him something orally as well. Amar gave the nurse a great reward, and sent congratulations to Dilavez and praised her sympathetic feelings very highly.

[Amar and his officers paid a visit to Khvajah Arbab; they politely ate the elaborate dinner.] Amar, searching out the opening of the tunnel, sat Adi down beside it and said, "Whoever sticks his head out, squeeze his throat with both hands and pull him out, so that not a sound escapes from his lips, and he's absolutely unable to speak. All the other champions will be standing near you, they won't budge from this spot. You keep on seizing the men and passing them on to the others; they'll keep their mouths covered as you have done, and will keep sending them along into confinement; they'll do just as I have said. And be warned—if anyone should slip through your fingers, then just the way I've fed you, I'll rip open your stomach!" Adi squatted down by the hole like a bread-baker, on his haunches, so that when anybody stuck a head through, he could pull it out deftly, all light and puffy like a fluffy roll, and do just as Amar had ordered.

. . . In the meantime, someone stuck his head out of the hole. Adi was sitting like the Angel of Death to cut off his breath: he seized his throat and pulled him upward, and passed him on to the other officers. They took him in this choked condition and locked him up. When the second man stuck his head out, the same thing happened to him. In short, in no time at all Adi seized four hundred champions. . . . In the morning, Amar had the four hundred chiefs of the enemy army who had been seized, together with Khvajah Arbab, hanged on a scaffold; he didn't leave even one alive. And he closed up the end of the tunnel with lead, so that there was absolutely no way to come or go. Hurmuz and Faramarz wrote down all these events in a letter, and sent it off to Naushervan by the hand of Sabir the Felt-robed; they entered the whole story in their petition.

26. [The Amir marries Raihan Pari, in an attempt to reach the World.]

Now please hear a bit about the Sahib-qiran's situation. Asman Pari had sworn in the presence of Khvajahs Khizr and Elias, and taken the most solemn oaths and vows, that in six months she would send the Sahib-qiran back to the World, and would absolutely not break faith this time. When six months had passed, the Amir said to Asman Pari, "There—the period of this vow is over too! Now send me to my own land; in God's name, this time keep your promise!" Asman Pari said, "I'll send you in a year. Stay one more year. For my sake, force yourself to be patient."

The Amir, growing angry when he heard this, said sharply, "Asman Pari, have you no fear even of God? People ought to fear God, and not do things that will ensnare them in God's wrath! You swore in the presence of two Prophets that in six months you would, with the most complete certainty, send me to my country, and convey me to the Realm of the World. Today you're again making new promises!" Asman Pari replied, "I'm the one who'll be punished for swearing false oaths! What's it to you?"

The Amir, displeased, went to the king. . . . The king treated the Amir very kindly, and comforted him. At once seating the Amir on a throne, he summoned four Devs and enjoined them, "Take the Sahib-qiran to the Realm of the World; obey this order of mine with your whole heart and soul."

. . . Asman Pari, weeping, went to her home; she was very grieved at the Amir's departure. Sending for Rizvan Parizad, she said, "Go to the Sahib-qiran on the excuse of taking leave of him, and give my order quickly to the Devs who are bearing the throne: tell them that they are to abandon the Amir in the Desert of Wonders and come back here, and not go a foot beyond that wilderness. Otherwise I'll treat them very harshly—they'll taste the fruits of their disobedience!"

Rizvan, flying swiftly, went to the Amir; in the space of a breath he reached him. The Amir, seeing Rizvan, said, "His arrival is not without meaning—no doubt about it, there's something behind all this! Asman Pari is very treacherous." To the throne-bearing Devs he said, "Go back to Shahpal; do as I say!" The Devs began to make excuses. The Amir, resting his hand on his sword-hilt, said, "If you don't go, then I won't leave a single one of you alive! Remember that—I'll break the heads of every one of you!" The Devs, having no choice, took the Amir to the king; according to his order, they brought the Amir back to Shahpal.

King Shahpal, seeing the Amir, said, "Oh Amir, is everything all right? How have you happened to come back, what has caused you to return?" The Sahib-qiran replied, "I've come to ask you whether you intend to send me to my home—or to have me left wandering again in some wilderness, and to cause me such confusion as you did the first time?" The king swore, "I willingly send you to the World! It's truly my pleasure that you go to your native land, and have the joy of seeing your friends and relatives." The Amir replied, "If this is so, then please make the throne-bearing Devs swear by Hazrat Solomon before you send me off; enjoin them most strictly to take me to the World, before you give them leave to go."

When the king told the Devs to take the oath, they excused themselves: "We won't swear, because Asman Pari has ordered us not to take the Amir to the World, not to do this deed against her wishes. We would only disobey the princess' order if we were tired of our lives, if we had no idea what was for or against our interests!" The king, looking at Asman Pari, said, "What is this vileness?" Asman Pari replied, "What do you have to do with it? He's my husband, and I don't consent to his going! I don't like being separated from him, his absence is very oppressive to my heart."

The Amir, coming down from the throne, groaned so loudly that the fort trembled, and said, "Asman Pari, you swore an oath before two Prophets as witnesses, and then betrayed me! If God Most High wills, the wrath of the Lord will fall on you—your high fortune will slip away from you! I'm going into the wilderness, placing my trust in God." With these words, he set out toward the wilderness like a madman.

Shahpal said to Asman Pari, "Oh Asman Pari, by treating the Earthquake of Qaf so badly you've disgraced and dishonored me in all Qaf! Your improper behavior has made me low and base in everyone's eyes." Asman Pari replied, "I'm willing to have you disgraced and dishonored, but I'm not willing to have my life ruined!" With these words, she had the proclamation made that the Earthquake of Qaf had left Garden of Iram, and whoever should give him shelter, or take him to his own country, would be killed by her own hand along with his wife and children, he would be punished most terribly.

Now please hear about the Sahib-qiran. Leaving Garden of Iram, he went on for seven days and nights into the wilderness. On the eighth day, he fainted from lack of food, and collapsed in a garden. The next day, coming to his senses, he ate from the bread-bun bestowed on him by Hazrat Khizr, and began to look around the area.

After a little while, what did he see but a Dev, powerful of body and tall of stature, coming along—the very sight of whom would make the heart flutter with fear. When the Dev came near, he recognized the Amir and saluted him. The Amir asked him, "Oh Dev, how far is the World from here? I need to find out the distance." The Dev said, "Oh Earthquake of Qaf, Younger Solomon, if a human wants to go on his own, and get himself to the Realm of the World, he'll arrive in five hundred years. The ordinary Devs can take you in six months. The messenger Dev will take you in forty days; he'll take you faster than all the others. And a Dev like me, in seven days."

The Amir said, "If you'll take me to my house, you'll do me a great kindness." The Dev replied, "If I didn't have to return to this land, I'd certainly take you to the World, and disobey my ruler! But Asman Pari has proclaimed in the whole land of Qaf, that anyone who takes the Sahib-qiran to the World she will not leave alive, nor his wife and children—she'll break their heads!" The Amir called to him to come closer, and tried to put the fear of God into him. The Dev replied, "I'm not such a fool as to come near you, and have you beat me, and sit on my head, and somehow force me to go to the World! What could I do then? I'd be entirely in your power!" With these words, he saluted and flew away.

The Amir, losing hope, said to himself, "Hamzah, no Dev or Parizad will take you to your country; you'll never reach your goal through them. Instead, trust to fortune and go on your own. The Lord is merciful: if He wishes, He will guide you there." With these words, he set out toward the wilderness. Jungle after jungle, forest after forest, desert after desert, sometimes weeping, sometimes laughing, he went on; he endured thousands of kinds of grief and distress.

On the fifteenth day, the Amir saw a fort; on it Jinns were praying, bareheaded, to the Lord of Oneness. And a Dev, ill-formed, huge, with elephant ears, stood as immovable as a mountain, having surrounded the fort with his army. The Amir felt pity for those inside the fort, he was grieved at their plight. [He challenged the Dev, then fought and killed him.]

The king, coming out of the fort, embraced the Amir; seizing his hand, he took him into the fort and seated him on a throne. He treated him with great honor and generosity, and said, "I am that same Jinn, *Sabz-qaba, Shahpal's brother, whom you liberated from the tilism of Solomon's Chessboard,[26] and saved from that mortal peril." With these words, he took the Amir into the fort of Sabz-nigar and caused all, great and small, to pay their respects to him, and introduced him to them all.

Arranging for a royal celebration, he inquired about the Amir's situation. The Amir, telling him the whole story of his experiences, said, "Oh Sabz-qaba Jinn, I'm afraid to trust you either! For you're the older brother of King Shahpal, you're still part of that family. So I can't by any means hope for faithfulness from you!" The king replied, "Why, what are you saying? I'm your slave and obedient servant." The Amir said, "May the Lord keep you well! In truth, men hope for so many things from their friends." Then he continued, "Instead of sacrificing your life for me, do me only this much of a favor: take me to my country. I'll be grateful to you my whole life long."

The king, after some thought, called Khvajah Rauf the Jinn and said, "Tell the Amir, 'If you will take *Raihan Pari, who is my daughter and loves you, as your wife, and will have no doubt or hesitation about this, then nine days from today I'll take you to your home; I pledge myself to bring this to pass.' " The Amir, after first refusing, finally consented, and obtained the king's oath as well for his part of the bargain. Sabz-qaba the Jinn celebrated Raihan Pari's marriage to the Amir with great pomp and splendor; he was proud to take the Amir as a son-in-law.

But at night, when the Amir went to lie down with Raihan Pari, he put a sword between them. She felt that it must be a custom of the Amir's country to sleep on this occasion with a sword in between, and lie down together like this on the first night. Both, turning their backs to each other, settled down on their own sides of the bed and went to sleep; there was no involvement between them, there was no true union. That night the Amir suddenly saw Mihr Nigar in a dream—he saw her very much distressed by the separation. Waking with a start, he ran out toward the wilderness like a madman.

. . . Now please hear a bit about Asman Pari. One day, wearing red clothing, she came into the king's court. Looking at Abdur Rahman, she said, "See where the Amir is these days—tell me truly where he is, according to your rules of geomancy." Abdur Rahman, using geomancy, said only this and nothing more: "The Amir, thanks to you, is wandering around in distress."

Since Asman Pari was seated just beside him, and herself had some knowledge of geomancy, she looked at the diagram and exclaimed, "Oh God, oh God! To think that Sabz-qaba the Jinn, although he's my uncle, should marry his daughter to my husband, and should have no regard for my honor and reputation, no fear of my wrath and fury! It seems he's not my uncle, but my rival. For an uncle to do such a thing is extraordinary—to knowingly and deliberately make Raihan Pari my co-wife. If I don't burn down his country into black dust, if I don't punish him, I won't claim the name Asman Pari!" With these words, taking a fierce army with her, she seated herself on a throne and set out toward the fort of Sabz-nigar.

27. Asman Pari goes with a powerful army to the fort of Sabz-nigar, lays waste the city, takes captive Sabz-qaba the Jinn and Raihan Pari, punishes Sabz-qaba the Jinn, and imprisons Raihan Pari in the Dungeon of Solomon.

The narrator writes that Asman Pari arrived near the fort of Sabz-nigar. Sabz-qaba the Jinn, taking some gifts with him, went to welcome Asman Pari, and escorted her into the city with perfect honor and respect, and behaved toward her with the greatest love and courtesy. Asman Pari, arriving in his court, ordered, and commanded her people, "Bind Sabz-qaba the Jinn and Raihan Pari hand and foot—don't delay even a moment in carrying out my order!" Her followers bound them both and presented them. Asman Pari, having laid waste the city, went back to Garden of Iram. For a number of days she had a thousand lashes each given daily to Sabz-qaba the Jinn and Raihan Pari; then she confined Raihan Pari in the Dungeon of Solomon.

News reached Shahpal that Asman Pari had dishonored Sabz-qaba the Jinn in this way. Rending his garments, bareheaded and barefooted, weeping uncontrollably, Shahpal ran there. Asman Pari had already gone to her home. Shahpal took Sabz-qaba the Jinn away to his own home, and showed him extreme kindness. He fell at Sabz-qaba's feet and wept bitterly; with many apologies, he washed the dust of displeasure and unhappiness from Sabz-qaba's heart. And he said, "That shameless wretch has really insulted not you but me—in truth, she's caused pain not to you but to me!"

Although King Shahpal said all this, Sabz-qaba was not consoled; the resentment didn't leave his heart. Like a madman he rose and struck the fortress gate of Garden of Iram hard with his hand, and spoke; he opened his mouth to petition in utter submission and desolation before God, "Oh Divine Presence, as Asman Pari has so behaved toward me, and has without right or reason caused me grief, in return for it send down Your wrath upon her!" With these words, weeping, he went off to his city; he went off calling down curses upon her.

Please hear about the effect of that curse. In the seventh region of Qaf a Dev named *Rad the Deceitful, who in Hazrat Solomon's time had acted as a messenger, was said by everyone to be peerless in courage and hardihood. Hazrat Solomon's seven magic rivers were famous, for no Dev or Jinn could cross them—in fact, no one could even bear the sound of their noise and tumult. Anyway, Hazrat Solomon departed this world, and went on the final journey. Rad the Deceitful, who was the nephew of Ifrit Dev, built two forts beyond those seven rivers: one he named Black Land, and the other White Land. And he prepared a tilism, and adorned and strengthened them in every way.

He had recently heard of the killing of Ifrit Dev. . . . The moment Rad the Deceitful heard the news, he burned like fire. At once taking Hazrat Solomon's net—which after Solomon's death had fallen into his hands somehow, and which he had obtained by some means—he flew up from the fort of Black Land, seized everyone in Garden of Iram, imprisoned them, and ordered the prison guards to torment them. Abdur Rahman, who had taken leave and gone to his own house, was saved. [He went to Hamzah, and with much difficulty persuaded him to rescue the captives, promising him that the *Simurgh could help.]

Abdur Rahman seated the Amir on a throne, and said to four Jinns, "Take the Amir to King Simurgh's house; carry out this errand most carefully." The four Jinns, taking up the throne, rose into the sky like stars, to such a height that no dark land masses could be seen, only the bright water. For seven days and nights they bore the throne. On the eighth day, after about four hours had passed they put the Amir's throne down on a riverbank; constant traveling had made them very tired, and they rested a bit.

The Amir looked at the river. Its every wave reached as high as the blue river of the sky—not to speak of a man, even a bird would gasp at the sight of it. All along the riverbank such huge trees were growing that their branches reached up as high as the Tree of Paradise, and every tree shaded an area of five leagues. And atop those trees was a wooden fort, extremely strong and elegant, provided with everything necessary for luxury and enjoyment. [He discovered that it was the Simurgh's nest, from which the parent birds were absent.] When he looked at the Simurgh's chicks, he saw that although they were little naked balls of flesh, every one was larger than an elephant, every one had a body the size of a mountain, and they were screeching frantically. The Amir began to look around, to see what they'd seen that had made them recoil in fear.

As he looked, the Amir's eye fell on a serpent which was climbing steadily up that tree, with its flaming breath setting all the foliage on fire. The Amir killed the serpent with arrows, cut it into pieces, and fed it to the Simurgh chicks on the point of a spear; he saved them from that serpent. When the chicks' stomachs were filled, they settled down in their nest and went to sleep, free from the pangs of hunger.

. . . The Simurgh was very pleased with the Amir. Since the sun was falling on the Amir, he shaded him with one wing, and protected him from the intense heat of the sun. With the other wing, he began to fan him, so he would feel refreshed and restored. When the Amir felt the comfort, his eyes opened. . . . The Amir said, "I have come to you in need of help." The Simurgh said submissively, "I am your obedient follower and servant. Whatever order you give, I will carry out." The Amir said, "The Dev Rad the Deceitful has imprisoned King Shahpal and Asman Pari, together with their officers, in the fort of White Land, and has oppressed them grievously. Take me to where they are imprisoned, and show me that house." The Simurgh said, "Although the Devs of Qaf will be my enemies for this, and will harbor a grudge against me, still I'll take you there; I will certainly do this much for you. Please take with you on my back seven morsels of food, and seven sips of water; don't fail to carry out this plan. When I feel hungry, please give me one morsel of meat and one sip of water."

The Amir went hunting in the wilderness and killed seven nilgai, skinned them, and made water-skins. Filling them with sweet water, he took the water-skins and all seven nilgai with him as well, and mounted the Simurgh's back. He set out for the fort of White Land with the greatest urgency.

. . . The Simurgh, bearing the Amir, traveled to the heights of the skies. When the Amir looked carefully downward, the earth looked like the stone of a tiny ring. As far as the eye could see and the imagination could reach, there was only water to be seen. The Amir asked the Simurgh, "What is the name of this river?" He replied, "This is the first of the seven magic rivers; there are still six more that we have to cross." In short, the Simurgh, flying swiftly, traveled on; he labored hard to cross that river. When he reached the middle of the river, the Simurgh felt hungry. He said to the Amir, "Oh Amir, hurry and put a morsel of food in my mouth, for my strength is waning; hunger has overcome me." The Amir put a skinful of water and a nilgai into the Simurgh's mouth; he ate quickly. Somehow, in one day and night he crossed the first river.

On the second day, he went over the second river. The Amir, seeing darkness in that river, asked the Simurgh, "Where does this blackness come from? I can't see anything, I feel very anxious at heart!" The Simurgh replied, "This river is made of dust." When he reached the middle of the river, he asked the Amir for a morsel of food. The Amir put it in his mouth. In short, he crossed this river too. On the third and fourth days, eating morsels of food in the same way, he crossed the River of Mercury and the River of Blood as well; he never stopped even for breath. [Two more rivers were crossed.]

When the Simurgh passed over that river and flew over the seventh river, which was of fire, even though he flew very high the flames of that River of Fire—which rivaled the heavenly sphere of fire—caused the Simurgh to suffer very much. Although the Simurgh tried to control himself, his senses almost left him. At length the Simurgh, enduring all the fierce heat, reached the middle of the River of Fire and said to the Amir, "Oh Earthquake of Qaf, hurry and give me the morsel of food, for this is the time for hardihood and swift flying, the time for extreme struggle and courage."

When the Amir put the nilgai into his mouth, he pulled his hand back quickly because of the heat of the fire, and the nilgai didn't go into the Simurgh's mouth—it fell into the River of Fire and burned up, in a single moment its bones collapsed and it melted away. After flying a little further, the Simurgh asked for food. The Amir answered, "The seventh morsel that was left, I've just given you! Now where can I get food for you, what can I give you to eat?" The Simurgh said, "I didn't get that morsel, it didn't enter my stomach." And his strength began to wane. The Amir saw that it was a dire peril: in a few moments the Simurgh would fall with him into the River of Fire. At once he put the bread-bun given by Khizr into the Simurgh's mouth, and freed him from any worry about food. Thanks to the virtue of that bread-bun, the Simurgh crossed the river with his full force intact; all his helplessness was removed. [They arrived safely.]

The Amir said to the Simurgh, "Well, farewell, and may God protect you. You've done me a great favor in bringing me this far." The Simurgh, plucking out three feathers from his wing, gave them to the Amir and said, "If somehow, God forbid, you should encounter some difficulty, please put this feather on the fire. I will instantly appear and present myself; whatever you command, I will do. And after you reach the World, please put this second feather in your horse's plume, and make him beautiful. And please give the third feather to Khvajah Amar Ayyar as a gift from me; please do as I have said." With these words, the Simurgh took his leave and flew off toward his nest.

The Amir set out toward those forts. When he had gone a little way, a lion came at the Amir and attacked him, and blocked his way. The Amir, striking a blow with the Scorpion of Solomon, cut the lion in two; removing its skin, he placed it on his shoulders. And he reflected, "When I reach the World, I'll have a long coat made from this, for my use. I've heard somehow that a lion-skin coat was worn by Rustam the son of Zal, and due to its fearsome and awesome aspect he was infinitely successful in every venture."

. . . The Amir, standing by the gate, began to reflect, "I wonder whether King Shahpal, Asman Pari, etc., are in the fort of Black Land, or the fort of White Land." From the Unseen a voice came, "Oh Amir, King Shahpal and Asman Pari are imprisoned in the fort of White Land." The Amir went toward that fort. When he reached the gate, he saw that the fort had a hundred battlements, and on every battlement was a Dev—one with a tiger's head, one with a horse's head, one with a snake's head, one with a crow's head, one with a wolf's head, all fully armed and busy reciting magic spells, each of them in his own form keeping watch over the fort. And at the gate was a fire-breathing serpent, shooting out flames from his mouth in a manner beyond description. His mouth was so wide that it filled up the whole gate, as though his jaws were a noose around the neck of the gate.

The Amir was troubled: "How can I get in, by what means can I enter the fort?"—when again a voice came from the Unseen: "Hamzah, it is not for you to conquer this tilism, it is not your task to break it. A grandson of yours, who will be named Rustam the Second,[27] will conquer it; he alone will step with manly hardihood into this encounter." The Amir said to himself, "I myself am still a mere boy—God knows best when a son of mine will be born, and when a grandson will come into the world! And as for the people who are prisoners in here, how long will they have to stay in captivity like this, how will they endure the misery of confinement for their whole lives?" For the second time a voice came, "You must think only of freeing the captives, not of breaking the tilism! Breathe the Great Name on this serpent; he will go away, you will have power over him."

The Sahib-qiran breathed the Great Name over the Serpent; the serpent went away from the gate. [Hamzah went in, and found the captives.] Asman Pari was thoroughly repentant; falling at the Amir's feet, she began to say, "Oh Amir, at least now please pardon my sin—in six months I'll certainly send you to the World, I swear that this time I won't be treacherous!" The Amir gave her no answer, and paid no attention to her words. Taking everyone along, he came out of the fort. . . . The Amir, taking Shahpal, etc., went to Garden of Iram. Reaching their homeland, they were all at peace.

When six months had passed, the Amir once again had a painful dream. Waking with a start from sleep, he began to weep, he began to string the pearls of tears. Asman Pari, awakened by the sound, began to ask, "Is everything all right? Oh Amir, why do you weep, why are you so grieved?" The Amir said, "Oh Asman Pari, fear the Lord, and send me to my country! For I'm distraught with grief at the separation from my near and dear ones." Asman Pari replied, "Oh Sahib-qiran, in a year I'll send you to your country; this time I won't break my vow!" The Sahib-qiran, displeased with this speech of Asman Pari's, went to the king, and began to complain of Asman Pari and to describe her heartlessness. Shahpal, comforting the Amir, at once seated him on a throne, and ordered the Devs, "Take the Sahib-qiran to the World; do as I command you."

When the Sahib-qiran set out, Asman Pari said to a Parizad, "Go and tell the throne-bearing Devs to abandon the Amir in the Hunting-grounds of Solomon and not—absolutely *not*—to take him to the World." When that Parizad met the Amir on the way, the Amir, seeing him, guessed that he had come to dissuade the Devs, and was bringing the same message from Asman Pari as before. The Amir went back to Shahpal, and complained of all this. Asman Pari too was in attendance then. Shahpal said angrily, "Oh Asman Pari, you're never through with your devilish tricks!" Asman Pari replied, "Don't meddle in this matter! Am I to break up my well-settled home on your say-so?" The Amir, hearing this speech, stood up. Cursing Asman Pari, he set out for the wilderness; in the grief of separation he wept blood instead of tears.

Some write that the Amir divorced Asman Pari that day, and some do not accept this version, but hold this story to be false. The narrator writes that after the Amir's departure Shahpal too, because of Asman Pari's unworthy speech, became a *faqir and withdrew to a mountain; he washed his hands of the kingship.

28. Zuhrah of Egypt disappears from the roof of the fort, and comes before Asman Pari.

Asman Pari, assuming the throne, began to rule, and had the proclamation made throughout Qaf that anyone who took the Sahib-qiran to the World would be treated with great harshness—he would be severely punished for his deed. After that, she said to Khvajah Abdur Rahman, "Look and see what that woman's like whom Hamzah dotes on, and where she is. I hear that she's renowned among great and small for her beauty and radiance." Abdur Rahman, after practicing geomancy, said, "In truth, Hamzah's claim was correct. Even her maidservants are more beautiful than you; every one has a face as bright as the moon and a brow like Venus. And she is in the fort of Devdad, in that country."

Asman Pari, causing a map of that fort to be drawn, gave it to a number of Parizads and ordered them, "Go to the World, to the fort that looks like this. Snatch up Mihr Nigar from it, and bring her here; bring her before me quickly." The moment the Parizads received the order, they took the map of the fort and set off, to bring Mihr Nigar before Asman Pari.

. . . Now please hear a few sentences of the dastan of that afflicted victim of separation, utterly given over to longing, Princess Mihr Nigar, who night and day spent herself in weeping and lamentation over the Amir's absence. She ate nothing but pieces of her own torn heart, she drank nothing but her own heart's blood. She lay dishevelled and disarrayed on her canopied bed. If Zuhrah of Egypt or Tarrar-e Khuban or some other companion told her to wash her face, she washed it in bloody tears. And if someone told her to adorn herself, she strung teardrop pearls on her eyelashes.

Her companions were afraid that she would gradually go mad. Each one wanted to divert her sad heart in some way, to distract her with some game or entertainment. They all used to join in persuading her and promising her, "Princess, so much time has passed, and only a little is left! . . . If you grieve yourself to death, then what's the point? Then when the Amir comes, whom will he see, and who will see him? Come along, please take a little stroll on the roof and enjoy the fresh air. For the Lord's sake, don't cause us any more grief!"

In short, after much persuasion they took Mihr Nigar up to the roof of the palace; they began showing her the beauties of the flourishing forest greenery, and diverting her mind with casual conversation. Before very much time had passed, a spot of cloud appeared; a black cloud arose in the sky, and slowly, slowly that cloud moved over the palace and spread around it on all sides. Dazzling lightning began to flash, thunder began to rumble. Suddenly and without warning a hand took shape from within the cloud, a hand appeared from the Unseen. It picked up Zuhrah of Egypt, who was standing next to Mihr Nigar, and bore her away; in the blink of an eye it seized her and carried her off.

[She was taken before Asman Pari.] Asman Pari, seeing her beauty and radiance, was thunderstruck; seeing her face and form, she was astonished. She said, "Hamzah had right on his side. How should he not suffer in his separation from her, in her absence how should he not be wretched?" Then looking toward Zuhrah of Egypt and addressing her, she asked, "Are you Mihr Nigar, the daughter of Naushervan, are you the one whose beauty is renowned in the universe and celebrated with admiration by young and old?"

Zuhrah of Egypt, saluting her respectfully, said, "I am the daughter of Abdul Aziz, King of Egypt, and the wife of a slave of Hamzah's named Muqbil the Faithful. How could I possibly presume to be the equal of Mihr Nigar? My name is Zuhrah of Egypt. Mihr Nigar has among her maidservants four hundred daughters of the kings of Arabia, Persia, China, Central Asia, etc., each one of them more beautiful than I; they are proud to serve her, and are always ready to bear her company."

Asman Pari, seeing Zuhrah of Egypt's courtesy and refinement, was very pleased. And she asked, "Tell the truth, Zuhrah of Egypt, I adjure you by Hamzah's head—am I more beautiful, or is Mihr Nigar more beautiful?" Zuhrah of Egypt, with hands respectfully folded, said, "It's impolite to say it, but there's not as much beauty in you as in the soles of the feet of Mihr Nigar's maidservants. How can the sun be compared to a dull grain of dust!" Asman Pari, hearing Zuhrah of Egypt's words, grew angry and ordered, "Indeed! Give her into the custody of the executioners, and let them strike off her head! She's utterly mischievous and rude, how could this boor be fit for my company?" The executioners took Zuhrah of Egypt to the execution-ground.

It happened that Quraishah, carrying a dagger, was going into the court. She was seven years old at the time, but her loveliness and radiance would have caused a fourteen-year-old beauty to pale with envy, and the *Houris of Paradise, seeing her, would have blushed with shame. Seeing a crowd of people, she went toward Zuhrah of Egypt. She asked the executioner, "Who is this, and what offense has she committed, that you want to kill her? Why do you raise a knife to the neck of this innocent one?" The executioner said, "I don't know anything of who she is or what offense she's committed. But the Ruler of the Paris has given the order."

Quraishah asked Zuhrah of Egypt about her situation; Zuhrah of Egypt told her in detail. Quraishah began to tremble with anger. And taking Zuhrah of Egypt with her into the court, she said to Asman Pari, "What has she done to you, that you brought her here from the Realm of the World and gave the order to kill her? It seems clear that if Mihr Nigar had come, you would have had her killed as well! You wouldn't have spared a thought for the Sahib-qiran, or feared the wrath of the Lord! Listen: Mihr Nigar too is a part of the Sahib-qiran's honor, and is hundreds of thousands of ranks above you in honor and purity, for she is the Sahib-qiran's first wife, and superior to you in every way. What can I do? You're my mother! Otherwise, for this misdeed I'd cut you in half with a dagger, I wouldn't be afraid of anyone!"

Asman Pari, seeing Quraishah's fury, trembled. She was silent and made no reply; she didn't open her mouth at all. Finally Quraishah mounted Zuhrah of Egypt on a throne that very moment, and ordered the Devs who had brought it, "Take her back exactly where you brought her from, do just as I say!" The bearers, lifting the throne, set out.

. . . Please hear about Khvajah Amar. When he heard the noise and confusion, he went into the palace. He was informed that a hand had appeared from the sky, picked up Zuhrah of Egypt, and carried her off. Trembling with anger, he said to Mihr Nigar, "I've explained to you a hundred thousand times, and told you over and over, not to do anything without asking me! But my words had no effect. If that hand had picked you up and carried you off, what could I have said to Hamzah, and how could I have found you again? My twelve years of labor would have been wasted, and I would have been disgraced and humiliated in everyone's eyes!" With these words, he struck Mihr Nigar three blows on the back with his whip, so hard that she suffered great pain. From the force of the whiplashes, she moaned and sobbed, and began to writhe in pain on the floor like a ground-tumbler pigeon.

This misdeed of Amar's angered Mihr Nigar very much, she was extremely disgusted with Amar. She said to herself, "If I hadn't fallen in love with the Amir, I would never have been whipped by some petty son of a camel-driver, I'd never have endured such sufferings! There are slaves in my house who are higher in rank than he is, and who have a good reputation in every kind of service!" At that time she said nothing. But when half the night was over, she lowered a rope and let herself down from the fort. . . . Putting on men's attire and veiling her face, she mounted a horse and set out for the forest; she went beyond the range of Amar's sight.

Please hear about Amar. After whipping Mihr Nigar, he left the palace, and that night, out of shame, he did not go back to it. He decided that he would go in the morning and placate Mihr Nigar and obtain her forgiveness. Toward the end of the night, the Amir came to him in a dream and said, "Well, Amar, is that any way to behave—the way you've treated Mihr Nigar, and caused her so much pain? Because of this misdeed of yours she has set out into the wilderness, she's involved in thousands of difficulties!" When Amar, after this troubled dream, grew anxious and entered the palace, he was told that indeed Mihr Nigar was not in her bed. He searched here, he searched there, but he found no trace of her.

. . . Mihr Nigar, by the next day, had gone a number of days' journey away from there. She was faint with hunger—when just then she saw a melon field. Then she felt comforted. She asked the melon farmer for a cantaloupe. He brought a number of cantaloupes and placed them before her. Mihr Nigar began to eat the cantaloupes, and recovered her strength. She was so hungry that she ate them all. And that despicable bastard, who couldn't have been less than ninety years old, began saying to Mihr Nigar, "Oh sweetheart, if you'll stay with me, I'll keep you in wonderful style, I'll give you whatever you ask for!" Mihr Nigar was astonished: "What is this buffoon jabbering about?"

When she had eaten her fill of the cantaloupes and felt her hunger assuaged, she asked him, "Don't you have any family?" He replied, "I have ten sons and eleven daughters and a wife." Mihr Nigar said, "When you already have a wife, how can I stay with you, how could I be happy here?" The old bastard replied, "I'll divorce her, for your sake I'll make her live separately." Mihr Nigar said, "All right, go and divorce her; I'll sit here and wait for you." That simpleton went to divorce his wife, and Mihr Nigar, leaving the price of his cantaloupes, mounted her horse and went on.

When the old melon farmer, having divorced his wife, returned to the melon field, he found no Mihr Nigar. He began to shriek, "Oh Pari, alas Pari, where have you gone? You've left me miserable!" His wife, bringing the landlord along to the field to make her husband see reason, came and found him saying "Oh Pari, alas Pari!" and weeping. They all concluded that his mind was clouded, that the Jinns had possessed him.[28]

As Mihr Nigar traveled on from there, evening found her in a jungle. Wherever she looked, she saw beasts of prey like the tiger, the cheetah, the hyena, the wolf, the bison, the rhinoceros, the bear, the langur, and the monkey, which devour everything they find. Leaving her horse, she climbed a tree and settled herself in its branches. In the morning a tiger appeared, killed Mihr Nigar's horse, and went back where it had come from. Mihr Nigar, climbing down from the tree, tied the horse's saddle to the tree. She felt very sad at the loss of her horse, and set out from there on foot.

In the evening she came to a very large artificial pond, just beyond some fields near a village. Next to the pond she saw a splendid big tree. The princess climbed into the tree and settled herself there. In the morning, the village headman, wanting to bathe, sent his maidservant to bring water from the pond. The maidservant saw Mihr Nigar's face reflected in the pond, and thought it was the image of her own. With great conceit, she took the empty pots and went back to the house. The headman asked, "Have you brought the water?" She replied, "Hah! As beautiful and radiant as I am, am I to carry water? Am I to do chores for you like a maidservant?" The headman, beating her quite sufficiently with his shoe, said, "Go, you whore, bring water at once—and don't dawdle even a moment! For I want to bathe; I'm tired of feeling dirty, and I'll have a good bath."

Again she took the pot and went to the pond. Mihr Nigar was still there, and again she saw Mihr Nigar's reflection and was extremely excited. Without bringing water, she went back to the house, and repeated just what she had said before. . . . Mihr Nigar realized that if the girl returned to the pond once more, there would be mischief afoot, some new danger would surely come about. Climbing down from the tree, she set out, with no particular direction in mind.

When the maidservant again spoke in such a way to her master, he, having no choice, showed her a mirror and said, "Look at your face, you bitch! Is *this* what you're so proud of?" When she looked in the mirror, she saw a repulsive face. Then, after thinking hard, she replied, "Come to the pond and look at my face in the water, and see whether I'm telling the truth or not!" Grudgingly, the landlord, taking some more men along, went with her to the pond. Although she saw that her face, in the water too, was just as she had seen it in the mirror, she shamelessly kept on saying, "With such beauty and radiance I won't carry water, I absolutely won't do such a lowly task!" People said that perhaps some Pari had disturbed her mind,[29] and she ought to be given treatment.

[Amar followed Mihr Nigar's trail by means of hints and rumors.] He came upon the melon farmer in his field: hearing "Oh Pari, alas Pari!" on the farmer's lips, he knew that it could only have been she, her fate had brought her to all these places. From there he reached the jungle where the tiger had killed her horse, and Mihr Nigar had tied the saddle to a tree and passed on. Amar untied the saddle from the tree, and confided it to Zanbil. And from there he arrived in the village where the headman's crazed maidservant lived. [From there, disguised as a faqir, he reached a faqir's encampment where Mihr Nigar had taken refuge. He revealed his identity to her.] The Khvajah, with tears in his eyes, said, "Oh Princess, I'm not a faqir, I'm your slave Amar. I repent of my offense. I'm your old servant, and I've combed so many lands in search of you!" When the princess saw Amar, she flung her arms around him and began to weep.

[On the way back, they were ambushed by Hurmuz's forces, and were in serious danger.] In the space of a moment the Veiled One Dressed in Orange, with forty thousand horsemen, arrived; at God's command, he came to Amar's aid. Killing Jahandar of Kabul and Jahangir of Kabul, Zhopin's brothers, he scattered Hurmuz and Faramarz's whole party, and put all their companions to confusion. Many infidels were killed; only those who preferred flight over fighting survived, they escaped the circle of the slain. Hurmuz and Faramarz, defeated, low in spirits, mourning for Jahandar of Kabul and Jahangir of Kabul, went back to their camp; they had suffered a great shock.

The Veiled One, escorting Amar to his fort, set out for his own dwelling. Amar, entering the fort, brought Mihr Nigar into her palace, and felt free of concern about her. Again begging her forgiveness, he was pardoned for his fault; through attentive service he made her forget all her grief and distress.

29. [THE AMIR TRIES AGAIN TO LEAVE QAF, AND AGAIN IS UNWILLINGLY REUNITED WITH ASMAN PARI.]

Now, before I come back to their dastan,[30] I will tell a few sentences of the dastan of the Sahib-qiran, the World-conqueror. Leaving the fort of Garden of Iram, he wandered like a madman in the wilderness for forty days. Disgusted by those people's bad faith, he went off entirely alone. On the forty-first day, he came to his senses.

[He encountered, fought, and killed a Dev.] After killing him, the Amir entered a verandah. There he found two boys, attractive and beautiful, sitting loaded with jewelry and ornaments. The Amir asked, "Who are you?" They replied, "We're the sons of a merchant. Our father is dead. The Dev whose house this is seized us and brought us here, the tyrant involved us in this distress. Please tell us, who are you?" The Amir said, "They call me the Power of God, the Sword of God, the Power of the Beneficent One, the Earthquake of Qaf, the Younger Solomon; for courage and hardihood I am thought by everyone to be unique in this age. I have come from the World and killed all the Devs of Qaf. I have also just killed the Dev who seized you and brought you here, I've taken my revenge on that vexatious creature. Now take heart: I'll take you to the World, I'll do that much for you."

Then the boys fell at the Amir's feet, and were delighted. The Sahib-qiran asked, "What are your names?" One replied, "They call me *Khvajah Ashob," and the other said, "My name is Khvajah Bahlol." The Amir said, "If God Most High wills, when we reach the World I will make one of you my vazir, I'll give him a high position; and I'll make the other a minister." They replied, "When we reach the World alive, then we can be vazir and minister! We know that we'll never get free, we'll die in this distress." The Amir comforted them both, and reassured them very much: "If the Lord wills, we'll soon get to the Earth, we'll get out of this disaster." With these words, he took them along and left the fort.

. . . On the fifth day, on a riverbank they saw a large and splendid ship. Goods were being loaded into it. Drawing near, the Amir asked the stevedores, "Whose is this ship, and where is it going? In which city will it anchor?" They replied, "This is the ship of Said the Merchant, and it's going to the World—that's its destination, it will anchor there." The Amir said, "We three persons are also going to the World. Whatever rate you ask, we too will pay, and take passage in the ship, and thank you for your kindness." . . . Khvajah Said treated them very courteously, and said to the Amir, "The price is, that you marry my daughter." The Amir recoiled: "This cannot be—I refuse to marry! I feel a distaste for this deed." The Amir rose and went away; the merchant's speech did not please him at all. But the two boys said to the merchant, "If you arrange marriages for us as well, then we'll make the Amir agree. We take this upon ourselves." The merchant said, "I agree."

The boys said to the Amir, "Dear Power of God, why don't you marry? You will not only reach the World, and get a woman for free, but also enjoy so many kinds of pleasures!" The Amir said, "I am not willing to marry, I absolutely won't take a step along *that* road!" The boys replied, "Dear Power of God, you will have to marry! Your refusal will count for nothing; we see that it will only cause you grief." The Amir said, "Am I to marry under pressure from you, and ensnare myself in difficulties?" The boys said, "Certainly you must marry under pressure from us!" The Amir burst out laughing at this conversation, and said, "All right, if you insist like this, then I'll marry; I won't cause you any kind of disappointment."

The boys joyfully ran to the merchant, and reported the conversation, and said, "There, sir, we made him agree, we made him give us a firm promise about it! Now please marry him to your daughter, arrange for the wedding festivities." The merchant instantly married the Amir to his daughter, and married the boys to the daughters of some other person; he brought this task to a successful conclusion. In the morning, when the Amir looked, Asman Pari was sleeping beside him, and that merchant was Abdur Rahman! It was a strange affair, a novel situation. Since the Amir, in a rage, had divorced Asman Pari, Abdur Rahman had used this scheme to make the Amir marry Asman Pari a second time, and thus made her permissible to him according to religious law.

Asman Pari, falling at the Amir's feet, began beseeching and imploring him, and showing utter submissiveness. And Abdur Rahman too touched the Amir's feet, he behaved with great humility: "Whatever offenses have been committed up to today, please pardon them—please don't think any more about the past! If from now on any offense should occur, don't pardon it: please give whatever sort of punishment you wish." Asman Pari also spoke: "Oh Amir, in truth I will send you now to the World, I swear that now I won't commit any fault." Having no choice, the Amir, together with those two boys, went along with Asman Pari to Garden of Iram. Asman Pari celebrated with festivities for six months.

Then the Amir again said one day to Asman Pari, "Oh Asman Pari, now send me off to the World! For I'm very tired of staying here, I have suffered very much at the separation from my near and dear ones." Asman Pari replied, "Oh Amir, if God Most High wills, I'll send you off tomorrow morning. But please tell me if you'll come here again sometime, if you'll let us see your face again sometime." The Amir said, "Oh Queen of Qaf, just as here I long for Mihr Nigar, there I'll long for you; my heart will be eager to see you." Asman Pari was very pleased with this answer of the Amir's.

In the morning, seating herself on the royal throne, she summoned those four Devs who had always borne the Amir, and first gave them a reward. Then she sent for a large throne, and had gifts from Qaf placed on it, and said to the Amir, "In the name of God, please mount, please prepare to leave." The Amir was just about to mount the throne, when suddenly there was a turmoil and commotion in the distance, a tumult like Doomsday broke out. [Word of Shahpal's death was brought.] Asman Pari, the moment she heard this news, fell from the throne, and worked herself into a bad state. All of Garden of Iram became a house of mourning; the noise and tumult were like Doomsday. All, great and small, dressed in black; they wept and wept until they fainted.

Asman Pari, with hands submissively folded, said to the Amir, "Oh Amir, where you have stayed for seventeen years, please stay for forty days more, for my sake please endure the grief of separation from your near and dear ones for a few days more, so that I can go and bury Shahpal's body in the City of Gold, and convey him to this ancient cemetery. I will mourn him for forty days, and grieve over his death. When I come back from there, I'll send you off, I'll allow you to depart from here." The Sahib-qiran said, "All right, go; I'll stay here, I'll do as you say."

Asman Pari said, "I don't want you to become sad and go off somewhere, and cause me to grieve once again over your absence! I will leave Salasil Pari with you when I go. If you are restless, you can take the keys from her and enjoy the Forty Wonders of Solomon, so you won't feel bored or grow uneasy." With these words, she took Shahpal's body with her and set out for the City of Gold.

[Hamzah began to enter the various chambers of the Wonders of Solomon.] In short, in thirty-nine days the Amir entered thirty-nine chambers, and greatly entertained himself with seeing their marvels and wonders. On the fortieth day, he said to Salasil Pari, "Open this fortieth chamber, so I can enter it also, and enjoy its wonders." She said, "I cannot open this door, I cannot possibly undertake it. This is the Dungeon of Solomon." The Amir insisted. She replied, "I don't have the key to it." The Amir snatched the keys from her hand, opened the chamber, and went in. Salasil Pari ran to tell Asman Pari that the Amir had opened and entered the fortieth chamber too, paying no heed to her refusal.

The narrator writes that when the Amir entered the fortieth chamber, he saw that thousands of Devs, Jinns, and Parizads were imprisoned in it. . . . The Amir took pity on them all. Cutting their shackles, he freed them all from this confinement. Each one fell at the Amir's feet, then took leave and set out for his own house. Suddenly from one side the sound of a horse's hooves fell on the Amir's ear. When he turned his gaze to that side, and went in that direction, he saw that a colt, unbroken, rose-colored, was wandering there. From head to foot he looked as pretty as a picture, he was extremely handsome and had a beautiful gait. Almost four hundred rosettes could be seen on his body, looking altogether elegant and fine, and each rosette seemed to bloom like a thousand roses.

When the Amir saw the colt he was very pleased; the colt too, seeing the Amir, began neighing and prancing. Running up to the Amir, he kicked out at the Amir's foot. Although the Amir was wearing armor under his clothing, he still felt a good deal of pain. The Amir grew angry at receiving such a blow from the colt's hoof. He ran after him. The colt ran off, and entered a house. The Amir followed him, he didn't hesitate for a moment. The house was quite dark. The Amir, taking the Night-glowing Pearl in his hand, went on by its light.

He had gone a little way, when a voice fell on his ear. Someone said, "Oh my master, I am in a very oppressed condition now—come quickly and release me, rescue us from this misery!" When the Amir went forward, he saw that *Lanisah and *Arnais sat weeping and lamenting, in great distress and suffering. The Amir said, "Wait a minute—a colt kicked me, and ran away. I'll kill him and then free you." Arnais and Lanisah petitioned, "Oh Sahib-qiran, he is our son. He did not know who you were. Please pardon the fault he committed, and consider all of us your obedient servants."

The Amir, when he heard this, was surprised, and asked, "You are a Dev and your wife is a Pari—how does it happen that your child is a horse? Tell me about this in detail, inform me of the facts concerning it." They told him all the circumstances,[31] and said, "We have named him *Ashqar." Arnais, calling Ashqar, made him fall at the Amir's feet, and made the Amir pardon his fault. The Amir freed them all from bondage, he did them this kindness. And he commanded, "You sit here, I'll go and have a look at what's ahead; I'll go see some more wonders of this place, then come back."

The Amir went on ahead. He saw a house with two female Parizads in it. Their hair was bound up, and they were hanging upside down, striking their foreheads in their misery. The Amir, taking pity on them, released them too. Going on, he saw that Raihan Pari and Qamar Chahrah,[32] whom he had married, were sitting with their feet in shackles, they were sitting there extremely sorrowful and downcast. When the Amir saw them, his eyes filled with tears. They too, seeing the Amir, began to weep, they began to cry their hearts out. The Amir, taking them along, taking Arnais and Lanisah with him as well, came out of the chamber.

That night he slept with Raihan Pari and Qamar Chahrah in Asman Pari's bed, he possessed and enjoyed them both. By the power of the Lord, both became pregnant that night. The narrator writes that the son who will be born to Raihan Pari will be named Pearl the Pearl-robed and the name of Qamar Chahrah's son will be Qamarzad. The dastan of both those princes will be written in the section called *Bala Bakhtar*[33]; it will be described in its proper place. In short, in the morning the Amir said farewell to both the Parizads, and they went to their homes.

The Amir said to Arnais, "Now, can you take me to the World?" He replied, "I'm at your service." The Amir, taking the two boys, seated himself on the throne, and Arnais and Lanisah, lifting the throne to their shoulders, soared up until they looked like glowing stars in the sky. When about four hours remained in the day, they came down by a riverbank. The Amir saw a dazzling, shining building, very strange and agreeable in its design. He went inside it, and admired every door and wall, for he had never seen such charm in any house, he had never seen a building of such elegance. He discovered that this was the Mirror-palace of Hazrat Solomon. It is famous because in the evening the house by itself glows so brilliantly that if hundreds of thousands of lamps were lighted, they would not be as bright. When four hours remained in the night, the Amir, taking the boys, went to sleep. And Arnais too, taking Lanisah, went to sleep in a chamber. But Ashqar went out to enjoy the forest.

30. [The Amir is helped by Asifa Basafa to escape from Asman Pari, and leave Qaf.]

Now please hear a few sentences of the dastan of Asman Pari. When she had completed her father's fortieth-day ceremony, she gave the kings and lords of the realms of Qaf leave to depart, she gave them all rewards and robes of honor according to their rank, and she herself too set out for Garden of Iram. Salasil Pari saluted her on the way, and said, "The Earthquake of Qaf released the prisoners in the Dungeon of Solomon, he freed all the captives from confinement." Asman Pari said, "He did well. Hazrat Solomon's words have come true; what the Hazrat predicted has come to pass." Salasil Pari said, "He released Arnais and Lanisah as well, he showed so much favor to them as well." She replied, "Well, it's all right."

Salasil Pari said, "He released Raihan Pari and Qamar Chahrah as well." Asman Pari replied, "He did badly. He ought not to have freed my rivals." She asked, "Then what happened?" Salasil Pari said, "Only this much occurred while I was there; I don't know what happened afterwards." As they were speaking, another Pari came and reported, "The Sahib-qiran took Raihan Pari and Qamar Chahrah to sleep with him for the whole night in your bed. They both enjoyed themselves very much. And in the morning, he said farewell to them and mounted a throne. Lanisah and Arnais, taking him up, set out for the World."

Hearing this, Asman Pari was furious, and said, "I myself wanted to give the Sahib-qiran leave to go. But why did he have to sleep with my co-wives in my bed? Perhaps he wanted to make me jealous! Just wait and see what I do to the Sahib-qiran in revenge for this, what disasters and calamities I bring down on his head!" With these words, she mounted a throne and set out, with a fierce army, in search of the Sahib-qiran. As she went along, when she came to the Mirror-palace she was informed that the Sahib-qiran was in it. As fate would have it, she first entered the chamber where Arnais and Lanisah were sleeping. Drawing her sword, with one blow she separated both their heads from their bodies; murdering them, she vented her spleen on them.

Having slain them both, she went into the other chamber and raised that same bloodstained sword above the Amir's head. Quraishah, who was with her, snatched the sword away from her and said, "What can I do? I'm restrained by the fact that you're my mother! Otherwise I'd slash you open right now with a dagger and let your guts fall out in a heap, I'd make sure you were through with life! Do you have the gall —not just while I'm alive, but while I'm right before you!—to raise a hand against my father, and think to murder him?" Asman Pari controlled herself. Writing a note, she placed it on the Sahib-qiran's bed and went straight back to Garden of Iram; she didn't stay with the Amir for even a day.

When morning came, Ashqar returned from the forest and found his mother and father dead; he began weeping and sobbing loudly. At the sound of his weeping, the Amir's eyes opened. He saw that Arnais and Lanisah both lay headless, these innocent ones lay murdered on the ground. He lamented very much. And he consoled Ashqar. . . . Causing Arnais and Lanisah to be properly buried, he stayed there for seven days, he remained extremely downcast with grief for them both. On the eight day, he said, with tears in his eyes, "Now how will I get to the World? I'll never possibly escape from Asman Pari's clutches! It seems that I'm destined to wander here in Qaf itself, and die within its borders." Ashqar, hearing this, said to the Amir, "Why are you sorrowful? I'll take you to the World, I won't have the least fear of Asman Pari! Please mount on my back, and get ready to leave." The Amir said, "What can I do with those two boys, how can I leave them here?" He replied, "Please mount them on my back also." The Amir made two baskets and seated the two boys in them, and hung them one on each side like stirrups. And he himself mounted on Ashqar's back.

Ashqar, bearing the Amir, flew off from there. They say that in the course of the day Ashqar covered a thousand leagues; in the space of a breath he conveyed himself to his chosen destination. In short, Ashqar flew over the waters. When he reached dry land, he set foot on the earth, and planted his foot there. When he ran on, the wind was left behind him, the wind applauded the swiftness of his flight. When four hours remained in the day, he arrived in the foothills of the Mountain of Light. The Amir, taking the boys, dismounted. They saw that Hazrats Khizr and Elias were coming down from the mountain and heading in their direction. The Amir ran to kiss their feet, and petitioned, "Oh Hazrats, Asman Pari has made my life wretched! I'm sick of staying in this land!"

They said, "Oh Amir, don't be upset. This time you'll assuredly go to the World, you'll have the comfort of seeing your near and dear ones. Come along. Our revered mother, whose name is Bibi *Asifa Basafa, has sent for you to bid you farewell. She feels compassion for your plight." The Amir, with the two boys, went up the mountain. He saw a dome with rays of light, which illuminated every corner of the mountain, streaming down into it from the sky. When he went into the dome, he found a venerable old lady, whose face was full of light, sitting on a prayer-carpet, with prayer-beads in her hand, absorbed in the worship of God. He felt in his heart the greatest awe for her. The Amir respectfully saluted her.

Bibi Asifa, clasping his head to her breast, said, "Oh son, I've been longing very much to see you. It's well that you've come here, and shown me the auspicious radiance of your face. Now, through the Lord's grace, you will soon reach the World." With these words, she gave him a noose a yard and a quarter long, and commanded, "Give this noose to Amar from me, and tell him that this noose was made by my own hands, he should keep it with him carefully. It will be of great use to him, it will show him great marvels. When he wishes, this noose will bind a Dev, it will help him in every task. And when he recites the praises of the Prophet and blows the words over the noose, it will become a thousand yards long." After that she commanded, "Tonight you must be my guest." The Amir said, "To attend upon Your Grace is an honor for me."

In the morning, when the Amir had offered his prayers, Hazrat Khizr said, "Amir, this horse must be shod; otherwise he won't be able to cross the Desert of Qaf, he won't be able to pass through that bloodthirsty wasteland." With these words, he cut off Ashqar's wings and made the shoes from them, and drove in nails to hold them. The Amir asked, "Hazrat, how long can these feather-shoes last—how can they be secure?" Hazrat Khizr said, "As long as you live they won't break, and they won't come off his feet. When the horseshoe falls from his fourth foot, then you'll know that the cup of your life is full, and it's time for you to go from this world to the world of Nothingness." Giving the Amir a saddle, he said, "Put this saddle on his back. Alexander spent the tribute of the Seven Realms to have this saddle made." The Amir, girding the saddle on Ashqar, prepared to leave; he thanked Hazrat Khizr for his favor.

Now I will say a few sentences about the affairs of Asman Pari, I'll inform you about her. . . . Arriving like the wind, she surrounded the Mountain of Light; with an army of Devs she besieged the mountain. Drawing her sword, she went before Bibi Asifa Basafa and said, "Well, Bibi, have you no regard for me, that you've resolved to send my husband to his country? You don't know that my anger is quickly aroused!"

Bibi Asifa Basafa, hearing her rude words, said, "Oh you wretch, what nonsense are you jabbering? What do *you* amount to, and what can you do against me? May fire burn in your body, for you have no fear of the Lord, and you talk to me like this!" The moment Bibi Asifa Basafa said this, flames sprang out of Asman Pari's body as though her whole body were a fireplace; she began to burn and repent.

Abdur Rahman ran and said to Quraishah, "Now in a few minutes Asman Pari will burn to ashes! Go quick and plead with the Amir, fall at his feet, so he'll ask Asifa Basafa to pardon her offense, so he'll take pity on you and persuade her!" Quraishah ran and fell at the Amir's feet and said, "Oh dear father, for the Lord's sake, pardon mother her offense!" The Amir rose and interceded for her with Bibi Asifa Basafa, he adjured the Bibi to pardon her offense. Granting the Amir's request, the Bibi sprinkled the water from her religious ablutions over Asman Pari. Instantly the fire went out, she was saved from burning. Asman Pari fainted and fell to the ground. The Parizads laid her on a throne and took her away to Garden of Iram.

The Bibi kept the Amir as her guest that night as well. In the morning, she said to Hazrat Khizr, "Go and see the Amir safely across the Bloodthirsty River, do as I say at once." The Amir, saluting the Bibi, suspended the boys in the baskets; in this way he carried them with him. And he himself mounted and set off with Hazrat Khizr. After they had gone about thirty miles, a river appeared. Hazrat Khizr said, "Oh Amir, this is the Bloodthirsty River. All of you close your eyes, you must not by any means look at the turbulence and tumult of the water." The Amir and the boys closed their eyes. Hazrat Khizr went seven steps onward and commanded, "Now open your eyes." When the Amir opened his eyes, he saw that the river was flowing behind his back, and Hazrat Khizr had vanished.

The narrator writes that the Amir traveled on, stage by stage, for forty days. On the forty-first day, he reached the Green River. He saw that it was a remarkable kind of river, immeasurably wide, so that there was no sign of its other bank; it was so frightening that no one could bear to stand on its bank. The Amir went along the riverbank. On the tenth day, a fort could be seen; reaching it, they stopped for a little while. The Amir began to inspect the fort from below. That city belonged to the Cow-heads. One of them saw the Amir and recognized him, and informed his king.

That king was named Samrat Shah Cow-head. Hearing that the Earthquake of Qaf had come, he was very happy. Coming out of the fort, he touched the dust of the Amir's footsteps to his eyes. Everyone treated the Amir with extreme honor; taking him into the fort, they showed him great hospitality, and celebrated for a number of days. The Amir said to Samrat Shah, "Can you convey us across that river?" He replied, "If you'll marry my daughter, whose name is Arvanah, then why not? I'll convey you across the river, and carry out your order." The Amir refused.

But the boys said to Samrat Shah, "Prepare for the marriage, we'll make the Amir agree; we'll insist in the matter." The king prepared for the marriage according to their custom, and ordered his officers to collect the necessary items. The boys persuaded the Amir to go through with the marriage, they delighted the king with this outcome. That night, when the Amir lay down next to Arvanah, she wanted to embrace the Amir and kiss him, to give herself joy. The Amir slapped her so hard on the mouth that her front teeth were knocked out. Weeping, very sad and downcast, she went to her father and told him the whole story.

He sent for the two boys and asked, "Why has the Earthquake of Qaf done this mischief, why did he strike my daughter?" The boys said, "It's the custom of our country to knock out the bride's teeth on the first night, so that the night will be memorable. And we sons of Adam only sleep with our brides for the first time in the middle of a river, and not in any other situation." Since the king was of the Dev race, he believed it must be true. At once he ordered a boat and placed his daughter in it, and prepared all the supplies necessary for a river trip. And he said to the boys, "Inform the Amir, so that he too may enter the boat."

Both boys, delighted, went to the Amir, and recounted all these matters to him, and reported all the conversation that had taken place, and said, "Please come along and enter the boat!" The Amir, hearing the boys' words, laughed out loud, and went with them and entered the boat. When they were on the river, Arvanah wished to sleep with the Amir, she told him this longing of her heart. The Amir bound her hands and threw her in the river, he drowned the poor thing in the river of suffering. And he said to the captain, "Take us across quickly! Otherwise I won't leave one of you alive, I'll break all your heads!" The captain, out of fear, hoisted four or five sails on the mast and took them across at once, he did as the Amir had said.

The Amir, taking the boys, got out on the bank. Seating himself on the wolf-skin, the Amir pulled out the bread-bun of Khizr; he himself ate, and he fed Khvajahs Ashob and Bahlol as well and relieved them of hunger. He went on from there. The next day when they felt hungry, the Amir said, "Now I'm fed up with eating and eating that bread-bun! I can't help but crave something spicy to eat, I want to cook something flavorful!" Just as he was saying this, a deer emerged nearby. The Amir killed it and made kabobs. He himself ate some, and he fed both the boys as well.

[In the course of his wanderings the Amir encountered Zuhrah of Egypt, and killed a Dev who was holding her captive. He took her along with him.] In the evening, he was standing in the foothills planning where they should spend the night, when from one side came the sound of "Peace be upon you"; someone had spoken from the Unseen. When he looked around, he couldn't see anyone, there was no trace of the speaker to be found. There was a Tree before him; when his gaze fell upon it, he saw that all its fruits hung there in the form of human heads, and the voice was coming from that Tree; God's power was showing him its wondrous sights. The Amir, in awe at the Lord's power, returned the greeting, he answered as a Muslim should.

Again the voice came: "Oh Sahib-qiran, my name is *Vaq. Once Alexander spent the night in my shade, I showed him hospitality. Today I will show you hospitality as well; of my own free will I invite you as my guest. Please rest here the whole night, and delight yourself with the sights and scenes here." After these words, a fruit fell from the Tree into the Amir's lap. The Amir cut it open and ate some of it himself, and fed it to Zuhrah of Egypt and the two boys as well. They experienced such relish as they had never had from fruit before, and they felt thoroughly satisfied. Then they made their beds under the Tree.

Through the whole night the Tree talked to the Amir, and delighted him with its eloquence. It said, "Oh Sahib-qiran, on just the same spot where you are sitting, Alexander once made his bed, he too rested in this pleasing atmosphere. He asked me, 'When will I die, when will I take leave of this world?' I said, 'When the earth is iron and the sky is gold, then beyond all doubt you will take leave of this world.' Two or three days afterwards, he arrived in Solomon's Desert of Seven Wanderings, which is only a little way beyond this place, and in which there's not even a hint of a tree. And he was distressed by the heat of the sun, the intense heat made his condition extremely grave. His companions spread out their chain-mail as bedding, and used their shields to shade his head; in this way they gave him some relief. At that very moment Alexander's soul was seized."

The Amir asked, "Oh Tree, tell me also: when will I die?" It answered, "When no shoes remain on Ashqar's feet, then realize that you are about to take leave of the world, and your life is over; the morning of your life has turned to evening. But there's a long time yet till then." In this way the Tree talked with the Amir the whole night long. When morning came, the Amir took leave of the Tree and set off.

31. [The Amir is joyfully reunited with Mihr Nigar and all his old companions.]

[The Amir went on ahead of his companions to Amar's fort.]

He saw that the fort was smallish, but there were twelve battlements and the walls were well manned. If even a bird sought to fly over, it would be hunted down. On one side of the fort was a mountain, on the second side a river, and on the third side a forest. For many miles marigolds in full bloom could be seen, the number of which was absolutely beyond imagining. Here and there attractive fruit-bearing trees were to be seen; everyone who even looked at their fruit—much less ate it—felt refreshed and restored to life. On the fourth side, where the main gate was, was a dry wasteland. Safely out of range of the fort, Naushervan with his large army was camped; all the officers' tents stood in their proper places.

And Amar, atop the Elephant-proof Gate, was sitting under a pavilion of gold and Chinese brocade, on a jewel-adorned chair, so arrogantly that even the King of the Seven Realms was nothing compared to him; he was so imposing and overbearing that no one was bold enough to speak a word to him. To his right stood kings and companion princes, alert and attentive; to his left stood Muqbil the Faithful, with twelve hundred archers. The Amir, seeing Amar in such lavish splendor, laughed very much. He spread his wolf-skin beneath the walls of the fort and sat down, using the wall itself as a backrest; he seated himself as faqirs do. And he commanded Ashqar Devzad, in the language of the Jinns, "Go into the forest below the fort and have something to eat. Eat whatever you can find. But don't fall into anyone's hands!" Ashqar set out for the forest.

Please hear about the Ayyar and King of Ayyars. That day he went to Mihr Nigar, whom he found in a very bad state, grieving over the Amir. . . . Mihr Nigar said, "Oh Khvajah, patience too must come to an end sometime! How long can I be patient, how can I calm my heart? Today the Amir has been gone for eighteen full years!" Amar replied, "It's still a long time till evening. If by evening the Amir should come, and arrive safe and well, that wouldn't be at all beyond the Lord's power."

[When Amar came to interrogate him, the seeming "faqir" mentioned casually that he'd seen Hamzah.] Amar, hearing this, sat down. He asked, "How long has it been since you've seen Hamzah?" The Amir said, "It's been just six months since he and I were in the same place." Amar said, "The Amir must have given you some message?" The Amir said, "As we parted, he only said that when I reached Mecca I was to salute his father on his behalf and assure him that the Amir was well." Amar said, "He must have said something more?" He replied, "Yes, he also said that if I saw his companions, I was to ask how they were." Amar said, "He must have given you some other message for somebody?" The Amir said, "He told me one thing with great earnestness to be told to Mihr Nigar."

Amar asked, "What was that? In the Lord's name, tell me quickly!" The Amir replied, "I won't tell you, I won't go against his order. I'll say it in Mihr Nigar's ear, because that's what the Amir commanded me to do." Amar said, "Hazrat, what is this that you're pleased to command, what words are these that you bring to your lips? How could Mihr Nigar appear before you? She lives in retirement!" The Amir said, "If she doesn't, then I won't say it." Amar said, "Oh faqir, take five hundred tumans of gold, and tell me the Amir's message!" The Amir said, "I've told you once, and made it very clear to you, that if Mihr Nigar wants to hear it she must send for me and hear it in her ear. And if she doesn't, then what's the point of arguing? It will be her own fault if she doesn't hear the message!"

Amar, having no choice, entered the palace. [He told Mihr Nigar about the faqir.] Mihr Nigar was agitated, and said, "Khvajah, for the Lord's sake, bring that faqir here at once!" Amar went again and said to the Amir, "Oh mendicant, I'll give you a thousand gold tumans, if you'll tell me Hamzah's message, if you'll do as I say." The Amir said, "What's the point of talking nonsense? Take me before Mihr Nigar, if you and she want to hear the message. I've told you not once but a thousand times, that I won't tell it to anyone but Mihr Nigar, I'll never disobey my instructions." Amar, having no choice, said, "All right, please come along."

. . . Amar took the Amir into the palace, seated him near the pardah-screen, and said, "Oh mendicant, Mihr Nigar is sitting right behind this screen. Deliver the Amir's message." The Amir said, "Hamzah made me swear by his own head to say it into Mihr Nigar's ear. So how can I go against my oath? If she wants to hear it, then let Mihr Nigar come before me and hear her husband's message. If not, then I'll go." With these words, the Amir rose and began to leave.

Having no choice, Amar went behind the screen, wrapped Fitnah Bano, the daughter of Mihr Nigar's nurse, in a large shawl, and seated her there; instead of Mihr Nigar he brought this girl before the Amir, and said, "There, darvesh—here is Mihr Nigar! Say whatever you have to say, break your silence." The Amir said, "Show me her face, so I can see whether it's Mihr Nigar or someone else." When Amar pulled aside the shawl from Fitnah's face, when he showed her face to the Amir, the Amir said, "This is not Mihr Nigar, this is Fitnah! Hamzah told me how to recognize her as well, he told me all about her."

Then, since there was no choice, Mihr Nigar herself came before the Amir; unwillingly, she showed him her face. The Amir saw that she was in a strange condition: with a pale face, dry lips, and wet eyes, wearing dirty clothing. Tears came into the Amir's eyes, but he averted his face and suppressed them, so that his hidden secret would not be revealed, and no one would see him weep and guess it. Amar said, "There, faqir—this indeed is Mihr Nigar; now speak." The Amir said, "I still say the same thing: I'll say Hamzah's message into Mihr Nigar's ear, I'll do just as I have previously said." Amar, growing furious, sent

THE SAHIB-QIRAN RETURNS FROM QAF TO THE FORT WHERE PRINCESS MIHR NIGAR IS, AND SUDDENLY MAKES HIMSELF KNOWN, AND MIHR NIGAR AND THE AMIR FAINT, AND AFTER THAT THEY CELEBRATE WITH HAPPINESS A HUNDREDFOLD.

for Muqbil, etc.—some of the officers—and said, "All of you stand ready with swords drawn. With this faqir leaves, kill him, cut the insolent wretch into pieces!"

In the meantime, Mihr Nigar inclined her ear, she brought her head near him. The Amir said softly, "Oh my dearest, I'm Hamzah, I'm no faqir!" With these words, he removed the turban from his head. Mihr Nigar could see the dark mole and the Hashimite vein and the lock of hair of Abraham. On seeing them, Mihr Nigar shrieked, and the Amir gave a loud groan. Both fainted; from extreme passion they lost consciousness. When Amar looked attentively at the Amir's forehead, he recognized him, and knew for sure that this was Hamzah himself; and he repeatedly made the gesture of warding off evil from the Amir onto himself.

Everyone learned that the Amir had come. They sprinkled rose-water and musk-willow perfume on the faces of Mihr Nigar and the Amir, and began to fan them from all directions. Both the senseless ones gradually came to themselves. The Amir pressed Amar and Muqbil to his breast, and treated everyone with kindness. And he began to weep uncontrollably, they all began to weep and sob aloud. From one end of the palace to the other, that day was like the festival of *Id.

[Asman Pari eventually arrived and set up camp nearby; Hamzah went to visit her.] When the Amir arrived at the Pavilion of Solomon, he left everyone else at the door and himself went into the tent. Asman Pari, with Quraishah, came to the door of the pavilion to welcome the Amir, she brought all her attendants and companions with her. Laughing, she said to the Amir, "You left me behind, but finally I myself have come to you, and I've brought with me the things for Princess Mihr Nigar's wedding!" The Amir asked, "What kind of things have you brought? First tell me everything in detail, then show me every single thing." Asman Pari said, "The Pavilion of Solomon, the Drum of Solomon, the four bazaars of the Queen of Sheba, and every kind of jewel, and gifts from Qaf, and ermine and red squirrel and velvet and gold-embroidered brocade."

The Amir was very much delighted. Kissing Quraishah on the forehead, he embraced her, and he embraced Asman Pari too and kissed her many times. Asman Pari said, "You should sit on the throne." The Amir did not agree; he sat on the chair of Asif Barkhiya. All the chiefs of the Devs and Jinns and Paris who had come with Asman Pari made obeisance to the Amir. The Amir honored them all with his attention, and inquired kindly about each one; he spoke to each of them individually. And he said to Asman Pari, "That Amar Ayyar whom I always used to praise to you—he's arrived, and is very eager to meet you. You should accept whatever presents he's brought you." Asman Pari said, "Send for him, let him come in."

. . . The queen gave orders, and commanded her attendants to put the Kohl of Solomon on Amar's right eye, and let him see the effects of this kohl. It should be understood that if the Kohl of Solomon is put on the right eye, Devs become visible; and if it is put on the left eye, Parizads and Paris become visible. When the kohl was put on Amar's right eye, Amar began to see the forms of the Devs, the whole crowd of Devs came within Amar's vision. Muttering many prayers of repentance,[34] he asked the Amir, "Which of these is your honorable wife, the Queen? For the Lord's sake, tell me quickly, point her out to me!" The Amir laughed very much at these words of Amar's, and the queen too laughed and laughed until she almost fell off her throne.

The queen ordered that the Kohl be put on Amar's left eye as well, to make him able to see her own form. . . . Approaching the throne, Amar saluted the queen. And he said to the Sahib-qiran, "So this is Queen Asman Pari? Oh Sahib-qiran, for *this* face you wasted eighteen years of your life? I take refuge in God![35] For such a face I wouldn't have stayed even a day, I'd never have suffered as you did. From such a woman I wouldn't even accept a pot of water to use after the toilet! I wouldn't even eat a plum, if her hands had touched it!" The queen was mortified, her eyes filled with tears.

The Amir said to Asman Pari in the language of the Jinns, "Why are you downcast? He's a jester, this is merely a small pleasantry of his. Why, you haven't seen anything yet! You'll see what strange things he does, what kinds of tricks he shows you. When I told you about him in Qaf, didn't I say that he was such a mischief-maker that people were amazed at his tricks, they were thunderstruck by them? Do one thing: just give him something, right now—then see what happens!" Asman Pari, wiping her eyes, bestowed on Amar a robe decorated with many jewels, and gave him with it a suitable amount of cash as well.

Amar, putting on the robe, saluted her and, snapping his fingers rhythmically, sang this verse two or three times; acting like a clown, he began to clap his hands:

> "How can your beauty be described aright—oh God, oh God!
> For it's equal to the *Chapter of Light—oh God, oh God!"

And looking at the Amir, he said, "Oh Sahib-qiran, even before this I felt sure that you must have found some moon-faced one whom you were reluctant to leave in order to come back. In truth, if a man gets his hands on such a beautiful beloved, why shouldn't he forget about the World and all it contains? Before this I used to think that in all the world only Mihr Nigar was truly beautiful, that she was incomparable in her loveliness. But compared to this queen who rivals the sun, she doesn't have even as much sparkle or brightness as a grain of sand! . . . How can a daughter of Adam compare with a Parizad?"

Asman Pari was very pleased with these words of Amar's. She

laughed uncontrollably and said, "Go away, you worthless creature!" Then she gave Amar so many jewels and gifts of Qaf that he was ecstatic. Afterwards, Asman Pari sent for the nobles and officers and champions of the Amir's army, and dressed each one in a robe of honor suited to his rank, and gave each one, according to his rank, cash and gifts, the like of which even the sky could never have seen, or even imagined. . . . The Amir, after staying three days with Asman Pari, on the fourth day returned to his camp; for four days, he couldn't manage to leave Asman Pari's side.

32. [The Amir marries Mihr Nigar, and she gives birth to Qubad.]

On the day of the wedding procession, the Amir put on a royal robe of honor, and mounted Ashqar Devzad. The kings and princes of the age, flinging gold and jewels to the poor for the Amir's sake, walked along on all sides of his horse. Twelve thousand beautiful Jinn children, carrying lighted camphor-white candles in crystal candelabra and colorful jeweled lanterns, marched before the Amir's horse. All the attendants did their proper and appointed work most scrupulously and carefully. Forty thousand Jinns marched along, setting off fireworks from Qaf in the air, and gurgling and squealing to each other with happiness. Twenty thousand Parizads on flying thrones displayed their singing and dancing, and played their musical instruments, on both sides of the Amir's entourage. The Drum of Solomon was borne by winged camels, and resounded as it went along. Things which no one had ever seen or heard of before, could be seen by everybody.

And the Ayyar and King of Ayyars, the enemy-killer, Khvajah Amar bin Umayyah Zamiri, accompanied by four thousand four hundred forty-four ayyars in ornate costumes, went along overseeing the Amir's progress, he supervised everything with the greatest joy and happiness. . . . Dressing Mihr Nigar in bridal attire, Asman Pari gave away trays and boxes full of jewels in charity for her sake; in delight and amazement she offered up heaps of gold and jewels. Seeing Mihr Nigar's glory at that moment, Asman Pari herself fell in love with her, she was beside herself, enraptured. With the greatest happiness she busied herself in arranging the marriage celebration.

. . . When four hours remained in the night, Khvajah Buzurchmihr joined the Amir with Mihr Nigar in marriage according to sacred religious law. Just before dawn, the bridegroom was sent for from within the palace. When the Amir arrived at the outer door of the palace, Queen Asman Pari closed the door and said, "The door will be opened when you pay over Mihr Nigar's dowry, and fulfill this religious debt." The Amir gave Muqbil the Faithful, together with forty thousand horsemen and slaves with golden sashes, as Mihr Nigar's dowry. Queen Asman Pari opened the door. Then, closing the second door, she demanded the price of seeing Mihr Nigar's face. The Amir gave his sword, the Scorpion of Solomon, together with his horse Black Constellation. Whatever Asman Pari said to do, he did.

In short, in this way at seven doors Asman Pari took seven things from him for Mihr Nigar. He gave without arguing. Then she allowed him to set foot in the inner chamber. The Amir saw Mihr Nigar in bridal attire among a group of Pari-like women with faces bright as the moon. He saw her seated on a throne. Then, like a rose when it blooms, he could hardly contain himself. He gave thanks to the Lord that he had obtained this bride who would captivate even a Houri. After the bride had fed sugar-crystal to the groom, and the groom had looked at the bride's face in a concealed mirror,[36] the Amir took the bride in his arms and carried her to the canopied bed.

Like *Majnun, dying with love for this *Laila-like one, he pressed her breast against his own and began to suck the red fruit of her lips. After some time, as happens in such cases, the bride and groom struggled playfully together. The Amir, cajoling and seducing her, obtained from that ocean of beauty the pearl he sought, with perfect composure and satisfaction he achieved his desire. And through the power of the Lord, that pearl of the ocean of belovedness became heavy with a rare pearl.

In the morning the Amir bathed and changed his clothes; glowing and smiling, he entered the Pavilion of Solomon. All the courtiers had the honor and pride of attending upon him. He spent the whole day celebrating. That night he went to the bed of Queen Asman Pari. The following night, he took Princess Raihan Pari to lie in his arms, and took his pleasure with her as well. And the third night he slept with Saman Sima[37] Parizad, he took her to bed too. In this way the Amir enjoyed himself with one wife every night, with them all he found the pleasure of life. For forty days the kings of Qaf and the princes of the World were absorbed in celebrating with the Amir. All work was suspended except luxury and enjoyment.

One day, after the celebrations were over, the Amir rode out to enjoy the Four Arcades. In his entourage were all his heralds and attendants. They had just left the drum-house, when suddenly out of the sky came a Dev—the brother of Rad the Deceitful whom the Amir had killed. He landed on the earth; seeing that the Amir was alone, he struck a blow with his mace at the Amir's head. The Amir, dismounting from his horse, warded off the attack, caught hold of the Dev's waist, spun him around above his head three times, and hurled him to the ground with such force that he was ready to cry for his mother; all his senses were scattered. He wanted to get up and run away, but the Amir, holding down one of his feet under his own foot, took the Dev's other foot in his hand and easily ripped him in half and flung him aside like a worn-out piece of cloth, he tore him in two like a scrap of paper. The onlookers were dumbfounded, they were all amazed; many great heroes and warriors stood with their mouths hanging open.

. . . Queen Asman Pari, presenting the Amir with the gifts of Qaf she had brought especially for him, asked leave to depart. The Amir embraced her and said, "As much as I was unhappy with you before, I'm now that much pleased with you and obliged to you, I'm indebted to your kindness. Any time you send for me, if I'm not involved in some battle I'll set out at once to go to you, I won't delay at all. And this is your house, after all—any time you wish, come and adorn it with your presence, and enjoy the pleasure of my company." And embracing Quraishah, he kissed her several times on the forehead, and gave her leave to depart; and he presented her with whatever gifts were suitable for her. Raihan Pari and Saman Sima Pari too took leave of the Amir, and went with the queen.

The Sahib-qiran gave the whole region of the West to the King of the Western Dominion, and made him ruler of that realm. But he, appointing a viceroy to govern the land, accompanied the Amir. The next day the Amir sent the vanguard on toward Mecca the Great. And turning over authority to his son named *Amr bin Hamzah—who was born from the womb of Princess Nahid Maryam, daughter of Shah Faredun of Greece—he became absorbed in luxury and enjoyment with Mihr Nigar. He himself abandoned all the work of governing, and gave the entire authority to his son.

[One day Adi, in a state of drunkenness, quarreled with Landhaur.]

Amr bin Hamzah, seeing this situation, threatened Adi, "Why are you being so rowdy, why are you acting so superior?" Adi was drunk, after all; he replied impulsively, "What business is it of yours? It's between Landhaur and me! Keep quiet, and don't meddle in the matter." The *Amir's son rose, and dealt Adi a buffet, so that Adi fell to the ground. . . . Since this misdeed of the Amir's son seemed very wrong to all the chiefs and champions, a remarkable tumult and commotion arose in the gathering. The Amir, feeling anxious, came outside; seeing the situation, he was very much disturbed. Finding out the long and the short of it, he commanded his son, "Beware—don't ever do such a misdeed to anyone again! Landhaur and Adi would have worked it out with each other; what right did you have to interfere between them?"

The Amir's son grew furious and replied, "If Adi ever treats me so disrespectfully again, I'll cut off his ears and throw him out of the city!" The Amir, displeased, said, "Such impertinence is not right; I don't like this kind of talk. If you say such things again, I'll pick you up and hurl you to the ground, so your brain will ooze out your ears, and you'll forget all your boasting!" The Amir's son was in the flower of his youth. He resented his father's counsel. He replied impulsively, "Who can strike me—who is strong enough, who has the power?"

The Amir, angered, seized Amr's hand and led him out to the field of combat. Both father and son mounted their horses and prepared to fight. The beholders began to watch this combat of father and son, to see the skill of both their arms. The Amir summoned Amr to attack first. But however much Amr whipped his horse, the horse didn't take a step forward. The Amir said, "Oh you little fool, learn manners from a simple beast!" Amr leaped down from his horse. The Amir too got down, and prepared to wrestle. Amr, seizing the Amir's belt, used all the strength at his command, but he couldn't dislodge the Amir's wrestling-stance. Feeling helpless, he released him, and separated himself from him.

But the Amir, grasping Amr's waist, lifted him above his head—then put him gently down on the ground, and kissed his forehead. The Amir's son too bowed his head at his father's feet, and apologized very much for his insolence. The Amir, embracing him, said, "Oh life of your father, one can only rule by means of champions; it's through people of this kind that every sort of thing gets done. In all circumstances, it's necessary to pay them attention and respect their honor; in every way they must be shown courtesy and regard." The Amir's son, feeling abashed, returned to the gathering and began to watch the dance; he was very much ashamed at heart over what had occurred.

The reporters of news write that in the ninth month sons were born from the wombs of Mihr Nigar and Amr bin Hamzah's wife. The Amir, hearing this good news, was very happy. While he named his grandson *Sad, he didn't name his own son himself. He commanded Amar Ayyar, "Go and inform Naushervan, and ask him to please name the child himself." Amar, after some days, reached Ctesiphon, and after making obeisance to Naushervan he submitted, "Congratulations—you have a grandson! The Amir begs that Your Majesty will yourself name the boy, that you must certainly name him out of regard for the Amir."

Naushervan was very happy at this good news; bestowing on Amar a resplendent robe of honor, he ordered a celebration on the fortieth day after the birth, and arranged the requisites for joyous festivities. And he named the boy *Qubad. . . . When Qubad and Sad were both four years old, the Amir entrusted both boys to Amar, to be taught courtesy and refinement. When they reached the age of five years, the beholders who saw them said that such beautiful, radiant, well-bred boys had never been seen or heard of before, the eye of the sky could never have seen their like. Even at that age, the signs of valor were manifest in their faces, the marks of hardihood were visible in their forms. The Amir, morning and evening, recited holy verses and blew them over the boys; out of love, he constantly made the gesture of taking their misfortunes onto himself.

33. [The Amir suffers three terrible bereavements.]

After Queen Asman Pari had gone, the Amir asked his companions in court, "I wonder where the infidels have gone?" Amar submitted, "I've heard that they've gone to Kashmir, and taken refuge with the ruler of Kashmir, who is named Jafar; he has aided the infidels." Amr bin Hamzah spoke up: "If I am commanded, I'll go to Kashmir and wipe them out—through the grace of God, I won't leave even one infidel alive!" The Amir said, "That's fine." The Amir's son, taking with him Amar, Adi, *Farhad bin Landhaur, Istaftanosh, etc.—seven champions—and an army, set out for Kashmir.

After a time, the Amir's son entered Kashmir. The infidels, in terror, shut themselves up in their fort. The Amir's son surrounded the fort from all four sides; with his army, he besieged it heavily. It happened that one day a wild ass came out of the forest into the army of Islam, and wounded many with its teeth and hooves. It kicked some, and attacked others with its teeth. The Amir's son heard about this. He mounted, and followed the wild ass. [He pursued it up into the mountains.] On the way, he saw a city; its people and atmosphere pleased him very much. He asked people the name of the city. They said, "It's called Farkhar, it's said to be the envy of the eight gardens of Paradise. Zhopin's sister, who is named Gulchahrah, lives here; all the people recognize her as their king." Suddenly she herself looked down from her balcony at the Amir's son. The moment she saw him she fell in love with him, she was beside herself with love. She sent a eunuch to summon that young man, to bring him to her in any way possible.

. . . Gulchahrah treated the Amir's son most hospitably, and asked, "What is your name, and what country do you come from? On what business have you come here?" The Amir's son replied, "Amr bin Hamzah is my name. My father's renown is on the lips of great and small." She said, "For a long time I've been pining to meet you, I've been weeping and wailing and lamenting night and day, I've endured thousands of kinds of grief and sorrow in my passionate desire to see you! And today the Lord has fulfilled my wish without my lifting a finger, and satisfied my longing."

With these words, she ordered the meal. She had the dining cloth spread; she ate, and she fed the Amir's son as well. Afterwards, flagons of rosy wine began to circulate. The Amir's son grew inebriated, and she herself too became very intoxicated. She asked for lovemaking. The Amir's son said, "A sister of yours is married to me. I won't get involved with you, I will never by any means do a deed so contrary to religious law." She insisted. Having no choice, the Amir's son said, "All right. My champions are besieging the fort of Kashmir. I'll send for them and ask them, and see what their opinion is about this. If they agree to it, I'll go to bed with you, I'll take my pleasure with you." That wretched Gulchahrah at once sent a messenger, summoned the champions, and informed them of this matter.

. . . The next day Adi, etc., presented themselves in the service of the Amir's son. Gulchahrah behaved toward them with respect and dignity; they all enjoyed her company very much. She entertained them elegantly, and revealed to them her love for the Amir's son: she made known to them the wish of her heart. Adi said to the Amir's son, "Why do you make this poor thing die a living death? Do people torment their lovers like this, do they harass them beyond endurance?" The Amir's son, hearing these words, laughed and replied, "Oh Adi, when something is simply not to be done, how should I do it? Should I set foot on a path where I will lose my way?" Adi said, "Do it or don't do it, it's up to you. I only took pity on her lamentations, I was sorry to see her so restless, so I spoke to you as I did."

In short, that night, when the Amir's son had become intoxicated with wine and passed out, Gulchahrah, extremely intoxicated, wrapped herself around him, from her extreme passion she lost control of herself and held him tight. The Amir's son said, "Oh you shameless creature, what impudence is this, what immodest thoughts do you cherish in your heart? I won't commit such a dirty deed!" And, a bit playfully, he gave her a slap as well.

Gulchahrah was disappointed in her hope for enjoyment. She said to herself, "He's in love with my sister—and I burn in the fire of love for him, night and day I wring my hands with grief and longing! It's better if, as someone put it, 'Neither yours nor mine—here, go throw it in the fire!' " Suddenly and forcefully she drew her sword and struck one blow at his neck. Amr bin Hamzah's head was separated from his body.

[After the murder was discovered, Adi and the others interrogated her.] Binding that whore's arms, they asked her, "Why did you kill the Amir's son?" She replied, "I was in the grip of love—I couldn't bear it, I was helpless. I committed this crime. Now punish me however you wish, murder me too in revenge for him!" The companions said to each other, "A man must not lift his hand against a woman—if we're to kill her, then how can we do it? We're sorely perplexed in this matter, we're very much troubled and concerned."

The Amir suddenly dreamed that he saw Amr writhing in a pool of blood. Fearful, he awoke with a start, and repeated his dream to Amar. Amar left that very instant for Kashmir. Eventually he arrived in Kashmir. He learned that the Amir's son was in the city of Farkhar, in Zhopin's house with his sister. At once he went there, traveling like the wind, and arrived at that wretch's palace. Adi, etc., fell at his feet and told him the whole state of affairs. Amar, flinging dust on his head and beating his breast, left that place and came to the Amir, and said, "It seems that the Prince lies wounded in Farkhar, in Zhopin's house, and has sent for you very urgently. This servant has come to take you there." The Amir at once mounted Ashqar Devzad and prepared to go there.

. . . When they entered the city, his companions saw the Amir, and began to weep and wail. The Amir asked, "Is everything all right? Why this weeping and wailing?" They said, "Your son has been killed at the hands of Zhopin's sister." The Amir commanded, "Take her to Amr's mother, take this whore to her. And tell her, 'She has killed your son.' " Amar took Gulchahrah before the mother of the Amir's son and said, "This is the murderer of your beloved son. The moment she heard these words, she said, "Alas, my son!" and died; the moment the news reached her her life departed.

The Amir was doubly bereaved and grief-stricken. For forty days he mourned for his son. He sent his son's body, together with Gulchahrah, to Sadan in Fort Kaus. Sadan killed his sister Gulchahrah with his own hands, he took revenge in this way for Amr bin Hamzah's blood.

The Amir commanded, "This ill-omened place[38] should be laid waste, for here my son was killed; I will surely destroy it, I'll never by any means let this house stand." With these words, he smashed in the doors with his mace. Entering the fort, he began to massacre everyone. Hurmuz escaped through a small secret gate, and set out for Ctesiphon. Most of Hurmuz's companions were slain by the Amir, and some became Muslims. Finally the Amir turned his sword on the Kashmiris, he drew his sword to slaughter them all. Their ruler sought mercy from the Amir. The Amir granted him peace; out of mercy he granted him his life; and then the Amir set out for Fort Kaus.

. . . It happened that an ayyar whose name was Blanket-robed said to Naushervan, "If you command, I'll cut off the heads of all the Arab chiefs, one by one, and bring them to you—I'll pack them all off to the land of Nothingness!" Naushervan said, "What could be better?" That very night at midnight, that ayyar reached the Arab camp and approached the tent of Prince Qubad. He saw that two ayyars named Victory and Triumph were standing guard beside Qubad's tent. Blanket, staying out of their sight, pulled up a tent-peg and went into the tent. Finding Qubad sound asleep, he cut off his head with a dagger and left the tent.

Amar's ayyars, who were on guard, captured him, they didn't let him escape. Seeing Qubad's head in his hand, they began to weep and lament. The Arab officers, coming out of their own tents, entered Qubad's tent; they all came and gathered there. They saw that Qubad was lying headless on his bed. In the camp of Islam it was all at once as though Doomsday had come. On all sides was tumult and lamentation and mourning. All, great and small, were extremely grieved. When Mihr Nigar heard, she was in such a dreadful state, her heart was so charred in the fire of grief, that very few can have felt such grief over their sons. In the morning, Blanket was torn to pieces. When Nausher-van heard this bad news, he too mourned for his grandson, he grieved beyond measure. For forty days there was mourning for Qubad in both camps, there was great grief and sorrow. After the fortieth-day ceremony, both armies arrayed their ranks, and a great battle took place.

. . . Meanwhile, Zhopin realized, "The coast is clear—except for Mihr Nigar, there's nobody in the camp. Come on, I'll carry off Mihr Nigar, I'll use this chance to get her in my power!" With this plan in mind, he slipped into the camp of Islam. Killing some guards who were at the gate of the camp, he reached Mihr Nigar's quarters, he entered her private apartments. Mihr Nigar shot so many arrows into his malicious breast, that his breast became full of holes like a wasps' nest. Zhopin realized that she would not accept him. Feeling irritated and slighted, he struck a blow with his sword at Mihr Nigar's beautiful body.

He was about to strike a second blow—when the Amir was suddenly upon him. Zhopin had no chance to flee; having no choice, he struck a blow at the Amir too. The Amir parried his attack and struck him, as he tried to flee, with a blow that cleaved through his skull, his neckbone, and his backbone, ending at his pelvic bones. He fell on the spot, all in a heap. The Amir, approaching Mihr Nigar, saw that she lay at death's door. At once he sent Amar to bring Khvajah Buzurchmihr and have him see to Mihr Nigar. Amar went to bring the Khvajah. Meanwhile, Mihr Nigar submitted her life to God, she went to live among the Houris in Paradise. The Amir, with a loud groan, fainted.

After a time, when the Amir regained consciousness, he was like a madman: sometimes he laughed, sometimes he wept, he was almost dying of sorrow. . . . The Amir had one coffin made for Mihr Nigar, a second for Prince Qubad, and a third for Amr, and set out for Mecca; he accompanied the coffins, along with a large number of mourners, both relatives and strangers. Eventually he arrived near Mecca. The Amir had three graves dug in a pleasant meadow, and buried the three coffins, and stayed there for the night. He did not feel like going into the city, so he camped in the forest.

The narrator writes that the twenty-first day passed. It was the night of the twenty-second day when the Amir saw Hazrat Abraham in a dream, and drank a glass of wine from his hands. The Hazrat gave the Amir this counsel: "Oh son, to get yourself in such a bad condition over one woman is very far from wisdom. If you live, you'll get thousands like her, better and higher-ranking women than Mihr Nigar will enter your service." When the Amir's eyes opened, he began asking Amar bin Umayyah, "Where am I, and what has happened to me? Tell me truly, in what condition have I been?" Amar told him the whole state of affairs, he reported everything that had befallen him. The Amir described to them all what he had seen in the dream. His comrades said, "Oh Hazrat, you are his son—if he didn't come to console you, then who would? Is it possible that anyone wouldn't feel his child's grief?"

The Amir said, "Come what may, I have made a vow to Mihr Nigar. In order to fulfill it, I will certainly live here as the devoted attendant at her tomb, I'll stay here at her tomb until I die. You people go off to your homes; for the Lord's sake, don't torment me." Although Amar reasoned with him a great deal, the Amir paid no attention to his persuasions. Sending them all away, he seated his grandson, Sad bin Amr, on the throne, and sent him off to Egypt.[39] Amar said, "Oh Amir, don't make me leave you, don't make me suffer the grief of parting from you!" The Amir commanded, "It's quite sufficient for Muqbil to stay with me, I don't need anyone else. There's no necessity for you to stay."

When they had all left, the Amir had his head shaved, and assumed the dress of a faqir. Wearing an ascetic's loose robe, night and day he began to sweep out and care for Mihr Nigar's tomb. He began to live right there. Whenever sleep overpowered him, he lay down at the foot of Mihr Nigar's tomb.

34. [The Amir marries new wives, and discovers a son.]

[Hamzah's enemies took advantage of his vulnerability by kidnapping and torturing him; he finally escaped from their clutches, and took his revenge. After that, he left Mihr Nigar's tomb and resumed his former life. Then the Veiled One Dressed in Orange came to his camp one day, and revealed herself as Naranj Pari, who had performed her protective mission out of love for him. Hamzah was overjoyed, and eagerly married her.

Then one day, as the long war continued, a strange champion appeared before Naushervan's army, and challenged them to battle; he was known as the Prince of Rum, and no one could stand against him.]

Naushervan's whole army lost heart, the fighters' spirits collapsed in fear. For a time, the prince continued to challenge them to battle, but no one came forth from the infidel army to confront him, no one dared to encounter him. Having no choice, he turned his horse's head toward the army of Islam and challenged them; he called out in a loud voice, "Oh Arabs, whoever among you has a heart for battle, let him come before me, let him show me his prowess and martial skills!"

Farhad, obtaining the Amir's permission, urged his elephant forward. . . . They both began to fight, mace against mace. The prince saw that Farhad too was very skilled in mace-fighting. Leaping down from his horse, he picked up Farhad together with his elephant. Giving a battle-cry, he hurled them both to the ground and said, "Now go, and send someone else at once, for there's no strength left in you, you have no further power to fight."

The narrator writes that if Farhad had not hastily leaped down from the elephant, his bones too would have been smashed like those of the elephant, his skull would have burst from the impact. But even as it was, Farhad was somewhat wounded, he suffered much pain from the shock. From both armies came the sound of admiration and praise. The Amir said, "We have heard it said of Rustam, that he used to lift up his opponent along with his elephant and throw them to the ground. But I've seen this prince with my own eyes!" People replied, " 'How can hearing be like seeing?' That is a mere tale and story, this happened right before our eyes!" Farhad petitioned the Amir, "The prince told me to go and send someone else to encounter him."

The Amir made a sign to King Landhaur, he commanded him to fight. Landhaur, seizing Shabrang's reins, went before the Prince of Rum. The prince, spurring his horse, rode over until he was stirrup-to-stirrup with Landhaur. Seizing Landhaur by the waist, he picked him up from the horse's back, lifted him a number of hands-breadths above his head, hurled him to the ground, and said, "Go, send someone else from your army."

Sad bin Amr bin Hamzah, spurring his horse, went to encounter the prince. Both seized each other's belts and began to exert their strength. Both exerted so much strength that their horses gradually sank into the ground up to their knees; they were trapped like this a number of times. The Prince of Rum, releasing Sad, said, "Go, and send Hamzah. I'll see how strong he is! I hear that he's a man of valor and hardihood." Sad returned and gave his message to the Amir, he informed the Amir of his intention and his claim. Landhaur said to the Amir, "Oh Sahib-qiran, this prince seems to me to be of your blood. The Amir said, "If he were of my blood, he wouldn't fight with my comrades!" Landhaur said, "Amr too fought with you. He must want to test himself."

Finally, the Amir galloped Ashqar into the field like a master rider. Bakhtak said to Naushervan, "This prince, without any doubt or question, is of Hamzah's blood. The Amir's sons normally act just like this. Please enjoy the show—a battle between father and son, a peerless combat, like the combat of Rustam and Suhrab!" Naushervan replied, "It wouldn't be so surprising." In short, the Amir brought his horse over within reach of the prince's horse, he came to encounter him. The prince put his hand to the Amir's waist; the Amir too gripped the prince's leather belt. Father and son began to exert their strength.

Finally the Amir, giving a battle-cry, picked up the prince and lifted him off his horse. He was about to hurl him to the ground, when a voice came from the Unseen, an angel told him the good news, "Be warned, Hamzah, don't hurl him down with force! He is your son!" The Amir, hearing the angel from the Unseen, gently put him down on the ground and asked, "What is your name?" He replied, "Alam Sher of Rum." With these words, he fell at the Amir's feet. The Amir embraced him and kissed his mouth repeatedly. Sounding the celebration-drums, they entered the camp. The Amir, having found him, felt very much at peace. He named the prince *Rustam Pil-tan, the Lion who Overthrows Ranks.

The Amir said, "You've behaved very disrespectfully! You overthrew my comrades' battle-lines, and stood against even me." The prince petitioned, "My brother Amr also did such mischief, and I've committed the same offense." The Amir introduced him to all his comrades, and obtained their pardon for the prince. Since he was the Amir's beloved son, everyone treated him most affectionately, and the celebrations went on for seven days and nights.

. . . That night, an ayyar came and told Naushervan, "King Tasavvuran has sent his daughter, who has no equal anywhere for beauty and radiance, for you to marry. Please send for her to come to you, please give her leave to arrive here." Naushervan, hearing this good news, was very happy, and sent Khvajah Buzurchmihr to bring her. The Khvajah brought her and caused her to enter the ladies' apartments. Naushervan was very much delighted at her arrival.

The narrator writes that that princess had previously seen a picture of Hamzah, and longed with her whole heart and soul to see him. After some days, one night she found herself at liberty. Putting on a thief's dress, she entered Hamzah's camp; uprooting a tent-peg from the back of Hamzah's tent, she entered the tent. She saw that the Amir was deep in slumber. When she placed a knockout drug in the Amir's nostrils, the Amir sneezed and fell unconscious. Tying the Amir into a bundle, she went out the way she had come in; she took him into a trench, she brought him away without letting anyone see her. Giving the Amir an antidote to the knockout drug, she told him how she had come to love him; she revealed the hidden secret of her heart.

The Amir asked, "Who are you?" She said, "My name is Zar Angez, daughter of King Tasavvuran; in beauty and radiance, who is my equal? And now I'm the wife of Naushervan." The Amir said, "He is my father-in-law. Furthermore, you already have a husband. I'll never commit such a sin; such a deed is forbidden in our religion." However much she said provocative things to him, the Amir paid her no attention at all, he absolutely didn't pay her any heed. When she saw that the Amir would not be persuaded, she threatened him, and told him, "If you don't accept me, then, Hamzah, I'll kill you." The Amir said, "If that fate is to befall me, then how can I prevent it? But your doing this evil deed will achieve no purpose." During this argument, morning came. She left the Amir imprisoned in that place, and went to her own tent.

In the morning, tumult broke out in the Amir's camp: the Amir had disappeared from his tent! They all began to search for him everywhere. Gradually the news reached the infidels' camp also, and they too were astonished. Kayumars began to put on airs before Naushervan: "Hamzah has run off to save his life. From fear of my poisoned spear, he's fled and hidden himself, to escape death!" With these words, he had the battle-drum sounded, and arrayed his army's ranks in the field. Then the combat between the two armies began again. The army of Islam, appointing Rustam Pil-tan to command in the Amir's place, formed their ranks. [Kayumars succeeded in dominating the field.] Meanwhile evening came. In both armies the retiring-drums sounded; all the soldiers went to their proper camps.

That night, that whore again went to the Amir, and informed him, "Today such-and-such three champions from your army were wounded at Kayumars' hands. I felt very sad, to see such champions in such a state." The Amir said, "Alas, that at such a time you keep me captive! Release me, so I can make Kayumars taste the fruits of spear fighting;

with my well-tempered sword I'll make him taste the sherbet of death!" That whore replied, "Until I get what I want, I'll never release you—I'll never give up pursuing my purpose!" The Amir said, "Release me or don't release me—I'll never do such a vile deed, I'll never do this deed forbidden by religious law." In short, that night too came to its end in discussion like this. That madwoman, leaving the Amir there as she had before, went to her own tent.

Kayumars again entered the field and challenged them, he raised a powerful battle-cry, "Whoever has Death playing dice with his head, let him come before me, let him spur his horse into the field of battle!" Sad of Yemen, obtaining Prince Rustam's permission, went and confronted Kayumars. Kayumars hurled a spear at him, he made an attack on him. Sad parried it. After four or five spear exchanges, Kayumars, catching Sad off his guard, wounded him too. Meanwhile, evening came; both armies returned from the battlefield.

That night, that adulteress again came to attend upon the Amir, and began to avow her passion with a thousand tears and laments; she placed her head on his feet. It happened that Amar bin Umayyah, searching for the Amir, passed by that way. Hearing the words of that deceiver, he went and confronted her. The moment she saw Amar's face, she fled. Amar asked the Amir, "Who was that? If you give the command, I'll kill him, I'll spill his brains out of his head!" The Amir commanded, "Let her go, don't kill her. She's a woman; let it pass. The bitch is a new wife of Naushervan's, he feels great affection for her."

Amar wanted to unfasten the Amir's bonds. The Amir himself exerted his strength: all the bonds snapped in an instant. Amar said, "Why didn't you exert your strength and free yourself from captivity two days ago, why didn't you break your bonds before?" The Amir said, "All actions depend upon their proper time. And it was the Lord's will that a worthless woman should bind me." With these words, he came out of the trench, and gave thanks to the Lord. Sending for his weapons and Ashqar, he mounted and went from there straight to the battlefield.

. . . That same day Naushervan had the battle-drum sounded. Taking the army of Gilan and Mazindaran, he arrayed his ranks in the field. The Amir too arranged his army to confront him. As yet no one from either army had come onto the field, when a cloud of dust arose from the forest. Both armies began looking to see who was coming to help whom, whose friend had brought such a numerous army to whose assistance.

The moment the dust cleared, a horseman, spear in hand, could be seen, whose powerful appearance impressed everyone. At a sedate and easy pace, he entered the field. Looking over the armies of both sides, he challenged the army of Islam to battle; they were all astonished at his courage and hardihood. Sher-mar of Shirvan, obtaining the Amir's permission, came and fought with him. The horseman from the forest, in the very first attack, struck him with his spear and knocked him down from his horse; with his great strength, he wounded him. The horseman said, "You're not worth killing. Go, and send someone else!" Taz Turk came and confronted him. Putting a hand to Taz Turk's waist, he threw him to the ground and said, "Go, send another." Kaus of Shirvan went and confronted him. The same thing happened to Kaus, and meanwhile evening came, the fighting was ended. Kaus turned back to his tent, and the horseman turned back toward the forest.

The Amir, taking Amar with him, set out after the horseman to find out who he was. [They followed the horseman home and found that she was a princess called *Geli Savar.] The princess, going into the pavilion, took off her weapons and men's clothing, and put on women's clothing. Welcoming the Amir, she brought him into the pavilion, seated him on a cushion, and showed him great respect and honor. Having joined the Amir in an elegant dinner, she summoned the silver-faced cupbearers. First filling a crystalline cup with rose-colored wine, she gave it with her own hands to the Amir. She made him intoxicated with the wine; afterwards, she herself drank. When they had drunk three or four cups, the princess grew happy and elevated. Lifting aside the veil from her face, she came and sat in the Amir's lap, she abandoned all shame and modesty.

When the Amir looked into the eyes of that moon-faced one, the arrows of her eyelashes, shot by the bows of her eyebrows, buried themselves in the Amir's heart and made deep wounds there. Eagerly he begged her to marry him, he clearly proposed a marriage between them. After all, the feeling was already there in her heart: she agreed. Khvajah Amar immediately read the marriage ceremony, he married them most willingly. Both, in a canopied bed, paid due heed to the claims of pleasure; the Amir had great luxury and enjoyment with her.

. . . One night the Amir was sleeping with Geli Savar in the garden, when Zar Angez, the wife of Naushervan, who had kept the Amir prisoner for three days in a trench, put on thief's clothing, took a bow and arrow in her hand, and entered the garden. There she saw the situation: the Amir was sleeping, with Geli Savar in his arms. It was as though a snake crawled over her heart. She said to herself, "Hamzah refused me, and he's married Geli Savar. He has caused me so much pain! I'll kill them both at once, I won't by any means spare them!" She was about to make her attack. Geli Savar's eyes opened; seeing her, Geli Savar arose from the canopied bed.

Zar Angez leaped down from the edge of the roof. Geli Savar too came down from the roof. Zar Angez mounted her horse and hastily fled, out of fear. Geli Savar mounted and followed her. When they had both left the garden and entered an open field, that whore turned and confronted Geli Savar, and said, "I fled from the garden for fear of Hamzah. Why should I fear you, what threat or danger could I find from you?" With these words, she shot an arrow at Geli Savar. Geli Savar cut the arrow in half with her sword. Spurring her horse, she galloped like lightning right up to Zar Angez, until they were stirrup to stirrup. She struck such a sword-blow at her, that Zar Angez was cut in half and fell to the ground; after that one blow she never took another breath, she left this world for a visit to the world of Nothingness.

The Amir was watching the show from a distance. When Geli Savar killed Zar Angez, the Amir called out, "Oh Geli Savar, what have you done? Naushervan will think that I killed her, and will be ashamed before me for no reason; he'll be very much embarrassed by this!" Geli Savar replied, "What was to happen has happened, what can be done about it now?" The Amir, taking Geli Savar, went back into the garden, and rested.

In the morning, word was brought to Naushervan that Zar Angez was lying dead in a field, she was lying without shroud or tomb in the wilderness. He sent ayyars to take up the body and bring it to him. And expressing great regret, he said, "It seems that this bitch had gone to Hamzah, and he killed her." With these words, he said to his slaves, "I've reigned for a long time. Now I want to wander around from country to country, seeing the sights." They replied, "We're your servants, we'll obey you in every way. Whatever you order, we will carry out, we'll do just as you command." Naushervan, at midnight, packed many goods and jewels, and much cash, into saddlebags, took a thousand slaves with him, left the city, and set out on the road for Khotan. If anyone asked him, he said he was a merchant; he hid his true identity from everyone.

Meanwhile, in the morning a tumult arose in the camp—Naushervan had disappeared! Some said that the Amir had killed him, others maintained that Amar had carried him off. But Buzurchmihr said, "If

Hamzah had killed him, or Amar had carried him off, why would a thousand horses be missing? Naushervan has been shamed by this misdeed of Zar Angez's, and has gone off somewhere." Crown Prince Hurmuz sent people off in all directions to search for him. At the counsel of his friends and relations and the nobles of the court, Hurmuz seated himself on the throne. He began to conduct the affairs of the kingdom, he began to do everything in place of Naushervan.

35. Dastan of the birth of Prince Badi uz-Zaman from the womb of Geli Savar daughter of Ganjal, and the prince's being shut up in a box and floated down the river, and his rescue and upbringing by Quraishah daughter of Asman Pari, at Hazrat Khizr's order.

[The Amir rescued Naushervan from his wanderings, which ended unhappily in the Fire-Temple of Nimrod, and restored him to his throne.]

The narrator writes that when the Amir had set out for Mount Alburz, he had confided Geli Savar, who was pregnant, to Ganjal, so that she was a trust he had left with him. Ganjal, that ingrate, ordered the maidservants and midwives . . . to kill the baby at once, to slay him immediately. The midwife, seeing his sweet sweet little face, took pity on him, she didn't at all approve of Ganjal's words. She said to King Ganjal, "If you give me the order, I'll bury him alive; if you command, that's what I'll do." He replied, "That's a very good idea." The midwife, shutting the baby up in a box, floated him off down the river, she confided the child to God's care.

It happened that Asman Pari and Quraishah had come that day for an excursion on the river. The box, drifting along, floated over to the bank on which they stood, and lodged there. When they took the box out of the water and opened it, they saw a baby boy who would rouse the sun to envy, who would put the moon to shame, sucking his thumb. Love for the baby sprang up in their hearts. When they saw a black mark shining on his forehead, Asman Pari said, "This mark is the sign of Abraham, the Friend of God; this child is high in God's favor." Meanwhile, Hazrat Khizr appeared and said to Asman Pari, "This boy is Hamzah's son. Bring him up very carefully. When he grows up, send him to Hamzah. And name him *Badi uz-Zaman." With these words, Hazrat Khizr disappeared.

Quraishah lifted Badi uz-Zaman into her lap and took him to Qaf. Nursing him with the milk of Paris, she began to bring him up with great care and attention. When he reached the age of seven years, Quraishah, making him a master of the military arts, gave him weapons; she taught him all the skills of soldiery. And when she had to go somewhere on some military expedition, she took him with her as well, and had him witness the battle. When he entered his eleventh year, he asked Quraishah, "What are my parents' names, and where are they? In which city do they live? Tell me where they are!" Quraishah replied, "You have the same father as I do; he rules in the Realm of the World. He is the Sahib-qiran, World-conqueror, Earthquake of Qaf, Younger Solomon, Father of Greatness—that is, Amir Hamzah bin Abdul Muttalib. As for the rest, I don't know your mother's name—who she is, or where she is; where to find her, or what her origins are." And she told him the whole story of the box in detail, she informed him about the whole matter.

Badi uz-Zaman said, "Send me to my father, do me this much of a kindness." Asman Pari, sending many gifts of Qaf with him, confided him to the Paris and Quraishah: "Take him with the greatest care to Mount Alburz, to the army of Islam; see that he encounters no hardships on the way." When he was leaving she explained to him and told him, "All your brothers have fought with the Amir at their first meeting. You too must fight him, before you attend upon him; don't neglect the custom of your family." And she told him the names of all his relatives.

In short, Badi uz-Zaman took leave of Queen Asman Pari, and went to Mount Alburz. He saw that the armies on both sides were arrayed in ranks; the young men had come into the battlefield to test their swords. The Paris told Badi uz-Zaman about the banners of both sides, they showed him how the camps were arranged: "This is your father's army, and that is the enemy's army." They themselves, hidden from everyone's gaze, began to watch the spectacle.

Badi uz-Zaman, standing between the two armies, turned his face toward the army of Islam and challenged them: he called out in a loud voice, "Oh my dear friends, whoever longs for union with the beautiful beloved Death, let him come before me, let him show his courage and hardihood!" Both armies, seeing Badi uz-Zaman's beauty and radiance, and his clothing and weapons, were astonished: "We've never seen a young man like him, and we've never beheld such weapons and clothing. From what country does he come, and where did he get his equipment?"

[He overcame several of Hamzah's champions.] And he said, "Go, send Rustam Pil-tan—for I'm very eager to meet him, so that he too can see my prowess." Rustam came and did battle with Badi uz-Zaman. After three hours of struggle Badi uz-Zaman subdued Rustam as well, and said, "Send Sad bin Amr." Sad bin Amr came and fought with him, and was subdued by Badi uz-Zaman. He said to Sad, "Send your grandfather Hamzah, so that I can have some pleasure in fighting!" Sad came and told this to the Amir.

The Amir came into the field, he set forth to confront him. Badi uz-Zaman, spurring his horse, galloped like lightning to the Amir's side, and instantly seized the Amir's belt. The Amir too put a hand to his waist. Both exerted so much strength that their horses almost collapsed; if they had not gotten down, their horses' backs would certainly have broken. When the Amir felt himself in a sweat, he gave a battle-cry and strove to dislodge Badi uz-Zaman's wrestling stance, he strove to lift him up above his head. But even then Badi uz-Zaman was not moved. The Amir gave another battle-cry, but this one had no effect either. Bakhtak began to say, "It wouldn't be surprising if Hamzah were killed at this young man's hands, if he were defeated today by this young man!"

The narrator writes that that day the Amir gave repeated battle-cries, but Badi uz-Zaman was not affected by the terrifying power of the battle-cry—he hardly even heard it. Finally the Amir, infuriated, drew Samsam and Qamqam from their scabbards, and wanted to strike at Badi uz-Zaman, he wanted to attack that young man with his well-tempered sword—when Quraishah appeared and seized the Amir's hand, and made him aware: "Dear father, this is your son, my brother!" The Amir was astonished: "Whose womb is he from?" Quraishah told the whole story of the box, and of what Hazrat Khizr had said, to the Amir in full detail; she bared that hidden secret before the Amir.

The Amir, with complete delight, embraced Badi uz-Zaman; love for him flowed warmly in his heart. He called Amar and said, "This noble son is mine, the Creator has sent him to help me." With these words, having the celebration-drums sounded, he entered his camp. And ordering a forty-days' celebration, he became absorbed in luxury and enjoyment; all the requisites for pleasure were provided.

[Afterwards, battle was resumed.] In the morning, as usual, the ranks were arrayed. Zhopin Iron-body, entering the battlefield, began to challenge them all, he began to call out to everyone by name, "If the time has come for any one among you to die, let him appear before me! It's not possible for anyone to fight me and come away alive!" [Finally Hamzah managed to conquer him and take him captive.]

Meanwhile, the champions went in a body to Amar bin Umayyah and said, "Zhopin has disgraced and humiliated us all in battle, he has given us all a great shock. If he remains alive, we'll never be able to look him in the eye! If by some means he were to be killed, then our trouble would disappear." Amar said, "The Amir will never have a champion like Zhopin killed! Rather, he'll hold him dearer than all the rest, since champions of such magnificent strength are not easy to find. Brave warriors who know men's worth would never even dream of killing such a valiant young man!" When they bribed Amar and appealed to his greed, Amar said to Hardam, "You melt some lead and pour it down Zhopin's throat. If the Amir should be displeased, I'll be answerable, I'll reconcile him somehow." Hardam, having some lead melted, poured it down Zhopin's throat; Zhopin's heart and liver immediately melted.

When the Amir came out of the palace, he sent for Zhopin. He was informed that Hardam had poured molten lead down his throat and taken his life, he had treated him in such an improper way. The Amir was very angry at Hardam. Hardam petitioned, "I did it on Amar bin Umayyah's say-so, on his instructions I poured the lead down his throat. I haven't committed any offense in this—I could never have dared to do such a thing on my own! His blood will be on Amar bin Umayyah's head." The Amir, displeased, asked Amar, "What did he ever do to you, that you killed him?" Amar replied, "Oh Amir, that gallows-bait deserved to be killed, so the people could be free of his tyrannous hand." The Amir said, "What can I do? If it had been anyone other than Amar, then, by the Lord of the Kabah, I would have poured molten lead down his throat too and killed him!" Nevertheless, he gave Amar seven lashes with a whip, and commanded, "If you ever again do such a thing without my order, I'll punish you very severely, I'll bring down a great disaster on your head!"

Amar said, "If I don't give the Amir seventy lashes, in revenge for those seven lashes, then I'm no son of Umayyah Zamiri!" With these words, he went straight off into Naushervan's presence, and said, "Oh King of Kings, what troubles I took upon myself for that Arab, how many times I risked my life! And in return for it all, he's given me seven lashes for the sake of an infidel, he's disgraced and humiliated me in the eyes of all the champions. If Your Majesty will take me into your service, I'll remain in attendance upon you, I'll serve you with my whole heart and soul." Naushervan happily said, "Oh Amar, you'll be the light of my eyes." With these words, he exalted him with a resplendent robe of honor, and raised him above all his companions. He gave him a chair to sit in, he showed him much respect and honor.

When the Amir heard this news, he was so fearful that he stayed awake all night, he practiced every sort of vigilance. And Amar, every night, watched and waited for his chance against the Amir—but, finding him awake, he stole away. At last one night the Amir went to sleep; in the grip of human weakness, he was deep in slumber. Amar was just waiting for this chance. Finding the Amir lost in sleep, he blew knockout powder into his nostrils with a blowpipe, and made him unconscious. Binding him with a noose, he carried him off into the forest, tied him tightly to a massive tree, and revived him; in revenge for those lashes, he humiliated him like this.

The Amir, finding himself tied to a tree, was very much astonished; he felt thoroughly ashamed. Amar cut off a branch from the tree and gave the Amir seventy blows with it, counting every one. The Amir smiled and said, "All right, you trickster and thief! If I don't shed your blood, then my name isn't Hamzah! Now I'll have no rest or peace until I kill you." With these words, he exerted his strength and broke the noose that bound him. Amar fled from the Amir like a runaway camel. The Amir took his bow and arrow in hand.

Amar realized, "The Amir's arrows never go astray. I'll be killed for nothing, I won't escape from his hands!" He ran over to the Amir and said, "Oh Amir, pardon my offense!" The Amir said, "I have sworn an oath that I'll shed your blood, that I'll punish you for this!" Amar said, "If that's your pleasure, then I'm at your service—please strike off my head, don't hesitate to separate my head from my body." The Amir, in order to fulfill his oath, pulled out a razor and caused a bit of blood to flow from Amar's veins. Afterwards, taking Amar, he went back to his camp.

36. The Amir sets out toward Nayastan, and kills Stonethrower the Bloodthirsty of Nayastan, the lord of that place.

[Naushervan sent a false physician who brought Hamzah and his friends a "salve" for their eyes that made them blind. After much hardship and many prayers, Khizr came and restored their sight.]

Amar bin Umayyah said to the Amir, "It seems that all this mischief was the work of that benighted Bakhtak. If you command, I'll punish him, I'll take revenge upon him for this misdeed." The Amir replied, "He will inevitably receive the punishment he's earned. What's the point of causing anyone pain?" Amar was poisonously bitter against Bakhtak, how could he rest? At that time he kept silent, for fear of the Amir he said nothing. That night, he took on the appearance of a cook, and went to Bakhtak's tent. He said to the door-keeper, "Tell the vazir, inform him at once, that a cook has come from Rum. Although he makes all main dishes and sweets very well, he cooks meat stew so excellently that he has no equal in the world."

Bakhtak called him into the tent, he ordered him brought before him. But he was afraid that this might be Amar. Then he said to himself that Amar was blind, so this must surely be a real cook. But even so, he sent some ayyars to see whether Amar was with Hamzah or not. The ayyars, leaving the tent, took counsel together: "If by any chance this person is indeed Amar, then if we betray him he'll hold a grudge against us in the future." With this thought, they went off a little way, then returned and said to Bakhtak, "Amar is with Hamzah." Bakhtak was reassured. He ordered Amar to cook meat stew, he at once provided him with all that he needed for it. Amar cooked an extremely fine meat stew.

Bakhtak went to Naushervan and told him, with great praise and admiration, about this cook, and informed him of his excellence. Naushervan made him the chief of his kitchen, he gave him every kind of authority. Amar began to cook new kinds of food every day and serve them to him. One night he put a hundred-and-fifty-pound pot on the cooking fire, but he put no meat, etc., in it—only water to boil. When half the night had passed, he made the cooks unconscious and went into Bakhtak's tent. He saw that Bakhtak was snoring like a trumpet, and all those around him were deep in slumber. He put several pinches of knockout powder in Bakhtak's nose. Bakhtak sneezed, and lost consciousness.

Amar, wrapping him up in a blanket, brought him into the kitchen, and put him into that pot of boiling water. When he had been scalded, Amar buried his head and skin in the ground, with ingenuity and prudence he put them under the earth. With the remaining parts of his body Amar cooked meat stew, and in the morning he placed it on the king's dining cloth. The king bestowed portions of it on a number of nobles, and himself began to eat it, with much approval; he began to praise Amar's cooking skills to everyone.

It happened that a finger was found in the stew, and on that finger was a ring bestowed by the king. Naushervan, seeing the finger, withdrew his hand from the dish. He asked the cook, "Whose finger is this? How has it gotten into the food? Why have you cooked it?" The cook said nothing, but the king recognized the ring as Bakhtak's. He commanded, "See what Bakhtak is doing; call him, bring him to me at once." When people went into Bakhtak's tent, they found his bed empty. They didn't know what had happened, what misfortune had overtaken him. They searched here and there, and submitted, "Bakhtak has disappeared from his tent." The king realized that the stew had been made of Bakhtak's flesh. He vomited and vomited until he made himself ill, from this terrible trouble he was in a very bad state. Amar, vanishing from there, went back and stayed with the Amir.

[Naushervan incited several frightful cannibal kings against Hamzah. In Hamzah's absence, Rustam led an army against one of the worst of them, Ahriman Sher-e Gurdan.] Ahriman approached Rustam's army and challenged, "Oh goats, whoever is eager to have his throat cut, let him come before me, let him come into the field and be slaughtered!" Qunduz Sar-e Shuban, obtaining Rustam's permission, fought with him, and was martyred. The cannibals rushed to divide up every morsel of his flesh; they chewed up his bones, rib-cage and all.

Aljosh went and struck Ahriman so forceful a blow in the stomach, that his long dagger and even his hand sank into Ahriman's stomach, but Ahriman was not injured at all, he never even felt the blow at all.

Ahriman Sher-e gurdan, seizing Aljosh, wanted to crunch him up also. But Aljosh, with the greatest difficulty, got free and began to attack him. Finally, as they fought and fought, that cannibal seized Aljosh and ate him raw.

Rustam saw that two renowned champions had been martyred. Enraged, he seized his horse's reins and went to confront him, he showed his valor. Ahriman Sher-e Gurdan struck at Rustam with his mace. Rustam blocked the blow with his shield, and struck such a sword-blow that if it had fallen on him, he would have been cut in two, nothing would have been left of him. But he warded it off. Rustam, leaping down from his horse, seized both Ahriman's arms and exerted so much strength that the wall of his stomach burst.

. . . When the Amir, after his hunting trip, came to Jamshediyah and saw signs that an army had camped there, he said to Amar, "It seems that Rustam has come here, undoubtedly he has passed through this way. He's left Jamshediyah topsy-turvy, and gone on toward Bakhtar. May the Lord protect him from anyone's evil eye, and show him to me safe and sound! My heart keeps sinking for no reason, my heart is in my mouth." With these words, the Amir set out for Bakhtar. When he drew near it, all his comrades and sons, bareheaded and barefooted, weeping, fell at his feet. When the Amir heard of the deaths of Rustam and Qunduz and Aljosh, he fell from his horse to the ground, and began to roll in the dust. He was utterly distraught, he suffered the greatest grief and pain.

[Hamzah fought with Ahriman, and subdued him.] He said to Amar, "Bind him." Amar bound Ahriman and took him away. And the Amir, drawing his sword, penetrated the enemy ranks. Those who became Muslims were reprieved, the rest were slain by the harsh sword. All the champions said to Amar, "The Amir won't kill Ahriman either! You must take due revenge for Rustam's death." Amar at once heated lead and poured it into Ahriman's ears. That petty creature was sent to Hell. The Amir came back and commanded Amar, "Bring Ahriman before me." Amar said, "Due vengeance has been taken upon him for Rustam's death." The Amir fell silent.

The next day the Amir commanded, "Dig tunnels, place explosives, and blow up the cannibals who have shut themselves up in their fort." Amar at once dug tunnels, placed explosives, and blew up the fort, he did as the Amir had said. All the cannibals went into the flames of Hell. The Amir, having won the war against Ahriman Sher-e Gurdan, set out.

[He next prepared to fight with another cannibal king, *Gaolangi.] Gaolangi, seeing how short in stature the Amir was, suspected that it was some other champion. He said, "Oh champion, I have business with Hamzah, I have nothing to do with you. It's not my practice to fight with mediocre champions! Go and send Hamzah, let him come and confront me." The Amir said, "I myself am Hamzah bin Abdul Muttalib." Gaolangi replied, "Oh Amir, I thought you would be taller of stature and more powerful of body than I! With a stature like this, did you really defeat and subdue thousands of high-headed champions, and bring high-handed Devs under your hand in Qaf?" The Amir said, "If I'm insignificant in size, what of it? My Helper is very powerful: compared to Him, the earth and sky are insubstantial!"

[They fought for twenty-one days and nights.] The Amir commanded, "Be warned—I'm going to give a battle-cry!" He replied, "You can make as much noise as your heart desires! I'm not a boy, to tremble at the sound of your voice, or feel afraid of it." When the Amir gave the battle-cry "God is great!" the desert shook for thirty-two miles all around. Lifting Gaolangi above his head, he spun him around and put him gently on the ground; he proved all his claims to be false.

Then he commanded Amar, "Bind him, and don't give him any chance to escape." Gaolangi replied, "Amir, why should you bind me? I'm bound by my pledge of obedience to you!" The Amir commanded, "Then accept Islam." He at once, with a sincere heart, said the profession of faith. The Amir embraced him, and told everyone the good news of his becoming a Muslim. And taking him into his tent, he introduced him to all the champions. Gaolangi took the Amir, together with his companions, into his city, and kept the Amir absorbed in celebrations for forty days.

[The Amir then attacked, overcame, and killed two kings who ruled nearby cannibal cities.] The narrator writes that after exterminating Irash, the Amir asked Gaolangi, "Now what city lies ahead of us?" Gaolangi submitted, "It is Nayastan, a large and splendid city. The ruler of the city is named Stonethrower the Bloodthirsty of Nayastan, and his army too is very fierce and full of hardihood. His height is one hundred ninety yards. His eyes glow like ovens, and his soldiers are innumerable. The way there is so narrow that two men can't walk abreast, not even birds can enter there. And on both sides of the road flames of fire shoot out of the ground, so hot that they melt even mountains."

The Amir paid no heed to his words, and set out for Nayastan. When the Amir reached that place, his army couldn't bear it, they couldn't stand the hardship; people began to die from the heat of the flames. Then the Amir placed the noose of Khvajah Khizr[40] on the ground, and commanded, "Take hold of the end of this and come ahead, don't have any doubt now in your hearts." The narrator writes that the Amir's whole army, with their mounts, burned up. One champion mounted on a camel, and three hundred foot-soldiers, seized the rope and crossed that river of fire; all the rest of his soldiers set out for the land of Nothingness.

At length, with the greatest difficulty, the Amir arrived near the city. Stonethrower the Bloodthirsty of Nayastan, who was its king, heard of the Amir's arrival and came out of the city with his soldiers, he brought his whole army to confront him. The Amir saw that around each soldier's neck hung a bag filled with stones. Seeing the Amir, they all with one accord began to hurl stones. Among the Amir's companions seventy-one men survived; all the rest were stoned to death by the enemy. The Amir, seeing this, felt sorely helpless and under pressure.

The Amir, drawing his sword, rushed into their army the way a tiger enters a herd of goats. He began to wield swords in both hands, he began to strike off their heads from their necks. So many bloodthirsty soldiers were killed that their blood began to form a river. Finally Stonethrower the Bloodthirsty of Nayastan came and struck a sword-blow at the Amir's head. The Amir warded it off. When he began to lift his mace, the Amir made a leap and struck him such a sword-blow that both his legs were cut off at the knees and sank into the ground. The Amir struck a second sword-blow that sent him off to Hell. And the surviving enemy soldiers, who had shut themselves up in their fort, he caused to be burned to death by fire, he reduced them all to ashes.

And he said, "I've heard Buzurchmihr say that I would emerge from the Dark Regions with seventy friends, that I would defeat and subdue all those enemies. Now seventy-one men are with me. It remains to be seen which one of them is fated to die, which one's name is erased from the page of life." With these words, he fell into deep grief. The narrator says that the Amir said to Gaolangi, "Oh my friend, a hundred thousand horsemen and footmen were with me, and out of all of them only these seventy-one men have survived, all the rest have been finished off! I am very much grieved at their death. Now tell me, what city lies ahead of us?"

[The Amir continued his travels.] One day he asked Gaolangi, "Now you must tell me what further evil menaces remain, you must give me some fresh news!" Gaolangi replied, "All the mischiefs and menaces from Bakhtar to the Dark Regions have been wiped out. Now please come to Alabaster and rest for a while, please come along with me. Let us go from this place to Alabaster, let us enter that noble city." Gaolangi arranged a celebration for the Amir, with the greatest elegance; he ordered his attendants to prepare all the requisites for the feast.

After the celebration was over, they went out of the city to hunt—when suddenly Badi uz-Zaman saw a deer. He wanted to kill it. The deer, bounding along, went on ahead. Badi uz-Zaman urged his horse after it, he prepared his gun to shoot it. After it had gone a little way, the deer leaped into a large artificial pool. Badi uz-Zaman urged his horse into the pool. The Amir too, with his comrades, leaped into the pool.

When they opened their eyes and looked, they saw a wide plain, they found a strange kind of wilderness. However much they searched here and there for Badi uz-Zaman, they found no trace of him. The Amir, with tears in his eyes, said to his comrades, and told them with great, great grief and pain, "Now seventy men are left; the seventy-first was Badi uz-Zaman, who has disappeared. Alas, that one more fresh hole has been made in my heart! I am ravaged by grief." His comrades comforted the Amir in their own way: "Oh Amir, no one can fight against fate. Except for the balm of patience, there's no cure for this deep wound." The Amir didn't say a word except of patience and gratitude to God. He saw no refuge except in silence.

37. The Amir sets out for Mecca the Great, and is martyred at the ever-victorious side of the Master of the Universe, God's peace and blessing be upon him, and the dastan is concluded.

The narrators who weigh their words tell this interesting dastan in this way: When the Amir had become somewhat resigned, and his heart had found some peace after its anguish, Gaolangi said, "You said that you'd cause me to kiss the feet of the *Final Prophet of the Age, God's peace and blessing be upon him, and would surely show me his auspicious beauty. So please now proceed to

Mecca." The Amir, taking Gaolangi and his companions, set out for Mecca. . . . After some days of traveling, he drew near to Mecca. Gaolangi and all the Amir's companions, kissing the feet of the Final Prophet of the Age, God's peace and blessing be upon him and his family, were ennobled by Islam, they were well thought of by everyone.

One day the Final Prophet of the Age, God's peace and blessing be upon him and his family, was in the mosque, when a Bedouin submitted, "Oh Prophet of God, God's peace and blessing be upon you and your family. The infidels of Egypt and Rum and Syria have joined together to create turmoil, they have brought a numerous army with them."

First Hazrat sent Amir Hamzah, with other warriors, to Mount Abu Qubais. Later, he himself went there. The infidels arrayed their ranks. The Amir gave Gaolangi permission to fight. An infidel powerful of body made many proud boasts before Gaolangi. Gaolangi lifted him up from the ground and spun him around so many times that he was half-killed, he was extremely helpless and shocked. When Gaolangi hurled him to the ground, the small breath of life that was left in him went out of his body. Another infidel came. The same thing happened to him. In this way a number of infidels died at Gaolangi's hands. The infidel army was utterly terrified; no one came out to confront Gaolangi, all their hearts were full of fear.

Finally the Prince of Hind, whose name was Pur-e Hindi, urged his horse into the field. Doing battle with Gaolangi, he gave him such a spear-thrust in the chest that the spear came out through Gaolangi's back, and from this thrust Gaolangi rendered up his soul. The Amir was very sorrowful at this. Growing angry, he himself came to confront him. Pur-e Hindi said, "Oh old man, why have you come to give up your life, what half-baked notion do you have in your heart? Whereas even the young men don't have the courage to confront me! Anyway, tell me your name, so you won't die anonymously."

The Amir said, "Oh you jabberer of nonsense, my name is Hamzah bin Abdul Muttalib." He replied, "I've heard that Hamzah has gone to Bakhtar." The Amir said, "That's true. I've been back from there for some days. Come on, show me—what kind of an attack can you make?" Pur-e Hindi aimed his spear straight at the Amir. The Amir, seizing its hilt, snatched the spear away, and left him helpless. And he drove that same spear into his liver, so that it came out through his back. Pur-e Hindi fell from his horse and died, he gave up his soul at once.

The Amir, raising a battle-cry, fell on his army, and killed many infidels; thousands of wretches were killed. The infidels, helpless before the Amir, took the path of flight, they all alike showed their backs. The Home of Prophethood, God's peace and blessing be upon him and his family, took the Amir and entered Mecca, victorious and triumphant; he returned thanks to the Lord for this victory.

The narrator writes that Pur-e Hindi's mother, hearing of her son's death, came to Ctesiphon with the kings of Hind, Rum, Syria, China, Zanzibar, and Turkestan, and a fierce army. She demanded justice from Hurmuz. Hurmuz too, with an army, joined her. Eventually, all these armies drew near to Mecca. The Prophet, God's peace and blessing be upon him and his family, hearing of this, said, "My uncle Hamzah by himself is sufficient to destroy these armies." Since Hazrat had not first uttered, "If God Most High wills," the Indivisible One was displeased.

When Hazrat, with his companions, went to confront the infidels, Hurmuz said to his army, "Don't fight these Arabs one by one! Fall on them all together, and kill them hand-to-hand; otherwise you won't prevail over them." Hurmuz's army burst on the army of Islam all together. Landhaur, and Sad bin Amr bin Hamzah, and Adi, etc., all the comrades of Amir Hamzah were martyred, to the last man. And the infidels began to rain arrows on Hazrat Ali bin Abi Talib, God be pleased with him; arrows began to come at him from all directions. And one infidel, throwing a stone, martyred the tooth of the Prophet, God's peace and blessing be upon him and his family and companions.

Amar bin Umayyah Zamiri gave this news to Amir Hamzah, he informed him of this mortal peril. The Amir armed himself and mounted his horse, he prepared to kill the infidels. And he slaughtered the infidels until he reached Hurmuz himself. Hurmuz, seeing Amir Hamzah, jumped down from his throne and ran away. His army too fled, no one had the hardihood to remain. The Amir pursued them for eight miles, and in a number of places he piled up heaps of the slain. At length, victorious and triumphant, he turned back toward Mecca.

On the road *Hindah, the mother of Pur-e Hindi, who was lying in ambush for him with an army, came from behind and struck Ashqar such a sword-blow that all his four feet were cut off. Amir Hamzah was not alert; the moment his horse fell he landed on the ground. That ruinous bitch struck such a blow with her blood-drenched, poisoned sword at Amir Hamzah's blessed head, that the Amir's head was separated from his body. And cutting open the Amir's stomach, she pulled out his liver and ate it, and she cut his blessed body into seventy pieces.

Afterwards, when her intoxication of heedlessness abated, she was worried: "When Quraishah, Amir Hamzah's daughter, hears of her father's martyrdom, she'll come with an army of Devs and Jinns and take vengeance on me!" With this thought, she went to the Prophet, God's peace and blessing be upon him and his family, and sought refuge with him, and pleaded and wept a great deal before the Prophet, God's peace and blessing be upon him and his family. And she accepted Islam. Hazrat commanded, "Show me the corpse of my revered uncle, show me where that Lion of the Lord is."

Hindah, taking Hazrat with her, showed him the Amir's body, she brought Hazrat to where Amir Hamzah's body lay. The Hazrat, God's peace and blessing be upon him and his family, collecting the pieces of the Amir's body, said a separate prayer over every piece. And at that time Hazrat stood on tiptoe. After burying the body, people asked him why he had said the prayers while standing on tiptoe. Hazrat said, "I stood like that because there were so many angels that there was no room in the field, and the angels offered prayers seventy times over every piece of the body." He gave everyone the good news of this exalted rank and holiness.

At last, when Hazrat returned after burying the Amir, Hindah came before the Prophet, God's peace and blessing be upon him and his family. The Hazrat turned his face away from her, he paid her no attention at all. Just then a revelation descended: "Oh my dear one, Hamzah has been martyred. But look up into the sky!" Hazrat lifted his head and saw Amir Hamzah seated on a jewel-encrusted throne in Paradise, while Houris and youthful slaves stood before him with folded hands. Hazrat, God's peace and blessing be upon him, smiled and gave redoubled thanks to the Lord.

After some days, Quraishah, with a countless army, presented herself in the Hazrat's service, and demanded her father's murderer. Hazrat showed her the heavenly rank of Commander of the Faithful attained by Hamzah, God be pleased with him, and commanded, "Be very happy, and give thanks to the Lord. Oh Quraishah, if your father had not been martyred, he would not have attained this rank, why would God Most High have raised him to such a station? Thus you must give up your revenge." The narrator writes that it was then that the *Chapter of the Jinn descended. Finally Quraishah, as Hazrat, God's peace and blessing be upon him and his family, had ordered, gave up her revenge, she spoke no more of vengeance. Taking leave, she went to her own land.

One school of thought holds that Hazrat, without saying, "If God Most High wills," had said, "My uncle by himself is sufficient to destroy this army, this warrior by himself is sufficient to slaughter hundreds of thousands of infidels." These words displeased the Most High Presence, and for this reason Amir Hamzah's blessed body was cut into seventy pieces, and the Hazrat's blessed tooth was martyred.

And the second account is that one night *Aishah the Truthful, God be pleased with her, was mending her robe, she was sewing up and putting to rights her torn garments, when the Hazrat came in, and it happened that the lamp was blown out, and the thread slipped out of the needle's eye; the Mother of the Believers was very distressed. The Hazrat smiled. In the light of his teeth, Hazrat Aishah, God be pleased with her, threaded the needle. Hazrat said, "Do you see how bright my teeth are? You threaded the needle in their light! My teeth served as a candle." These words displeased the Most High Presence, and for this reason the Hazrat's tooth was martyred.

And in this same battle an arrowhead broke off in the foot of Hazrat Ali, may God exalt him, the Commander of the Faithful, and remained lodged there. However much the surgeons sought to pull the arrowhead out of the wound, it wouldn't come out. However, when Hazrat was performing the final prostration of his prayers, the Prophet, God's peace and blessing be upon him and his family, commanded, "Pull out the arrowhead from Ali's foot, God be pleased with him, right now, so he won't feel the pain."

Some champions seized the arrowhead in a pair of forceps and pulled it out. The Hazrat was not at all aware of it. When he had finished his prayers, he saw the blood and asked, "Where does this blood come from, when did you pull the arrowhead out of my wound?" His companions told him what had occurred, and asked, "Oh Hazrat, did you really not know?" He said, "*La vallah la*"[41]—that is, "I swear by God, I didn't know at all when the arrowhead was pulled out."

Oh Lord, by virtue of the martyrdom of the blessed tooth of the Prophet, God's peace and blessing be upon him and his family, and through the grace of the wound in the blessed foot and the prayers and humility of Ali ibn Abi Talib, God be pleased with him, may this translator and writer come to a good end in the world to come, and not be indebted to anyone in this world, and be honored as much as he wishes with treasures of the Unseen; and may the truth or falsehood of this qissah be attributed to the inventive narrators.

Notes

1. The name is explicitly given in the text as 'Amar bi'l Fatḥ, thus fixing its pronunciation as Amar, rather than the more correct Arabic 'Amr (the diminutive form of the name 'Umar).

2. The Persianized *"naẓar kardah karnā"* literally means "to make (someone) looked-at." A common Sufi concept, it rests on the belief that a person of high spiritual authority can cast an intent and concentrated look at someone in order to endow that person with special powers and increased mystical insight.

3. This Arabic phrase is conventionally used to express uncertainty or skepticism.

4. All these titles apply to Hazrat *Ali.

5. The *"āfat band"* seems to be otherwise unknown; since Buzurg Ummid boasts of its uniqueness, perhaps this is not surprising.

6. That is, in the hands of the oral narrator presumed to be telling the story.

7. Ṣābir Bilgrāmī, an extremely obscure poet, was perhaps a friend of the author, 'Abdullāh Bilgrāmī. Both were from Bilgram, a town northwest of Lucknow.

8. A verse by Naẓīr Akbarābādī (1740–1830). She is called a disaster because of the devastating effects of her beauty.

9. A special *"chahal kunjī,"* or "forty-key [bowl]," inscribed with prayers and containing forty tiny keys, was filled with water which the sick person then drank; it was thought to guard against supernatural afflictions.

10. These two verses from a ghazal by Rind (1797–1857) are well-known. The first line of the second verse has been altered: instead of ending in *"chand roz"* (a few days) as it does in the original, it has been made to end in *"thoṛī der"* (a little while).

11. The name Gurāz ud-dīn is farcical and insulting, a parody of many Muslim names which end in "of the Faith." The pig is of course an unclean and prohibited animal, and even the grammar of the name violates rules: the Persian word *"gurāz"* cannot properly be used with the Arabic phrase *"ud-dīn."*

12. The Qur'ān says (2:34) that Iblīs (Satan) refused to bow down before Adam; as a creature of light he refused to humble himself before a creature of dust. For this arrogance God punished him with banishment from Heaven.

13. The verse is in Persian.

14. In South Asian Muslim practice, charitable offerings are often made to the poor, etc., in someone else's name, so that the religious merit will accrue to that person. Sweet things are often included in such offerings, especially offerings made in the name of someone absent. Sweetening the river with sugar is presumably an act of general charity and goodwill.

15. Muslims sacrifice goats to commemorate Abraham's readiness to sacrifice his own son. The phrase used here, "*bal bakrā,*" also suggests a Hindu sacrifice (*bali*); in Bengal goats are sacrificed to the goddess Durgā.

16. The verse is in Persian, but incorporates a famous short prayer in Arabic.

17. Amar says "*valī allāh kā.*" He thus suggests—but does not quite claim—that he is a "*valī ullāh,*" a "Friend of God," a title suited only to certain venerable religious figures.

18. The meaning of "*ṭakoṛī*" is not clear.

19. Of the names not in common use, most refer to tribal groups.

20. The reference is to the gleaming metal counters used in such shops.

21. The verse is in Persian.

22. In fact, on that occasion Amar rallies the champions by sending them letters, not by running around to each one.

23. No such event is described in the present text. But Amar is still alive after Hamzah's death, and so are a few of Hamzah's sons, so there is room for it to occur.

24. This is the only reference to this character in the present text; it is impossible to tell who he is or why he kills the king.

25. This famous Urdu proverb, equally well-known in its Persian form, conveys something like "There's many a slip twixt the cup and the lip."

26. The tilism of Solomon's Chessboard appears earlier in the dastan, but Sabz-qaba the Jinn doesn't figure in it at all. Hamzah did, however, liberate him from another tilism.

27. Rustam the Second (Rustam-e S̤ānī), actually Hamzah's great-grandson, figures in the Long Version of the dastan, especially in the volumes of *Āftāb-e shujā'at.*

28. Possession by Jinns is the cause of many forms of erratic behavior, according to an Arab folk belief that goes back to pre-Islamic days.

29. Paris do not possess people, but can disturb their minds by revealing themselves in all their bewitching beauty.

30. That is, the story of Amar, Mihr Nigar, and their companions.

31. Arnais was in the form of a horse when he impregnated Lanisah.

32. Qamar Chahrah, "Moon-faced," appears only in this one episode. If Hamzah has indeed married her, we have not been told about it.

33. *Bālā bāḳhtar*, the "(Book of the) Upper West," is one of the volumes of the Long Version. But neither Pearl the Pearl-robed (Durr-e Durdar Posh) nor Qamarzād, "Son of the Moon," appears in it.

34. Such a reaction suggests disgust rather than fear.

35. Another expression of disgust.

36. The bride's feeding of sugar to the groom, and the mirror ritual, are characteristically Indo-Muslim. In the latter, a copy of the Qur'ān is held open above the bride and groom like a canopy. A mirror is placed between the pair, and the groom is allowed to see the bride's face in the mirror.

37. Saman Sīmā, "Jasmine-browed," appears only in this one episode. Perhaps she is Qamar Chahrah by another name.

38. Presumably the fortress of Jafar, King of Kashmir, who has allied himself with Naushervan.

39. Apparently Hamzah is now separating the area of his own conquests from Naushervan's realm, and declaring Sad bin Amr king of this personal domain.

40. Perhaps this is the noose sent to Amar by Bibi Asifa Basafa, Khizr's mother.

41. In Arabic, "No, by God, no."

Glossary

[The glossary identifies important characters, places, and other references from the translated adventures. Transliterated forms show spellings as used in the text. The entries are described from the point of view of the dastan itself, disregarding problems of historicity, etc. The bracketed number after each entry identifies the chapter in which it first appears.]

Abraham (Ibrāhīm). An early Prophet who upheld monotheism and built the Kabah; he appears to people in dreams and converts them to Islam. [1]

Abdul Muttalib (ʻAbd ul-Muṯṯalib). Hamzah's father, ruler of Mecca and head of the tribe of Hashim. [1]

Abdur Rahman the Jinn (ʻAbd ur-Raḥmān Jinnī). Shahpal's vazir, virtuous and skilled in divination. [1]

Adam (Ādam). A Prophet, and the father of the human race. [2]

Adi Madikarab (ʻĀdī Maʻdīkarab). The son of Hamzah's wet-nurse, Adiyah Bano; he becomes one of Hamzah's close companions. Adi was a highway robber until Hamzah conquered and converted him, and is known for his insatiable gluttony and immense strength. [1]

Adiyah Bano (ʻĀdiyah Bāno). The wet-nurse of Hamzah, Amar, and Muqbil, and mother of Adi Madikarab. [1]

Ahriman (Ahriman). A Dev, the father of Ifrit. His name is that of the Zoroastrian principle of evil. [18]

Aishah (ʻĀʻishah). The Prophet's youngest and favorite wife. [37]

Alburz, Mount (Koh-e Alburz). A famous high mountain range north of Teheran. [25]

Aleppo (Ḥalab). A city in northern Syria. [14]

Alexander (Sikandar). Alexander the Great, the exemplary world-conqueror, a name to conjure with in Islamic story tradition. He is once referred to as "the Two-horned" (Żūʼl-qarnain), a title of uncertain significance. [11]

Ali ibn Abi Talib (ʻAlī ibn Abī Ṯālib). The nephew and son-in-law of the Prophet; he is especially revered by Shiites. [3]

Amar bin Umayyah Zamiri (ʻAmar bin Umayyah Ẕamīrī). Hamzah's adopted brother and loyal comrade, the son of a Meccan camel driver. Amar is the supreme *ayyar of his age; his special talents include music and fast running. His name would normally be read as "Amr," but the text itself instructs us differently in his case. [1]

Amir (Amīr). "Chief, lord." An honorific title given to Hamzah. [1]

Amir's son (Amīrzādah). A title used for Amr bin Hamzah. [32]

Amr bin Hamzah ('Amr bin Ḥamzah). Hamzah's eldest son, by Nahid Maryam. [32]

Angel of Death (Malak ul-Maut). The angel sent by God to claim the souls of those whose time has come to die. [11]

Arnais (Arnā'īs). From "arnā," a male buffalo. A Dev, father of Ashqar. [29]

Ashqar Devzad (Ashqar Devzād). A beautiful winged colt, son of Arnais and Lanisah; he bears Hamzah home from Qaf and stays with him to the death. [29]

Asif Barkhiya (Āṣif Barḳhiyā). Solomon's vazir. [3]

Asifa Basafa, Bibi (Bībī Āṣifā Bāṣafā). "Lady Asifa the Pure." The mother of Khizr and Elias; she lives on the Mountain of Light. [30]

Asman Pari (Āsmān Parī). "Sky Pari." Daughter of Shahpal, and later herself Queen of Qaf. She falls in love with Hamzah, marries him, and holds him captive by love and violence for eighteen years. She bears him one daughter, Quraishah. [2]

ayyar *('ayyār)*. A practitioner of the profession of *ayyari. [1]

Ayyar and King of Ayyars (Shāh-e 'Ayyārān 'Ayyār). A title of Amar's. [25]

ayyari *('ayyārī)*. The special art of trickery, deceit, dirty tricks, disguise, espionage, reconnaissance, and guerrilla warfare in which Amar is expert. Ayyari is a profession, with its own dress and private language; ayyars may serve different masters, but they recognize each other as fellow professionals. [4]

Badi uz-Zaman (Badī' uz-Zamāṅ). "Wonder of the Age." Hamzah's son by Geli Savar. [35]

Bahram Gurd, Emperor of China (Bahrām Gurd Ḳhāqān-e Chīn). One of Hamzah's close companions, ruler of the land of *China. [6]

Bakhtak (Baḳhtak). "Small Fortune." Naushervan's evil counselor, hostile to Hamzah, always ready for major or minor mischief. [1]

Bakhtyarak (Baḳhtyārak). "Small Master of Fortune." Bakhtak's son. [20]

Basra (Baṣrah). A city in Iraq, on the Persian Gulf. [10]

Black Constellation (Siyāh Qīṭās). Hamzah's horse, whom Gabriel brings for him from the stables of the Prophet Isaac. [3]

bread-bun of Khizr *(kalīchah-e 'ināyat-e ḥaẓrat Ḳhiẓr)*. A bread-bun that never diminishes no matter how much is eaten from it. [11]

Buraq (Burāq). The horse-like creature ridden by the Prophet during his night journey to Jerusalem and his ascent into Heaven. [24]

Buzurchmihr (Buzurchmihr). "Great Sun." Naushervan's virtuous vazir, skilled in divination and esoteric knowledge; he is secretly a Muslim. [1]

Buzurg Ummid (Buzurg Ummīd). "Great Hope." Buzurchmihr's son. [4]

Chain of Justice *(zanjīr-e ʻadālat).* A chain which hung down outside the palace wall but sounded a bell in Naushervan's presence, so that any subject could petition for redress of grievances. [14]

Chapter of the Jinn (Sūrat al-Jinn). The seventy-second chapter of the Quran; it describes the conversion of some of the Jinns to Islam. [37]

Chapter of Light (Sūrat an-Nūr). The twenty-fourth chapter of the Quran, especially beautiful for its mystical imagery of God as Light. [31]

China (Chīn). A vaguely defined Central Asian land that seems to include both Uzbekistan and Kabul. [6]

Dark Regions (Ẕulmāt). A land somewhere near Qaf, inhabited by a non-human species. [20]

David (Dā'ūd). A Prophet, and a notable musician; his gifts include Amar's two-stringed Lute of David, and his singing ability. [3]

Dev (Dev). A species of immensely huge, powerful, strong demons, mostly violent and brutal; they are invisible to ordinary human eyes, and can fly. They live in Qaf, and are kept in subjugation by Shahpal. Some are cannibalistic. Their females seem usually to be magicians. [1]

dinar *(dīnār).* A well-known ancient gold coin, of varying value. [10]

divining-dice *(qurʻah).* These were thrown, often as part of a form of divination called geomancy. [1]

Earthquake of Qaf (Zalāzil-e Qāf). A title of Hamzah's, which he earns through his subjugation of the rebellious Devs of Qaf. [18]

Elias (Ilyās). A Prophet, described as Khizr's brother. [10]

faqir *(faqīr).* A Muslim ascetic, usually a solitary wanderer living on the voluntary gifts of the pious. [27]

Faramarz (Farāmarz). Naushervan's younger son. [1]

Farhad bin Landhaur (Farhād bin Landhaur). Landhaur's older son. [33]

Father of Greatness (Abu'l-ulā). One of Hamzah's titles, often used in intimate, affectionate situations. [14]

Father of the Runners of the World (Bābā-e Davindagān-e ʻĀlam). An epithet of Amar's. [4]

Final Prophet of the Age (Paiġhambar-e Āḳhir uz-Zamāñ). The Prophet Muhammad, God's own special and final Messenger, on the basis of whose revelation Islam was founded. [37]

Fitnah Bano (Fitnah Bāno). "Lady Mischief." Mihr Nigar's chief confidante, the daughter of her old nurse. She is half-comically engaged to Amar. [9]

Friends of God (Auliyā' Allāh). In the dastan, a group of holy persons highly honored by God's special favor and often charged by Him with special commissions. Among them are Gabriel, Khizr, and Ali. [3]

Gabriel (Jibra'īl). An angel of God who is sent on errands to men. [3]

Gaolangi (Gā'olangī). Known for his gigantic stature, he is the ruler of Alabaster, in the Dark Regions; he becomes a Muslim and Hamzah's ally. [36]

Garden of Iram (Gulistān-e Iram). Shahpal's capital city, named after one of the gardens of Paradise. [2]

Geli Savar (Gelī Savār). A warrior princess, daughter of King Ganjal; Hamzah marries her, and she gives birth to Badi uz-Zaman. [34]

geomancy *(ramal).* A method of divination by drawing lines and figures on the ground; it is often accompanied by use of the divining-dice. [2]

gesture of taking someone's misfortunes onto oneself *(kisī kī balā'eñ lenā; kisī par taṣadduq honā).* Making this gesture usually consists of running the palms of the hands down the other person's cheeks, then bringing the hands to one's own cheeks, making fists, and cracking the knuckles. An alternative form of the gesture is to walk several times clockwise around the person. [22]

ghost *(bhūt).* In Indic folk tradition, a mischievous spirit bent on harrassment; it often appears dirty and disheveled. [8]

"God is great!" *(allāhu akbar).* An all-purpose pious phrase. It is Hamzah's battle-cry, used at the climactic moment of a single combat; it can also cause enemy armies to faint, grow deaf, or panic. [5]

gold piece *(ashrafī).* A gold coin used in medieval India, and on into the nineteenth century, most often weighing ten grams and worth 18 rupees. [1]

Gurshasp (Gurshāsp). One of Rustam bin Zal's ancestors. [3]

Hamzah (Ḥamzah). The hero of the dastan; he is the son of Abdul Muttalib, and the paternal uncle of the Prophet. [1]

Hashimite vein *(rag-e ḥāshimī).* A special vein in Hamzah's forehead; the name implies that it is a sign of his Hashimite ancestry. [14]

Hazrat (Ḥaẓrat). "The Presence." An extremely respectful title of honor, normally reserved for kings and Prophets and other dignitaries of the highest rank. [1]

Hell-cave Bano (Saqar Ġhār Bāno). Bakhtak's mother. [13]

Hindah (Hindah). The mother of Pur-e Hindi; she ambushes and murders Hamzah to avenge her son's death, then accepts Islam to protect herself. [37]

Houri (Ḥūr). A female companion of the righteous in Paradise. [28]

Hud (Ḥūd). One of the earlier Prophets mentioned in the Quran. [3]

Hurmuz (Hurmuz). Naushervan's eldest son, the Crown Prince. [1]

Id (ʿĪd). The most important Muslim festival; a day of celebration that follows the annual month of dawn-to-dusk fasting. [31]

Ifrit (ʿIfrīt). "Demon." The most powerful and terrifying of the Devs who rebel against Shahpal. "Ifrit" is normally a species name, but here it is the name of a single individual. [16]

Jam (Jam). See *Jamshed. [25]

Jamshed (Jamshed). An ancient Persian king, known as a magician. [17]

Jinn (Jinn). A species of Qaf-dwellers, invisible to ordinary human eyes; they can fly. They seem to be intermarried with the Paris: Shahpal's brother Sabz-qaba is described as a Jinn. [1]

Kabah (Kaʿbah). The holiest place of Islam, located in Mecca; it is the place of pilgrimage, and defines the direction Muslims face in prayer. [1]

Khizr (Ḳhiẓr). "Green." A well-established figure in Islamic story tradition, here called a Prophet. Khizr is associated with water (often with Alexander and the Water of Life), fertility, and right guidance; he bears messages and help from the Unseen to Hamzah and his companions. His mother is named Asifa Basafa, and Elias is his brother. [3]

Khvajah (Ḳhvājah). "Lord, master." Often used as an honorific title for a man of high rank. [1]

Khvajah Ashob and Khvajah Bahlol (Āshob, "Devastation"; Bahlol, "Jester"). Two mischievous boys, held captive by a Dev, whom Hamzah rescues and takes with him out of Qaf. [29]

King of Egypt (ʿAzīz-e Miṣr). An ally of Naushervan's, who betrays Hamzah and is later captured and killed under humiliating circumstances. [15]

King of Kings (Shāhanshāh). The official title of an emperor. [16]

Kohl of Solomon *(surmah-e sulaimānī)*. A special collyrium that enables human eyes to see Devs and Paris. [2]

Laila (Lailā). "Night." The faithful beloved of the legendary Majnun. [32]

Landhaur bin Sadan, Emperor of Hindustan (Landhaur bin Saʿdān Ḳhusrav-e Hindūstān). One of Hamzah's closest companions, famous for his prowess in mace-fighting and for his elephant, Maimunah. [10]

Lanisah (Lānīsah). A Pari, the mother of Ashqar. [29]

Lat and Manat (Lāt o Manāt). Two goddesses worshiped by the pre-Islamic Meccans and denounced in the Quran [53:19–20]. They are sometimes invoked by Naushervan and members of his court. [13]

lock of hair of Abraham *(kalālah-e ibrāhīmī)*. One of several tokens by which Hamzah can be recognized; its nature never becomes very clear. [16]

Maimunah (Maimūnah). "Fortunate." Landhaur's elephant, whom he rides into battle. [12]

Majnun (Majnūn). "Jinn-possessed." The most famous mad lover in Islamic story tradition; he sacrificed everything for his love of Laila. [32]

Malunah Jadu (Mal'ūnah Jādū). "Cursed woman the Magician." Ifrit's mother, a formidable magician. [21]

Manzar Shah of Yemen (Manẓar Shāh Yamanī). King of Yemen, and one of Hamzah's close companions. [4]

maund *(man)*. A traditional Indian measure of weight, usually about eighty pounds. [4]

merman *(jal mānus)*. A humanoid water-creature from Indic folk tradition. [25]

Mihr Angez (Mihr Angez). "Affection-evoking." Naushervan's wife, daughter of the Emperor of *China; she is the mother of Hurmuz, Faramarz, and Mihr Nigar. [1]

Mihr Nigar (Mihr Nigār). "Affection-adorning." Naushervan's daughter, Hamzah's true love; she waits eighteen years to marry Hamzah, and bears him one son, Qubad. [1]

Muqbil the Faithful (Muqbil Vafādār). The son of a slave of Abdul Muttalib's, he is Hamzah's adopted "brother" from birth, and a peerless archer. [1]

Nahid Maryam (Nāhīd Maryam). Nāhīd: a name for the planet Venus; Maryam: "Mary." Hamzah's first wife, the daughter of King Faredun of Greece; she is the mother of Amr bin Hamzah. [14]

Name *(ism)*. An invocation of the power of the one named, in order to achieve special feats or break magic spells; the virtuous usually use one of the Names, or even the esoteric Great Name, of God. [11]

Naranj Pari (Nārang Parī). "Orange Pari." The real identity of the *Veiled One Dressed in Orange. She eventually marries Hamzah.

Nariman (Narīmān). Rustam bin Zal's great-grandfather. [1]

Naushervan (Naushervān). The King of Kings of the Seven Realms, who rules with his Sasanians at Ctesiphon in Iran; Hamzah becomes his son-in-law through marriage to Mihr Nigar. [1]

Nimrod (Namrūd). Traditionally, the idolatrous king who threw Abraham into the fire [Quran 21:70]; here treated as a a Zoroastrian figure. [14]

Pari (Parī). "Fairy." The dominant race of Qaf-dwellers. Creatures of fire, invisible to ordinary human eyes, they have the power of flight, and many other powers as well. They seem to be about the size of humans, and are often extremely beautiful; they can visit the World at will. [1]

Parizad (Parīzād). "Pari-born." The name commonly used for the males of the *Pari race; sometimes female Paris too are referred as Parizads. [2]

perfume-orange *(turanj ḳhushbū kā)*. A fragile spherical perfume-holder, designed to break on impact and perfume the person it was thrown at; it was used during Iranian wedding celebrations. [22]

Pillarless Mountain (Koh-e Besutūn). The huge stone mountain through which Farhad, the Mountain-digger of Persian story tradition, had to carve a channel in order to win his beloved Shirin. [12]

Prophet (Nabī). A human being appointed by God as a messenger to his own people, and charged with a message specifically addressed to them. [3]

Qaf (Qāf). The region inhabited by Paris, Parizads, Devs, Jinns, and other non-human species, under the dominion of Shahpal bin Shahrukh. It is often called Mount Qaf (Koh-e Qāf). [1]

Qubad (Qubād). Hamzah's son by Mihr Nigar. [32]

Quraishah (Quraishah). "Woman of the Quraish." The daughter of Hamzah and Asman Pari. [23]

Rad the Deceitful (Ra'd-e Shāṭir). Ra'd, "Lightning." Ifrit's nephew, a powerful Dev. [27]

Raihan Pari (Raiḥān Parī). "Sweet-basil Pari." Asman Pari's cousin, who also marries Hamzah. [26]

Rustam bin Zal (Rustam bin Zāl). The mightiest and most famous hero from the Persian epic tradition. His best-known combat was with his son Suhrab: not recognizing each other, father and son fought to the death, and in the end Rustam killed Suhrab. [1]

Rustam Pil-tan (Rustam Pīl-tan). "Rustam Elephant-body." Hamzah's son by a princess of Khursanah called Rabiah the Sackcloth-dressed. [34]

Sabz-qaba (Sabz Qabā). "Green-robe." Shahpal's older brother; he marries his daughter Raihan Pari to Hamzah. [26]

Sad bin Amr bin Hamzah (Sa'd bin 'Amr bin Ḥamzah). The Amir's first grandson, born to the wife of his eldest son Amr bin Hamzah. [32]

Sahib-qiran (Ṣāḥib qirān). "Lord of the conjunction." A title of Hamzah's, referring to his birth at an auspicious astrological moment. The title is a sign of Hamzah's special destiny: he is sometimes referred to as the "Sahib-qiran of the Age." [4]

Salasil Parizad (Salāsil Parīzād). Salāsil, "Chains." A courtier of Qaf. [21]

Salih (Ṣāliḥ). One of the earlier Prophets mentioned in the Quran. [3]

Sam bin Nariman (Sām bin Narīmān). Rustam bin Zal's grandfather. [3]

Samiri (Sāmirī). In the Quran [20:85–97], the maker of the golden calf; in Persian story tradition, a powerful magician. [21]

Samsam and Qamqam (Ṣamṣām o Qamqām). Ṣamṣām, "Bold"; Qamqām, "Lofty." Two swords given to Hamzah by Gabriel. [3]

Sarandip (Sarandīp). Part of Landhaur's realm of Hindustan; it seems to be an island, and may represent Sri Lanka. [11]

Sasanians (Sāsānī). The nobles of Naushervan's court. [6]

Scorpion of Solomon ('Aqrab-e Sulaimānī). Hamzah's favorite sword, given him by Shahpal; it originally belonged to Solomon. [18]

Shahpal bin Shahrukh (Shahpāl bin Shāhruḳh). King of Kings of Qaf, and father of Asman Pari. It is he who summons Hamzah to Qaf. [1]

sherbet *(sharbat)*. A cooling sweet drink made of fruit juice, sugar, and water, often served on festive and ceremonial occasions. [1]

Simurgh (Sīmurġh). An immense, powerful bird, who can talk; he is an important and dignified figure in Persian story tradition. [27]

Solomon (Sulaimān). Solomon is described in the Quran as having authority over the Jinns [27:16–17], by God's special grace. He thus represents virtuous esoteric power, a kind of counter-magic sponsored by God. [2]

Suhrab (Suhrāb). Rustam bin Zal's son. [3]

Sultan Bakht of Maghrib (Sulṭān Baḳht Maġhribī). The prince of Maghrib, one of Hamzah's close companions. [4]

Tal Shad Kam (Tal Shād Kām). "Hill of Joy and Success." The Amir's encampment in Ctesiphon, where he lives with his retinue and army. [13]

Tauq bin Haran (Ṭauq bin Ḥarān). "Neck-ring son of Haran." One of Hamzah's close companions, a former highwayman who intimidated travelers with a ferocious tiger until Hamzah conquered and converted him. [4]

throne *(taḳht)*. A raised platform on which a king sits to hold court; when borne aloft by Devs, it becomes a flying vehicle. [16]

tilism *(ṭilism)*. A magic world created by a magician. Nothing in a tilism is necessarily what it seems. Special counterspells must be used to break the tilism; the magician who made it then usually dies. [16]

tuman *(tuman)*. "Ten thousand." A sum of money equal in theory to ten thousand of the Persian coins called dirhams. [4]

Vaq (Vāq). A prophetic tree near Qaf, with fruits like human heads. [30]

Veiled One Dressed in Orange (Naqābdār Nāranjī Posh). The mysterious rescuer who appears at the last moment to save Amar in times of disaster, during Hamzah's absence in Qaf. [19]

Verse of the Throne (Āyat al-Kursī). This verse [Quran 2:255] is a glorification of God. [8]

Wall of Alexander *(sadd-e sikandarī)*. A wall built by Alexander out of copper, to keep Gog and Magog out of the inhabited world. [12]

Water of Life *(āb-e ḥayāt)*. The legendary revivifying water that can restore the dead to life and grant immortality. [5]

water-flask of Khizr *(mashkīzah-e Ḳhiẓr)*. A water-flask that never runs dry no matter how much is drunk from it. [11]

White Dev (Safed Dev). A powerful Dev of Qaf who torments Hamzah. [24]

witch *(cuṛail)*. In Indic folk tradition, a female ghost or demon of horrifying aspect. [14]

World (Dunyā). The region of the earth inhabited by humans. [1]

World-conqueror (Getī Sitān). An epithet of Hamzah's. [21]

Yazid (Yazīd). The ruler whose armies killed Husain at Karbala; to Muslims, the archetypal sinner. [15]

Younger Solomon (Sulaimān-e S̈ānī). A title of Hamzah's, referring to his power of subduing Devs. Solomon is described as having predicted Hamzah's adventures in Qaf in some detail. [18]

Zanbil (Zanbīl). Amar's bag, out of which anything can be taken, and into which anything can be put; when touched, it gives shape-shifting powers. [12]

Zhopin Kaus (Zhopīn Kā'ūs). Zhopīn, "Spear." One of Naushervan's generals, a treacherous and dangerous enemy of Hamzah's. [16]

Zuhrah of Egypt (Zuhrah Miṣrī). Zuhrah: a name for the planet Venus. The daughter of the King of Egypt, who accepts Islam and is engaged to Muqbil the Faithful. [15]

Bibliography

A. Works in English

Basgöz, Ilhan. "Turkish *Hikaye*-Telling Tradition in Azerbaijan, Iran." *Journal of American Folklore* 83(330):391–405, 1970.

Bausani, Alessandro. "An Islamic Echo of the 'Trickster'? The '*Ayyars* of Indo-Persian and Malay Romances." In *Gururājamañjarikā: Studi in Onore di Giuseppe Tucci,* 2:457–67. Naples: Istituto Universitario Orientale, 1974.

Beer, Gillian. *The Romance.* London: Methuen, 1970.

Blackburn, Stuart H. et al., eds. *Oral Epic in India.* Berkeley: University of California Press, 1989.

Faridany-Akhavan, Zahra. "The Problems of the Mughal Manuscript of the Hamza-Nama 1562–77: A Reconstruction." Ph.D. dissertation, Harvard University, 1989.

Field, P. J. C. *Romance and Chronicle: A Study of Malory's Prose Style.* London: Barrie and Jenkins, 1971.

Hanaway, William L. "Formal Elements in the Persian Popular Romances." *Review of National Literatures* 2:139–60, Spring 1971.

Hanaway, William L. "Persian Popular Romances Before the Safavid Era." Ph.D. dissertation, Columbia University, 1970.

Hanaway, William L., trans. and ed. *Love and War; Adventures from the Firuz Shah Nama of Sheikh Bighami.* Delmar, N.Y.: Scholars' Facsimiles Reprints, 1974.

Husain, Shaikh Sajjad. *The Amir Hamza, an Oriental Novel.* Calcutta, 1892. (Part 1 only; apparently no more was ever published.)

Lang, D. M., and G. M. Meredith-Owens. "*Amiran-Darejaniani:* A Georgian Romance and its English Rendering." *Bulletin of the School of Oriental and African Studies* 22(3):454–90, 1959.

Levy, Reuben, trans. and ed. *The Epic of the Kings.* London: Routledge and Kegan Paul, 1967.

Mannan, Qazi Abdul. *The Emergence and Development of Dobhasi Literature in Bengal (up to 1855 A.D.).* Dacca: University of Dacca, 1966.

Page, Mary Ellen. "Naqqali and Ferdowsi: Creativity in the Iranian National Tradition." Ph.D. dissertation, University of Pennsylvania, 1977.

Pritchett, Frances W. "Emperor of India: Landhaur bin Sa'dan in the *Hamza* Cycle." In: Christopher Shackle, ed., *Urdu and Muslim South Asia: Studies in Honour of Ralph Russell*, pp. 67–75. London: School of Oriental and African Studies, 1989.

Pritchett, Frances W. *Marvelous Encounters: Folk Romance in Urdu and Hindi.* New Delhi: Manohar Publications; and Riverdale, Md.: The Riverdale Company, 1985.

Russell, Ralph. "The Development of the Modern Novel in Urdu." In: T. W. Clark, ed., *The Novel in India: Its Birth and Development*, pp. 102–41. London: George Allen and Unwin, 1970.

Russell, Ralph and Khurshidul Islam, trans. and eds. *Ghalib, 1979–1869; Volume I: Life and Letters.* London: George Allen and Unwin, 1969.

Schimmel, Annemarie. *Classical Urdu Literature from the Beginning to Iqbal.* Wiesbaden: Otto Harrassowitz, 1975. (Vol. 8, Fasc. 3 of *A History of Indian Literature*, Jan Gonda, ed.; 8 vols.)

Southgate, Minoo S. *Iskandarnamah; a Persian Medieval Alexander-Romance.* New York: Columbia University Press, 1978.

B. WORKS IN URDU

Amān, Ḳhvājah, trans. *Ḥadā'iq-e anẕār.* Delhi: Maḥmūd ul-Maṯābi', 1866. (A translation of vol. 1 of Ḳhiyāl's *Bostān-e Ḳhiyāl.*)

Ashk, Ḳhalīl 'Alī Ḳhān. *Dāstān-e amīr Ḥamzah.* Bombay: Maṭba' Ḥaidarī, 1289 A.H. [1863–64]. (Original ed. 1801.)

'Askarī, Muḥammad Ḥasan. *Intiḳhāb-e ṯilism-e hoshrubā.* Lahore: Maktabah-e Jadīd, 1953. "Muqaddamah" by 'Azīz Aḥmad, pp. 1–16.

Bilgrāmī, 'Abdullāh Ḥusain. *Dāstān-e amīr Ḥamzah.* Lucknow: Maṯba' Munshī Naval Kishor, 1871 (India Office Library).

Bilgrāmī, 'Abdullāh Ḥusain. *Dāstān-e amīr Ḥamzah.* Lucknow: Maṯba' Naval Kishor, 1874 (2d ed.).

Bilgrāmī, 'Abdullāh Ḥusain. *Dāstān-e amīr Ḥamzah.* Lucknow: Maṯba' Naval Kishor, 1927. 7th printing.

Bilgrāmī, 'Abdullāh Ḥusain. *Dāstān-e amīr Ḥamzah.* Lucknow: Maṯba' Tej Kumār, 1969. 11th printing.

Farmān Fatḥpūrī, Dildār 'Alī. *Urdū kī manẕūm dāstāneñ.* Karachi: Anjuman Taraqqī-e Urdū, 1971.

Ġhālib Lakhnavī, Navāb Mirzā Amān 'Alī Ḳhān Bahādur. *Tarjamah-e dāstān-e ṣāḥib qirān getī sitān (āl-e) paiġhambar-e āḳhir uz-zamān amīr Ḥamzah bin 'Abd ul-Muṯṯalib bin Hāshim bin 'Abd ul-Manāf kā.* Calcutta: Maṯba'-e Ḥakīm Ṣāḥib, 1855.

Gyān Chand Jain. *Urdū kī nas̤rī dāstāneñ*. Karachi: Anjuman Taraqqī-e Urdū, 1969 (2d ed.).

Ḥasanī, Yūnus. "Dāstān kā fan." *Qaumī Zabān* 44(7):11–15, July 1972.

Ḥamīd Buk Ḍipo. *Aṣlī mukammal dāstān-e amīr Ḥamzah urdū bataṣvīr*. Lahore: Ḥāmid Buk Ḍipo, 1985–86(?).

Ibn-e Kanval. *Hindūstānī tahżīb bostān-e ḳhiyāl ke tanāẓur meñ*. Delhi: Urdū Akādamī, 1988.

Ja'frī, Ra'īs Aḥmad, ed. *T̤ilism-e hoshrubā*. Lahore: Shaiḳh Ġhulām 'Alī and Sons, 1959. Abridged.

Jāh, Muḥammad Ḥusain. *T̤ilism-e hoshrubā*. Lucknow: Mat̤ba' Munshī Naval Kishor, 1881 (vol. 1); 1884 (vol. 2); 1888–1889 (vol. 3); 1890 (vol. 4).

Jāh, Muḥammad Ḥusain. *T̤ilism-e hoshrubā; urdū kī dilcasptarīn dāstān-e musalsal, mukammal, bilā talḳhīs, qist vār*. Sayyid Qāsim Maḥmūd, ed. Lahore: Maktabah Shāhkār, 1978– (published serially in monthly installments).

Jahāngīr Buk Ḍipo. *Mukammal o bataṣvīr dāstān-e amīr Ḥamzah*. Lahore: Jahāngīr Buk Ḍipo, 1987(?).

Kalīm ud-dīn Aḥmad. *Urdū zabān aur fann-e dāstān go'ī*. Lucknow: Idārah-e Furoġh-e Urdū, 1972.

Ḳhān, M. Ḥabīb. *Urdū kī qadīm dāstāneñ*. Aligarh: Indian Book House, 1974.

Mubīn ur-Raḥmān, Muḥammad. *Dāstān-e amīr Ḥamzah*. Karachi: Farīd-e Mubīn Pablisharz, 1986–87(?).

Niyāz Aḥmad Ḳhān. *Dāstān-e amīr Ḥamzah*. Meerut: Raḥmānī Pres, 1892.

Rāhī Ma'sūm Riẓā. *T̤ilism-e hoshrubā; ek mut̤āli'ah*. Bombay: Ḳhayābān Publications, 1979.

Ratan ainḍ Kampanī. *Dāstān-e amīr Ḥamzah mukammal chār ḥiṣṣe*. Delhi: Ratan ainḍ Kampanī, n.d. [mid-20th c.].

Rāz Yazdānī. "Dāstān-e Ḥamzah." *Nigār* (September):25–30, 1959.

Rāz Yazdānī. "Mat̤bū'ah-e t̤ilism-e hoshrubā." *Nigār* (November):6–12, 1959.

Rāz Yazdānī. "Urdū dāstānoñ par kām kā tajziyah aur tabṣirah." *Ājkal* 18:27–34, July 1960.

Rāz Yazdānī. "Urdū meñ dāstān go'ī aur dāstān navīsī." *Ājkal* 18:3–9, May 1960.

Riẓā, Rāhī Ma'sūm. *T̤ilism-e hoshrubā; ek mut̤āli'ah*. Bombay: Ḳhayābān Pablikeshanz, 1979.

Riẓvī, Sayyid Aḳhtar Mas'ūd. "Kuchh 'ayyāroñ ke bāre meñ." In: *Fikrī kāvisheñ*, pp. 5–28. Peshawar: Maktabah-e Shāhīn, n.d.

Sharar, ʻAbdul Ḥalīm. *Guẓashtah Lakhna'ū; mashriqī tamaddun kā āḳhirī namūnah.* Lucknow: Nasīm Buk Ḍipo, 1965. (Original ed. 1914–1916.)

Shāyān, Ṭoṭārām. *Ṭilism-e shāyān maʻrūf bah dāstān-e amīr Ḥamzah.* Lucknow: Naval Kishor Press, 1862.

Ṣubūḥī Dihlavī, Ashraf. "Mīr Bāqir ʻAlī." In: *Dillī kī chand ʻajīb hastiyāñ.* Delhi: Anjuman Taraqqī-e Urdū, 1943.

Suhail Aḥmad Ḳhān. *Dāstānoñ kī ʻalāmatī kā'ināt.* Lahore: Panjab University, 1987.

Suhail Aḥmad Ḳhān, ed. *Dāstān dar dāstān; dāstānoñ kī ẓāhirī o bāṭinī maʻnau'iyat par mantaḳhab maẓāmīn.* Lahore: Qausain, 1987.

Suhail Buḳhārī. *Urdū dāstān, taḥqīqī o tanqīdī muṭāliʻah.* Islamabad: Muqtadārah-e Qaumī Zabān, 1987.

Suhail Buḳhārī. "Urdū dāstān kā fannī tajziyah." *Nuqūsh* 105:84–99, April-June 1966.

Taḥsīn Sarvarī. "Mīr Bāqir ʻAlī dāstān go." *Qaumī Zabān* 28(5):54, 72–74, May 1966.

Viqār ʻAẓīm, Sayyid. *Hamārī dāstāneñ.* Lahore: Urdū Markaz, 1964.

Yūsuf Buḳhārī Dihlavī, Sayyid. "Mīr Bāqir ʻAlī dāstān go." *Urdū Nāmah* 23:51–65, February 1961. Reprinted in *Yārān-e raftah,* pp. 19–38. Karachi: Maktabah-e Uslūb, 1987.

C. *DĀSTĀN-E AMĪR ḤAMZAH*: THE LONG VERSION BY THE NAVAL KISHOR PRESS

(The dates given are based on Gyān Chand, *Nas̤rī dāstāneñ,* pp. 473–74, as emended by S. R. Fārūqī's more recent unpublished research.)

DAFTAR-E AVVAL

Naushervān nāmah, vol. 1, 1893, Taṣadduq Ḥusain; vol. 2, 1898–89, Taṣadduq Ḥusain.

Hurmuz nāmah, 1 vol., 1900, Taṣadduq Ḥusain.

Homān nāmah, 1 vol., 1900, Qamar.

DAFTAR-E DUVVUM

Kocak bāḳhtar, 1 vol., after 1892, Taṣadduq Ḥusain.

DAFTAR-E SUVVUM

Bālā bāḳhtar, 1 vol., 1899, Taṣadduq Ḥusain.

DAFTAR-E CHAHĀRUM

Īraj nāmah, vol. 1, 1893, Taṣadduq Ḥusain; vol. 2, after 1893, Taṣadduq Ḥusain.

DAFTAR-E PANJUM

Ṭilism-e hoshrubā, vol. 1, 1883, Jāh; vol. 2, 1884, Jāh; vol. 3, 1888–89, Jāh; vol. 4, 1890, Jāh; vol. 5, part 1, 1891, Qamar; vol. 5, part 2, 1891, Qamar; vol. 6, 1892, Qamar; vol. 7, 1893(?), Qamar.

DAFTAR-E SHASHUM

Sandalī nāmah, 1 vol., 1895, Ismā'īl Asar.

DAFTAR-E HAFTUM

Tūraj nāmah, vol. 1, 1896, Pyāre Mirzā, Taṣadduq Ḥusain; vol. 2, 1897(?), Taṣadduq Ḥusain, Ismā'īl Asar.

DAFTAR-E HASHTUM

La'l nāmah, vol. 1, 1896, Taṣadduq Ḥusain; vol. 2, 1896(?), Taṣadduq Ḥusain.

Āftāb-e shujā'at, vol. 1, 1903(?), Taṣadduq Ḥusain; vol. 2, 1903, Taṣadduq Ḥusain; vol. 3, 1904, Taṣadduq Ḥusain; vol. 4, 1905, Taṣadduq Ḥusain; vol. 5, part 1, 1908, Taṣadduq Ḥusain; vol. 5, part 2, 1908, Taṣadduq Ḥusain.

Gulistān-e bāḳhtar, vol. 1, 1909, Taṣadduq Ḥusain, Ismā'īl Asar; vol. 2, 1909, Taṣadduq Ḥusain, Ismā'īl Asar; vol. 3, 1917, Taṣadduq Ḥusain, Ismā'īl Asar.

Ṭilism-e fitnah-e nūr afshāñ, vol. 1, 1896(?), Qamar; vol. 2, 1896, Qamar; vol. 3, 1896(?), Qamar.

Baqiyah-e ṭilism-e hoshrubā, vol. 1, 1897, Qamar; vol. 2, 1897, Qamar.

Ṭilism-e haft paikar, vol. 1, 1897, Qamar; vol. 2, 1897, Qamar; vol. 3, 1897, Qamar.

Ṭilism-e ḳhiyāl-e sikandarī, vol. 1, 1897(?), Qamar; vol. 2, 1897(?), Qamar; vol. 3, 1897(?), Qamar.

Ṭilism-e nauḳhez-e jamshedī, vol. 1, 1901, Qamar; vol. 2, 1902, Qamar; vol. 3, 1902, Qamar.

Ṭilism-e za'frānzār-e sulaimānī, vol. 1, 1905(?), Qamar, Taṣadduq Ḥusain, ed. by Ismā'īl Asar; vol. 2, 1905, Qamar, Taṣadduq Ḥusain, ed. by Ismā'īl Asar.

D. WORKS IN OTHER LANGUAGES

Gaillard, Marina. *Le livre de Samak-e 'Ayyār; Structure et idéologie du roman persan médiéval.* Paris: Institut d'études Iraniennes, Université de la Sorbonne, 1987. (French)

Glück, Heinrich. *Die Indischen Miniaturen des Haemzae-Romanes im Österreichischen Museum für Kunst und Industrie in Wien und in anderen Sammlungen.* Zurich: Amalthea-Verlag, 1925. (German)

Ḥājī Qiṣṣah-k̲hvān Hamadānī. *Zubdat ur-rumūz.* Manuscript, c. 1613–14. Khudabakhsh Library, Patna, No. 728. (Persian)

Ja'far Shi'ār, ed. *Qiṣṣah-e Ḥamzah.* Teheran: University of Teheran Press, A.H. 1347 [1968–69]. 2 vols. (Persian)

Kālīcharan and Maheshdatt. *Amīr Hamzā kī dāstān jis meñ Ālā Ūdal kī sī shūrtā bīrtā vikhyāt hai* . . . . Lucknow: Naval Kishor Pres, 1879. (Hindi)

Kitāb-e rumūz-e Ḥamzah. Teheran, A.H. 1274–76 [1857–59]. (British Museum Library.) (Persian)

Mirzā Muḥammad K̲hān malik ul-kuttāb. *Kitāb-e dāstān-e amīr Ḥamzah ṣāḥib qirān.* Bombay: Maṭba'-e Sipihr-e Maṯla', A.H. 1327 [1909]. (Persian)

Razavi, Frédérique, trans. *Samak-e 'Ayyār,* vol. 1 (Paris: Editions G.-P. Maisonneuve & Larose, 1972). (French)

Van Ronkel, Ph. S. *De Roman van Amir Hamza.* Leiden: E. J. Brill, 1895. (Dutch)